THE CAREER MAKERS

THE
CAREER
MAKERS

*America's Top 100
Executive Recruiters*

JOHN SIBBALD

1817

HARPER BUSINESS

A Division of Harper & Row Publishers, New York

*Grand Rapids, Philadelphia, St. Louis, San Francisco
London, Singapore, Sydney, Tokyo, Toronto*

International Standard Book Number: 0-88730-391-9

Library of Congress Catalog Card Number: 89-45778

Printed in the United States of America

Library of Congress Cataloging-in-Publication Data
Sibbald, John (John R.)
    The career makers: America's top 100 executive recruiters/John Sibbald.
        p.   cm.
    ISBN 0-88730-391-9: $21.95
    1. Executives—United States—Recruiting—Directories. I. Title.
HD38.25.U6S53   1990
858.4'07111'02573—dc20   89-45778
                                                                                        CIP

Book design by C. Linda Dingler
90 91 92 AT/HC 9 8 7 6 5 4 3 2 1

Dedicated to:

the professional who yearns to get ahead,
the high achiever who gets approached,
the job seeker who prays he will be,
     and the recent graduate who one day might be.

Also, to the university that needs a president,
the President who seeks both cabinet and staff,
the government official who wants a corporate job,
the military officer stepping into civilian clothes,
the classroom teacher with boardroom goals,
the search committee that seeks consensus,
the hospital that quests a healer,
the company that needs a leader . . .

     and to those who can make it all happen—
     the 100 best matchmakers this side of Cupid.

Contents

Careers are like an investment portfolio.
Only the best-managed ones ever build an estate.

—JOHN SIBBALD

Acknowledgments

This book would not have been possible without the exceptional cooperation of the heads or principal contacts of 311 retainer-type executive search firms and the Chief Executive Officers or senior personnel executives of well over 600 client organizations of all types. The questionnaires that both groups completed form the core of the project. Thanks are also due the 200 recruiters who were nominated by both clients and peers and who completed the individual survey forms used to rank them among their peers. Particular appreciation goes to individuals who qualified as being in the Top 100 and therefore completed a detailed questionnaire—often obtaining client approval—as well as providing us with a recent photograph. Every recruiter who qualified as one of this country's 200 most accomplished recruiters is included in the book.

The Career Makers: America's Top 100 Executive Recruiters owes its title and readability to Virginia Smith, my oh-so-patient executive editor at Harper & Row. Her gentle persuasion, encouragement, and sage counsel at times when this neophyte author was about to drown in data or concede that there was no way that we would ever obtain every recruiter's information kept me from forsaking the project and going back full-time to the infinitely easier task of headhunting for our clients instead of headhunting the headhunters themselves.

A very special thanks is also due to those staff members in

my own firm who had less help from me during the months I was preoccupied with this effort. But my largest debt of gratitude is reserved for my associate, Kathryn Costick. Her attention to detail, follow-through, ingenuity, and determination were matched only by her selflessness and commitment. She was a sounding board to me from start to finish. Few others would have managed the multiplicity of tasks with as much organization and good humor.

Introduction

This is a book for only two groups of Americans—the professionals in every field of work who either need a job *now* or aspire to a better one and the employers who spend countless hours and dollars trying to find them. Each is constantly looking for the other, but they have the darndest time getting together.

Accordingly, this book will not prove valuable to nor should it be purloined, purchased, or perused by such other significant groups as

Recent graduates on their way up, unless they need to earn over $50,000 a year someday;

Retired people who have earned their lives of economic peace, except in those virtually unheard of instances where they still fret about a son, daughter, or grandchild not progressing in their careers as well as they might be;

Hourly workers of all types who enjoy paying union dues and want no part of ever becoming salaried;

Those of enormous wealth, who dwell on tropical islands, have no less-well-off family members or relatives, and vastly prefer Hermès boutiques to bookstores;

Prisoners while they are still behind bars;

Past Presidents of the United States—except as the book might be a gift from them to friendly out-of-office senators, representatives, cabinet members, party officials, and former military officers.

Fortunately for both the professionals interested in a new job now or in the future and the employers who need them, they have some highly accomplished helpmates. For the job seeker lucky enough to be known by them, these Good Samaritans of the job market can grease the skids to the perfect job. But alas, they are an elusive group and terribly whimsical. When they want you, you may not want them; and when you need them the most, they're nowhere to be found.

These keepers of the key to many of this country's best opportunities in every field of endeavor go by a variety of titles: executive recruiter, executive search consultant, searcher, or headhunter—a name some of them bristle at. But whatever they're called, they all stand for the same thing. The business press increasingly labels them kingmakers because of the significance of the top management positions they fill. Career makers might well be the best title of all because in the final analysis that's really what they do.

The careers they touch span the universe of opportunities. When the leveraged buyout aces at Kohlberg Kravis Roberts & Co. needed a new Chief Executive Officer for recently acquired RJR Nabisco Inc., they went to Tom Neff of SpencerStuart Associates. When Apple Computer sought a president who was a consumer marketing whiz, they called on Gerry Roche of Heidrick & Struggles. When Southern Methodist University needed a new president, they engaged Steve Garrison of Ward Howell International. And when the Los Angeles Olympic Organizing Committee went looking for an executive director, they brought in Richard Ferry of Korn/Ferry International. The list could go on and on.

But these chief executive officer searches represent only the tip of the executive recruiting iceberg. The 90 percent that is below the surface is where the bulk of the search work goes on in this country's executive employment marketplace. When you reach the $50,000 salary level or have reasonable aspirations for that salary, you've stepped into the hunting grounds of America's headhunters. As you'll find in reading further, this is *not* the time to keep your head down.

The other important message in the examples of the senior searches referred to above is that these clients, whether they are corporations, universities, associations, or any other type of employer, have chosen a specific individual recruiter and not necessarily the firm they're associated with to assist them with their very significant searches. The executive search industry evolved this way, and while there are many very large recruiting firms, the business is still conducted by individuals. Knowing the right headhunter for the right search is as critical to a job seeker as it is to an employer.

In the minds of most of us, executive recruiters do their work in the corporate jungle. Most of it *is* done there. They're the people we spot behind the potted palm in the Union League Club, sleuthing out the next Chairman of Leviathan Intercosmic, Inc., or the Vice President–Technology for Pet Rock, Ltd. Yet there is a large and growing number of recruiters who have an eye especially calibrated only for university presidents, hospital administrators, school superintendents, physicians, lawyers, association executives, municipal and government officials, and many other nonbusiness-sector types. In fact the headhunter lurking behind that potted palm in the Union League Club just might be sizing up its club manager and not assessing a giant of industry.

Although executive recruiters may be directly engaged with only about 20 percent of all managerial and executive hiring done today, the positions they are asked to fill represent a disproportionate number of the highest-paying and most prestigious jobs in the United States and abroad. *Thus, for an executive in any line of work, or the manager who aspires to becoming an executive, and for every young professional on the way up, it is prudent to know one or more executive recruiters,* especially those recruiters who specialize in searches in one's particular line of work.

Executive recruiting in America is big business. Estimates of the revenues generated by the 10,000 (some say double that) men and women who practice the art range from $2 billion to $4 billion a year. Recognizing that most search consultants charge their clients 33 percent of the first-year compensation of those they place, these purveyors of opportunity fill positions

worth close to $10 billion in earnings for professionals in vir-
tually every field of endeavor. To this sizable chunk of the wage
pool, add the $1 or $2 billion in employee compensation recruiters account for when they gratuitously do a favor for a
good client by simply referring a talented candidate they have
met and the client hires the individual.

Executive recruiting in America is also significant work.
Most leading search firms will not recruit at salary levels below
$50,000. Some will go no lower than $100,000; and a few claim
they will not recruit at any level below $300,000 in base salary
and seek only Presidents and members of Boards of Directors.
The clients that recruiters serve add to the significance of their
work. Organizations tend to fill their less consequential positions on their own; for the tough ones, often of great confidentiality and sensitivity, they frequently call in a search consultant.
A number of the key jobs in Washington are filled with the help
of executive recruiters. When boards and committees are
involved in senior staff selections, they too turn more and more
to headhunters.

Up to now, we've been speaking about the value of knowing a search consultant from the employee or job seeker's
aspect. *It is every bit as important for employers to know individual
recruiters—the right recruiter for the specific need they're out to fill.*
Sometimes the choice is easy because the organization has used
the recruiter for a similar successful search in the past. But what
if that search did not go well? Or what if the job to be filled is
a new one or in a field where the recruiter customarily used has
never worked? Although many of the most senior headhunters
profess to be generalists able to recruit for any position in any
field, the truth is that they all have functional areas, industries,
or professions in which they are considerably more proficient.
An employer who ignores this modern fact of executive recruiting is, in effect, entrusting a general medical practitioner to perform brain surgery.

To emphasize this point, our firm recently took over a
search for a major consumer packaged goods company that had
been using another executive search firm for over ten months
and still had no placement to show for it. As the frustrated President of the company told us, he doubted whether the recruiter
handling the search had ever previously done an assignment for

a consumer marketing executive. He recalled that the other recruiter's background had been in marketing but in marketing for a bank. He added that on several occasions the former recruiter slipped into such banker's jargon as "client prospecting" and "call programs." It was the kind of costly mismatch between client need and recruiter's inexperience that never should have happened yet too often does.

So where does the savvy employer turn to locate the best individual executive recruiter in America to help fill the highly specialized and supercritical job that can make or break the entire organization? For starters, the employer can make some phone calls to friends—but is it safe to let others know about this need and how crucial it is or to reveal that the employer is planning to replace the incumbent in the job? Fortunately, there are a number of reference guides to executive search firms. The most helpful of these, an annual publication titled *The Directory of Executive Recruiters* (Kennedy & Kennedy, Templeton Road, Fitzwilliam, NH 03447), contains listings of almost all executive search firms and also cross-indexes the firms by areas of particular expertise and geographic location.

Useful as this guide is, and several others like it, there is no way in it *to identify those few specific individual recruiters best equipped to handle the employer's all-important search.* Thus, the process of finding the most effective recruiter to help the employer fill a specific need comes down to the time-consuming and risky process of calling each of the search firms listed under the directory heading of particular interest and trusting those called to be candid about their expertise in recruiting in a particular field. Without intending to impugn the integrity of any executive search firm, the margin of distortion in firms' statements of apparent qualifications or preeminence can range from complete truth to downright fiction.

Complicating the situation further for both the professional seeking a new opportunity and the employer scouring the universe for an employee who walks on water is this cruel fact: There are recruiters and there are recruiters. This is not a book about those who hunt heads for a bounty. Recruiters who work on a contingency basis are paid when and if they are successful in bagging the right body for the right job opening. Such recruiters serve a worthwhile purpose in satisfying many organizations' recruitment needs, but they are most effective in filling lower-level jobs. Because they don't receive any up-front money to do extensive long-distance telephone calling, travel, and otherwise canvass the marketplace, they usually can afford to work only with those candidates who have sent them resumes and are already in the job market. The great majority of contingency recruiters would have a hard time *personally* introducing their candidates to their client—because they've rarely enjoyed the luxury of being able to meet their candidates beforehand.

Those headhunters who are not contingency recruiters are called retained recruiters and belong to retainer-type executive search firms. The most ethical of these firms do not do any search work on a contingency basis—even in the grip of recession. Retainer firms pride themselves on standards of ethical conduct and performance that they believe reflect well on the calibre of clients they serve and the candidates they place. They get paid whether they're successful in the search or not, with the first one-third of their ultimate fee usually coming as their retainer at the time they start the search. Their professional fees are generally 33 percent of their ultimate placement's first-year compensation—base salary plus anticipated bonus. Some also will work on a flat-fee basis. All out-of-pocket expenses incurred in searching the marketplace for a proverbial needle in the haystack are reimbursable to them. They can afford to take the time and make the effort to identify and induce the right candidate to take the job—or at least that's what their glossy brochures promise.

The Career Makers: America's Top 100 Executive Recruiters is a book about a very select few of the thousands of men and women employed with retainer-type executive search firms. This is not a book about the firms themselves because in my twenty years in the search business, both as partner in the large consulting organization of Booz, Allen & Hamilton and in the firm I now run, I've never known a recruiting organization to make a placement: *Individual recruiters make placements, not recruiting firms.* Just ask any client or candidate and the recruiters themselves.

Until now, lists of the so-called leading retainer-type executive search firms were the best guides available to help job seekers and outplacement firms direct resumes and to provide grist for the business press. They also encouraged ambitious smaller firms to try to catch up with the leading firms. But these celebrations of size or reputed eminence do nothing to help satisfy the needs of the only two constituencies a search firm really serves—the professionals worth recruiting and the clients who pay for and deserve the recruiters' best efforts. Both of these groups want to know which recruiters, *by name and recruiting areas of specialization,* can help them the most. They need specificity to improve their chances for success.

This book breaks new ground and opens more direct avenues for job seekers and employers alike in reaching their respective employment goals. *The Career Makers: America's Top 100 Executive Recruiters* spotlights for the first time the individual recruiters most worth knowing. America's most effective and reputable recruiters—the industry's *crème de la crème*—are identified, categorized by areas of competency, and profiled so that professionals looking for work or advancement and employers searching for just the right headhunter have a precise way to reach them.

The book is divided into two parts for ease in use. Part I, "Working with the Top Executive Recruiters," contains four chapters. The first of these describes how the Top 100 recruiters were selected and the characteristics they share, both from their own and clients' points of view. Chapter 2 is intended primarily for job seekers and those who contemplate changing employers or careers at some time in the future. Employing organizations of all types will find Chapter 3 helpful to them in pointing out how to work most effectively with executive recruiters. Chapter 4 is for your easy reading pleasure. Yet there are important messages for job seekers and employers alike in the real-life war stories included in this chapter, each one selected from this headhunter's diary.

In Part II of this book the most accomplished 1 percent of all of America's executive recruiters are individually profiled, perhaps a better term is *exposed.* For once, the headhunters have had the tables turned on them. Readers can see where they grew up, went to school, worked previously, and what their outside interests are. Each profile reveals what these top recruiters look for in candidates and describes five placements each considers representative of their work. The phantoms of the employment world have stepped out of their closets for the first time—and even shown their faces.

Part II also contains a chapter on what we have called the Top 2 Percenters. These are the 100 women and men recruiters who came closest among their thousands of colleagues to qualifying for the Top 100. Many missed inclusion by only a nomination or two. While these highly accomplished recruiters are not individually profiled, they are ranked along with those from the Top 100 in their respective areas of competency. Many actually stand higher in their functional or organizational specialties than those from the Top 100. Chapter 7, Areas of Recruiter Specialization, ranks all of the 200 recruiters who qualified for this book in the order of their expertise as seen through the eyes of clients and fellow recruiters alike.

There are also some things this book is not intended to be. An employer will not find information here on how to negotiate a compensation package or conduct the ultimate interview. Likewise, an individual will not discover how to compose the perfect resume or launch the most successful job search in history. Bookshelves are sagging with these types of guides now. Astute users of this book—whether they are job seekers or employers—will find that their days of shotgunning the marketplace in search of the right recruiters to help them have ended. *The Career Makers: America's Top 100 Executive Recruiters* gives its readers a chance to use the accuracy of a rifle to take clear aim at their target for the first time.

PART I

WORKING WITH THE TOP EXECUTIVE RECRUITERS

1

The Top 100 Recruiters:
Their Selection and Characteristics

The woods are full of schlocky headhunters—a fair number of whom could telemarket the trees they're hiding in as the perfect raw material for the hull of a nuclear submarine. Fortunately, reasonably alert professionals should be able to spot these charlatans almost immediately. Their pitch often starts out like this:

> "Hi there, Jack." (Your name is John and you've always detested being called Jack.)

> "This is Cash McCool, your friendly headhunter. Have I ever got an opportunity for you!" (Background noise is either a stuck elevator or an off-balance washing machine. Unfortunately he goes on.)

> "Our mutual friend, Sherwin Wastewater, told me to give you a call because you'd be perfect for my client." (You go through a quick mental test to recall a Sherwin Wastewater, but the best you can come up with is Herman Westwater, an old boyfriend of your first wife.)

If you're wise, at this point you'll end the conversation by saying something like this:

> "I can't talk any longer, Mr. McCool, because my boss just walked into my office."

Another equally terminal response is,

"My secretary has just gone into labor."

Either way, extricate yourself expeditiously.

Regrettably, many headhunters fit McCool's profile. They are often well-meaning but untrained individuals who think that executive recruiting is a quick trip to a Rolls-Royce. Sometimes they open an office on a month-to-month basis, but more frequently they work from home. Call them back and you'll usually get an answering machine. These kinds of recruiters spring up when the country is in a tight employment market, and they vanish at the first breeze of recessionary winds. Their comings and goings, however, and how they conduct themselves have helped perpetuate the negative connotations of the term *headhunter*.

There are, fortunately, thousands of ethical, effective headhunters. With few exceptions, these individuals conduct themselves professionally and discreetly and fully appreciate the trust their candidates and clients give them. They are trained in the business, belong to respected recruiting firms of all sizes and types, and follow acceptable industry practices and codes of ethics. These recruiters might be with contingency types of recruiting organizations or retainer firms. This book is concerned only with recruiters from retainer firms. Among the thousands of retainer recruiters are a few especially talented individuals who stand apart from their colleagues in the minds of both their fellow headhunters and clients. The pages that follow are about them.

For individuals to be selected as among the 100 best search consultants in America means that they stand in the top 1 percent of all of their recruiting peers nationwide. This is a noteworthy accomplishment—especially in a personal services business seemingly unable to establish for itself any type of individual certification of competency.

In the absence of any industry certification of recruiter proficiency, it was difficult to decide how to begin to identify the Top 100. Executive recruiters skills are on display to only three groups: the clients they serve, their peers in the business, and the candidates with whom they deal. This third group was rejected as a survey category because of the transitory nature of candidate contacts with recruiters, their consequential lack of perspective or objectivity, and the logistical difficulties of locat-ing them to solicit their responses. Accordingly, the focus of the selection process was on surveying clients and peers of recrui-ters, both competitors and those employed in the same search firms. The career makers featured in this book have been iden-tified by what the marketplace thinks of them and not by the arbitrary and subjective judgments of a few self-styled industry experts and the largest search firms' public relations agencies.

Because the book was intended from its inception to be of value to the widest possible range of professionals—not just those in business—questionnaires were sent to the Chief Exec-utive Officers, or their equivalents, of America's

  1,000 largest public corporations, from the *Fortune* 500 lists
    of industrial and service companies,
  500 largest privately held companies, from *Forbes* magazine
    and the *Macmillan Directory of Leading Private Companies*,
    1989 edition,
  143 largest hospitals and health care providers,
  200 leading public and private colleges and universities,
  130 largest professional societies and trade associations,
  125 major hospitality organizations including hotel and res-
    taurant chains, private clubs, and resorts,
  15 governmental and quasigovernmental agencies known to
    have used search firms.

These chief executives (or more immediately involved senior officers) were asked, "In your own opinion, who are the most effective *individual recruiters* (by name and firm) who have served your organization in the last several years?" The respondents were asked to list no more than five recruiters and not neces-sarily in order of preference. The list of recruiter nominees was further refined by this question: "If you were personally respon-sible—*to such an extent that your own job was on the line*—for recruiting the next Chief Executive Officer of your organization, to which *individual recruiter* would you entrust that search?" Completed forms were received from just over 30 percent of all client organizations surveyed, a statistically significant response rate.

To balance the employer or client side of the picture, a similar inquiry was made to key contacts or managing principals at 366 retainer executive search firms based in the United States. For firms with more than one office or key contact, the mailing was made to the principal headquarters listed. One question asked of these recruiters was, "In your opinion, who are the most effective *individual recruiters* within your *entire organization* (including those in other offices), working with U.S.-based clients, who actually handle client searches directly—not those who act as managers or overseers of more junior consultants who actually do the majority of the work?"

As with the clients, the heads of the search firms were asked to limit their nominees to no more than six from their own organizations. Again, in order to establish the most capable individual of those they listed, the addressees were asked: "If the entire reputation and future of your firm rested on the success of one exceptionally significant search, to which of those you nominated would you entrust that search?" The last question asked of the recruiter group was to provide the names of up to six of the most effective headhunters from executive search firms *other than their own.* Survey forms came back from 311 of the 366 search firms queried, a response rate of approximately 85 percent.

The combined survey responses from both client organizations and executive search firms resulted in a total of 837 individual executive recruiters who received at least one nomination for excellence. Because many of these came close to qualifying for a spot among the Top 100 listed in Chapter 5, a second group of 100 recruiters has been compiled and ranked along with their Top 100 peers in Chapter 7. This group of Top 2 Percenters has achieved a very high standing among 10,000 colleagues. Many of these individuals actually outrank those from the Top 100 in their areas of recruiting specialization.

The Weighting System Used to Select and Rank Nominees

Recruiter nominations have been valued differently depending on their source. An individual could be nominated only once by his or her own firm, but this seems to be the most highly valued of all mentions and has been assigned five points. Mention by a competitor search firm was worth only one point. Information about the quality of a search consultant's work, especially from a competitor's vantage point, is definitely not as valid as the assessment made by one's own firm. Nominations from clients were viewed as falling about midway between the two or three points each. To be judged as the very best recruiter by either a client or by one's own recruiting organization was worth an additional two points.

Some might quibble with this weighting formula and the point allocations, yet we could find no fairer system. They might contend that to be nominated by a very large search firm like Korn/Ferry International or Russell Reynolds Associates should be worth more than the nomination from a very small firm, but the nominee of a small firm may be every bit as vital to its effectiveness and survival as the nominees of Russell Reynolds and Korn/Ferry are to them. The critic who maintains that to be nominated by General Motors should be worth more points than to be mentioned by AON Corporation, the smallest company on the *Fortune* 500 lists, should realize that the work the headhunter did for the folks at AON was probably as consequential to them, maybe more so, than what the other headhunter did for General Motors.

Some recruiters might say that the data are methodologically flawed because questionnaires to clients were directed to the corporate offices and specifically to their Chief Executive Officers. They might say they have conducted thirteen successful searches in a row for a multibillion dollar corporation's division located in an alkali flat outside Winnemucca, Nevada. This geographically disadvantaged but stellar headhunter doubts whether the CEO of the parent company back on Park Avenue even knows that the division exists, let alone that he has enticed into Winnemucca everyone from the division's Chief Scorpion Exterminator to its Senior Rocket Scientist. On the other hand, the Vice President of Human Resources or some other officer somehow may have heard about this recruiter and mentioned to the CEO what a superior headhunter he was. But if no one did, that's why the CEO knows only those who have managed to progress beyond recruiting in plants, divisions, subsidiaries, or the Australian outback and found themselves searching—for better or worse—in corporate offices. Most of us who believe that cream rises to the top also can appreciate that the same might hold true for those offering professional services to organizations.

The profiles of the Top 100 are arranged in the book alphabetically, and within the Areas of Recruiter Specialization chapter individuals are ranked on a frequency-of-mention basis. Each of the Top 100 was asked to select up to ten functional areas of recruiting competence and up to ten organizational specialties. Choices were listed in descending order of the recruiter's own preference and experience. Recruiters qualifying as Top 2 Percenters had the same selection opportunities.

A weighting formula was also applied to the Areas of Recruiter Specialization compilation in arriving at the actual rankings of recruiters within each category. Although a few of the old guard may differ with me, it is my conviction that no recruiter can be equally competent in every choice of functional or organizational expertise. Accordingly, a sequential reduction of 10 percent of the recruiter's total nomination points was made for each selection below a first choice. As an example, recruiters who accumulate an overall point total of 85 received full value for their first choice in both the functional area and organizational preferences. But their point totals—and thus their place in the rankings—for their fifth choices would be 51, a reduction of 40 percentage points. Their tenth-place choices, if they selected that many, would give them a point total of 10 percent of their overall total or 8.5 points.

Search consultants who work almost exclusively in specific fields like health care, hospitality, and legal, are ranked only in the organizational categories in which they concentrate. Their choice of functional competencies, however, are treated in the same way as those who do not specialize. With this in mind, the user of this book should consult the rankings of both functional preferences *and* organizational specialization in selecting those recruiters to contact. Failing to cross-reference could result in the mutually wasteful consideration of a recruiter who is experienced only in health care searches being approached by either an employer or individual seeking a General Manager's position in industry—simply because the health care recruiter ranked relatively high in the functional area of general management yet does no recruiting at all in industry.

Characteristics of the Top 100

The Top 100 are a diverse group. Who, for instance, would believe that a headhunter, stuffy as they are perceived to be, would claim collecting erotic art as a special interest? Or that several of them know that a Royal Coachman belongs more appropriately amid the riffles of the Beaverkill River than the pomp of Buckingham Palace? Back on dry land, there's the recruiter who jumps horses and studies the Enneagram. The principal difference in her interests is that one concerns itself with the behavior of a four-legged animal, the other with the personality of a two-legged variation.

Geographically, those in the Top 100 hail from all over the United States, but most have found their professional bases in the major cities. As one might expect, New York is the home office for the greatest number (forty-six) with Chicago living up to its reputation as second city. The West Coast is well represented, but the Southeast, Pacific Northwest, the Plains states, Mountain states, and Middle Atlantic are not. One recruiter who must not mind the vicissitudes of travel has recently set up shop in Marco Island, Florida.

They are a well-educated group. Only five lack an undergraduate degree, and almost half possess master's or law degrees. Although many of the clients and candidates they serve have graduate business degrees from premier business schools, relatively few of the Top 100 have similar degrees from prestigious institutions.

The Top 100 are also well seasoned. They are not young hot-shots like the investment community brags about—or at least used to. The average age of America's most accomplished recruiters is an AARP-qualifying fifty-four. The youngest is thirty-seven, as of this writing, and the oldest is eighty-five. Perhaps even more impressive is that these recruiters average nearly nineteen years of executive recruiting experience. It clearly takes many years to build up the relationships, credibility, and reputation to make it into the top 1 percent. Once there, though, few step down at sixty-five. It might be said that old headhunters never die, they just dial away.

Virtually all the top recruiters have worked for more than one employer in the search business. Most of these prior employers have been other executive search firms, but others have been with general management consulting or public accounting firms. Frequently, those who cut their teeth in consulting firms were part of those organizations' recruiting divisions.

If there is a so-called academy firm known for developing good search consultants in the same vein that Procter & Gamble trains top consumer marketing professionals, it is Booz, Allen & Hamilton. Thirteen of the Top 100 recruiters received their initial training in this leading general management consulting firm. Booz, Allen, whose leadership became increasingly skittish about executive recruiting, finally dissolved its search arm in 1979. Ironically, the combined revenues of the many search firms spawned and staffed by Booz, Allen & Hamilton alumni exceed severalfold the annual billings of their venerable alma mater.

Recruiters have long debated about the type of work background that leads to a successful career in the search business. Many have claimed that a strong grounding in personnel or human resources is desirable and gives the search consultant a considerable advantage. A review of the backgrounds of the Top 100 recruiters shows that almost half of the top recruiters have personnel backgrounds but the majority do not. General management or marketing and sales is the functional career path of two in five. Thirteen trained in the financial function.

Unlike their colleagues in other personal services vocations like medicine, teaching, law, public accounting, banking, and the ministry, it is probable that not one of the Top 100 ever planned a career in executive recruiting. Serendipity was how they found their way into the career they now excel at, and not one recruiter that I have talked with thinks of leaving it.

Search legends Paul R. Ray, Sr., and Gardner W. Heidrick have seen their sons follow in their footsteps, including joining them among the elite profiled in this book. The Top 100 also includes a husband and wife team: Barbara L. Provus is a Partner with Sweeney Shepherd Bueschel Provus Harbert & Mummert and her husband, Frederick W. Wackerle, is Partner with McFeely Wackerle Jett. Two of those in the Top 100 were founders of major search firms still bearing their names, but they themselves have left and hung out their own shingles elsewhere. Gardner W. Heidrick left Heidrick & Struggles, Inc. to link up with son Robert and fit into The Heidrick Partners, and Bob Lamalie has started over again after selling Lamalie Associates to its employees.

An Executive Recruiter's Twelve Most Important Personal and Professional Qualities

One of the most interesting results of the surveys done of both client organizations and recruiting firms was the response to this open-ended question posed to both groups: "What personal and professional qualities do you ascribe to the most effective executive recruiters you know?" The descriptors were selected by the respondents themselves. Tables 1-1 and 1-2 list those responses, which offer some important messages for recruiters and clients alike.

Before analyzing the significance of what the two groups have to say about the qualities of effective headhunters, it is

Table 1-1.   Client Choices.

Quality	Percentage of Clients Mentioning
Knowledge of our business/industry	51%
Integrity/honesty	48
Communications	16
Thoroughness	13
Presence/image	13
Intelligence	10
Assessment/interviewing skills	10
Discretion/confidentiality	9
Tenacity/hard-working	7
Judgment	7
Well connected	6
Creativity/resourcefulness	5

Table 1-2.   Recruiter Choices.

Quality	Percentage of Recruiters Mentioning
Integrity/honesty	39%
Tenacity/hard-working	25
Intelligence	14
Judgment	10
Good listener	9
Persuasiveness	8
Enthusiasm/energy level	8
Thorough	8
Closer/negotiator	7
Intuition	7
Empathy	6
Commitment to client	6

important to remember that clients will perceive those who serve them in a quite different light from how headhunters view themselves. Both groups consider integrity and honesty to be very important but vary in their assessments of other qualities. Clients, perhaps understandably, place a greater premium on what might be considered more pragmatic descriptors. Highest on their list is the requirement for "knowledge on the part of the recruiter about our business and industry." Communication from the recruiter also ranks high with clients. Although both of these major qualities may be universally appreciated by recruiters, neither makes it into their top dozen choices. Both view thoroughness as nearly equal in importance, but clients place recruiter presence and image high on their list. Presence doesn't show up on the recruiters' rankings at all. Both value tenacity and being hard-working, although the recruiters view this as far more important than their clients.

Headhunters can clearly benefit from what clients say they are looking for, but clients themselves need to be more searching in selecting the criteria by which they judge recruiters. The average recruiter questionnaire had eight qualities ascribed to the best recruiters, while the average client questionnaire—of which over 600 were returned—contained only three qualities. Clients consistently listed knowledge of our business and industry and recruiter integrity as very important but were less diligent in identifying additional recruiter qualities. Surely the

selection of an outstanding recruiter or the right search consultant to use on a significant search merits more client discrimination than only two or three criteria for qualification.

The biggest surprise to executive recruiters in general is
that the survey reveals that with the exception of a few search
consultants who concentrate their work in a single area of specialization, *none of the Top 100 who recruit essentially in industry
enjoys anything close to preeminence in the minds of managers of client
organizations.* This fact from the real world of executive employment is probably the greatest revelation to be derived from all
of the survey data.

The functional area of general management, as listed in
Chapter 7, affords the best opportunity to determine which
executive recruiter might lay claim to being the best of the best.
Although Gerry Roche of Heidrick & Struggles, Inc. leads this
functional area, which virtually all of the recruiters selected as
an area of strength, he accomplished this feat with minimal help
from client nominations. He received a maximum number of
points from his own firm, but what boosted him above all others in this category were the substantial number of nominations
from recruiters with competing search firms.

It is little different with many of the other recruiters ranking in the top ten in the general management category. In fact,
a number of headhunters as far down the list as in the thirties
and forties received more client nominations than Mr. Roche
and the majority of the others in the top ten. But outside of
their number of clients, who clearly think well of them, these
individuals farther down the list are not yet well known among
their recruiting colleagues. As with all assessments of excellence,
what may be *perceived* as true counts just as much, sometimes
even more, than all the cold hard facts in the world.

Unlike recruiters in the industrial recruiting areas described
above, recruiters serving only specialized categories often dom-
inated their fields. The highest-ranking headhunters in such specific fields as health care and hospitality enjoy commanding
shares of those markets. One of these individuals received nominations from twenty different client organizations, fifteen of
which also considered this recruiter the best in their field.

Taking a broad projective view of what the survey data tell
us about recruiters in general and the clients they serve seems

to indicate that the future for America's headhunters looks promising in every aspect. Notwithstanding the growth of large firms, many with their own international arms or affiliates, executive recruiting is still a business of individuals. Recruiters may band together in large, medium-sized, and small firms, but what counts most is how well they perform as individuals. Both clients and the recruiters themselves strongly agree on this point. Almost 99 percent of all client organizations surveyed said that it was the individual recruiter, not the recruiter's firm, that made the difference in whom they selected to serve them, and 97 percent of the recruiters agreed. This response suggests a need for growing specialization on the parts of individual recruiters, if not firms themselves. Clients appear to be increasingly sensitive to search firm fees, especially where a fair percentage of search time is spent by a consultant who is simply getting up to speed in a business or area of activity.

The fact that no single recruiter is dominating the general industrial and business marketplace—by far the largest sector—means that opportunities to achieve individual excellence abound today and will likely multiply in the future. Because there is a limit to the number of clients that any recruiter can serve well, it is understandable why top recruiters want to work on only the most senior searches, which offer high fee prospects. This means that there will be increasing opportunities both now and in the future for other recruiters to advance in the business. Moreover, sectors like academia, municipalities, and government agencies, which have been limited users of retainer recruiters in the past, are increasing their use of these recruiters.

Just over the horizon may be the greatest boon of all for the headhunters of America—a skilled labor shortage the likes of which this country has never witnessed before. There is a rosy future for those who ply their trade as headhunters, but the promises of the future must be balanced against this prophetic and sobering maxim. When you're an executive recruiter, you're only as good as your last search.

Bestowing on any group of individuals the mantle of the best or the Top 100 or the Top 2 Percenters is bound to stir the hackles of those who didn't quite qualify but believe they fully merit the same recognition. This is especially true the first time such a culling of competence is attempted. Notwithstanding the tiny tempests likely to swirl around this pioneering selection of the top executive recruiters of America, the book is designed to help those who most need it. In *The Career Makers: America's Top 100 Executive Recruiters,* every professional anxious to move up, whether their interest in making a change is self-initiated or employer-induced, can find a helpmate—or a number of them. The same holds true for employers of all types that pursue excellence of performance among the executive search consultants they retain at such lofty fees.

2

Cultivating the Top Recruiters and Gaining Their Help

How would you like to be on the inside and have a way of knowing about unpublicized jobs that become available in your field of work or interest—opportunities you would otherwise never know of? Wishful thinking, you may say. No, individuals just like you, hunkered down in employers' trenches, enjoy all the real and psychic benefits of such a pipeline of privileged information. They do so because they're plugged in with the *right* executive recruiters. Perhaps surprisingly, your current line of work or level of management responsibility makes little difference in your access to these recruiters. If you are a professional in any field, a distinct career advantage is also open to you.

All it takes is getting to know personally at least a few of America's top 200 executive recruiters. How to accomplish this is another matter. Bear in mind that the only thing a search consultant really sells is time, and every hour and fraction thereof is precious. The most accomplished practitioners—the ones this book is about and who handle the most significant and attractive jobs in the field—guard their time zealously. But you've got TSD—talent, smarts, and determination—on your side. In today's job market cultivating some top recruiters should be your highest priority. Don't sit back passively any longer! Once you get aggressive and find these people, you can make them into collaborators in your career progress and success.

Fortunately for you, every recruiter has time for talented or high-potential individuals who can help fill current or future search assignments. Regardless of how good a search consultant's personal research skills are or how good a firm's research staff is, recruiters are always looking for (and sometimes have forgotten about) highly capable prospects for top jobs in every field. The challenge to professionals who aspire to better opportunities is how to become known in the first place to the best headhunters and how to rekindle their interest when initial contact with them may have occurred long ago.

Simply sending a resume to every individual in this book just won't work. The very busy men and women who qualify for mention here receive 30 to 100 unsolicited managerial and executive-level resumes every day. To that number, add another dozen or so unsolicited telephone calls. A standard resume or telephone call by itself seldom pays off. Attempting to be clever or cutesy with a resume is no better. A few of the latter, however, have stood out in my mind from the tide of a half million or so resumes that have washed across my desk in the last twenty years. Some of the following real-world examples of what *not* to send will be worth far more to you than some general admonitions against so-called creative resumes.

An especially memorable example of a too-cute resume was a four-page all-color resume sent from a man in New Mexico. Page one was a giant photographic close-up of his outstretched hand with the word *MEET* in boldface upper-case letters. Page two had his name and a full-page shot of his face, with the lens clearly too close to his nose. The third page showed the job seeker full-length, Samson-like, apparently holding up the arches of a Spanish mission somewhere. Page four finally got around to stating his interest in finding a new job, presumably in construction—or was it demolition?

Then there have been the product resumes. A lemon came in a small, brown cardboard box, accompanied by a meticulously folded resume proclaiming that the sender was not a lemon. A marketing man taped a very shiny aluminum bolt to his resume to show off one of his greatest new product successes. For some reason he chose not to send the nut.

Baseball cards have been designed to show work history, accompanied by a note saying that the sender wished to be traded. A three-foot telegram once arrived from a suburb fifteen minutes from our offices. I've seen all sorts of questionnaires, advertisements for the sender, reader response cards, comic strips, videos, and portraits, most of the latter looking like they came from the post office wall. And as might be expected, not all of these ingenious creations were conceived in the fertile minds of men. I remember receiving a lady's white glove with a note stapled to it saying, "Shall we dance?" Inside was a folded resume—along with a dance card neatly filled in with the names of twelve companies to which she wanted to be introduced.

Regrettably, weaknesses in this woman's resume made it evident why she probably remained a wallflower for most of her career. The same held true for the other individuals who composed the most memorable of the creative resumes. I can't recall a single instance where the sender was invited in for an interview. Our staff always enjoys receiving such efforts, and we chuckle over many of them. A high reading on the laugh meter, however, does not seem to warrant a face-to-face session with a gimmicky resume creator.

So if novel resumes don't work, how *does* one begin to establish contact with the most effective headhunters? Resumes that are properly directed—that are rifle-shot to the right recruiters—can and do work. But so do some other techniques—sometimes even better.

The best time to start looking for a job is before you have to. This is especially true if you hope to get maximum assistance from America's top headhunters. There are ways to reach out for help when you're already out of a job or on outplacement, and we'll talk about these techniques later in this chapter. But the surest way to gain a headhunter's assistance is to acquaint yourself with the right ones before you really need their help. The more the merrier, and the earlier in your career you can do this, the better.

Initiating a Relationship with the Recruiters Who Count

Except for those fortunate few who are approached regularly by the *right* headhunters, most of us have to be the initiators of the relationships we establish with recruiters—and that is what it is, a relationship. To think that any recruiter is going to jump through hoops for you just because you believe that your resume paints the picture of an exceptional talent is naive. Not only do search consultants get many resumes every day "over the transom," but most of these resumes never are seen by the recruiters they're addressed to. Search firms, except for the smallest, have research departments, and these unsolicited resumes are first screened at the hands of researchers. Only if a background appears to meet the specific needs of a current search is the resume passed along to the recruiter handling that search. The chances of your unsolicited resume fitting an ongoing search, even in one of the largest search firms, is probably less than one in a hundred. The odds are worse in smaller firms.

Some recruiters never consider an unsolicited resume. They always generate their own candidates, or so they say. Consider this type of headhunter to be about as smart as the miner panning for gold who throws away the nugget that gets wedged between his toes because he didn't find it in the bottom of his pan. In short, don't be discouraged by such claims. The recruiters good enough to be listed in this book are savvy enough to accept any favor, including those that come unexpectedly over the transom.

Tough as the odds are of using a resume to start building the all-important relationship with the right recruiters, there are some ways to dramatically improve your chances. It comes down to basic marketing. If you think of yourself as a new product—a very good new product—that you're launching, then your resume represents that new product. Your resume reflects what your product is made of, what it has been able to do in the past, and what its potential is for the future.

But an appealing new product by itself is not enough in today's job market. Your consumer—in this case, a headhunter—must want to pick your new product off a shelf that's already glutted with both old and other new products. What your new product needs is what we call a "handle"—a special attractor that positions your new product (consider it packaging) and causes your consumer to reach out and select it from all the others on the shelf. The handle we're talking about can be presented best in the cover letter that accompanies your resume. The cover letter should not take up more than three to five paragraphs and never exceed a page in length. But most important is what the cover letter says and to whom.

Virtually all resumes that reach our top recruiters are accompanied by cover letters. Yet not one cover letter in fifty contains an effective handle. This deficiency is even more pronounced with the standardized cover letters (to say nothing about resumes) pouring out of guide books on how to write a resume and from the boilerplate files of outplacement firms. *Finding the handle that makes your resume stand out to the right executive recruiters is the single most important objective for smart job seekers today.*

This book gives you more opportunities for coming up with handles that sell than have ever been available before. You should start your search for these handles by first identifying the recruiters who should be the targets of your new product marketing effort. Let's say that your background and future interests happen to be in the high-tech, electronics, and office machinery industries. A quick turn to Chapter 7, Areas of Recruiter Specialization, and the subheading of Organizational or Industry Specialization will give you a list of individual search consultants most heavily involved in these industries. There are plenty of recruiters to choose from—for your purposes, perhaps too many. Your interests then should be further refined to include your functional areas of competence. Let's say that they are in general management and industrial marketing. Under Chapter 7's other subheading, Functional Specialization, you can find recruiters with significant recruiting experience and clients in these two functional areas. Look for the overlap of those who have proficiency in both the *organization and industry* areas of interest and the *functional* areas you prefer. The list of recruiters you generate from this cross-referencing will become your own personal target list of executive recruiters.

As you can expect, the more specialized and esoteric your interests, the fewer the number of headhunters who will be on your target list. Opening up your criteria somewhat will give you a larger number of headhunters to cultivate. For example, the merchandising manager interested in getting into television broadcasting should include recruiters with strengths in functional areas such as editorial and advertising/promotion, in

addition to recruiters listed with organization and industry specialties of communications and radio/television broadcasting.
Incidentally, while the top recruiters have indicated the "minimum salary level at which I work," do not be dissuaded from
including them on your target list just because your current
earnings fall short by $20,000 to $30,000 of that level. With few
exceptions, these top recruiters have considerable flexibility, and
a fair amount of inflation creeps into their proclaimed recruiting minimums. It is also worth noting that almost two-thirds of
the Top 100 and Top 2 Percenters combined will recruit at salary levels between $50,000 and $100,000.

Those in the executive recruiting business get turned off by
some of the utterly unrealistic interests expressed by job seekers. A recent one I remember was the thirty-seven-year-old who
loved skiing and trout fishing and would only "consider a position in Colorado Springs, Jackson Hole, or the Lake Tahoe
area," as he put it. His entire work experience had been in
pharmaceutical research, but to my knowledge there are no drug
companies anywhere close to these locations. Another was the
ex–Deputy Undersecretary of Agriculture who wrote indicating
his readiness to "take on a Chief Executive Officer's position in
a multibillion dollar agribusiness company." Umpteen school
teachers have written about their preparation to run large
departments in the business world because as one put it, "If you
can manage their children, you can manage their parents."

But let's assume that your goals are more realistic, and
armed now with your target list of names of recruiters, it's time
to get personal. Chapter 5 contains the profiles in alphabetical
order of America's 100 top recruiters. As will be shown, there
are many opportunities to find handles for those with profiles.
But your target list may also include some recruiters in the Top
2 Percenter group, since they are also ranked in Chapter 7 in
the Areas of Recruiter Specialization. Although no profiles are
provided for these highly accomplished runners-up, Chapter 6
contains their names and firm addresses. This information can
serve as an adequate handle to begin developing them to
become your future helpmates, just as you would with recruiters
from the Top 100. Do not concern yourself with where any of
the recruiters in this book are based. They serve clients nationwide and, in some instances, internationally as well.

Study the profiles of the recruiters from the Top 100 who make your list. In addition to the obvious handle you already have—that they recruit in your areas of functional and organizational interest—there are many other opportunities to find additional handles on which to capitalize. Our goal is to find as many common threads of interest, contacts, or coattails as we can.

The possibilities are limited only by one's resourcefulness and luck. I remember when one of America's largest search firms would interview almost anybody who graduated from Yale. (And not coincidentally, many of their original staff hailed from that esteemed Ivy League institution.) Another senior recruiter was an avid supporter of Ducks Unlimited. He was never blind (pardon the pun) to meeting with those who shared his water-fowl hunting interest. The old school tie has great appeal for many recruiters, as does the locale where they grew up. If you can establish a link to either and communicate that effectively, your chances of meeting that headhunter face-to-face soar. Belonging to the same private club, or knowing someone influential who does, can also increase your chances appreciably.

Each of the top recruiters has been asked to describe *in their own words* what they look for in a candidate. The adroit professional who picks up on what a recruiter says about candidates who have "the right stuff" and draws a convincing parallel, or offers a sharp rebuttal, often is rewarded with some form of dialogue with that recruiter. Headhunters, even busy ones, are great philosophers and generalizers and love spirited discourse. The range of their anecdotes is exceeded in modern times only by Ronald Reagan's.

There are two other major areas of opportunity for finding a handle in each profile. The first of these is in the recruiter's employment history. Perhaps you were toiling in the textile stretch department of Jockey International at the same time your target recruiter was over in marketing warming up Jim Palmer for his classic underwear ads. Reference to a former employer held in common works even better when you were higher up in the organization than the recruiter—unless, of course, you were part of the reason the recruiter left, in which case it may be more astute for you to skip to the next individual on your target list. (Search consultants have long memories for setbacks.)

Another highly effective area of opportunity for identifying a handle is the recruiter's list of "significant and representative placements." Perhaps you know one of the five that most of the Top 100 have named, or you might know a senior executive who works in a placement's organization. Few handles are as likely to capture a headhunter's attention as a specific reference to a past or current client. Although you can certainly refer to the individual you know either in your cover letter or in a telephone contact, by far the most successful way of exploiting this handle is to have your friend in the client organization make the connection for you. It's astonishing how accessible headhunters are when a client is doing your bidding for you.

By this time you probably have the picture: The way to get the initial attention of top recruiters is to employ a handle that plays to their background and special interests or makes clear that you know someone who has the current or potential clout to either help or hurt that recruiter. But exercise good judgment in this last area. Stating that you know or are being referred by major public or professional figures and celebrities can backfire on you. I'm reminded in particular of a cover letter I received from an investment banker who said he was referred to me by "our mutual good friend, Ivan Boesky." No one in my office had ever met or had any contact with Mr. Boesky, whose position atop the arbitrage world came tumbling down about the time I received the banker's letter.

You don't need many handles with each recruiter on your target list. One will do nicely, more if you have them, but don't force them on the headhunters you wish to cultivate. I recommend writing about the handle in your cover letter. Getting past a headhunter's secretary via the telephone is about as easy as reaching the IRS with a question at tax return time.

Some job seekers may not be able to come up with any handles at all for some of the search consultants on their target lists. Among them may be the ones highest on their list. What then? Well, you're reasonably fortunate already because you know precisely which recruiters to attempt to establish relationships with—the ones in your fields of particular interest. These same recruiters also have some interest in getting to know you because you have experience in the fields in which they do much of their work. Their research departments or secretaries may have instructions to forward such resumes to them with or without handles.

Or you can be audacious and solicit the help of a gadfly or two. Every industry and every profession seems to have a few of them. They can be both a curse and salvation for an executive recruiter. A gadfly is that unusual person who seems to know everything going on in a given industry or occupation and all the right people to influence. Gadflies get their name because they are endowed with a special antenna for picking up scuttle-butt and then passing it along with about as much discretion as your local barber or hairdresser.

Executive recruiters enjoy a love/hate relationship with gad-flies: On the one hand they appreciate the industry information and names that gadflies volunteer so readily; but on the other, gadflies have no qualms about breaking a confidence—which, for many searches, can spell disaster. Enlisting the aid of a gadfly can help you make a connection with a recruiter. Gad-flies know the recruiters who work in their fields, and whether recruiters like it or not, they are to some extent dependent on referrals from these individuals. So take a gadfly to lunch—at least once. It can work wonders for you in opening recruiters' doors.

Gadflies usually work in organizations other than your own. Yet there may well be individuals within your own organiza-tion—former supervisors, peers, or subordinates—who are in a position to help you become known to those on your target list. Let me tell you about one company where this type of network has served many former and current employees very well. Proc-ter & Gamble is one of the most difficult companies to pene-trate for information about its people. Unless a caller has a specific name to offer, P&G's switchboard operators and secre-taries will neither refer your call nor provide a name. In short, the company is a very tough nut to crack for any recruiter or employer.

P&G is very happy that its managerial talent is well insu-lated from those seeking to recruit them. For someone who works for Procter & Gamble and may wish to leave the com-pany, however, this stringent security blanket greatly reduces access to outside opportunities. Fortunately, there has existed in P&G for many years a small group of senior individuals who

have a wide range of contacts with executive recruiters who specialize in work in the consumer packaged goods field. While
these Procter & Gamble managers are still with the company,
they have been the clandestine vehicle by which many of their
former colleagues have jumped ship and gone on to opportunities elsewhere. Most P&Gers know who these valuable confidants are. You may have similar individuals within your own
organization. Make it a point to get to know them—discreetly,
of course.

Staying in The Recruiter's Mind
Until the Right Job Comes Along

Whether you have used resumes with smart cover letters or
the intercessions of contacts, sooner or later your efforts will be
rewarded with a call or letter from those on your target list.
When this happens, you can consider yourself to be on the
brink of being in the recruiter's system. You want that with a
passion. Most often the first communication from the headhunters you're trying to cultivate will come in the form of a telephone call. How you handle that contact determines how much
of a prospect, and perhaps later a candidate, you become to that
recruiter.

The best recruiters do not make idle telephone calls. When
one calls you, you can be sure that the recruiter is doing one
or more of these three things: (1) sounding you out as a possible candidate; (2) determining whether you might be a source—
in other words, whether you can suggest a candidate or two; or
(3) repaying a favor to a client, former client, prospective client,
a prior placement, a fellow recruiter, a current candidate, or a
gadfly. Regardless of the recruiter's motives for calling you, do
something on your end of the line to cause that recruiter to
have good reason to either arrange a personal visit or make a
mental note to keep in touch with you. In brief, don't squander
the opportunity to make yourself memorable to that headhunter.

If you are fortunate enough to fit a search that the recruiter currently is working on, you'll have plenty of opportunities to make yourself memorable—even if something happens to cause you not to get the job. The search consultant who has brought you along as a candidate will have started a file on you. This file, or a printout of key elements in your background, will be available for years to come not only to the recruiter you first met but to all other search consultants in that firm, including branch offices as well.

But what if that first call is about a job you don't fit at all, or it's from that tireless headhunter we heard about earlier in this book who is the expert on recruiting in Winnemucca, Nevada. He's now looking for a Deputy Scorpion Exterminator, and you know your wife won't give up her tennis in Greenwich. Do you just say, "No, I'm not interested" and hang up? No, instead put your mind in gear to help that hapless headhunter. The light bulb goes on in your memory bank of seldom-used but hopefully useful facts, and out comes a response like this: "I'm sorry I'm not quite right for your search, but I do have a suggestion of a possible candidate for you. He and I were in Vector Control while we were both in the service. The last I heard he was an entomologist killing roaches for Raid up in Racine, Wisconsin. Would you like to know more about him?" Of course your recruiter friend would.

Or maybe your response is along these lines: "Try as I might, I don't have a single individual to suggest to you as a candidate, but I can give you the names of a couple of terrific sources. They own their own exterminating businesses, so aren't recruitable, but they know everybody who ever zapped a rat or killed bugs dead." In addition to gems like these, you might know of a trade journal on pest control or an association concerned with insect annihilation. Whatever you do, leave that recruiter whom you have worked so hard to cultivate with food for thought—and a nice warm feeling that you are a very worthwhile contact. Your name and phone number will go into the recruiter's workbook as a good source—someone for him to call again.

Then, as fate would have it, a week later you see in the trade press that Boyle-Midway, which markets a line of insecticides, is cutting back. Promptly you follow up with your recruiter friend by phone or with a copy of the news clipping. By this time most of the top 200 recruiters in this book will very likely have started a file on you even if you have not yet become a candidate on any of their searches.

Now it's a matter of gently but regularly stuffing the file folder with your name on it in that headhunter's office. You're in no immediate hurry to make a change, but you do want to know when an exceptional opportunity opens up. You remind yourself—and your spouse—that there really are tennis courts outside of Greenwich, Forest Hills, and Wimbledon.

This is as good a time as any to raise the issue of movable spouses and children. Today it is nearly as likely that it will be the female as the male partner getting the call from the head-hunter. Will her mate move? Will the children move? Address the subject head on and early on, so you don't end up leaving someone holding the bag later on. Every headhunter has dozens of war stories about the candidate who went all the way to the altar—had an offer, maybe even accepted it—and then found that the anchor at the homefront wouldn't budge. I've had experiences like this cover the gamut of everything from the eighteen-year-old Olympic diving hopeful who couldn't leave her coach in Florida to allow her father to take a major job in Washington, DC (she didn't qualify later in the Olympic trials) to the househusband who didn't want his wife to accept a new opportunity in Coatesville, Tennessee, because he was concerned about the quality of preschool education there to the trauma of losing a very senior executive who accepted a new job in Connecticut, bought a home there, permitted announcements to go out to the employees and press of his joining, and then vanished from the scene because his wife decided she couldn't bear to leave her mother in Southern California.

Hopefully, your anchor is free of these kinds of deterrents and for the right kind of opportunity in the right part of the country you're reasonably mobile. Having determined this, you're free to continue saturating your friendly headhunter's mind and file system with information that tells him how accomplished you are. He already has a copy of your resume. You sent him one previously, but did he keep it? Better send him a second one just to be sure, and attached to it might be a short note that says something along these lines: "Just thought you'd like to add this most recent information on me to your file. My current compensation is a base of $65,000 with a bonus paid last February of $15,000. I remain keenly interested in a Vice President–Marketing job in the insecticide field."

Don't be concerned if no acknowledgments come from your recruiter. Keep adding to his file on you. Some always helpful items are company news releases or house organs that talk about your department or division or *Advertising Age* or some other trade journal that has an article that talks about you or a new product you've launched.

If you happen to be with a government agency, school system, college or university, hospital, hotel, or association, the same logic holds. Take advantage of articles and stories that talk about you and what you are responsible for. But please do not send complete curriculums that you've worked on for your high school, a copy of the Federal Budget for the United States of America with a paperclip on the page that refers to your department in a footnote, or the membership directory for the University Club—copies of each of which I have received in the past.

Annual reports can be good or bad. Unless you are President, Chairman, or the Vice President of Communications responsible for its production, do not send the full report. Select a summary page from the financials or those pages from the President's letter or from the report somewhere that refer to you and your department. Annual reports pollute headhunter's offices and take up valuable space in the circular files already overflowing with ill-directed resumes.

Now what's this we hear? You've won election to your local school board, you've been selected for the board of the National Pest Council of America. That is major news for your file so send it in. Membership, but especially leadership, in your association is one of the most important credentials you can add to your attributes in furthering your relationship with those on your target list. One of the most well-worn directories in any recruiter's office is the *Encyclopedia of Associations*. Few searches neglect contacting the leadership of trade associations or professional societies. The fact that your peers think enough of you to elect you to a leadership role in your field of work is one of the very strongest credentials any professional can have. Broadcast it.

In the final analysis, what every smart professional is really after is *visibility* with those on your target list. Very few of us become renowned in our own fields. We can dream about writing an article or a book or a scientific discovery of great merit that catches everyone's attention. But most of what goes into our file with our headhunter friends will be a steady accumulation of little things that eventually add up to a significant record of achievement. Never forget that visibility also can be acquired by what Daniel Patrick Moynihan has called "creeping gradualism." It may not be as exciting as achieving instant fame but often proves far more enduring.

What ranks at the top of my own list as one of the most savvy examples of a job seeker's ingenuity in getting my attention and appreciation occurred about five years ago. I received a telephone call from an individual whose name I only faintly recalled and whom I had never met. After identifying himself he told me that he had just learned that his trade association was going to replace their Executive Director and if I was interested in doing the search for his successor I should get in touch immediately with their President. I did so, presented our qualifications in the industry, and got the search with no competition. We subsequently did four more searches for the same association. Needless to say, my firm worked especially hard to find the right next job for the thoughtful job seeker who had done us such a favor. Within six months we had placed him in the General Manager's position he had been seeking and still holds today.

As one might expect, some things go into your file that you have not provided or even knew that your recruiter contact had. The headhunter you're out to win over will have made a note and put it in your file if you were abusive, devious, or pushy with his secretary. Or maybe he noticed that you wore short socks to your interview with him or that you bathed in so much perfume that he got a headache from your visit and couldn't work the rest of the day. Like many firms, my own has a form on which we evaluate every person we meet on such subjective factors as presence, energy level, listening ability, language facility, and many other personal factors. This too goes into your file although you will never see it. So will copies of the reference reports the recruiter does on you, including verification of your college degree—the single biggest item of candidate fabrication today and yet one of the easiest things for employers to check.

Perhaps you "forgot" in your resume to add a former employer you had for less than a year; a recruiter from your target list may discover this and add the information to your file. Or you might have made a "simple error" in calculation and overstated your earnings by 30 to 40 percent. When the recruiter uncovers that tidbit, another entry goes into your file. A cardinal rule for every headhunter is *no surprises for a client.* Your headhunter's entire reputation as a top professional rests on thoroughness. The best sniff out every fabrication. You can count on that from all of the Top 100 and Top 2 Percenters in this book.

It is hard for me to confess this, but even top search consultants have an endemic weakness. They are not very forgiving when a job seeker takes advantage of them. It is difficult for headhunters to build a relationship with a client and then win a search from that client. Recruiters do not take it kindly when a job seeker lets a headhunter down in such a way that it jeopardizes the relationship between consultant and client—or worst of all, ends it. Two of the most common embarrassments that recruiters suffer through are (1) when a candidate's spouse or family will not move after the breadwinner has proceeded all the way to the altar and received an offer and (2) when a candidate has received an offer from a new employer and then used that to extract a counteroffer from the old employer. Although black balls tend to take up too much file space, Avery Label makes a nice flat black dot that applies very neatly to an individual's file folder. Only the most foolish would risk that censure with any of the top 200. Many a professional who has taken advantage of a recruiter has discovered that even elephants don't survive as long as the memory of a headhunter wronged.

Fortunately, nothing like this is going to happen to you. You are out to develop the most positive possible relationship with the headhunters in your future. It might be interesting for you to scan the representative placements made by the Top 100. Impressive, aren't they? Remember too that these represent only a small fraction of that recruiter's work over the years. Those placements at one time were nothing more than names on a recruiter's long list of initial possibilities for that search. Some-how they prevailed over all the others. Each of them had a file started on them in that recruiter's office, probably years before they were ever placed. They very likely had files in other recrui-ters' offices too. Some had been placed by headhunter after headhunter throughout their rises to the top.

Many of America's top executives in every field of work have never really had to look for a job, even though they've had a number of different employers. The opportunities always came to them. In the majority of instances, the bearers of glad tidings were the headhunters they had met and cultivated along the way. Wouldn't it be nice to have the feeling that even while you have your head down working away at your current grindstone, someone out there is constantly sensitive to you and your aspi-rations? Your recruiter friends would be minding your career for you.

Even after you've succeeded in taking a new position with the help of a recruiter, don't just close the door on a relation-ship that took a long time to build and to pay off. A good recruiter is going to stay in touch with you, but that recruiter is more interested in hearing from you periodically. There may even come a time when you can reward your friend by passing along a search yourself. Just because you've been placed doesn't mean that your file goes into storage. Although no reputable recruiter is ever going to recruit you away from the client orga-nization where you were placed, the world of employment takes strange turns. Who knows when you may need your hard-earned friend again? Make that *friends.* You will want to keep in touch with all of those on your target list.

Cultivating the right headhunters can be the wisest invest-ment you'll ever make—one that pays dividends for a working lifetime and costs you nothing more than postage.

What to Do When the Axe Has Already Fallen

I've spent most of this chapter talking about ways to culti-vate headhunters. To get the best results and help from them requires time to build the relationship. Unfortunately, you may not have the luxury of time. What if you've been caught in one of the thousands of restructurings, downsizings, spinoffs, mega-mergers, LBOs, takeovers, and other similar traumas. Corporate raiders are as popular in the American workplace as Darth Vader or Muammar Qaddafi. In short, you're out of work—or "on the beach," as the headhunters put it.

If you're lucky, you've got outplacement help. If you're on your own, you need the information in these pages no less than those on outplacement. Either way, there's great urgency to your situation. This is not the time to worry about sending recruiters newsclippings to build your file. But neither is it the time to panic and shotgun several hundred boilerplate resumes to a long list of recruiting firms. Remember that until you're earning over $100,000 a year, only about 20 percent of your employment opportunities are going to involve executive recruiters. So your campaign to contact recruiters should be only one part of your master plan for finding a new job. (When you're earning $100,000 and up, that percentage shoots up to 30 percent or higher.)

The best way to start is to remind yourself that you have a giant advantage over every professional still working. While they're gainfully employed, working full-time, having to be super discreet if they're considering a change, *your full-time job is finding another one*. What an opportunity! You're free to find the perfect job for you now.

What's more, for the first time you have the chance to aim that part of your employment campaign involving headhunters directly at those individuals most likely to help you. They're no longer just a name listed in a directory with thousands of others. So turn quickly to Chapter 7, Areas of Recruiter Specialization. Create your own target list as described earlier in this chapter. Go first to the organization and industry subsection and then to the functional areas. Select a manageable number of recruiters who are ranked in both types of listings to constitute your target list. Choose anywhere from twenty to fifty individuals. If you come up with less than twenty, you're probably being too selective; more than fifty suggests you're not selective enough and your career itself may reflect a lack of direction.

The recruiters listed in your organization and industry selection should always take precedence over those listed under your functional specialty. The optimum choices are those recruiters you find listed in both the organization list *and* the functional list. The higher they stand on both lists, the higher on your target list they should be. It should make no difference to you whether those on your target list are those profiled in the Top 100 or whether they are Top 2 Percenters. Never forget that those Top 2 Percenters are just that: They rank among the top 2 percent of all of America's executive recruiters. At any given time, they, and not those in the Top 100, could be the ones working on the perfect job for you now.

From this point on, there are no special tricks to getting help from these top headhunters. Just hard work, diligence, follow-through, optimism, and fortuitous timing. Above all, this is not the time to passively sit back to wait for things to happen for you. They won't. And that new product you're launching, which happens to be you, has a limited shelf life. It's time to take charge of your career and job search. Go for the jugular. Here's how:

1. Study the profiles of the Top 100 on your target list.
2. Identify the handles you can use to help in making personal contact with them. You may want to refer to the section on handles earlier in this chapter. And don't forget to work on some handles for the Top 2 Percenters on your list either.
3. Incorporate your handles in a skillful cover letter—or in rare instances, they may be compelling enough to chance a telephone call to a specific recruiter.
4. Take another critical look at your resume. Does it really represent you well? Does it look attractive? Is it long enough? (Forget everything you've ever heard about a one-page resume.) Does it describe and not just name, your previous employers? Does it contain a clear description of what your job was and your accomplishments in it? Is it free of typos, grammatical errors, fabrications and distortions, and names of references? *Try to get a recruiter friend or someone in the employment field to critique it before you send it out.*
5. Contact the local chapter and national headquarters for your trade association or professional society. Which recruiters can they recommend to you? Are they willing to make a contact on your behalf?

6. Search out your gadflies and organization confidants. Don't forget to reach out for former colleagues who used to work with you and found new positions with the help of head-hunters. Which recruiters can they introduce you to?

7. Discover who your real friends are. Acquaint as many potentially helpful executives and contacts as you can with the great new product you're launching. What help can they give you in meeting the headhunters you need to know or possibly employers directly?

8. *Nurture, nurture, and nurture.* Follow up every lead, promote and market your new product like it's the next Big Mac, keep records of your job search, maintain a daily work schedule, and don't ever believe you are hounding anyone as much as you think you are.

If, after two months have gone by and you haven't made personal contact with at least a few of those on your target list, it's time to start over. One of those headhunters on your list may have just taken on a search that is tailor-made for you. Go for it.

3

An Employer's Guide to Working with the Top Recruiters

Pity the poor employer. Even when you believe you have engaged the right executive search firm to help you, the one that has served you so well in the past, your search for an absolutely essential new executive goes on and on. You're getting heat from the Chairman of the Board on down. You begin to wonder whether you've made the wrong choice of both recruiter and firm.

How well I remember what may have been the most difficult executive search in Booz, Allen & Hamilton's long history of executive recruiting. It started when the Chairman and Chief Executive Officer of one of America's largest diversified pharmaceutical firms engaged Booz, Allen to recruit an Executive Vice President to head up its then-fledgling hospital products group. The especially challenging twist to the search was that although the hospital group was the company's smallest at the time and least known, the ultimate placement had to have the near-term capability of becoming the corporate President and then Chief Executive Officer.

Booz, Allen had always done this drug company's search work, as well as virtually all of its general management consulting work. Without doubt, the company was one of the consulting firm's most significant clients. Adding to the sensitivity of the search was the fact that one of Booz, Allen's founding partners sat on the drug company's Board of Directors—no small embarrassment to the founder and a growing thorn in the side to the Chairman of the drug company as the search dragged on month by month with no sign of real progress. A year went by. Still no placement. The senior partners at Booz, Allen were wearing paths in the firm's Wedgwood-blue carpets pacing back and forth fretting over what to do. They could visualize their long-standing and very successful general management consulting work being jeopardized by the debacle of this highly visible but apparently doomed search. Three of the most senior professionals in the firm's Chicago search staff had tried and failed to find the right candidate. Booz, Allen then called in its New York recruiting arm and alerted the firm's worldwide staff of over 600 professionals to the urgency of this project. Word went out to the entire firm, support and professional personnel alike, that whoever could come up with the placement would receive a $5,000 bonus. But still no rabbits popped out of the hat.

One day, *twenty months after the start of the search,* the most junior recruiter in the consulting firm's New York office was thumbing through the annual report of a giant chemical company in connection with another search. Far in the back of the report was a small picture of an obscure divisional officer wearing a yellow hardhat apparently inspecting the chemical company's fermentation plant in Brazil. The individual in the hardhat was someone no researcher or anyone else in the firm had uncovered.

The mystery man in the yellow hardhat presides today over that drug company as its Chairman and CEO, just as planned. What did it ultimately cost the client company to recruit him? Booz, Allen in those days charged for its recruiting on a time and expense basis, like a law firm. Let's just say that the final percentage fee was probably the highest in recruiting history— about 85 percent of the placement's very hefty starting salary! And how about that alert young recruiter? Did he get his $5,000 bonus? Of course not! He was just doing his job.

After a horror story like that, an employer may wonder whether it's worth getting to know any executive recruiters at all. But would that drug company have found its new leader on their own? Very likely not. But did they pick the right recruiters to help them in the first place? That is certainly open to question. Was the huge fee they paid to find their future Chief Executive Officer worth it? Today they would answer with an unqualified yes.

Seventeen years have passed since that classic search. Much has changed in the world of executive employment. Four major reasons, some job-related and some personal, indicate why today it is even more important for employers of all types to know America's recruiters—especially the top ones:

1. You need to hire a talented professional right now.
2. You anticipate hiring a talented professional or a number of them in the not-distant future.
3. You want to be informed and realize it is savvy to know who the best recruiters are and their fields of specialization when a boss, fellow working associate, close friend, or family member asks you.
4. You possess the vision to realize that virtually all jobs today are subject to someone else's call. Today's employer is tomorrow's job seeker. You are wise enough to know that you may need help from America's best headhunters in a more intimate way—personally.

For whatever reason an employer initiates contact with an executive recruiter, the single most important decision is choosing the right individuals to serve you. Large search firms claim to provide resources to an employer that are unmatchable by smaller firms, and the small firms counter by emphasizing the personalized services they can offer and their access to a wider range of organizations they are free to probe for candidates. Both clients and recruiters agree, however, that the success of a search rests essentially with the skills and motivation of the individual recruiter handling the assignment.

Ironically, however, the most revealing piece of information derived from the comprehensive survey of several thousand client organizations and 366 executive search firms that forms the backbone of this project is that notwithstanding the prominence in the business press of a few New York-based headhunters *no single executive recruiter is preeminent in the minds of corporate clients.* As noted in an earlier chapter, some recruiters well down the lists of rankings actually received more nominations from client organizations than those standing in the top ten. In many other instances recruiters from the Top 2 Percenter group rank higher than individuals who qualified in the top 1 percent, the ones we have called the Top 100. Is it any wonder that employers of all types are frequently confused about whom to call when a need occurs either in their organization or for themselves personally?

Selecting the Recruiters to Get to Know

If you could persuade a headhunter to be completely open with you, and you asked this individual to tell you exactly which functions and types of industries or organizations he or she felt most competent and up-to-speed in, you would get the candid, marketplace-tested, first-of-its kind information you will discover later in this book. Unfortunately, at least for employers, organizations often approach recruiters with a question like this: "Tom, old friend, we're going to be looking for a new Senior Vice President of information services for our publishing division. Have you ever done a search like that?"

Tom, as eager as any other recruiter to book a search at a salary level well over $100,000 and not totally dishonest—after all, he did a search five years ago for a Director of Data Processing for a local newspaper—responds with, "Well, yes I have." Without further probing from the employer, one more search consultant who lacks the know-how and feel for the marketplace has just been qualified by an employer to perform a search they are not nearly as well equipped to carry out as others would be.

Can you blame the recruiter? Probably not. Ask a similar question of professionals in other competitive fields and you're likely to receive just as suspect an answer. Too many employers, whether they are in business or serve other types of organizations, are naive when it comes to selecting the right search consultants to serve them. They make three basic mistakes. The first of these is trusting good old Tom, who has recruited faithfully for them for years, to do all of their search work regardless of the functional area or business involved. The second occurs when an employer attempts to screen several recruiters for their competencies and makes the mistake of inquiring about their specific experience with no great diligence. The third mistake takes place when an employer calls a friend or contact who knows little regarding the exact need and inquires about which recruiter they have used in the past.

All three of these mistakes cost employers dearly. Not only should you as an employer wonder about the comprehensiveness of the universe for candidates ostensibly explored by a less-qualified recruiter, but you must also be concerned with the overall calibre of your placement—if, in fact, you achieved one. In addition, the reality is that a major part of the fee you paid that recruiter went to educate him or her about your industry or the function in which the search was conducted. *Fully one-third or more of the total fees paid to recruiters who are poorly chosen go toward helping them learn your business and then getting them up to speed in the specific areas they are called on to recruit.* All of this comes at your expense.

Those same dollars spent with the right executive recruiter go toward a precisely directed, decidedly more discriminating, and less time-consuming search. This usually leads to a considerably more successful ultimate placement. Until now, however, employers had few ways to identify the best-qualified recruiters to help them with each specific search. And major employers who hire many executives and other professionals every year often find themselves in a recruiting rut. They turn again and again to the same individual or individuals simply because they don't know better-qualified alternatives. Just as these organizations bring in fresh talent from the outside, they should periodically engage *well-qualified recruiters who are new to them.*

So you might ask, "How do I know whether I've been using the right recruiters to help me?" You've raised the right question. It's time to take advantage of the information in Chapter 7, Areas of Recruiter Specialization. Just as professionals looking for a new job were encouraged to do in the preceding chapter, turn to the section titled Organizational or Industry Specialization. If you have a recruitment need in the academic, association, health care, hospitality, or consulting areas, your recruiter choices are usually confined to those specialties alone. The same holds true for many industry areas of specialization. On the other hand, a number of industry classifications might warrant your inclusion of several different categories for recruiter consideration. For example, if your main business is in food products, the recruiters able to help you also could be listed in several other consumer product areas or possibly even under the holding company category. For the same reason, an employer whose principal business is in nonelectrical machinery may find it advantageous to consider recruiters listed under the fabricated metal products and electromechanical equipment categories.

In doing this initial sorting out of recruiters you are beginning to create your own target list of the right recruiters for you to become familiar with and possibly use in the near term or the future. You are likely to come up with a rather lengthy list of recruiters from this first screen, so it will be important to fine tune your list further. You can do this by referring next to the section titled Functional Areas of Specialization, which lists those recruiters reporting expertise in specific functional areas.

Some functions, like finance, planning, public relations, and human resources, can appear to be transferable to virtually any kind of industry or organization. Even so, there are subtle or not-so-subtle differences in the types of industries or organizations in which they operate. Whether one acknowledges this or not, your goal is to create a target list of recruiters whose names appear in your areas of choice in both the industry or organizational rankings *and* those for functional specialization. Again, you may find that you have more names of recruiters on your target list than you need or have the time to check out further. Narrow down your group of finalists for consideration to those standing highest in their respective rankings. Although most of these will be Top 100 recruiters, remember that Top 2 Percenters are no slouches when it comes to excellence of performance in their fields. If they make your short list for final consideration, they should be treated no differently than any of the Top 100.

When you have reduced your target list to a half dozen or so finalists, you're ready to make your first direct contacts with the recruiters themselves. Note that I say "recruiters themselves"—not their firms. Keep in mind that in using the information in this book, you are now able to do your own search, in effect, for the best individual recruiters to serve you or your organization. You have the right names and telephone numbers to use. Under no circumstances do you want to get passed along to some junior or less experienced recruiter who is a member of the same search firm. And unless your need is for an executive at the highest level of your organization, that's exactly what is likely to happen.

Accordingly, when you make your initial telephone calls to the finalists on your target list, ask who will actually handle your search. A number of other questions are equally important. And all of these qualifying or screening questions should be asked of the recruiters on your list themselves—not an associate, the administrative partner, the new business department, or even the recruiter's executive secretary. If you can't talk directly to the recruiter you're interested in doing business with, scratch that individual from the list of those to consider. Here's a rule of thumb: If you haven't had a return call within two days from the recruiter you're trying to reach—and you've already advised the recruiter's office that you are calling on a new business matter—assume that the recruiter is too lazy, too busy, or too disorganized to be of any help to you. Don't be patient. A recruiter like that will be no more attentive to you on a search.

Let's turn now to those key qualifying questions you will want to ask over the telephone. It is appropriate for you to identify yourself and your organization to the recruiter, *but don't tip your hand about the specific need you have in mind.* After identifying yourself, your flow of screening questions might go like this:

1. **In what industries and types of organizations do you personally do most of your work?** (How closely does this jibe with what your research from this book shows?)
2. **Are there functional areas in which you feel especially competent and current?** (Does this parallel your research findings?)
3. **How do you determine whether you personally handle the work or delegate it to another individual?** (This is a very important question, so listen carefully to the recruiter's response. Is the determination based on salary level, organization level, current search load, or what? Would your search qualify for the recruiter's personal handling or not?)
4. **Who does the research on the search, and is the researcher**

involved directly with the client? (The optimum is for the recruiter to personally handle the most important research. A recruiter who is fed all candidate information from a researcher is seldom as up-to-speed on a given industry as one who personally conducts research. One of the fringe benefits of a good search assignment is the industry scuttlebutt passed along by a recruiter. This type of super-timely market research can often be of competitive value to you.)

5. **Who makes the initial contact with a possible candidate— you, a junior recruiter, or a researcher?** (This is another very important question. Would you trust a more junior person, maybe someone who has never met you or sensed your organization's culture, to initiate that critical first contact in your behalf? Can a junior person represent your opportunity properly and at the same time maintain the confidentiality of your search? How well have you responded when junior recruiters or researchers called you?)

6. **When do you start reference checking, who conducts the references, and what kind of references do you ultimately provide a client?** (Are references checked before or after a client's first visit with the candidate? Does the recruiter or a less involved individual conduct them? Are references submitted in narrative form, attributable to those individuals offering specific comments, or simply summarized?)

7. **Approximately how long after you start the search will you, as the client, begin to meet candidates face-to-face?** (Is it the recruiter's practice to offer up a few "trial balloon" candidates within a few weeks of starting or to reserve candidate presentations until most of the research is completed?)

8. **How do you price your work?** (Is it a percentage of starting base salary only, or a percentage of first-year compensation? Will the recruiter work on a fixed-fee basis? What happens if you call off the search a few weeks into it? How are out-of-pocket expenses handled?)

9. **What kind of guarantee do you offer if a placement leaves or doesn't work out?** (Most will replace at no additional

professional fee, charging out-of-pocket expenses only, if the placement does not last a year.)

10. **What is your client block policy—that is, how long will you abstain from approaching any person in our organization after your last search with us?** (Most will refrain for two years, and a few longer than that, but it is also important to determine whether all of your divisions, subsidiaries, and plants are off limits—including those located outside the United States.)

These ten questions should give you enough information about your recruiter to help you decide whether you want to reveal more and possibly set up a direct visit, or politely close out the conversation and save both of you a considerable amount of time and later grief. Let's say, however, that the recruiter's answers seem satisfactory to you. Only then is it appropriate to be more specific about your staffing need. You should start by giving the recruiter a capsule description of the search you envision. It is essential that you tell the recruiter the title and scope of the job, who the position reports to, how soon you need it filled, and whether it is newly created or a replacement (and if the latter, why). The recruiter also should be told a bit about the expectations of the position and whether the search is a confidential one. After providing this background, you are ready to ask the recruiter a few final questions:

1. **Would you be personally interested in handling this search on the basis of what I've told you?** (A good straightforward question deserves a similar response. If it is no, or something like "I'd be pleased to oversee the work of one of our best associates," close the conversation with a comment to the effect that you will call the recruiter again sometime and place a quick call to the next one on your target list. You've got plenty to choose from.)

2. **Have you done a comparable or near-comparable search to this one? How recently?** (Again, listen carefully to the recruiter's answer. Does it sound credible? Has the work been done within the last year or so, or is it older than that?)

3. **May I ask you who your client was on that search? Are there some others for whom you've done similar searches?** (Many

of the top recruiters will be able to give you specific names of clients they have served, just as most of them have been willing to do in their profiles in this book. Others, however, may work for firms with more circumspect policies regarding the confidentiality of client information. Some client information is understandably off limits, but all client information should not be. Don't ever let a recruiter or recruiting firm hide behind a veil of total confidentiality. Why engage a recruiter who must be counted on to reference check candidates but who is unwilling to provide you with references on his or her own past performance?)

4. **What companies or organizations that might be good places to find candidates for my job will be off limits to you because of your firm's previous work with them?** (This is one of the most important but most infrequently asked questions of recruiters. If two or three of the most likely targets are blocked to this recruiter, you may be better off working with another one from your target list who is less restricted.)

5. **With your sense of the job market for the kind of person I'm looking for, what do you think will be the principal challenges in completing this search? How long do you estimate it will take to find our placement? And what do you think it will take in compensation to attract the right person?** (Weigh the recruiter's responses in light of your own hunches; and on the compensation issue, realize that to entice a high achiever is always going to involve a premium over what your current internal salary structure is.)

6. **Again, with your knowledge of the marketplace for this individual, what do you estimate your out-of-pocket expenses will run?** (Look for specificity, regardless of its magnitude. It can be an actual dollar range like $5,000 to $6,000 or a percentage of the professional fee. But watch out for an estimate like 10 to 15 percent of the professional fee on any search where the base salary is over $150,000—unless you also always fly first class, stay in $400 a night hotel rooms, and dine at five-star restaurants.)

If you still have an interested and interesting recruiter on the end of the line after posing these questions, this valuable resource should be asked to submit a formal proposal (complete with names of client references) and is worth inviting to your offices for a face-to-face visit. You should also invite one or two more. Recruiters do not jump up and down with glee over "shoot-outs," as they call them, where they have to compete head-to-head with others. But they're getting increasingly used to them. As employers become more sophisticated in their use of search consultants, especially as they become smarter in selecting the best qualified recruiter for a precise need—not just good old Tom every time—shoot-outs will become the norm, and ultimately to the benefit of employers and headhunters alike. Even good old Tom eventually will settle into his proper market niche.

Your selection process has now wound down to its last stage. It's the time to bring in your finalists and get specific with them. Each of them should receive the same overview and interview. Their visits ideally will occur on the same day or in close proximity. This is especially necessary where a search committee is involved or a group of individuals will be included in the selection process. You want impressions to be fresh in mind about all of those under consideration whether you alone or a group of individuals will be making the final selection of the right recruiter.

Allow about two hours for each recruiter, and have your agenda worked out in advance. If a brief plant tour or some other quick orientation is necessary, do that first. Then proceed to fill in the recruiter on all of the pertinent information to provide an accurate picture of your need. Above all, be honest. If others from your organization will be closely involved with the search or the product of that search, be sure to include them in these final screening sessions.

Your purpose is to select not only the most qualified recruiter from a technical aspect but the individual with whom you and your group have the highest comfort level personally. Much of your assessment of the recruiter's skills and knowledge of your industry or activity had been obtained in your initial telephone call. Now you're judging the intangible factors—the recruiter's sense of your culture, compatibility with you and the others involved, communication skills, intellect, sense of humor, and presence. In short, you're selecting a member of your team. There must be no hidden agendas or surprises for the recruiter down the line. Neither can there be a Human Resources Executive or Personnel Manager who feels threatened by the recruiter's work. Once you make your selection, you and your recruiter are in this project together. Although he or she may be the quarterback on this particular drive, you remain the captain of the team—and for the full season.

Following the recruiters' visits, and after polling those who sat in, you should be able to make the decision about your first choice. Assuming that the preferred recruiter's references have also been favorable, it is time for the advisory call to pass along the good news. The runners-up also deserve the courtesy of a phone call to advise them of your decision and to thank them for taking the time to meet with you. You may retain them one day too.

Getting These Top Recruiters to Perform Their Best for You

Congratulations. You've done a fine job in picking the right quarterback for your search from the 10,000 others who very likely would not score as well. Does this mean that you can just sit back and watch that recruiter do his or her thing? No way. The best results in any search come when both employer and recruiter interact together through the entire process—and beyond. We have referred previously to the need to function as a team, and that is exactly what it takes to obtain a successful search outcome.

Sounds easy enough doesn't it? After all, recognizing the importance of your search and what you are paying for it, why wouldn't you want to work as a team? Yet one of the harshest surprises every headhunter sooner or later discovers is that all searches are not truly on the level. There are instances where the client actually wants to see the search come up empty-handed or the candidate, once hired, fail miserably in the job.

Every recruiter has run into situations like this. Sometimes the hidden agenda of a client is apparent fairly early in the search, but usually it doesn't manifest itself until closure. I recently had an instance of this in connection with a search we were handling to find the new General Manager for one of this country's most prestigious private clubs. All had gone well on the search up to the point where four final candidates were being presented in one day to a search committee comprised of five members of the club's Board of Directors. As is our practice in such assignments, we organized the day so that each final candidate received a tour of the very beautiful clubhouse prior to meeting for an hour and a half with the full search committee. The tour was conducted by the Vice President of the club, who of course was also a member and who would sit in on the candidate's interview with the full committee.

At the end of each interview the chairman of the search committee asked each candidate whether he was more interested in the opportunity, having now visited the club, than before he arrived. Having interviewed all of the candidates before their visit, I knew that all four were highly attracted to the job. But by the end of the interviewing day I sensed something was amiss. The only candidate who had said he was more interested than before he made the visit was the weakest one of the four. While the committee was beginning to compare the four finalists at the end of the day, I escorted the last one, who ran a top club in Detroit, to the door and after a few comments to him about how he had handled the interview asked him point blank why he seemed less interested after his visit than before.

He paused a moment and then said: "You've got a snake in the grass on your search committee. That fellow who gave me the tour spent the whole thirty minutes telling me of all the problems in the club and why someone like me shouldn't risk taking the job. He really turned me off. Something tells me he wants the job himself." Armed with this information I pulled the chairman out of the meeting room and confronted him with this news. He looked distressed but not terribly surprised. He responded: "I was afraid of that. I've had suspicions for some time that our Vice President really wanted the General Manager's job himself. He's made several overtures to me about holding up on the search until next January. That just happens to be when he retires from his company. And that probably also explains why that one chap, the weakest of them all, was the only one he tried to turn on to the job. He knows that fellow wouldn't cut it for more than six months and then he'd be able to step in." The chairman the next day personally called the best of the candidates, presented the proper picture of the club and the opportunity, and brought this individual back for a detailed visit. The committee ultimately hired him.

Fortunately such counterplays are not the norm in searches, but they are far more frequent than most would imagine. Especially common is the situation where the client feels threatened by the calibre of the candidates being presented and seeks every possible avenue to disqualify each of them. Every recruiter has had their share of these types of clients.

There are no hidden agendas in your search, however, so we can get on with cultivating the kind of positive relationship you need with the top recruiter serving you. At the core of this relationship must be *trust*. It cuts both ways, with the employer and the recruiter. As an employer you must think of your recruiter as though he or she sits on your Board of Directors. So once you have made the selection of the right recruiter to serve you, it's time to get back together and open up with every bit of pertinent information. This includes sharing with your recruiter your organization's financial situation, the real problems and opportunities you see now and those that are on the horizon, the people relationships and issues that the new hire will have to contend with—in brief, where all the bodies lie in your organization. Especially important in times like these is trusting your recruiter with information as sensitive as the fact that your company may be on the block to be sold, merged, restructured, or susceptible to anything like these disruptive events so common today.

Your recruiter must assimilate all of this and incorporate what is relevant in a *candidate specification*—the vital document that sets forth the ideal personal and professional qualifications the candidate must possess in order to succeed in the job. Much of this outline will highlight personal traits and professional skills, but it must also convey in words the culture of your organization and the nuances of the actual work environment. A good candidate specification is a type of template; only the right candidates pass through it easily.

It is normally the employer's place to provide the *position description*, although on occasion the recruiter is asked to prepare this. The position description, equally as important as the candidate specification, details the basic functions of the job, reporting and supervisory responsibilities, coordinative relation-ships, and major duties and responsibilities in the position. The recruiter uses both the position description and the candidate specification in developing candidates for the job. It is impor-tant that both be well crafted and that you agree with what is said in both.

Armed with these materials, and with copies of your annual report and other organizational literature, your recruiter is equipped to sally forth in search of the needle in the haystack. But you want to know one more thing from your search con-sultant. What is the *work plan?* Although the sequence of the search may have been outlined in your recruiter's proposal let-ter, do you know more specifically which organizations by name will be probed? Are there some individuals or organizations on the recruiter's list that would prove awkward or embarrassing to you should they be approached? Do you think that the recruiter is soliciting candidates with the most appropriate titles and level in their current organizations? Do you know about some orga-nizations that might be good places to look for candidates but do not appear on the recruiter's list? Do you know some indi-viduals who would be helpful *sources*—people who may not be candidates themselves but might offer good suggestions of oth-ers? And are there some associations your recruiter should know about, conventions coming up, or trade journals that will prove helpful?

You're in this together. As the search goes forward you may hear of someone who might be a candidate or another good source. Let your recruiter know about that. For a search to go well there cannot be "your" candidates and "the recruiter's" candidates. They are all your team's candidates.

It is the recruiter's job to use all the resources and inge-nuity that can be mustered to generate an array of candidates who fit your job specifications to varying degrees, some better than others. It is also the recruiter's responsibility to perform the work ethically. One of the very unfortunate by-products of the pressure on researchers to obtain candidate names or orga-nization information can sometimes take the form of gross deception. There have been several recent incidents where researchers with search firms or with outside research suppliers have been caught using such surreptitious guises as saying they are performing research for an academic project or seeking names for *Who's Who* directories.

It is also the recruiter's responsibility to maintain the confidentiality of a confidential search and an appropriate degree of confidentiality even when a search is not a confidential one. No organization benefits from having its management needs broadcast to the world at large—except in those very rare instances where public awareness can help generate a candidate who might otherwise be nearly impossible to find. Searches for commissioners of major sports groups and heads of government agencies are often aided by wide public knowledge of the need.

As the employer, your responsibility is to see that the search proceeds on schedule and with regular feedback from you to the recruiter. If you haven't seen your first candidate within five or six weeks of the start of the search, something is awry. Either your recruiter is spending too much time on other assignments or having trouble getting a handle on your industry or area of activity. It's time to reconvene for a heart-to-heart talk. Maybe the marketplace is telling both you and the recruiter that your specifications are unrealistic. Your feedback to the recruiter is vital after you see each of the candidates for the first time and after each subsequent visit. Your availability for interviews with candidates is also expected.

Your role includes seeing that the recruiter you selected is still personally deeply involved with the search. Many search firms employ gifted "rainmakers." These are individuals who are especially accomplished at selling the assignment—they frequently are the ones who brag about "selling over a million dollars a year" in searches—but who are equally skilled at avoiding the trenches where the gruntwork on a good search really takes place. Rainmakers usually surround themselves with gofers, the bag people who do their work for them. Don't forget, *that's not what you contracted for when you selected one of the top recruiters.*

Throughout the search your recruiter has been doing various types of reference checking. Initially it is the kind of quick-and-dirty call or two to references the recruiter knows personally. The recruiter just wants to be sure there are no major flaws or flags with the candidate. The fine-tuned, in-depth references are reserved for your actual finalists, usually not more than one or two. Here's another place where your top recruiter earns his or her pay—and be sure that it is your recruiter doing your reference checking, not some underling.

Reference checks may not constitute the most critical element in the outcome of a search, but they are everything in predicting the ultimate performance of the candidate once in the job. Quality reference checking is the single most important ingredient in a search well done. Many a candidate, especially one who has had considerable prior interviewing experience, can fool an employer or the most seasoned recruiter in an interview regardless of its length or apparent thoroughness. I repeat, *references are everything*. Regrettably, they are getting much more difficult to do. The Privacy of Information acts and other regulatory restraints make reference checking difficult to conduct, and too many employers and recruiters alike shy away from any but the most cursory and superficial ones. Do not allow your recruiter to avoid doing in-depth references. Good thorough reference checking can still be accomplished. It just takes the right knowledge, skills, contacts, and the instincts of Peter Falk's Columbo. Speaking personally, I've always felt that thorough reference checking is as much in a candidate's best interests as it is in the employer's. Who in their right mind would ever want to be placed in a job where a limitation in their background, which could be uncovered through good reference checking, was going to cause them to fail?

The skills of your top recruiter also come into play when it's time to put together the hiring package with your preferred candidate. It is a bad mistake for employers to get directly involved with a candidate in negotiating a compensation package. Even though some employers seem to get ego gratification out of negotiating a deal with a candidate, I've never seen a single instance where a competent recruiter was not able to structure a better deal for both parties. And I've seen a number of potentially good corporate marriages fall apart when clients and candidates attempt to negotiate on their own. Your role as the employer is to give your recruiter the parameters to work with but then trust that the deal can be worked out between candidate and recruiter. You, however, should be the one who extends the ultimate formal offer, not your recruiter.

We work in a time of more job uncertainty and career chaos than in any period since the Great Depression. Megamergers, LBOs, downsizing, spinoffs, takeovers, and other employment discombobulations have wreaked havoc on hundreds of thousands of American lives. The net result of this is that our job market today is full of outstanding professionals of all types who five to eight years ago never would have found themselves anxiously looking for new opportunities. I'm sure I'm not alone among my headhunter colleagues in observing that a remarkably high percentage of the seventy-five or so unsolicited resumes that cross my desk every day come from high achievers we would have had to scout hard for and pry out of their organizations in the past.

Now, many of these talented professionals find themselves looking for jobs on their own or with the help of outplacement firms. In the recent past, most employers would turn their noses up at those "in the job market." And they were to a certain extent correct in that feeling. This attitude should no longer exist on the part of any hiring organization. Consequently, your recruiter should be encouraged as never before to consider those high achievers who send their resumes over the transom as objectively as any other candidates whom the search identifies. There is almost as much likelihood today of finding your perfect placement among the write-ins at the recruiter's office as there is in turning every stone out there in the field of the yet-employed.

Working together for the past three months, give or take a few, your team has succeeded in finding and hiring the right individual for your very significant need. Does this mean that you and your recruiter part company until the next search that appears right for him or for her? It should not. Even as the new hire comes aboard and settles into your organization, little tips might better be communicated to the placement by your search consultant than by you personally. Call them informal pieces of constructive criticism to correct small habits or traits that might become larger problems worth formal mention later on. Your recruiter is also going to want to speak with you every few months about how the new hire is performing. Like doctors, headhunters' egos need to know that the operation was not only a success but the patient is thriving.

Early in this chapter we said that there were four major reasons that employers needed to know America's top recruiters. The last of these four suggested that it would be wise to get to know the best headhunters personally—because you too someday might find yourself in the ranks of the unemployed. If that motivation was one of the reasons you read this chapter, may I suggest you turn back and read very carefully Chapter 2. It will give you all the advice you need.

4

War Stories From
A Headhunter's Diary

We came to the end of what had been a routine screening interview. I rose and began to lead the tall, blond, rather large-boned
woman toward the door out of my office. Suddenly she grabbed
my arm and spun me around to face her. She stood before me,
looking twice as large as she had before, her jaw set firmly as
her eyes locked on mine.

"Look," she said evenly, "I don't want any bullshit from you.
Do I get the job or not?"

I didn't know whether to laugh or duck. I must have hesi-
tated too long because the next thing I knew she had her other
hand up around the knot on my tie, Mickey Spillane style. I was
startled, and if she actually hadn't been choking me, I would
have taken it all as some big joke.

Somehow I gurgled that the client was the only one who
could make that decision. This must not have been good enough
because she now stepped between me and the door, and pulled
up harder on my tie. I was on my toes. "I need to know now,"
she ordered. "Now! Do you hear me?" It was not difficult for me
to give her my most sincere look, and I managed to gasp out
that if I had anything to do with it, she would surely get the job.
In fact, I croaked, I'd personally go see the client about her.

Slowly she released her hand from my tie, gave me a last
hard look, declared, "I'll expect a call from you later today,"

turned, and stalked out. She strutted down the hall past our receptionist like a horse that had just thrown its rider.

She never got her call, but she did get a courier-delivered letter from my client that very afternoon reporting that he had decided she didn't quite fit his needs. Nevertheless, I watched where I went the next several months.

No other interview has been as memorable to me as that one. Yet that very brief but intense confrontation with human nature is just one example of what every search consultant encounters at unexpected moments throughout a recruiting career. They're as likely to happen after twenty-five *years* of headhunting as they are in the first twenty-five *days* of being a recruiter. It's a big part of the reason that headhunters never find their work routine and explains why their skin gets as thick as rhinoceros hide.

As stated in the introduction, this book is intended for only two groups of Americans—our most talented professionals and the employers who seek them. But the book is, above all, written about some of the accomplished individuals who bring those two parties together. No discussion of the demographics or the individual profiles of the Top 100 can begin to do justice to portraying the day-to-day work of this country's retained recruiters. Some idea of what they deal with may be instructive for job seekers and employers alike because in few other vocations are the frailties of human nature as nakedly displayed. After all, how many decisions put at risk a job, earnings, family, community, emotional and physical well-being, *all at one time?* The personal experiences—one might aptly call them war stories—of the recruiters in this book could fill volumes. In offering a few of my own, I do so fully realizing that many other headhunters can surpass them with their own tales.

The war stories that follow are true; only the names of certain clients, candidates, and fellow recruiters have been changed to protect their further discreditation. Although it is unlikely that these events will happen to you, there are messages for all of us—professionals, employers, and recruiters—in what they tell us about the private world of headhunters. Perhaps a few of the following vignettes will quickly clear up the misconception that headhunters can do no wrong.

Recruiters . . . the Heroes of These Skirmishes. or Are They?

Ray Rightguard had been one of Booz, Allen & Hamilton's senior and premier executive search consultants. But he was also inclined to desperation sometimes when a key client progress meeting was coming up and he lacked suitable candidates. On one occasion Consultant Rightguard managed to pull together his dozen candidates by making liberal use of the firm's old files and presented himself to the eagerly awaiting client to discuss them. As the progress meeting droned on, Rightguard sensed that he hadn't excited his client about any of the candidates he had thus far discussed. He decided to really play up the next background included in his report and proceeded to do so. This candidate, he said, not only had all of the requisites desired for the job but was the most interested of all. The client, who was a major one for the firm, appeared very interested. He said to Rightguard: "I knew this individual once, and he was everything you said of him. How recently did you speak to him?" Consultant Rightguard, sniffing success, responded eagerly: "Why just this morning. In fact he is extremely interested in the opportunity." The client paused a bit and then said: "I find it so encouraging that he is—because I attended his funeral a week ago Saturday." (Ray Rightguard started his own job search shortly after this meeting.)

*   *   *   *   *

Many years ago, I too was one of Booz, Allen's up-and-coming young consultants. I hold the dubious honor of confusing Morristown, New Jersey, with Moorestown, New Jersey, and because of that raced via rental car in a rainstorm to the former while my candidate was waiting 100 miles away in the latter. Finally getting oriented, I sped south to Moorestown, where I discovered that the candidate had long since given up and gone home. Foolishly undaunted and now some three hours late for the original interview, I called the candidate at his home, was kindly invited to visit there, but was attacked first in the yard by the candidate's Doberman pinscher and then soundly berated in the house by the man's wife for trying to entice her husband into leaving New Jersey. (Fortunately, a better job with more money spoke louder to the candidate from Moorestown than the barks of both dog and wife, and I succeeded in moving them all—probably to the consternation of his new neighbors—to a Chicago suburb.)

*   *   *   *   *

Executive recruiting, perhaps more than any other line of work, requires many instant identifications in crowded places of people you've never in your life seen before. Most of these take place in airports as individuals debark from flights. Sometimes these ever-tentative chance glances for recognition occur in lounges, restaurants, or lobbies. To have to approach individual after individual and inquire, "Are you Mr. Garbanzo?" takes fortitude. After three or four disappointments your self-consciousness is palpable. Sometimes your Mr. Garbanzo doesn't bother to show up at all.

Penelope Snidely was one of our firm's most diligent recruiters. She also possessed the admirable trait of always being punctual, and usually early, for every appointment. True to her reputation, she arrived fifteen minutes early for an appointment to interview a candidate in a private club high up in the Sears Tower in Chicago. Our offices at the time were in the same building fourteen floors below the club. About twenty minutes after her scheduled appointment, Searcher Snidely telephoned our offices. Had the candidate called, she asked, because he hadn't shown up yet. She was told that he hadn't called and that she should continue to wait for him. It often took twenty minutes for people to make it up the elevators in that building—and those were the ones who had been there before.

Thirty minutes passed, and Searcher Snidely called again. "This guy is standing me up," she wailed. "I can't believe it. When I spoke to him on the phone he sounded like he really wanted the job. In fact, there's no one up here at all except some kook in a beard who's been reading *Rolling Stone* magazine ever since I've been here." My associate who had taken Searcher Snidely's call asked her if perhaps that man was her candidate. "No way," Snidely retorted. "My candidate couldn't possibly look like that." Curious herself now, my associate went up to the club, which at 4 P.M. in the afternoon was empty of members. In the main reception area sat Searcher Snidely, and directly across from her sat a bearded man with his head down reading *Rolling Stone*. My associate waved briefly to Snidely, went up to the man, and said: "Pardon me, by any chance are you waiting for Penelope Snidely?" He jumped to his feet and responded: "Well, yes I am. Are you her?"

"No, I'm not," replied my associate, "but she is here. She's been sitting right across from you for the last hour."

"Oh, my gosh," he blurted. "I didn't think anyone who looked like her could be a headhunter."

*   *   *   *   *

The birdcage at the Intercontinental New York Hotel, formerly the Barclay, has always been a good meeting spot for recruiters and candidates who have never met before. I once stood waiting expectantly and increasingly anxiously for a candidate who was forty-five minutes late. Finally, a well-dressed executive, complete with briefcase, who fit the general description given me previously, burst through the revolving doors from Lexington Avenue. He strode rapidly to me and greeted me with an apology for being late. Greatly relieved at his arrival, I suggested stepping up to the mezzanine level for a cocktail, where we made casual small talk as we took our first sips. Finally getting down to the interview at hand, I said, "Well, why don't we exchange literature. I've got some things for you to look over, and it appears you might have some things for me." He said, "I sure do." We quickly exchanged packets of information. As I glanced at what he had given me, and he did the same with what I gave him, we looked up at each other and burst into laughter. I'd given him a job description and annual report; he'd given me the manuscript to a play. Back to the birdcage we went to await our proper parties.

*   *   *   *   *

The follies of recruiters could fill this book. Once a fellow recruiter flew from Chicago to New York over a weekend to interview a very senior executive who was willing to meet him only at his home in Fairfield County, Connecticut. On Monday morning, we anxiously asked our recruiter colleague how his interview had gone. He looked down at his wingtips and responded that he had not been able to meet the man after all. Why not, we asked? "Well, it's like this," he said. "Have you ever tried to find where somebody lives when all your secretary has given you in the way of an address is his post office box—and he's got an unlisted phone number?"

*   *   *   *   *

Most recruiters are highly resourceful, but they are not always honorable. I remember well an incident in the restaurant at O'Hare Airport. We had been trying for weeks to arrange an interview with a very busy and talented executive who was much publicized at the time because of his corporate turnaround skills. I had finally succeeded in getting him to have lunch with me between his flights in and out of O'Hare. We asked to be seated inconspicuously at a small table shielded from others in the room by a wall of tropical plants. As we progressed through our meal, I kept hearing a rustling in the plants next to me. We finished our meal and interview, and I encouraged my candidate to go ahead to catch his plane while I paid the bill. He left, and I decided to check on who or what had been playing around in the plants over my shoulder. Expecting to find a child, I parted the greenery and discovered a former colleague of mine from Booz, Allen & Hamilton, now with another search firm.

He was seated by himself and with a huge grin and laugh said, "Boy, do I owe you a lot. I've been trying for months to get an interview with that guy with no success. I knew that you were also considering him for a search you're handling, and two days ago his secretary told me that he would be connecting through Chicago on his trip back from Germany but would be meeting someone there. I took a chance that it might be you. So I saw you waiting for someone at the international arrivals area and followed the two of you here. I owe you more than a drink. I got the same notes on him that you did!"

*   *   *   *   *

Especially high on my list of memorable recruiter stories is my own visit to the Nixon White House. This occurred in late 1972, well before the blossoming of Watergate, and I remember how flattered I was to be invited for an interview to become a member of the Nixon Administration's recruiting staff. After passing through various security checks in the Old Executive Office Building, I was ushered into the office of an executive recruiter who was on assignment to the Administration and who had invited me. He shook hands and motioned for me to take a seat. I looked around the office and all I could see was the loveseat he was beginning to sit down in and, of all things, a barber's chair. Separating the two was a small jungle of bushy green plants. I stopped dead in my tracks and said to him: "I'm sorry, I don't see a chair in here except for that barber chair, and I'm sure not going to sit in that."

"Why not?" he responded. "Everyone else does."

"You mean when you interview people for President Nixon or the Cabinet they sit in that chair?"

"They sure do," he said cockily. "If it's good enough for them, it should be good enough for you. Don't you agree?"

I did not sit in the barber chair, stood and spoke to the recruiter for fifteen minutes, and then excused myself. I never heard again from the Nixon White House, which was probably just as well. Our styles were different.

*　*　*　*　*

Even as you read this book, new and better war stories involving America's headhunters are being acted out in the real world. Headhunters are true gluttons for punishment. The fathers and mothers of this land, even those who are recruiters themselves, have had the wisdom and compassion to discourage their children from becoming headhunters. Graduate schools of business, even as courses of all other descriptions proliferate, have wisely abstained from adding a course on how to become a headhunter. Headhunters are born; they are not made. The best headhunters are too irrepressible to train, too restless to be happy at anything else, too curious for their own comfort, and so incurably optimistic that they believe there is always a needle in the haystack—even when there isn't.

Candidates . . . Who Goes There? Are You Friend or Foe?

Candidates, on the other hand, are sometimes no swifter than the recruiters pursuing them. I remember receiving an overseas telephone call very early one morning from a troubled client in London. The client had gone to Heathrow to pick up our candidate for an executive position with his British computer firm. Inexplicably, the candidate was not on the flight he was supposed to be on. I tried to reassure the client that the candidate must be on the Pan Am flight because I had personally talked with him while he was at the departure gate at Kennedy International Airport the previous afternoon. I encouraged the client to stand by at the airport while I checked with Pan Am in New York.

After the usual number of frustrating telephone calls, I was finally able to reach someone at Pan Am who told me what had happened. During the flight's three-hour delay in New York, our candidate managed to get himself thoroughly snockered in an adjacent lounge, and security would not allow him to board the plane. He capped off his eviction by taking a swipe at a security person with the umbrella he was anticipating using in London. Suffice to say he never made the trip to England or to any of our other client locations.

*   *   *   *   *

Few candidate antics, though, are as aggravating and damaging to a recruiter as the job seeker who goes all the way to the altar, receives a job offer from the client, and then declines. One of our staff had worked patiently for several months to woo a well-regarded general manager from a country club in midstate Illinois to a much more prestigious club near Chicago. With the help of the club's search committee, an attractive offer was extended to the candidate, and he accepted. He would start work a month later.

Two weeks after that, however, the candidate had second thoughts and declined the offer. He claimed that his wife, a teacher, felt she could not obtain a position for her specialty in the new community. The recruiter handling the search began to process various back-up candidates. A few weeks went by when without warning the original candidate resurfaced. He called the President of the Chicago area club directly and told him that he and his wife had reconsidered. While skeptical, the recruiter began to requalify the candidate who had disappointed us previously. The President of the club meanwhile had gone to the local school board and had determined that the candidate's wife would be able to get a job in her specialty within that school district. Everything came together very nicely. The job offer was reextended, the wife signed her teaching contract for the upcoming year in the new district, and announcements went out to the club membership of 800 families that their new general manager would join them beginning September 2. What had been an earlier disappointment had been resolved happily. Wrong. On September 1, the candidate called the recruiter to decline a second time. His wife finally concluded she could not move ninety miles away from the town in which she had grown up.

*   *   *   *   *

The search had been one of those protracted ones that severely strain the client/recruiter relationship. At long last, however, the perfect candidate was located and presented pro-testing (but not too much so) to the eagerly anticipating client. It was love at first sight. Eldon Belcher was just what the besieged President of Airsick Electronics needed to become his Vice President of Manufacturing and stimulate greater produc-tivity at the company's major consumer electronics manufactur-ing facilities. Candidate Belcher recovered enough from his earlier resistance to receive an offer and accept it to become Airsick's new manufacturing head. But alas, Belcher's old employer would have none of it. The day before Belcher was to join Airsick his old employer counteroffered handsomely and Belcher caved in to their insistence—*a week after the announcement of his joining had been distributed to employees and stockholders alike.*

Normally the story would end here—but unfortunately for poor Belcher it did not. Mysterious events were unfolding behind the scenes for both Candidate Belcher and the President of Airsick. Belcher's company had been quietly put on the block and sold. And as fate would have it in the complicated world of executive employment, the successful buyer of Candidate Belch-er's company sought out and hired as its new President *none other than the President of Airsick Electronics.* Candidate Belcher now found himself reporting to the person he had thoroughly embarrassed three months earlier. Needless to say, only a very few individuals knew why Belcher's employment lasted only a few days after the new President arrived on the scene.

*   *   *   *   *

Clients, prior to their own meeting with a candidate, frequently ask headhunters to describe what the individual looks like. It takes some practice, but eventually most recruiters are able to convey a reasonably graphic word picture with the individual's work history. Consultants often find it useful to use entertainers and public figures who either look, speak, or have mannerisms like the candidates in question. We've had look-alikes to Richard Nixon, George Hamilton, Mister Magoo, Miss Piggy, and Kermit the Frog pass through our doors, among many others. Sometimes familiarity with zoo creatures is helpful in describing candidates to clients. We have had giraffes, whooping cranes, various great apes, penguins, a tapir, and pigmy hippos visit with us. We have also seen the fashion products of everyone from Albert Nipon to Omar the Tentmaker. We have savored scents ranging from Halston, through Old Spice, to old barnyard.

Much as I would like to, because such information is helpful in particular to job seekers, it would not be propitious for me to give specific examples, except perhaps for one man whose most distinctive characteristic has not yet been identified by any group in our society as being a target for discrimination. The particular chap in mention was with a major advertising agency in New York and had succeeded in raising elements of the handle-bar mustache to new heights. He had sprouted exceptionally long eyebrows *between* his eyes and then twisted and waxed these three-inch-long feelers into one very pronounced spike. It was extremely difficult to interview this fellow; I found myself getting cross-eyed as we conversed. I also had a terrible time keeping a straight face in describing him to a client. In our firm we called him Unicorn Man. To the enormous credit of one of our clients, however, he was hired.

*   *   *   *   *

I have had several experiences where without invitation candidates have brought their wives along on their initial interviews with me. This is disconcerting enough in itself, but particularly distracting was a wife who bore a striking resemblance to Minnie Pearl. She did not wear Minnie's hat, but she brought her knitting with her. She kept her head down supposedly knitting away while I spoke with her husband but periodically peered over her granny glasses and interrupted with her own questions as the interview proceeded. Another wife brought a tape recorder to her husband's interview session because, as she put it, "Elmer doesn't hear well and often can't remember things." Unlike the good fortune of Unicorn Man, I don't believe any of these candidates was distinctive enough to present to our clients.

*   *   *   *   *

Many of our candidate presentations to a client involve an interview with a committee. We usually sit in on these interviews. One of the hardest lessons to learn as a recruiter is that the candidate who had been so poised and so impressive with you one-on-one can turn out to be a jellyfish in front of a committee. I've had the devastating experience of watching a candidate freeze in front of a group, literally unable to utter any response at all to the group's questions. On the other hand, I've watched people run off at the mouth to the point where I wanted to reach across the table and stuff a wad of paper between their gums.

I've seen candidates of all cholesterol levels ooze so much perspiration down their brows, onto their noses, and drop by drop onto boardroom tables that the drought in the far West could be eased if we had collected it instead of just leaving it to create watermarks on the oak. And everyone around that table just ached to offer the poor fellow a handkerchief. I've died a little when a female candidate who looked so professional when I interviewed her arrived for her meeting with a client with enough mascara to shame Tammy Bakker and sufficient fragrance to resurrect the Mongol hordes. On top of that she lit up a cigarette in the interview, took notes with a nineteen-cent ballpoint, and had runs in her stockings, and the half-inch heels on her shoes looked like she watered the horses before coming to the interview.

*   *   *   *   *

Candidates, even more so than clients, are the reason headhunters do not age gracefully. It takes only a few searches like the next one to add wrinkles to a young female recruiter's face or to encourage male-pattern baldness to make another bold advance on a victim like me.

A major property/casualty insurance company in the Mid-west asked us to find a new Chief Financial Officer for them. After sifting through sixty to eighty prospects to find just the right personality—to say nothing about technical skills—the search came down to a fine candidate who worked in Manhattan but lived in New Jersey. The front-runner, accompanied by wife and two teenage children, came to the Midwestern city to receive a formal offer and the chance to look at residential areas over a weekend. Late Sunday night the consultant spoke with the Chairman of the client company. The Chairman was clearly enthusiastic: "We've got him. We shook hands over it."

But bright and early Monday morning, the Chairman called back in great distress: "He's just called me and declined. He said that his wife now refused to move. That if he left, he'd leave without her. The children were no problem." Thoroughly perplexed, the consultant reread all of the candidate's references. There was no clue as to what might have changed the wife's mind. However, one reference who happened to live in the same New Jersey community, had closed his remarks by saying off-handedly that he'd be surprised if we could ever get the family to move. Further probed at the time, he had simply responded that they had always lived in the East.

The consultant decided to call back this reference and tell him what had occurred. After doing so, the consultant prodded the reference if there was anything more he could add that might explain why the wife had now dug her heels in. He paused for quite some time and then said: "Well, it won't help your client much, but almost everybody in this town except her husband knows that the wife has been carrying on a long-term affair with a local physician."

This saga, unfortunately does not end there. Devastated but still determined to make a placement, the consultant picked up the pieces of the search and went after the alternative candidate who lived in Milwaukee. The clandestine meetings occurred, the references were checked, and candidate number two received an offer and accepted on the spot. End of search? Not quite. When this candidate resigned to his CEO, all kinds of dollars and promises rained down on him. He capitulated. Our client was furious. "Damn it, Consultant, we've paid you $30,000 already. Get your buns up there and turn this guy around." The poor consultant, after much pleading, prevailed on the candidate to join him for dinner that same evening in Milwaukee and to bring his wife. Hours of persuasion later, and with the wife's help this time, the candidate came to the firm decision to go ahead with our client's opportunity. It was a relieved and happy consultant who drove home in the wee hours of the morning.

The candidate called the consultant early the following morning and told him that he had just seen his CEO and had resigned irrevocably. The consultant was elated and promptly called his client to give him the good news. There was a pause, and then the Chairman said: "You know, I got to thinking last night that I don't want that guy after what he put us through." No amount of discussion could change his mind. It was left to the consultant to work out a way for the unfortunate candidate, who had resigned, to regain his former position. With the grace of God, and motivated by the terror of a professional liability suit, the consultant somehow succeeded.

Clients . . . You Pay to Stay Above the Fray. But Do You?

As one might gather from the story above, not all clients are reasonable—even though all headhunters, like other consultants, grow up being told that the client is always right.

Sometimes that maxim is difficult to accept. I'm reminded of a search a few years ago for a St. Louis–based, multibillion dollar consumer products company. We were asked to find them a Senior Financial Analyst. The position was at the minimum salary level at which we would recruit at that time. Our client was the Assistant Treasurer, to whom the position would report. Six weeks into the project, I was called by the corporate Treasurer, who I had never met. After introducing himself, he told me that he had decided to upgrade the search. He was in need of a new Assistant Treasurer because he had decided to terminate our client.

We dutifully went to work to find more senior candidates. Two months into the upgraded search I received a call from the

Chief Financial Officer, another individual whom I had never met previously. He explained that he was aware of our search for an Assistant Treasurer but wanted to move it up a notch to the Treasurer's job. It seemed that he was going to encourage the current Treasurer, who was then our client, to take early retirement.

We put our heads down once again to ferret out Treasurer candidates. You guessed it. The next call was from the Chairman and CEO. He asked me to come to St. Louis to "talk about a very sensitive matter." Recruiters tend to be quite responsive to CEOs, so I quickly flew to St. Louis and met with him. After some small talk, he told me what was on his mind. "I know you're looking for a new Treasurer for us," he said, "but what we really need is a new Chief Financial Officer." I responded, "But sir, he's our client right now." The CEO looked at me and stated, "Don't you think I know that? But I'm not going to make it difficult for this company by firing him first and make it easy for you. I want you to find a Treasurer who is strong enough so that when our current Chief Financial Officer hires him, I can turn right around and fire the Chief Financial Officer." In a matter of five months, what had started out as a search for a Senior Financial Analyst at $60,000 had escalated into a search for a Chief Financial Officer at $260,000.

*   *   *   *   *

A few years before that search, a major British client of ours engaged us to find the new President of their U.S. subsidiary. Not unlike many other clients, they set their sights unrealistically high when it came to the qualifications of candidates. Nevertheless, we succeeded in enticing an outstanding candidate from a major air courier to the point where he received an offer. He returned to inform his boss of his decision to leave, whereupon the boss promptly doubled his salary and promoted him to President.

Three more times over the course of a year the same thing happened. The second candidate to receive an offer from the British client chose instead to join one of the world's largest airlines as its CEO. The third candidate to get an offer opted for the presidency of a major entertainment and land development company. The fourth candidate returned with offer in hand and was promptly promoted to CEO of the giant food company he had been with. All through this difficult period we had been encouraging our client to hire the back-up candidate to the first individual who had rejected the offer. Finally they listened to us and did so. (I'm happy to say that this individual has more than doubled sales and profits and last year won election to their board in London.)

*   *   *   *   *

Clients can make you scratch your head and wonder why you put up with them or can cause you to be terribly proud of them. Among those who I have wanted to stand up and cheer about is the current President and CEO of a multibillion dollar consumer products company headquartered in the upper Midwest. I had arranged for him to do a day's interviewing of candidates in our New York offices and had also scheduled several candidates from the East to come in to visit with him. The evening before this important day, the entire East coast was hit with a blizzard. Twelve inches of snow fell on Manhattan. All air travel and vehicle traffic was stopped, and the city was paralyzed. I had stayed in New York City that night and was certain that no one could get through. Nevertheless, I trudged through the traffic-less streets to our offices before 8 A.M. just to handle telephone calls from those who would be calling in but who obviously could not get in from out of town. Promptly at 8 A.M. I heard knocking on our front door. I opened it and standing there, looking a bit hassled but very alert, was my client. He had somehow patched together several flights to get him from the Midwest into Washington, D.C., and then caught a train that took the rest of the night to get into Manhattan. He had then walked almost two miles in the snow to make his appointment. Amazingly, our two leading candidates also conquered the blizzard to get there.

*   *   *   *   *

Then there are those clients who stand out because of their idiosyncracies. One favorite client of mine from London had a collection of hundreds of tie tacs. He always selected one that would be representative of what his principal mission was for that day. I remember in particular the day he flew in to New York, sporting a small gold hatchet as a tie tac, and proceeded to fire both the CEO and President of one of the major cosmetic companies he oversaw. Another much-admired client ran a steel fabricating company in a small town in central Michigan. The highlight of my visits with him in this community was lunch at the only restaurant in town. When most waitresses would come to your table at the end of a meal to ask if you would like dessert, the waitress in this restaurant always brought a bowl of toothpicks and passed them out one by one. This client's entire professional staff of some twenty people, all seated at the same long table, then sat and picked their teeth as a group for five or ten minutes.

I had another client from the United Kingdom who wanted us to find a President for their U.S. subsidiary, which manufactured electric storage batteries. My client, who had spent all of the preliminary weeks on the search in his London office, had sent his comments about the preferred candidate background. Among many other points, he had said that he felt the ideal candidate should be a genius. Every search consultant has heard that many times before, and frankly I didn't put a great deal of weight on that factor. We did, however, try to identify not only very qualified candidates from an industry aspect but also those we felt were well above average intellectually. Finally the weekend came for the first face-to-face meetings between my client who had come in from London and the five front-runners that we had lined up for him to see. The client had previously told me that he would be assisted by a friend from England. I called him the following Monday morning to inquire how the interviews had gone. He said: "Just miserably. My professor friend gave everyone the same IQ test, and there isn't anyone among these who scored over 180. I cannot tell you how disappointed I am in what you have done."

Needless to say, I realized now that when he meant a genius, he meant a genius. So the next week, while our client was still in the States, I worked feverishly and contacted two dozen universities with programs in electrical engineering. I rounded up a half-dozen assistant and associate professor candidates and arranged to interview them at a hotel in Hartford, Connecticut. I took with me the Miller Analogies Test and several other IQ tests. That's about all their interviews really consisted of. I found two who qualified as geniuses. Neither one had ever run a business, but our client wanted to see them anyway. So he did. And he hired one. He lasted six weeks.

I'm happy to say that our clients no longer discriminate on the basis of age, sex, race, creed, or national origin. They discriminate on other things. We have a client whose first name is Mel and will not interview anyone whose first name is Bruce. We have other clients who will not consider a candidate with facial hair. A number of our clients will no longer interview smokers. A very large percentage of our clients will not consider men who wear short-sleeved shirts or women with baggy pantyhose. And many of our clients have a distinct aversion to even interviewing a male candidate for a job who lives with a member of the same sex.

*   *   *   *   *

It may be fitting to conclude this sampling of war stories from one headhunter's diary with a tale that illustrates how interdependent consultants, candidates, and clients are—especially when they go down in flames together.

Among the most difficult of all executive search assignments is the placement of a university President. In the very early 1970s, shortly after a period of great campus unrest, we were called on to locate a President for a Big Ten university. The search went on and on. Candidates who were acceptable to the Faculty Committee were not acceptable to the Student Government Committee, and vice versa. Those who made it through the first two were invariably suspect to the Screening Committee of the Board of Trustees. However, after eight long months of the process the committees themselves were weakening. And the hapless consultant handling the search was able to get a very capable President of one of the State Universities of New York past all three groups to a formal luncheon with the full Board of Trustees.

The lunch was held in one of the dining rooms of a private club in the area. Fifteen trustees, one very hopeful consultant, and a composed candidate made up the attendees. The candidate, who was seated midway along the side of an elegantly set table, was adeptly fielding a wide range of questions. Sitting directly across from him was a white-haired, ultraconservative curmudgeon who was picking his way through his fruit salad.

Fixing his piercing eyes on the candidate, he inquired of him: "Who do you consider among the best university presidents today?" Without pausing long, the man responded, "Howard Johnson of MIT and Kingman Brewster of Yale." (Both were well known at the time as very liberal educators.) With that there was a loud pop from the throat of the crusty trustee, and a melon ball shot out of his mouth, across the table, and smacked the candidate in the middle of his forehead. It was all downhill after that for the candidate, the consulting firm, and the client. Some searches are simply not meant to be solved.

*   *   *   *   *

As you turn the following pages and look at the faces of the best of America's headhunters, bear in mind that they've all weathered many a campaign, won a lot and lost a few, gained no Purple Hearts or Congressional Medals of Honor, but survivors they are—with legions of merits.

PART II

AMERICA'S TOP EXECUTIVE RECRUITERS

5

Profiles of the
Top 100 Executive Recruiters

DONALD T. ALLERTON
President
Allerton, Heinze & Associates
208 South LaSalle Street,
  Suite 766
Chicago, IL 60604
Telephone: (312) 263-1075

Date of birth: January 4, 1940
Grew up in: New Jersey

Photo by Gregory Gaymont Inc.

HIGHER EDUCATION:
  Farleigh Dickinson University, Rutherford, NJ
    B.S. degree, business administration, 1965

EMPLOYMENT HISTORY:
  1978 to present: Allerton, Heinze & Associates
  1975 to 1978: Vice President and General Manager–Midwest Staub Warmbold
  1972 to 1975: Director, Corporate Employment, G.D. Searle & Company
  1969 to 1972: Celanese Corporation
  1965 to 1969: Warner-Lambert Company

REPRESENTATIVE AND SIGNIFICANT PLACEMENTS:
  Harry Kraemer, Vice President, Medical Specialties Group
    Baxter International, Inc.
  Wayne Wahlenmeier, Vice President and General Manager, Microsystems Division
    Fujitsu Microelectronics, Inc.
  Doug Reiff, Vice President, Marketing and Sales
    Marion Laboratories, Inc.
  Dr. Joseph Miraglia, Corporate Vice President and Assistant Director, Personnel
    Motorola, Inc.
  John Winke, Executive Director
    Orchard Association

WHAT I LOOK FOR IN GENERAL IN A CANDIDATE:
   Real ability—the ability to use information effectively—more than intelligence. The way the candidate thinks/conceptualizes and applies knowledge.

Chemistry—the interpersonal fit between the candidate and the hiring manager.

Communication skills—the ability to convey one's ideas and get others to buy in.

Adaptability/openness to change.

A sense of who they are, what they want, and where they're going.

MINIMUM SALARY LEVEL AT WHICH I WORK:
$100,000

GEOGRAPHIC SCOPE OF RECRUITING ACTIVITIES:
Clients nationwide and in Canada, Mexico, and Brazil

TOTAL YEARS OF RETAINER-TYPE RECRUITING EXPERIENCE:
14 years

JACQUES P. ANDRE
Senior Vice President
Paul R. Ray & Company, Inc.
825 Third Avenue
New York, NY 10022
Telephone: (212) 371-3000

Date of birth: August 29, 1937
Grew up in: Davenport, IA

HIGHER EDUCATION:
University of Miami
Photo by Bachrach
B.B.A. degree, personnel management, 1959

MILITARY:
Captain, United States Army Reserve, 1959 to 1967

EMPLOYMENT HISTORY:
1975 to present: Paul R. Ray & Company
1965 to 1975: Manager, Executive Search, Ernst & Young
1964 to 1965: Senior Employment Specialist, P. Ballantine & Sons
1960 to 1964: Assistant Personnel Director, Sealtest Foods

PRIVATE CLUBS:
Echo Lake Country Club
New York Board of Trade

SPECIAL INTERESTS AND HOBBIES:
Travel, sports, gardening

REPRESENTATIVE AND SIGNIFICANT PLACEMENTS:
Artur Walther, Partner (capital markets)
Goldman, Sachs & Company
John H. Copenhaver, Managing Director (derivative products)
Sumitomo Bank Capital Markets, Inc.
President of a futures subsidiary of a major money center bank
Joseph Pollack, Vice President, Taxes
GrandMet, USA, Inc.
John Grywalski, Jr., Partner, National Director, Health Care Services
Touche Ross & Company

WHAT I LOOK FOR IN GENERAL IN A CANDIDATE:
A candidate is evaluated for a specific opportunity with a
unique set of candidate specifications that normally consist of

educational, experiential, and personal trait requirements. Since achieving a good fit is in everyone's best interest, we hope that a candidate is open and forthright in discussing his or her background, personality, and interests. The process is most effective when the candidate answers questions fully and accurately. Therefore, honesty is important. Recognizing that interview styles differ widely, it is also important that the candidate help the interviewer accomplish his or her mission. Candidates who are too anxious and oversell do themselves a disservice. Similarly, candidates who are coy or undersell hurt themselves. Candidates should be well prepared and at their best in an interview.

MINIMUM SALARY LEVEL AT WHICH I WORK:
$75,000

GEOGRAPHIC SCOPE OF RECRUITING ACTIVITIES:
Clients nationwide and in North America, South America, Europe, and Asia

TOTAL YEARS OF RETAINER-TYPE RECRUITING EXPERIENCE:
24 years

MARTIN H. BAUMAN
President
Martin H. Bauman Associates, Inc.
410 Park Avenue, Suite 1600
New York, NY 10022
Telephone: (212) 752-6580

Date of birth: December 26, 1929
Grew up in: New York, NY

Photo by Bill Stone Photography

HIGHER EDUCATION:
New York University
B.S. degree, personnel management, 1956
M.B.A. degree, management, 1961

MILITARY:
Corporal, United States Army Signal Corps, 1951 to 1953

EMPLOYMENT HISTORY:
1968 to present: Martin H. Bauman Associates
1965 to 1968: Assistant Personnel Director, United Merchants & Manufacturers
1961 to 1965: Vice President, Personnel, Branch Motor Express
Five years prior experience in Personnel, Training, and Development in Retailing and Manufacturing

REPRESENTATIVE AND SIGNIFICANT PLACEMENTS:
Don Mayoras, placed as Industrial Engineer, presently Chairman and Owner
St. Johnsbury Trucking
A.B. "Ted" Ruhly, placed as Assistant to President, presently President and Chief Executive Officer
Maersk, Inc.
Robert F. Calman, placed as Treasurer, last position was Vice Chairman, presently Chairman, Echo Bay Mines, Ltd.
International Utilities
Don Marshall, placed as Regional Manager, presently President and Chief Executive Officer
Sun Distributors
Reuben Mark, Chairman and Chief Executive Officer, Colgate Palmolive
Placed on Board of Directors, Pearson P.L.C., London

WHAT I LOOK FOR IN GENERAL IN A CANDIDATE:

There are no specific criteria. Each recruit, each function, and each company have different sets of criteria. No two jobs are ever alike!

MINIMUM SALARY LEVEL AT WHICH I WORK:
$145,000

GEOGRAPHIC SCOPE OF RECRUITING ACTIVITIES:
Clients nationwide and in Canada and Great Britain

TOTAL YEARS OF RETAINER-TYPE RECRUITING EXPERIENCE:
21+ years

LYNN TENDLER BIGNELL
(formerly LYNN GILBERT)
Principal/Cofounder
Gilbert Tweed Associates, Inc.
630 Third Avenue
New York, NY 10017
Telephone: (212) 697-4260

Date of birth: April 26, 1938
Grew up in: Metropolitan New
York and Miami Beach

Photo courtesy of Gilbert Tweed Associates

HIGHER EDUCATION:
University of Florida
B.A. degree, mathematics, 1959

EMPLOYMENT HISTORY:
1972 to present: Gilbert Tweed Associates, Inc.
1963–67 and 1970–72: Director, Technical Recruiting, Dunhill Personnel
1960 to 1963: Associate, Personnel Associates

PRIVATE CLUBS:
Dutchess Valley Rod & Gun Club

SPECIAL INTERESTS AND HOBBIES:
Adventure travel, crafts, antiques, Outward Bound USA

REPRESENTATIVE AND SIGNIFICANT PLACEMENTS:
Jack Allen, Senior Vice President, C-E Environmental
Combustion Engineering
Herbert Hansen, General Manager
Interpace Corporation
Jacqueline Renner, Marketing Manager, Phosphorus Chemicals
FMC Corporation
Gary Whitehouse, Chief Operating Officer
Advanced Polymer Systems, Inc.
Martin Wiley, Vice President Sales/Hong Kong
Loctite Corporation

WHAT I LOOK FOR IN GENERAL IN A CANDIDATE:
I believe that my clients deserve candidates who can serve
aces, spin straw into gold, and turn dreams into reality. I fur-

ther believe that it is my responsibility to make certain that they settle for nothing less. I feel every candidate I recommend should add value to my client's organization.

Requisite skills, experience, chemistry, and cultural fit notwithstanding, it is a given that my candidates meet my clients' immediate needs. But more important, they must be able to contribute to the organization's ultimate long-term strategic objectives.

Accordingly, I must make certain that my candidates have that something extra to contribute—perspective, insight, vision, innovation. They must have unique skills and experience beyond what is needed today. My candidates aren't just bodies that fill today's position specifications. They are value-added individuals who must be a resource to my clients, contributing to the future fabric of their organizations.

MINIMUM SALARY LEVEL AT WHICH I WORK:
$75,000

GEOGRAPHIC SCOPE OF RECRUITING ACTIVITIES:
Clients nationwide and in Canada, Europe, Asia, and South America

TOTAL YEARS OF RETAINER-TYPE RECRUITING EXPERIENCE:
18 years

WILLIAM H. BILLINGTON, JR.
Chairman and Chief Executive Officer
Billington, Fox & Ellis, Inc.
20 North Wacker Drive
Chicago, IL 60606
Telephone: (312) 236-5000

Date of birth: March 23, 1924
Grew up in: Chicago, IL

HIGHER EDUCATION:

Photo courtesy of Billington, Fox & Ellis, Inc.

Northwestern University
    B.S. degree, business administration, 1949
    M.B.A. degree, 1956

EMPLOYMENT HISTORY:

1964 to present: Billington, Fox & Ellis, Inc.
1960 to 1964: Consultant, Booz, Allen & Hamilton, Inc.
1955 to 1959: Consultant, Fry Consultants
1952 to 1955: Salary Administrator, Chicago Title & Trust Co.
1950 to 1952: Consultant, Hewitt Associates

MILITARY:

Second Lieutenant (Pilot), United States Air Force, 1943 to 1945

PRIVATE CLUBS:

University Club
Economics Club
Executives Club

REPRESENTATIVE & SIGNIFICANT PLACEMENTS:

Chief Operating Officer
    NYSE-listed company
Chief Executive Officer
    Miniconglomerate Private
Chief Operating Officer
    NASDAQ-listed company
Vice President and Academic Dean
    Prominent graduate school
Directors
    NYSE-listed company (3); ASE-listed company (3); ASE-listed company (1); a substantial private firm (4)

WHAT I LOOK FOR IN GENERAL IN A CANDIDATE:

Before you can evaluate a potential candidate, it is critical that you and your firm know the client—the position, responsibility, leadership style involved in operating the firm. As we know, this is many times overlooked or made a surface evaluation or subsequently not communicated to the junior staff members, who, in nearly all of the large multioffice recruitment firms do the majority of the work. We seek out candidates based on experience requirements—industry (in most cases) and position. However, the assessment of personality characteristics is the critical factor. It is the key not only to the selection process but more important to subsequent job success and contribution. Ties me to the old statement: An individual can win medals, but teams win ball games. Characteristics: intelligence (with primary emphasis on "street smarts"), social skills, the ability to listen, physical impact, creativity/imagination, leadership style (democratic/autocratic), and both oral and written communication skills. Others can include educational attainment, increasing levels of responsibility (and increases in compensation.)

MINIMUM SALARY LEVEL AT WHICH I WORK:
No minimum

GEOGRAPHIC SCOPE OF RECRUITING ACTIVITIES:
Clients nationwide and in Canada and Europe

TOTAL YEARS OF RETAINER-TYPE RECRUITING EXPERIENCE:
34 years

OTIS H. BOWDEN, II
President
Bowden & Company, Inc.
5000 Rockside Road, Suite 120
Cleveland, OH 44131
Telephone: (216) 447-1800

Date of birth: January 2, 1928
Grew up in: Stuttgart, AR

HIGHER EDUCATION:

Photo courtesy of Bowden & Co., Inc.

Washington University, St. Louis, Missouri
   B.S. degree, business administration, 1950
   M.B.A. degree, 1953

EMPLOYMENT HISTORY:
   1972 to present: Bowden & Company, Inc.
   1967 to 1971: Vice President, Butler Associates, Inc.
   1963 to 1967: Director–Mass Transit Center, BF Goodrich Co.
   1953 to 1963: District Manager, TRW Inc.
   1950 to 1953: Financial Analyst, St. Louis Union Trust Co.

PRIVATE CLUBS:
   The Union Club, Cleveland
   Red Apple Country Club, Eden Isle, AR
   Rotary–Paul Harris Fellow

SPECIAL INTERESTS AND HOBBIES:
   Biking, photography, sailing

REPRESENTATIVE AND SIGNIFICANT PLACEMENTS:
   Placed as Controller at Nationwide Insurance,
      presently President, Property/Casualty Companies
   Placed as Division Manager at The Scott Fetzer Company,
      presently Group President, Household Products and Services
   Vice President and General Counsel
      GenCorp
   Placed as Plant Manager at SPI, Inc.,
      presently President (through leveraged buy-out)
   Vice President Engineering
      TRW Inc.

WHAT I LOOK FOR IN GENERAL IN A CANDIDATE:

First, I expect to understand the client's criterion and do original research leading to candidates well suited to such criterion. Then, I expect to spend two to three hours primarily listening to each qualified candidate in a guided interview so that I understand the candidate's career and qualification. I am particularly interested in the quantification, as well as qualification, of career accomplishments and contributions. Of equal important is the candidate's human chemistry aspect—i.e., the ability to work with and get along with and motivate people.

MINIMUM SALARY LEVEL AT WHICH I WORK:
$60,000

GEOGRAPHIC SCOPE OF RECRUITING ACTIVITIES:
Clients nationwide and in Canada and Western Europe

TOTAL YEARS OF RETAINER-TYPE RECRUITING EXPERIENCE:
22 years

WILLIAM J. BOWEN
Vice Chairman
Heidrick and Struggles, Inc.
125 South Wacker Drive, Suite 2800
Chicago, IL 60606
Telephone: (312) 372-8811

Date of birth: May 13, 1934
Grew up in: New York, NY

HIGHER EDUCATION:

Fordham University, New York

Photo courtesy of Heidrick & Struggles, Inc.

    B.S. degree, economics, 1956

New York University

    M.B.A. degree, investments, 1963

MILITARY

First Lieutenant, United States Air Force, 1956 to 1959

EMPLOYMENT HISTORY:

1973 to present: Heidrick and Struggles, Inc.

1969 to 1973: First Vice President, Shearson Hammill & Co., Inc.

1967 to 1969: Institutional Salesman, Hayden Stone, Inc.

1961 to 1967: Assistant Vice President, First National City Bank, New York

1959 to 1961: Trainee, Smith Barney & Co.

PRIVATE CLUBS:

Metropolitan Club, Chicago

Chicago Club

Union League Club of New York

Marco Polo, NY

Onwentsia Club, Lake Forest, IL

SPECIAL INTERESTS AND HOBBIES:

Golf, baseball, photography

REPRESENTATIVE AND SIGNIFICANT PLACEMENTS:

Lattie Coor, President

    Arizona State University

Robert O'Leary, President and Chief Executive Officer

    Voluntary Hospitals America

Peter Uebberoth, Commissioner
  Major League Baseball
Frank Rhodes, President
  Cornell University
John Petty, President and Chief Executive Officer
  Marine Midland Bank

WHAT I LOOK FOR IN GENERAL IN A CANDIDATE:

Integrity, leadership: A person with a "can do" attitude. Although executives should have a high degree of self-confidence, you want someone who can lead and motivate others as well as share the success—not an "I, I, I" type. A sense of humor doesn't hurt.

MINIMUM SALARY LEVEL AT WHICH I WORK:
  $150,000–$200,000

GEOGRAPHIC SCOPE OF RECRUITING ACTIVITIES:
  Clients nationwide

TOTAL YEARS OF RETAINER-TYPE RECRUITING EXPERIENCE:
  16 years

HOWARD BRATCHES
Partner
Thorndike Deland Associates
275 Madison Avenue
New York, NY 10016
Telephone: (212) 661-6200

Date of birth: June 1, 1929
Grew up in: Eastern United States

HIGHER EDUCATION:

Photo by Roberta F. Raeburn

Washington and Lee University, Lexington, VA
  B.A. degree, political science, 1951
  L.L.B. degree, 1953

EMPLOYMENT HISTORY:
  1969 to present: Thorndike Deland Associates
  1962 to 1969: Human Resources Management, General Foods Corp.
  1953 to 1962: Personnel/Labor Relations Manager, Shell Oil Co.

PRIVATE CLUBS:
  Union League Club of New York
  Manursing Island Club, Rye, NY

SPECIAL INTERESTS AND HOBBIES:
  Tennis, watercolor painting

REPRESENTATIVE AND SIGNIFICANT PLACEMENTS:
  Placed as Vice President Marketing, presently Executive Vice President
    Clorox
  Placed as President, presently Vice Chairman
    Brown & Williamson Tobacco
  Placed as Vice President Marketing Specialty Products, presently
    Vice President Consumer Products Division
    H. J. Heinz
  Placed as Vice President Marketing and Sales, presently President
    Fiorucci Foods
  Placed as Division Marketing Manager, presently President and Chief
    Operating Officer
    Advo Systems Inc.

WHAT I LOOK FOR IN GENERAL IN A CANDIDATE:

The ability to articulate job and career accomplishments in a manner that explains the candidate's involvement and contributions.

Also look for organization in a presentation, personality, attitude in dealing with peers, subordinates, and upper management.

A positive approach to the interview in terms of responses is a significant key.

MINIMUM SALARY LEVEL AT WHICH I WORK:

$75,000

GEOGRAPHIC SCOPE OF RECRUITING ACTIVITIES:

Clients nationwide

TOTAL YEARS OF RETAINER-TYPE RECRUITING EXPERIENCE:

20 years

SKOTT B. BURKLAND
President
Haley BDC
500 Fifth Avenue
New York, NY 10110
Telephone: (212) 768-1610

Date of birth: May 25, 1942
Grew up in: Media, PA

Photo courtesy of Haley BDC

HIGHER EDUCATION:
Dickinson College, Carlisle, PA
A.B. degree, political science, 1964

MILITARY:
Staff Sergeant, United States Army, 1965 to 1971

EMPLOYMENT HISTORY:
1974 to present: Haley BDC
1970 to 1974: Vice President Personnel–U.S. Consumer Products, The Singer Company
1969 to 1970: Personnel Manager–Area II Operating Group, Citibank
1968 to 1969: Director of Recruiting, W.R. Grace & Co.
1966 to 1967: Recruiter, The Sun Oil Company
1964 to 1966: Financial Analyst, E.I. DuPont DeNemours & Co.

PRIVATE CLUBS:
The New York Yacht Club

SPECIAL INTERESTS AND HOBBIES:
Ocean Sailing

REPRESENTATIVE AND SIGNIFICANT PLACEMENTS:
David F. Hale, President and Chief Executive Officer
Gensia Pharmaceuticals, Inc.
Dean Groussman, Vice President–General Merchandise Manager
Zale Corporation, Skillern Drug Division
Gordon V. Ramseier, President
Immunetech Pharmaceuticals, Inc.
Eugene Lewis, President
Baker Instruments, Inc.
Richard Perman, Vice President Finance–International
Estee Lauder Companies

WHAT I LOOK FOR IN GENERAL IN A CANDIDATE:

Previous performance and a forward moving track record is all important. Intelligence and a complete understanding of the business process, including how to read a profit and loss statement are additional critical factors in selection criteria. Energy, communication skills, appearance, loyalty, and a sense of humor round out candidates for important positions.

MINIMUM SALARY LEVEL AT WHICH I WORK:
$100,000

GEOGRAPHIC SCOPE OF RECRUITING ACTIVITIES:
Clients nationwide and in Western Europe

TOTAL YEARS OF RETAINER-TYPE RECRUITING EXPERIENCE:
15 years

JOHN H. CALLEN, JR.
President
Ward Howell International, Inc.
99 Park Avenue
New York, NY 10016
Telephone: (212) 697-3730

Date of birth: June 19, 1932
Grew up in: New Jersey

HIGHER EDUCATION:
  Trinity College
    B.A. degree, history, 1955

Photo courtesy of Ward Howell International, Inc.

MILITARY:
  First Lieutenant, United States Marine Corps Reserve, 1955 to 1958

EMPLOYMENT HISTORY:
  1977 to present: Ward Howell International, Inc.
  1958 to 1977: Burlington Industries
    1974 to 1977: President, Burlington Sportswear
    1973 to 1974: President, Galey and Lord
    1960 to 1973: Executive Vice President–Marketing, Burlington
    Madison Yarn Co.
    1958 to 1960: Sales Representative, Peerless Woolen Mills

PRIVATE CLUBS:
  Rumson Country Club, NJ
  Williams Club, NY

SPECIAL INTERESTS AND HOBBIES:
  Golf, paddle tennis, cross-country skiing, hiking, the environment,
    Association of Executive Search Consultants (AESC)

REPRESENTATIVE AND SIGNIFICANT PLACEMENTS:
  Director of Engineering
    Saudi Arabian government agency
  Chief Operating Officer (later promoted to President)
    Major textile knit fabric producer (acquired by a major holding
    company)
  Executive Director
    Influential environmental advocacy organization

Chief Operating Officer (later promoted to President)
   Well-established, privately owned men's tailored clothing manu-
   facturer
President
   Private college

WHAT I LOOK FOR IN GENERAL IN A CANDIDATE:

I look for signs of energy, intelligence, self-motivation, creative problem-solving ability, and if a high-level position, stature
becomes important. In this era, I also look for evidence of
strong interpersonal skills and a sense of humor. Also, I tend to
favor candidates who are active in their community or have
strong away-from-work interests.

When filling corporate positions in highly competitive
industries, I like to see evidence of a competitive spirit—particularly when filling marketing and general management positions.

MINIMUM SALARY LEVEL AT WHICH I WORK:
$120,000

GEOGRAPHIC SCOPE OF RECRUITING ACTIVITIES:
Clients nationwide and in Europe and the Middle East

TOTAL YEARS OF RETAINER-TYPE RECRUITING EXPERIENCE:
12 years

MICHAEL D. CAVER
**Managing Partner, Health Care
    Practice
Heidrick and Struggles, Inc.
125 South Wacker Drive, Suite
    2800
Chicago, IL 60606
Telephone: (312) 372-8811**

**Date of birth: April 7, 1942
Grew up in: Washington, DC, and
    Richmond, VA**

Photo courtesy of Heidrick & Struggles, Inc.

HIGHER EDUCATION:
   Hampden-Sydney College, VA
      B.S. degree, modern European history, 1964

EMPLOYMENT HISTORY:
   1979 to present: Heidrick and Struggles, Inc.
   1977 to 1979: Director, International Personnel Manager, Baxter-
      Travenol Labs.
   1976 to 1977: Manager International Personnel Administration, The
      Procter & Gamble Co.
   1972 to 1976: Director of Personnel Administration, The Procter &
      Gamble Co. of Canada, Ltd.
   1967 to 1972: Various Marketing, Sales and Personnel, The Procter
      & Gamble Co.

PRIVATE CLUBS:
   Metropolitan Club

SPECIAL INTERESTS AND HOBBIES:
   Photography, classical music, international travel

REPRESENTATIVE AND SIGNIFICANT PLACEMENTS:
   President and Chief Executive Officer
      One of the country's major national alliances of voluntary not-for-
      profit hospitals
   President and Chief Executive Officer
      Leading institute focusing on health, faith, and ethics
   President and Chief Executive Officer
      Large, successful, Midwestern multispecialty physician group prac-
      tice

President and Chief Executive Officer
Catholic-sponsored health care system
Start-up President and Chief Executive Officer
National alliance of teaching hospitals

WHAT I LOOK FOR IN GENERAL IN A CANDIDATE:

My objective is to identify candidates whose unique blend of experiences, concrete accomplishments, values, personalities, styles, ambitions, and family goals most closely match my client's *total* opportunity.

These clients are almost always undergoing fundamental change, and we are retained to help them achieve "critical mass" in senior executive strengths. Therefore it is important that candidates have demonstrated they consistently accomplish the priority objectives of their present mission while anticipating the future and properly positioning their organizations for future success.

Almost without exception my clients depend on our ability to present candidates of conspicuous character and integrity, well respected by their peers, committed to continuing professional development, balanced between collegial, participative, and directive styles as appropriate, with strong common sense, passionate about their commitments, inspiring, and sound developers of others. Such candidates are thoughtful about their affiliations, reluctant to leave as long as they are contributing and invariably make major impacts in all their involvements.

Especially appealing are those candidates who know themselves well and share their limitations and frustrations as well as their accomplishments and dreams.

MINIMUM SALARY LEVEL AT WHICH I WORK:
Focus on Chief Executive Officer and Chief Operating Officer projects

GEOGRAPHIC SCOPE OF RECRUITING ACTIVITIES:
Clients nationwide and internationally

TOTAL YEARS OF RETAINER-TYPE RECRUITING EXPERIENCE:
10 years

DAVID E. CHAMBERS
President
David Chambers & Associates,
   Inc.
6 East 43rd Street
New York, NY 10017
Telephone: (212) 986-8653

Date of birth: March 6, 1938
Grew up in: Mason City, IA

Photo by Bachrach

HIGHER EDUCATION:
   University of Arizona
      B.S. degree, business administration, 1961

MILITARY:
   Specialist Fourth Class, United States Army, 1961 to 1963

EMPLOYMENT HISTORY:
   1974 to present: David Chambers & Associates, Inc.
   1973 to 1974: President, Executive Search Division, Fry Consultants,
      Inc.
   1969 to 1973: Partner, Antell, Wright & Nagel
   1968 to 1969: Employment Director, Allied Chemical
   1967 to 1968: President, David Chambers Company
   1966 to 1967: Associate, Booz, Allen & Hamilton
   1965 to 1966: Employment Supervisor, Finance, Xerox Corporation
   1961 to 1965: Employment Representative, Pan American World
      Airways

PRIVATE CLUBS:
   Winged Foot Golf Club, New York
   The Boardroom, New York
   Union League Club, New York and Chicago
   Capital Hill, Washington, DC

SPECIAL INTERESTS AND HOBBIES:
   Golf, travel, people

REPRESENTATIVE AND SIGNIFICANT PLACEMENTS:
   James McIlhenny, President and Chief Executive Officer
      U.S. News and World Report

Stephen Munn, President and Chief Executive Officer
    Carlisle Companies Inc.
John McNiff, Vice President, Chief Financial Officer
    Dover Corporation
Edward Kata, Vice President–Mergers and Acquisitions
    Dover Corporation
Jefferson Amacker, President and Chief Executive Officer
    Leach Corporation

WHAT I LOOK FOR IN GENERAL IN A CANDIDATE:

In addition to personal chemistry and specific background and experience required on each search assignment, I am interested in the candidate's maturity, energy level, appearance, leadership skills, and other personal attributes.

Other considerations include family home life, outside interests, and other matters that show the person's "balance" and how he or she projects themselves.

MINIMUM SALARY LEVEL AT WHICH I WORK:
$100,000

GEOGRAPHIC SCOPE OF RECRUITING ACTIVITIES:
Clients nationwide, in Canada, and in Europe through affiliates in Paris and London

TOTAL YEARS OF RETAINER-TYPE RECRUITING EXPERIENCE:
20 years

DAVID H. CHARLSON
Executive Vice President and
Managing Partner
Chestnut Hill Partners
2345 Waukegan Road, Suite S-165
Deerfield, IL 60015
Telephone: (708) 940-9690

Date of birth: May 26, 1947
Grew up in: Pittsburgh, PA

HIGHER EDUCATION:

University of Arizona, Tucson

Photo courtesy of Chestnut Hill Partners

B.S. degree, business administration, 1969

EMPLOYMENT HISTORY:

1989 to present: Chestnut Hill Partners

1984 to 1989: Executive Vice President/Managing Director, Richards Consultants

1976 to 1984: Managing Director–Central Region, Korn/Ferry International

1975 to 1976: Staff Vice President, Staub Warmbold & Associates

1974 to 1975: Manager–Corporate Employment, General Foods Corp.

1970 to 1974: Personnel Director–International, Bank of America

1969 to 1970: Marketing Officer, Wells Fargo Bank

PRIVATE CLUBS:

University Club of Chicago

Bannockburn Bath & Tennis Club

SPECIAL INTERESTS AND HOBBIES:

Auto racing, golf, tennis

REPRESENTATIVE AND SIGNIFICANT PLACEMENTS:

O.B. Parrish, President–Pharmaceutical Group

G.D. Searle

James Armstrong, President and Chief Operating Officer

Norwest Bank Corp.

Dr. Joseph Davies, President–Searle Research and Development

G.D. Searle

Dr. David Steinberg, President

Lorax

Joseph E. Caprico, Director
United States Tennis Association

WHAT I LOOK FOR IN GENERAL IN A CANDIDATE:

I try to see a candidate through the eyes of my client and match as closely as possible his or her management style, work ethic, and personality to that of my client organization. I look for a demonstrated track record of success in more than one environment. Individuals who are bright, energetic, and articulate in both oral and written form. They must be self-assured and not easily threatened or intimidated and have the proven ability to recruit, hire, lead, manage, and control other professionals.

I look for candidates who can add value to my client's organization and have the ability to grow beyond the assignment they may be hired to perform.

Finally, I look for someone whose management style and expertise most closely align with my client organization.

MINIMUM SALARY LEVEL AT WHICH I WORK:
$75,000

GEOGRAPHIC SCOPE OF RECRUITING ACTIVITIES:
Clients nationwide and in England, France, Germany, Switzerland, Japan, and Brazil

TOTAL YEARS OF RETAINER-TYPE RECRUITING EXPERIENCE:
14 years

WILLIAM B. CLEMENS, JR.
Managing Director
Norman Broadbent International
Inc.
200 Park Avenue
New York, NY 10166
Telephone: (212) 953-6990

Date of birth: May 6, 1944
Grew up in: Lynchburg, VA

HIGHER EDUCATION:
Bloomfield College, NJ
B.A. degree, political science, 1967

Photo courtesy of Norman Broadbent International Inc.

EMPLOYMENT HISTORY:
1987 to present: Norman Broadbent International
1979 to 1987: Managing Director, Russell Reynolds Associates, Inc.
1972 to 1979: Director of Staffing, McKinsey & Company, Inc.
1969 to 1972: Personnel Manager, NL Industries
1967 to 1969: Recruiting Coordinator, Squibb Corporation

PRIVATE CLUBS:
University Club, NY
Norwalk Yacht Club, CT
Port Washington Yacht Club, NY

SPECIAL INTERESTS AND HOBBIES:
Sailing, skiing, racquet sports, traveling, theatre

REPRESENTATIVE AND SIGNIFICANT PLACEMENTS:
Steven Goldstein, President, Consumer Financial Services
American Express
Francis N. Bonsignore, Partner–National Director, Human Resources
Price Waterhouse
Donald G. Ogilvie, Executive Director
American Bankers Association
Ian Heap, Chairman and Chief Executive Officer
Exel Corporation
Quentin Smith (Retired Chairman, TPF&C), Member, Board of Directors
Guardian Life Insurance Company

WHAT I LOOK FOR IN GENERAL IN A CANDIDATE:

Our profession is an art, not a science. The quality of creative thinking the recruiter brings to his art, the judgment he uses in assessing prospects against client requirements, and the skill he uses to close in a manner beneficial to the client and candidate come only from experience. There is simply no substitute for experience.

One evaluates candidates against specific client needs. Personal characteristics, business skills, and personality traits are in part driven by the nature of the organization and the role for which we are recruiting. Nonetheless there are certain characteristics I look for in every candidate. Not necessarily in order they are a stable personal and professional history, series of successive accomplishments in their chosen field, strong sense of self, sense of humor, personal and professional ambition, positive and genuine personality but with a competitive edge, willingness to make decisions, ability to attract and develop people, intellectual curiosity, understanding of the economics of a business and how to make money and get things done, self-directed, highly motivated. Where we add value is assisting a client, within a given set of candidate parameters, select the most appropriate prospect in a timely fashion.

MINIMUM SALARY LEVEL AT WHICH I WORK:
$125,000

GEOGRAPHIC SCOPE OF RECRUITING ACTIVITIES:
Clients nationwide and in Europe

TOTAL YEARS OF RETAINER-TYPE RECRUITING EXPERIENCE:
22 years

JAMES H. CORNEHLSEN
Partner
Heidrick & Struggles, Inc.
245 Park Avenue, 32nd Floor
New York, NY 10167
Telephone: (212) 867-9876

Date of birth: June 11, 1942

HIGHER EDUCATION:
Dartmouth College
  B.A. degree, English, 1964

Photo courtesy of Handy Associates

MILITARY:
Yeoman First Class, United States Coast Guard, 1966 to 1972

EMPLOYMENT HISTORY:
1990 to present: Heidrick & Struggles
1983 to 1990: Handy Associates
1981 to 1983: Antell, Nagel, Moorehead (firm sold to Korn/Ferry)
1980 to 1981: President, Las Americas
1976 to 1979: Vice President–Marketing, Publishing Group, CBS, Inc.
1967 to 1975: McGraw-Hill, Inc.
1964 to 1967: General Electric Company

PRIVATE CLUBS:
Dartmouth Club
University Glee Club

REPRESENTATIVE AND SIGNIFICANT PLACEMENTS:
Group President
  $1 billion computer services company
President–U.S. Business
  $1 billion international publisher and direct marketing firm
Board of Directors–two members to guide global expansion
  $2 billion international holding company
President
  Consumer product/marketing firm
President
  Joint venture of three major corporations

WHAT I LOOK FOR IN GENERAL IN A CANDIDATE:
Leadership qualities
Vision and strategic insight

Motivational–sales marketing confidence
Communication ability
Flexibility
Personal presence
Creativity
Initiative–impact in past jobs
Attention to detail
Self-awareness
Strong personal ethics

MINIMUM SALARY LEVEL AT WHICH I WORK:
  $80,000

GEOGRAPHIC SCOPE OF RECRUITING ACTIVITIES:
  Clients nationwide and internationally

TOTAL YEARS OF RETAINER-TYPE RECRUITING EXPERIENCE:
  8 years

O.D. "DAN" CRUSE
Managing Director, High
** Technology Practice**
SpencerStuart
1717 Main Street, Suite 5300
Dallas, TX 75201
Telephone: (214) 658-1777

Date of birth: March 24, 1939
Grew up in: Texas

Photo by Gittings

HIGHER EDUCATION:
University of Dallas
   B.A. degree, liberal arts, 1961

EMPLOYMENT HISTORY:
1977 to present: SpencerStuart & Associates
1975 to 1977: Vice President Human Resources, Farah Manufacturing Company
1966 to 1975: Vice President Central Services, Tracor, Inc.
1963 to 1966: Labor Relations Specialist, General Electric Company

PRIVATE CLUBS:
Las Colinas Country Club
Tower Club

SPECIAL INTERESTS AND HOBBIES:
Golf, bird hunting, directorships

REPRESENTATIVE AND SIGNIFICANT PLACEMENTS:
Chief Executive Officer
   Leading technology trade association in industry
Chief Executive Officer
   $1 billion freestanding (prior to LBO) NYSE diversified electronics company
Chief Executive Officer
   Hotel enterprise for one of the country's leading business families
Chief Executive Officer
   For the turnaround of a $250 million NYSE technology company
Division President
   Recruited from GE who changed the culture of an old-line NYSE manufacturing company

WHAT I LOOK FOR IN GENERAL IN A CANDIDATE:

The functional discipline and/or progression within the candidate's career "is a given" at the levels we work with. Consequently, our focus is on accomplishments that distinguish the candidate and his or her fit within the client organization. Our contribution to the client is to identify candidates who have a demonstrated capacity for producing results (beyond the norm of good performance) that will have not only an immediate but a sustainable positive impact on results within the client organization. At the same time, we focus on fit, not just from a comfort standpoint but more important from a style/acceptability standpoint if the candidate makes an immediate and dramatic impact. Does the candidate have the interpersonal skills for acceptance if his or her actions potentially contribute to significant change and progress?

MINIMUM SALARY LEVEL AT WHICH I WORK:
$100,000

GEOGRAPHIC SCOPE OF RECRUITING ACTIVITIES:
Clients nationwide and in Japan, Germany, France, The Netherlands, Brazil, Austria, and Australia

TOTAL YEARS OF RETAINER-TYPE RECRUITING EXPERIENCE:
12+ years

RALPH E. DIECKMANN
President
Dieckmann & Associates, Ltd.
75 East Wacker Drive
Chicago, IL 60601
Telephone: (312) 372-4949

Date of birth: March 30, 1944
Grew up in: Cleveland, OH

Photo by Bachrach

HIGHER EDUCATION:
Northwestern University
  B.A. degree, psychology, 1966
Loyola University of Chicago
  M.S. degree, industrial relations, 1972

EMPLOYMENT HISTORY:
1981 to present: Dieckmann & Associates, Ltd.
1973 to 1981: Executive Search Division, Peat Marwick Main
1966 to 1973: Director of Recruiting, R.R. Donnelley & Sons Co.

PRIVATE CLUBS:
Tavern Club

SPECIAL INTERESTS AND HOBBIES:
Opera, symphony, tennis, cycling, cross-country skiing, sailing, travel, civic and charity boards

REPRESENTATIVE AND SIGNIFICANT PLACEMENTS:
William H. Bolinder, Chief Executive Officer
  Zurich Insurance Group–United States
John J. Avignone, Chief Executive Officer
  Auto Club Insurance Group
Newton Allen, President and Chief Executive Officer
  Farm Bureau Services
Glenn E. Stinson, President and Chief Executive Officer
  ABC Rail Corporation
George Doering, Group President
  MTS Systems

WHAT I LOOK FOR IN GENERAL IN A CANDIDATE:

An executive recruiter's greatest value-added service is helping a client determine which unique candidate talents will have a leveraging effect on results. Necessary to this process are understanding the complexities of the position within its organizational context and determining the skill sets required to appropriately complement the existing management corps.

Notwithstanding the unique aspects of every search, seventeen characteristics build a foundation for outstanding executive performance:

Communications excellence is the essence of the executive function. *Vision* provides the impetus for leadership and *realism* the boundaries to the vision. *Leadership* requires *charisma* to mobilize the emotional support systems and *drive* to achieve what charisma won't. *Common sense* allows one to lead in the right direction and *intelligence* to lead briskly. *Diversified interests* are a sign of intelligence and a foil for tunnel vision. *Perseverance* multiplies the effectiveness of intelligence. *Self-confidence* and *delegation* permit accepting new responsibilities by entrusting old ones to others. *Decisiveness* combats inertia, the cancer of organizations. *Flexibility* and *creativity* are the primary tools for coping with exponential change, with *staffing finesse* essential to frequent adaptation. Finally, a *sense of humor* is the best outlet for stress.

MINIMUM SALARY LEVEL AT WHICH I WORK:
  $150,000

GEOGRAPHIC SCOPE OF RECRUITING ACTIVITIES:
  Clients nationwide and internationally

TOTAL YEARS OF RETAINER-TYPE RECRUITING EXPERIENCE:
  15 years

ROBERT W. DINGMAN
President
Robert W. Dingman Company,
  Inc.
32131 West Lindero Canyon Road
Westlake Village, CA 91361
Telephone: (818) 991-5950

Date of birth: August 23, 1926
Grew up in: Eastern United States

HIGHER EDUCATION:
Houghton College, NY
  B.A. degree, 1950

Photo courtesy of Robert W. Dingman Company, Inc.

MILITARY:
Corporal, United States Army, 1944 to 1945

EMPLOYMENT HISTORY:
1979 to present: Robert W. Dingman Co.
1974 to 1979: Vice President and Partner, Billington, Fox & Ellis
1966 to 1974: Vice President and Partner, Wilkinson, Sedwick & Yelverton
1950 to 1966: Manager, Arthur Young & Co.
1951 to 1961: Personnel positions in industry, government and education

PRIVATE CLUBS:
Jonathon Club, Los Angeles
North Ranch Country Club, Westlake Village

SPECIAL INTERESTS AND HOBBIES:
Author of *The Complete Search Committee Guidebook,* Mission Aviation
  Fellowship board member

REPRESENTATIVE AND SIGNIFICANT PLACEMENTS:
Senior Vice Presidents of Finance, Marketing, and Operations
  Several airlines
President and Chief Executive Officer
  Electronics components firms
Vice Presidents of Marketing, Operations and Sales
  Consumer packaged goods company

Ten CEO searches
Religious parachurch organizations
CFO, General Counsel, Medical Director, Senior Vice President of
Marketing and Senior Vice President Alternate Delivery Systems
Major health care insurers

WHAT I LOOK FOR IN GENERAL IN A CANDIDATE:
There are three keys for a good fit:

1. What are the future plans of the client for the organization and the aspirations of the candidate? Are they compatible enough for at least a five-year good relationship?
2. Will the candidate and his or her boss have good personal chemistry? Are they in each other's comfort zone?
3. Both the client and the candidate need to be told the worst features each has and be willing to accept those and feel the good points far outweigh them. Discovering significant negatives after being hired kills the needed mutual trust.

Determining that a candidate has the required technical experience is essential, of course, but even a first-year recruiter can do that well. Finding the motivational patterns and interpersonal style is basic to making a key placement.

MINIMUM SALARY LEVEL AT WHICH I WORK:
$80,000 (excluding nonprofits)

GEOGRAPHIC SCOPE OF RECRUITING ACTIVITIES:
Clients nationwide

TOTAL YEARS OF RETAINER-TYPE RECRUITING EXPERIENCE:
30 years

MICHAEL S. DUNFORD
President
Michael S. Dunford, Inc.
478 Pennsylvania Avenue,
  Suite 301
Glen Ellyn, IL 60137
Telephone: (708) 858-3330

Date of birth: October 7, 1944
Grew up in: Appleton, WI

HIGHER EDUCATION:
Stout State University

Photo courtesy of Michael S. Dunford, Inc.

  B.S. degree, business administration, 1968
University of Wisconsin
  M.B.A. degree, marketing, 1971

MILITARY:
Ensign, United States Navy, 1968 to 1969

EMPLOYMENT HISTORY:
  1989 to present: Michael S. Dunford, Inc.
  1978 to 1989: Partner, Lamalie Associates, Inc.
  1973 to 1978: Associate, Booz, Allen & Hamilton, Inc.
  1971 to 1973: Marketing Manager-Refrigerated Foods Div., The Pillsbury Co.
  1971: Marketing Representative–Computer System Division, The RCA Corporation

PRIVATE CLUBS:
Knights of Columbus
Christian Business Men's Committee of USA

SPECIAL INTERESTS AND HOBBIES:
Church programs, American Legion participation, running, tennis

REPRESENTATIVE AND SIGNIFICANT PLACEMENTS:
Stephen F. Bollenbach, Senior Vice President–Finance
  Holiday Corporation
Judd R. Cool, Vice President–Human Resources
  Inland Steel Industries, Inc.
Thomas Herskovitz, President–Kraft/General Foods Frozen Products
  Kraft, Inc., Philip Morris Companies, Inc.

Robert E. Naylor, Group Vice President–Corporate Development,
    Technology, Research
    Rohn and Haas Co.
Jack W. Simpson, President
    Mead Data Central, Inc., Mead Corporation

WHAT I LOOK FOR IN GENERAL IN A CANDIDATE:

Each assignment comes with its specific requirements, but
there are several key elements that we look for in all executive
candidates. These can be divided into three categories: personality traits, professional capabilities, and personal interests. Our
primary focus centers on the individual's personality and character. Integrity, positive attitude, maturity, and strong communication and listening skills are heavily weighted. We look for a
balance between these traits and humility, common sense,
demeanor, confidence, and the ability to relate with others.

We examine previous employment experiences as an indication of current functional and industry knowledge and future
potential. Decision-making abilities, judgment, leadership and
management skills, a team orientation, and ability to handle
financial and corporate success and disappointment are also key
factors. The individual's major strengths and developmental
areas along with career interests and motivations are evaluated
and identified.

Personal interests such as exercise programs, religious activities, community involvement, and hobbies demonstrate the balanced life-style that we seek in a healthy, integrated executive.

MINIMUM SALARY LEVEL AT WHICH I WORK:
$100,000

GEOGRAPHIC SCOPE OF RECRUITING ACTIVITIES:
Clients nationwide and in Europe

TOTAL YEARS OF RETAINER-TYPE RECRUITING EXPERIENCE:
12 years

ANTOINETTE L. "TONI" FARLEY
Vice President
Kieffer, Ford & Associates, Ltd.
2015 Spring Road, Suite 510
Oak Brook, IL 60521
Telephone: (708) 990-1370

Date of birth: April 1, 1946
Grew up in: Evanston, IL

HIGHER EDUCATION:
University of Illinois

Photo courtesy of Kieffer, Ford & Associates, Inc.

B.S. degree, business administration, 1980

M.B.A. degree, finance and accounting, 1982

EMPLOYMENT HISTORY:
1985 to present: Kieffer, Ford & Associates, Ltd.

1982 to 1985: Manager, Encyclopedia Britannica USA, Inc.

1968 to 1982: University of Illinois:

Graduate Assistant, College of Business Administration

Manager, Nursing Personnel, Hospital and Health Care Colleges

Personnel Officer, Employment Administration

Personnel Officer, Wage and Salary Administration

Records Manager

1964 to 1967: Sales Associate, Marshall Field & Company

SPECIAL INTERESTS AND HOBBIES:
Jogging, reading, home restoration, news-politics-world events, family

REPRESENTATIVE AND SIGNIFICANT PLACEMENTS:
Ann Young Ameigh, Administrative Director of Nursing
Geisinger Medical Center

Bruce Rampage, President and Chief Executive Officer
St. Catherine's Hospital

Jim Long, Corporate Director of Productivity
Franciscan Health System

Jeffrey H. Liebman, Director of Cancer Center
Washington Hospital Center

Philip J. Glassanos, Senior Vice President of Corporate Development
South Shore Health and Educational Corporation

WHAT I LOOK FOR IN GENERAL IN A CANDIDATE:

The first step in a successful search is the establishment of a partnership between the client and the search consultant. Next comes a thorough assessment of the organization—its corporate culture and the unique needs of the position for which one is conducting the search. The third step is candid consultation with the client and feedback on the "degree of difficulty" of the search, the level of credentials, experience and track record required to meet the needs of the organization, and the personality and character traits sought for a good match. Although necessary credentials vary with functional area, there are certain characteristics that I look for in all candidates:

Has a professional appearance and executive bearing; is poised, polite, polished, but down-to-earth; has done their homework on the search firm and client in preparation for interview; possesses a healthy ego and sense of self-esteem but is not arrogant; is a visionary leader and calculated risk taker; can articulate accomplishments and relate them to the position for which he or she is interviewing; can state strengths and weaknesses; conveys a sense of enthusiasm and love for what he or she does; knows himself or herself very well and has a set of personal and professional goals; knows what motivates them; is able to explain value system; possesses a realistic picture of their own marketability and market worth; can share who or what has influenced them (books, people living or dead) and why; is a human being and can share what they have learned from their mistakes; possesses a sense of humor and does not take himself or herself too seriously; can handle constructive criticism and feedback and seeks it; has demonstrated leadership in other areas, e.g., active in community, professional organization; tries to get fun out of life and leads a balanced personal and professional life.

MINIMUM SALARY LEVEL AT WHICH I WORK:
$70,000

GEOGRAPHIC SCOPE OF RECRUITING ACTIVITIES:
Clients nationwide

TOTAL YEARS OF RETAINER-TYPE RECRUITING EXPERIENCE:
4+ years

LEON A. FARLEY
Managing Partner
Leon A. Farley Associates
468 Jackson Street
San Francisco, CA 94111
Telephone: (415) 989-0989

Date of birth: May 6, 1935
Grew up in: Southern California

Photo courtesy of Leon A. Farley Associates

HIGHER EDUCATION:
University of California at Los Angeles
 B.A. degree, English literature, 1956
University of California School of Law
 J.D., 1959

EMPLOYMENT HISTORY:
1976 to present: Leon A. Farley Associates
1974 to 1976: Vice President, Northwest Region, Korn/Ferry International (San Francisco)
1972 to 1974: Vice President, Korn/Ferry International (Los Angeles)
1970 to 1972: Executive Vice President, Business Development, ITT Aerospace Optical Division
1967 to 1970: Marketing Manager, Financial Operations Manager, Ford Aerospace
1963 to 1967: Contracts Manager, Ford Aeroneutronic Division
1959 to 1963: Contract Supervisor, Hughes Aircraft

SPECIAL INTERESTS AND HOBBIES:
Rugby, soccer, acting, tennis, travel

REPRESENTATIVE AND SIGNIFICANT PLACEMENTS:
Michael Chittick, President
 SeaAlaska Corporation
Michael Chan, President
 Kamehameha Schools–Bishop Estate
Pierre Madon, Director–Engineering
 Intelsat
Richard Pinto, President
 Thermco Allegheny International
Dick Latzer, Senior Vice President and Chief Investment Officer
 Transamerica Corporation

WHAT I LOOK FOR IN GENERAL IN A CANDIDATE:

It is a cliche in our business that "candidates are hired for what they know and fired for what they are." At the senior level at which we work, technical competence, functional knowledge, and requisite experience are almost a given. In my interviewing and evaluation of candidates, I strive to achieve the goal of understanding the whole person. General intelligence and business knowledge are necessary, but I especially focus on the manner in which individuals solve problems, their personal style, and the manner in which they interact with subordinates, peers, and superiors.

Usually the key to both motivation and interpersonal interaction lies in the formative years commencing with early childhood. Family patterns, experiences of love, sharing, rejection, and alienation affect individual self-esteem and inculcate values.

Providing our clients with individuals that bring the right mix of qualifications, credentials, values, and interpersonal skills is our responsibility. To do so correctly is a constant and continuing challenge. This is where we prove our value and derive our own satisfaction.

MINIMUM SALARY LEVEL AT WHICH I WORK:
$100,000

GEOGRAPHIC SCOPE OF RECRUITING ACTIVITIES:
Clients nationwide. International assignments are most often conducted through affiliates in Europe, the United Kingdom, Canada, Australia, and Hong Kong.

TOTAL YEARS OF RETAINER-TYPE RECRUITING EXPERIENCE:
17 years

RICHARD M. FERRY
President
Korn/Ferry International
1800 Century Park East
Los Angeles, CA 90067
Telephone: (213) 879-1834

Date of birth: September 26, 1937
Grew up in: Ohio

Photo courtesy of Korn/Ferry International

HIGHER EDUCATION:
   Kent State University
      B.S. degree, honors in accounting, 1959

EMPLOYMENT HISTORY:
   1969 to present: Korn/Ferry International
   1965 to 1969: Various titles to Partner, Peat, Marwick, Mitchell & Co.

PRIVATE CLUBS:
   The Regency Club
   California Club
   Valley Hunt Club
   Los Angeles Country Club
   Vintage Club

SPECIAL INTERESTS & HOBBIES:
   Numerous civic and charitable activities including Director of United
      Way (Los Angeles); Trustee, Occidental College; Board Member,
      The Music Center; Director Catholic Charities; Trustee, The Edu-
      cation Foundation of the Archdiocese of Los Angeles; Director,
      Paulist Productions; Director, Los Angeles Area Chamber of Com-
      merce; Board of Directors: 1st Business Bank, Los Angeles; Avery
      International, Pasadena; Centex Corporation, Dallas; Pacific
      Mutual Life Insurance Company, Newport Beach

REPRESENTATIVE AND SIGNIFICANT PLACEMENTS:
   Peter Ueberroth, Executive Director
      Los Angeles Olympic Organizing Committee
   Lawrence A. Del Santo, Chairman and Chief Executive Officer
      Lucky Stores
   Richard M. Kovacevich, President and Chief Operating Officer
      Norwest Corporation

Lawrence Hirsch, President and Chief Executive Officer
   Centex Corporation
Ray Irani, President and Chief Operating Officer
   Occidental Petroleum, Inc.

WHAT I LOOK FOR IN GENERAL IN A CANDIDATE:

I look for candidates who are preeminent in their field and who possess the personal qualities and passion to be chief executive officers. They must be bright, goal-oriented, creative, enthusiastic, singularly motivated, and have proven themselves in complex, demanding situations. In addition to being superb executives, they must be visionaries with superior communication skills to motivate their troops. They also must be outstanding human beings. I cannot overemphasize this point and the need to be ethical and absolutely above reproach. They must lead by example and must have a keen sense of social responsibility. Society will hold them accountable for their social actions, as Wall Street does for their financial performance.

MINIMUM SALARY LEVEL AT WHICH I WORK:
$250,000

GEOGRAPHIC SCOPE OF RECRUITING ACTIVITIES:
Clients nationwide and in countries served by the Korn/Ferry network of offices in Brussels, Caracas, Frankfurt, Geneva, Guadalajara, Hong Kong, Kuala Lumpur, London, Madrid, Melbourne, Paris, Sao Paulo, Singapore, Sydney, Tokyo, Zurich

TOTAL YEARS OF RETAINER-TYPE RECRUITING EXPERIENCE:
23 years

ROBERT M. FLANAGAN
President
Paul Stafford Associates, Ltd.
261 Madison Avenue
New York, NY 10016
Telephone: (212) 983-6666

Date of birth: March 19, 1940
Grew up in: Concord, NH

HIGHER EDUCATION:
Saint Anselm College, New Hampshire
A.B. degree, economics, 1962

Photo courtesy of Paul Stafford Associates, Ltd.

EMPLOYMENT HISTORY:
1980 to present: Paul Stafford Associates, Ltd.
1966 to 1980: Principal, Booz, Allen & Hamilton
1965 to 1966: Operations Manager, Milton Bradley Co.
1963 to 1965: Systems Analyst, American Mutual Insurance Co.
1962 to 1963: Operations Trainee, New England Merchants National
Bank

PRIVATE CLUBS:
The Union League Club of New York
Mount Kisco Country Club

SPECIAL INTERESTS AND HOBBIES:
Golf

REPRESENTATIVE AND SIGNIFICANT PLACEMENTS:
President
Major consumer services company
President
Major resort property
Chief Operating Officer
Worldwide electronics manufacturer
President–USA
Major UK-based services company
President
Major mortgage banking company

WHAT I LOOK FOR IN GENERAL IN A CANDIDATE:
Specific accomplishments in his or her field of endeavor
Quality of the candidate's background vis-à-vis education;

organizations he or she has been associated with;
outside interests including civic and public service
activities

An appropriate fit with the client organization relative to
his or her experience in dealing with issues, problems,
circumstances, that the candidate will be facing if
appointed to the position

A record of success in the candidate's background
beginning early in his or her career and including
academic, athletics, early work experience, and
progression through professional career

Leadership skills

MINIMUM SALARY LEVEL AT WHICH I WORK:
$100,000

GEOGRAPHIC SCOPE OF RECRUITING ACTIVITIES:
Clients nationwide and in Europe and the United Kingdom

TOTAL YEARS OF RETAINER-TYPE RECRUITING EXPERIENCE:
16 years

J. DANIEL FORD
Executive Vice President and Partner
Kieffer, Ford & Associates, Ltd.
2015 Spring Road, Suite 510
Oak Brook, IL 60521
Telephone: (708) 990-1370

Date of birth: August 22, 1942
Grew up in: Minnesota, South
 Dakota, Iowa

Photo courtesy of Kieffer, Ford & Associates, Ltd.

HIGHER EDUCATION:
 Jamestown College, ND
  B.S. degree, mathematics, 1964
 University of Chicago
  M.B.A. degree, health care administration, 1971

MILITARY:
 Lieutenant (Naval Aviator), United States Naval Reserve, 1964 to
 1969

EMPLOYMENT HISTORY:
 1984 to present: Kieffer, Ford & Associates, Ltd.
 1977 to 1984: Vice President, Western Region, Witt Associates
 1973 to 1976: Executive Director, Fox Valley Hospital Planning
 Council
 1971 to 1973: Director, Emergency Medical Services Planning, Chicago Hospital Council

SPECIAL INTERESTS AND HOBBIES:
 Family, church, music, photography, travel, and sports

REPRESENTATIVE AND SIGNIFICANT PLACEMENTS:
 Stanley Broadnax, Commissioner
  Department of Public Health, City of Cincinnati
 Robert Davidge, President and Chief Executive Officer
  Our Lady of the Lake Regional Medical Center
 Barbara Seebold, Vice President Operations
  Geisinger Medical Center
 W. William Noce, Jr., President and Chief Executive Officer
  St. Joseph Hospital of Orange California

Barry Connoley, President and Chief Executive Officer
Multicare Medical Center

WHAT I LOOK FOR IN GENERAL IN A CANDIDATE:

Values the person lives by (personal and professional)

Self-esteem—the person feels good about himself or herself

Positive attitude about life and people

Key influences on the person during his or her life (e.g., who would comprise a personal board of directors?)

Self-assessment—person's ability to assess their own life

Leadership, business, and communications skills (with strong emphasis on listening skills)

Self-starter, high energy level, assertive

Quality of personal life, including marriage (if applicable)

Career path understandable, productive, and generally positive

How he or she spends time when not working (hobbies, interests, personal-time activities)

Appropriate balance to life (work, personal, family, community, church, etc.)

MINIMUM SALARY LEVEL AT WHICH I WORK:
$60,000

GEOGRAPHIC SCOPE OF RECRUITING ACTIVITIES:
Clients nationwide

TOTAL YEARS OF RETAINER-TYPE RECRUITING EXPERIENCE:
12 years

SANDFORD I. GADIENT
President
Huntress Real Estate Executive
   Search
P.O. Box 8667
Kansas City, MO 64114
Telephone: (913) 451-0464

Date of birth: February 7, 1936
Grew up in: Davenport, IA

HIGHER EDUCATION:

Photo courtesy of Huntress Real Estate Executive Search

Arizona State University
   B.S. degree, business administration, 1956
University of Pennsylvania, Wharton School of Finance
   M.B.A. degree, finance and banking, 1978

EMPLOYMENT HISTORY:

1979 to present: Huntress Real Estate Executive Search
1966 to 1979: President, Condominium–Commercial Mortgages, Inc.
1962 to 1966: Executive Vice President, Financial Corp. of Arizona
1961 to 1962: Controller, Guaranty Bank (now United Bank)
1960 to 1961: Manager–Administrative Services, Arthur Anderson &
   Company
1959 to 1960: Management Consultant, McKinsey & Company
1957 to 1958: Budget Specialist, General Electric Co.–Computer
   Department

PRIVATE CLUBS:

Plaza Club, Honolulu
Lahaina Yacht Club, Maui

SPECIAL INTERESTS AND HOBBIES:

Antique collecting (particularly oriental pieces and art glass), golf,
   tennis, skindiving, travel

REPRESENTATIVE AND SIGNIFICANT PLACEMENTS:

Luke McCarthy, President
   Myers Capital Corporation
Don Crocker, President
   J. E. Robert Company

Richard Bliss, Senior Vice President–Real Estate Investments and
   Mortgages
   Mutual United of Omaha
Mark Hoewing, Executive Vice President and Managing Director
   National Association of Corporate Real Estate Executives
Ken McVearry, Senior Group Vice President
   Charles E. Smith Company

WHAT I LOOK FOR IN GENERAL IN A CANDIDATE:

In general, in recruiting candidates I try to determine the proper organizational fit for candidates to match clients' needs and objectives. Particular attention should be given to the value-added concept whereby candidates should be able to demonstrate specific accomplishments achieved to produce bottom-line earnings and positive results for every employer. Obvious factors such as age, education, experience, references, appearance, willingness to travel, aggressiveness, people skills, teamwork approach, and interviewing presence are important. Equally important, but sometimes more difficult to assess, are leadership skills, loyalty, perseverance in the face of adversity, stability, family support, negotiating abilities, work habits, and problem-solving skills. Perfect candidates are few and far between, yet it is the executive recruiter's responsibility to fully advise the client on each candidate's strengths and weaknesses relative to the position being filled.

MINIMUM SALARY LEVEL AT WHICH I WORK:
$100,000

GEOGRAPHIC SCOPE OF RECRUITING ACTIVITIES:
Clients nationwide and in English-language countries

TOTAL YEARS OF RETAINER-TYPE RECRUITING EXPERIENCE:
10 years

JAY GAINES
President
Jay Gaines & Company, Inc.
598 Madison Avenue
New York, NY 10021
Telephone: (212) 308-9222

Date of birth: April 18, 1947
Grew up in: Oceanside, Long
Island, NY

HIGHER EDUCATION:
George Washington University
   B.A. degree, psychology, 1968
Columbia University

Photo courtesy of Jay Gaines & Company, Inc.

   M.A. degree, industrial/personnel psychology, 1970

EMPLOYMENT HISTORY:
1982 to present: Jay Gaines & Co. Inc.
1976 to 1982: Vice President, Oliver and Rozner
1972 to 1976: Associate Recruiter, Halbrecht Associates
1968 to 1972: Teacher, Sixth Grade Special Service School, New York
   Board of Education

SPECIAL INTERESTS AND HOBBIES:
Power boating, the Long Island Sound, bicycling, reading

REPRESENTATIVE AND SIGNIFICANT PLACEMENTS:
Nunzio Tartaglia, Managing Director–Head of Automated Trading
   Morgan Stanley
Scott Abbey, Managing Director Information Technology
   Morgan Stanley
Jeff Jennings, Managing Director Investment Management
   Whitehead Sterling
John Logan, Executive Vice President, Asset/Liability Management
   and Treasurer
   First American Corp.
Doug Jacobs, President Real Estate Investment Banking Subsidiary
   Fleet/Norstar

WHAT I LOOK FOR IN GENERAL IN A CANDIDATE:
We look first for performance. Individuals should be performing at or near the top of their peer group with a demon-

strated record of substantive accomplishments relative to the needs of a particular client and assignment. Accomplishments must demonstrate initiative, staying power, and consistency. How well do individuals hold up under adversity? To what extent will they push for what they think is right? We want to know the individual's role and how difficult and how important their accomplishments were. Personal and professional integrity is important. We are most comfortable with individuals who have a well-developed sense of themselves. That includes understanding where they are today, why they have been successful in the past, recognizing the situations in which they operate best, and understanding the characteristics that differentiate them from their peers.

It also includes an ability to define and articulate a professional value system—what one wants to achieve, the rewards that are meaningful, and how they generally go about achieving it. We look for the accompanying sense of confidence and consistency in how they would approach any situation. We place an extremely high premium on thoughtfulness and insight. We look for and value in-depth professional/functional expertise combined with the instincts that come with seasoning and successful experience. We seek out a work ethic and commitment level that is substantially higher than the norm. However, we value the individual who has successfully managed his or her career along with their personal life. We want someone who ideally can bring an additional dimension and add substantial value to our client organization. Can the individual lead our clients and take them substantially further over time than where they are today? We want that person to deliver and be counted on over a long period of time.

MINIMUM SALARY LEVEL AT WHICH I WORK:
   $100,000

GEOGRAPHIC SCOPE OF RECRUITING ACTIVITIES:
   Clients nationwide and in London and Tokyo

TOTAL YEARS OF RETAINER-TYPE RECRUITING EXPERIENCE:
   17 years

FRANK A. GAROFOLO
President
Garofolo, Curtiss & Company
326 West Lancaster Avenue
Ardmore, PA 19003
Telephone: (215) 896-5080

Date of birth: May 2, 1938
Grew up in: Camden, NJ

HIGHER EDUCATION:
Drexel University

Photo courtesy of Garofolo Curtiss & Company

   B.A. degree, commerce and engineering, 1962

EMPLOYMENT HISTORY:
   1973 to present: Garofolo, Curtiss & Co.
   1971 to 1973: Vice President, Pappas, Coates & DelVecchio
   1969 to 1971: President, Pacesetter Management Systems Inc.
   1967 to 1969: Self-employed insurance broker

SPECIAL INTERESTS AND HOBBIES:
   Family, spiritual growth, sports, reading

REPRESENTATIVE AND SIGNIFICANT PLACEMENTS:
   Charles Pierce, Assistant Secretary Health of the State of New Jersey
      Delaware Valley Hospital Council
   Joseph Culver, President
      Woodward & Dickinson
   James McCaslin, Chief Operating Officer
      Episcopal Hospital
   Douglas J. Spurlock, President
      Polyclinic Medical Centers
   Maynard R. Stufft, President and Chief Executive Officer
      PHICO Insurance Co.

WHAT I LOOK FOR IN GENERAL IN A CANDIDATE:

Each candidate that the search consultant agrees to meet must have the personal technical background training and experience proposed by the client organization. Beyond this essential factor, personal chemistry or potential personal chemistry between the individual candidate and the client organization is the single most important condition that must be met. Everyone must be able to get along with each other, communicate well, and share ideas so that the required job can be effectively executed.

MINIMUM SALARY LEVEL AT WHICH I WORK:
  $75,000

GEOGRAPHIC SCOPE OF RECRUITING ACTIVITIES:
  Clients nationwide

TOTAL YEARS OF RETAINER-TYPE RECRUITING EXPERIENCE:
  16 years

STEPHEN A. GARRISON
Chairman and Chief Executive Officer
Ward Howell International, Inc.
1601 Elm Street, Suite 900
Dallas, TX 75201
Telephone: (214) 749-0099

Date of birth: May 10, 1940
Grew up in: Across the world

Photo by Gittings

HIGHER EDUCATION:
U.S. Naval Academy
    B.S. degree, naval science, 1962
Harvard University
    M.B.A. degree, finance, 1969

MILITARY:
Lieutenant, United States Navy, 1962 to 1967

EMPLOYMENT HISTORY:
1982 to present: Ward Howell International, Inc.
1973 to 1982: Senior Vice President, Heidrick and Struggles, Inc.
1970 to 1973: Vice President and Founder, Vaughan, Nelson & Boston, Inc.
1969 to 1970: Institutional Analyst, Underwood, Neuhaus & Company

PRIVATE CLUBS:
Dallas Club

SPECIAL INTERESTS AND HOBBIES:
Directorships of Buford Television, Inc.; North Texas Commission
Member-Associate, School of Business, Southern Methodist University
Dallas Partnership of Dallas Chamber of Commerce and Dallas Citizens Council

REPRESENTATIVE AND SIGNIFICANT PLACEMENTS:
Dean Groussman, President and Chief Executive Officer
    Canadian Tire Corporation, Ltd.
Roger Hemminghaus, Chairman and Chief Executive Officer
    Diamond Shamrock R&M Company

Charles Blackburn, Chairman and Chief Executive Officer
  Maxus Energy Corporation
A. Kenneth Pye, President
  Southern Methodist University
Hans Mark, Chancellor
  The University of Texas System

WHAT I LOOK FOR IN GENERAL IN A CANDIDATE:

Complexity: The candidate will have many layers of personality, only a few of which will be chosen to be shown to a given individual.

Ego: A large, well-defined, and controlled ego. The candidate believes that he is better than his peers and competitors. This ego is subordinated during interpersonal communications so as not to be threatening and dysfunctional to the discussion.

Street smarts: Rather than intelligence, which I believe is a negative correlator to success at very high levels, the candidate has a cunning that enables him or her to succeed on Wall Street or in the jungles of Brazil.

Luck or karma: Although success requires hard work, reasonable intelligence, and education (formal or self-taught), the consistently successful person will be in the right place at the right time and know how to capitalize on the circumstances.

MINIMUM SALARY LEVEL AT WHICH I WORK:
  $150,000

GEOGRAPHIC SCOPE OF RECRUITING ACTIVITIES:
  Clients nationwide and in The Netherlands, Belgium, Denmark, West Germany, the United Kingdom, Australia, New Zealand, Italy, Spain, Norway, France, Singapore, Japan, Canada, Mexico, Switzerland, Austria, Hong Kong

TOTAL YEARS OF RETAINER-TYPE RECRUITING EXPERIENCE:
  16 years

H. LELAND GETZ
Managing Director
Higdon, Joys & Mingle, Inc.
375 Park Avenue
New York, NY 10152
Telephone: (212) 752-9780

Date of birth: April 16, 1929
Grew up in: Scarsdale, NY

Photo courtesy of Higdon, Joys &
Mingle, Inc.

HIGHER EDUCATION:
Yale University
   B.A. degree, 1951

MILITARY:
Captain, United States Marine Corps, 1951 to 1954

EMPLOYMENT HISTORY:
1989 to present: Higdon, Joys & Mingle, Inc.
1969 to 1989: Founder, President, and Vice Chairman, Russell Reynolds Associates
1954 to 1969: Vice President, Manufacturers Hanover Trust Company

PRIVATE CLUBS:
New York:
   Links Club
   Downtown Association
   River Club
   Yale Club
Greenwich, CT:
   Round Hill Club
   The Field Club
   Bedford Golf & Tennis Club
   Mill Reef Club
   Edgartown Yacht Club

SPECIAL INTERESTS AND HOBBIES:
Golf, bridge, reading

REPRESENTATIVE AND SIGNIFICANT PLACEMENTS:
John Byrne, President and Chief Executive Officer to Chairman and Chief Executive Officer (now Chairman, Firemans' Fund)
GEICO

David Maxwell, President and Chief Executive Officer to Chairman
and Chief Executive Officer
F.N.M.A.

George Ball, President and Chief Executive Officer to Chairman and
Chief Executive Officer
Prudential Bache

Frank Cahouet, President and Chief Executive Officer to Chairman
and Chief Executive Officer (now Chairman, The Mellon Bank)
The Crocker Bank

Joseph DiMartino, Vice President to President and Chief Executive
Officer
The Dreyfus Corporation

WHAT I LOOK FOR IN GENERAL IN A CANDIDATE:

Integrity and intellectual honesty are sine qua nons

Next, a high level of intelligence, combined with strong
communications skills and self-confidence

A track record of accomplishment and demonstrated
ability as a leader

A strategic sense, combined with the drive and energy
required to implement strategic and tactical decisions

A good sense of humor, especially when combined with
some modesty and an ability to laugh at one's self,
contributes significantly to an ability to relate to others

A diversity of interests, effective management of one's
personal life, and a good sense of self-awareness

MINIMUM SALARY LEVEL AT WHICH I WORK:
$250,000–$300,000

GEOGRAPHIC SCOPE OF RECRUITING ACTIVITIES:
Clients nationwide and in Europe and Japan

TOTAL YEARS OF RETAINER-TYPE RECRUITING EXPERIENCE:
20 years

NELSON W. GIBSON
Chairman
N.W. Gibson International
5900 Wilshire Boulevard, Suite
760
Los Angeles, CA 90036
Telephone: (213) 930-1100

Grew up in: Hartford, CT

HIGHER EDUCATION:
Trinity College, CT
B.A. degree, English, 1944

Photo courtesy of N. W. Gibson International

EMPLOYMENT HISTORY:
1971 to present: N.W. Gibson International
1965 to 1971: Executive Vice President, Hergenrather Gibson Hanrahan
1962 to 1965: Vice President Industrial Relations, Litton Industries
1958 to 1961: Assistant Director of Personnel, Hughes Aircraft
1950 to 1958: Director of Industrial Relations, Sylvania Electric

SPECIAL INTERESTS AND HOBBIES:
Reading, tennis, fund raising (colleges, hospitals, charitable organizations)

REPRESENTATIVE AND SIGNIFICANT PLACEMENTS:
President
Mazda Motors USA
President to Chairman (also placed president to succeed him)
Motion picture production company
Executive Vice President (Corp.)
General Dynamics
President, U.S. Subsidiary
Thomson CSF–Paris
Vice President Finance and Administration
Northrop Corporation

WHAT I LOOK FOR IN GENERAL IN A CANDIDATE:

First impressions are important: Is the individual's attire appropriate? Is grooming (hair, nails, shoes, shirt) immaculate? Is the candidate's handshake firm, smile naturally pleasant, voice well modulated? Bearing confident and self-assured? Use of language fresh, grammar correct? Are questions intelligent, pertinent, succinct? Answers direct, substantive, unhesitating? Employment history unbroken or are gaps, if any, readily explained? Expressed interests in the position—principally about growth, challenge, quality of products, character of client company or about pensions, vacations, employment contract, insurance coverage? Is the individual's outlook open, outgoing, optimistic, inquisitive, or guarded, circumspect, negative? Is career path generally upward? Has incumbency in one or more line positions been followed by staff assignment? Comments about present and former employers and associates generally fair or derogatory? Expressions about people—peers, subordinates, superiors—generally respectful, considerate, complimentary? Finally, does he know how to manage for profit?

Clearly, no one rates a 10 on all of the above, and executives have succeeded without possessing many of them in large measure. My reactions serve, if nothing else, to eliminate the unqualified. These reactions are merely the beginning of the process.

MINIMUM SALARY LEVEL AT WHICH I WORK:
$100,000

GEOGRAPHIC SCOPE OF RECRUITING ACTIVITIES:
Clients nationwide

TOTAL YEARS OF RETAINER-TYPE RECRUITING EXPERIENCE:
24 years

WILLIAM E. GOULD
Managing Director
Gould & McCoy Inc.
551 Madison Avenue
New York, NY 10022
Telephone: (212) 688-8671

Date of birth: October 23, 1932
Grew up in: Watertown, NY

HIGHER EDUCATION:

Williams College, MA

Photo courtesy of Gould & McCoy Inc.

B.A. degree, chemistry, physics, 1957
Harvard Business School
M.B.A. degree; 1965

MILITARY:

Sergeant, United States Army, 1953 to 1955

EMPLOYMENT HISTORY:

1973 to present: Gould & McCoy Inc.

1969 to 1973: Vice President, Heidrick and Struggles, Inc.

1965 to 1969: Commercial Director, Mack Amax Aluminum Ltd., Subsidiary of Amax Corp.

1961 to 1965: Sales Manager, Varcum Chemical Division, Reichhold Chemicals Corp.

1957 to 1961: New Products Marketing Engineer, Carborundum Company

PRIVATE CLUBS:

Harvard Club
Williams Club

SPECIAL INTERESTS AND HOBBIES:

International business/cultural relations, geriatrics, second careers

REPRESENTATIVE AND SIGNIFICANT PLACEMENTS:

David W. Johnson, Chairman and Chief Executive Officer
Gerber Products Company
Daniel E. Gill, Chairman and Chief Executive Officer
Bausch & Lomb
Louis P. Mattis, President and Chief Operating Officer
Sterling Drug/Eastman Kodak

Burton A. Dole, Jr., Chairman and Chief Executive Officer
    Puritan-Bennett Corporation
Charles E. Cobb, Jr., Chairman and Chief Executive Officer
    Arvida Corporation

WHAT I LOOK FOR IN GENERAL IN A CANDIDATE:

I look for many elements. Cultural fit with the client is the most important or the person has a high probability of leaving within two years. The person's evolvement as a human being—how does he or she cope with adversity, with superiors/peers/subordinates—how mature is the person? What has the person done with his or her personal life—is the person a total human being or just one dimensional? What is the person's track record? Did they really do what they claimed to do? Is the person a leader or a follower, and how does that fit our client's requirements? What is the person's "life plan"? What are their goals? Do they have goals, and how does that fit with our client? What is the person's relationship with his or her spouse or, if single, is he or she fulfilled personally? Finally, the person should have a sense of humor. In my twenty years of retainer search experience, the successful people always had a sense of humor.

MINIMUM SALARY LEVEL AT WHICH I WORK:
$150,000

GEOGRAPHIC SCOPE OF RECRUITING ACTIVITIES:
Clients nationwide and in Europe, Brazil, and Argentina

TOTAL YEARS OF RETAINER-TYPE RECRUITING EXPERIENCE:
20 years

PETER G. GRIMM
Partner
Nordeman Grimm Inc.
717 Fifth Avenue
New York, NY 10017
Telephone: (212) 935-1000

Date of birth: May 23, 1933
Grew up in: Larchmont, NY

HIGHER EDUCATION:
  Cornell University

Photo courtesy of Nordeman Grimm Inc.

  B.S. degree, hotel administration, 1955

MILITARY:
  First Lieutenant, Single Engine Jet Instructors Pilot, United States
  Air Force, 1956 to 1959

EMPLOYMENT HISTORY:
  1968 to present: Nordeman Grimm Inc.
  1966 to 1968: Partner, Antell Wright & Nagel
  1961 to 1966: Senior Associate, Cresap McCormick & Paget
  1959 to 1961: Registered Representative, Merrill Lynch
  1955 to 1956: Sales, General Foods

PRIVATE CLUBS:
  University Club of New York
  University Club of Larchmont
  Winged Foot Golf Club
  Larchmont Yacht Club

SPECIAL INTERESTS AND HOBBIES:
  Golf, sailing, travel, reading, scuba

REPRESENTATIVE AND SIGNIFICANT PLACEMENTS:
  Bruce Allbright, Chairman and Chief Executive Officer
    Dayton Hudson
  Anthony Luiso, Chairman and Chief Executive Officer
    International Multifoods
  John Costello, President
    Nielsen Marketing
  Donald Donahue, Vice Chairman–Chief of Staff
    Continental Group

Kenneth Haas, Executive Director
Boston Symphony Orchestra

WHAT I LOOK FOR IN GENERAL IN A CANDIDATE:

The things I look for are

Intelligence—a sound thought process

Presence—the ability to present effectively

Energy—high energy is essential in today's competitive
environment

Work ethic—goes hand-in-hand with high energy

Competitive—in whatever he or she has done in school,
business, sports

Sound basic values—honesty, sensitivity to others

Success—the earlier the better

Luck—I look for the "lucky" executive; they usually make
their own luck

Consistency—some pattern in their lives and careers

Balance—something to balance the business part of their
lives—home, sports, travel

MINIMUM SALARY LEVEL AT WHICH I WORK:
$150,000

GEOGRAPHIC SCOPE OF RECRUITING ACTIVITIES:
Clients nationwide and internationally through foreign affiliates

TOTAL YEARS OF RETAINER-TYPE RECRUITING EXPERIENCE:
23 years

DAVID O. HARBERT
President
Sweeney Shepherd Bueschel
  Provus Harbert & Mummert,
  Inc.
777 South Harbour Island
  Boulevard
Tampa, FL 33602
Telephone: (813) 229-5360

Date of birth: April 14, 1940
Grew up in: Shaker Heights, OH

HIGHER EDUCATION:

University of Michigan

Photo courtesy of Sweeney Shepherd Bueschel Provus Harbert & Mummert, Inc.

B.B.A. degree, engineering and business, 1962
M.B.A. degree, finance and statistic methods, 1963

EMPLOYMENT HISTORY:

1986 to present: Sweeney Shepherd et al.
1981 to 1986: Vice President/Managing Director, Lamalie Associates
1979 to 1981: Vice President Finance and Chief Financial Officer,
  Austin Powder
1977 to 1979: Vice President Finance, Stanwood Corp.
1972 to 1977: President, Advisory Services Inc.
1968 to 1972: Manager Finance, Celanese Corp.
1965 to 1968: Senior Analyst, Standard Oil New Jersey (now Exxon)
1964 to 1965: Auditor/Consultant, Arthur Andersen & Co.

PRIVATE CLUBS:

Union Club of Cleveland

SPECIAL INTERESTS AND HOBBIES:

Physical fitness, music, stereo/video equipment, automobiles, travel

REPRESENTATIVE AND SIGNIFICANT PLACEMENTS:

Gaylon H. Simmons, President and Chief Executive Officer
  The Permian Corp.
Edward A. Hennig, President–Real Estate
  National Intergroup Inc.
Terrance W. Ravenscraft, Vice President–Finance and Administra-
  tion
  CHF Industries

Robert M. Alston, Senior Vice President–MIS
Foxmeyer Corp.

Bruce A. Henderson, Vice President Planning and Business Development–Occupant Restraint Systems
TRW Inc.

WHAT I LOOK FOR IN GENERAL IN A CANDIDATE:

My evaluation of candidates moves through several stages. Although individuals are being scrutinized at several levels throughout the search process, the following chronology tends to take place:

1. Technical skills—does the candidate meet the position's technical requirements? Have the appropriate steps and accomplishments successfully taken place? If so, I will then concentrate on:

2. Interpersonal skills and chemistry with my client—does the candidate present himself or herself in a manner compatible with the position and the environment? Typically this will include an evaluation of intelligence, aggressiveness, professionality, poise, articulation, candor, and sense of humor. Physical presentation is also considered—clothing, physical fitness, mannerisms, etc. I will then make judgments on:

3. Promotability—what is his or her potential to grow beyond the initial position?

4. The candidate's interests—will they be served? If not, he or she will probably fail in the position and therefore our client's needs will not be satisfied.

5. Recruitability—as I gain knowledge of the candidate, is it clear he or she can in fact be recruited, or are we wasting my client's time?

MINIMUM SALARY LEVEL AT WHICH I WORK:
$100,000

GEOGRAPHIC SCOPE OF RECRUITING ACTIVITIES:
Clients nationwide

TOTAL YEARS OF RETAINER-TYPE RECRUITING EXPERIENCE:
8 years

ANDREW D. HART, JR.
Managing Director
Russell Reynolds Associates Inc.
200 Park Avenue
New York, NY 10166
Telephone: (212) 351-2000

Date of birth: May 3, 1929
Grew up in: Charlottesville, VA

MILITARY:
First Lieutenant, United States Army,
1951 to 1954

Photo by Stanford Golob

EMPLOYMENT HISTORY:
1970 to present: Russell Reynolds Associates, Inc.
1969 to 1970: Associate, Boyden Associates, Inc.
1962 to 1969: General Sales Manager, Carton Division, Westvaco Corp.
1954 to 1962: Eastern Regional Sales Manager, Carton Division, Federal Paper Board Co.

PRIVATE CLUBS:
Siwanoy Country Club, NY
The Sky Club, NY
Farmington Country Club, VA

SPECIAL INTERESTS AND HOBBIES:
Education, Republican Party politics, fund raising, skiing, golf, tennis, reading, the arts

REPRESENTATIVE AND SIGNIFICANT PLACEMENTS:
Robert P. Bauman, Chairman and Chief Executive Officer
    Beecham Group plc
Maurice Segall, President and Chief Executive Officer
    Zayre Corporation
Reece A. Overcash, Jr., Chairman and Chief Operating Officer
    Associates Corporation of North America, Subsidiary Gulf + Western Inc.
William P. Panny, President and Chief Operating Officer
    Bendix Corporation
William M. Agee, Executive Vice President and Chief Financial Officer to President and Chief Executive Officer
    Bendix Corporation

WHAT I LOOK FOR IN GENERAL IN A CANDIDATE:

In personal terms, I look for leadership ability, interpersonal/communication skills, dedication, ambition, self-confidence, integrity, and good judgment. As to professional qualifications, I am interested in self-assessment of principal skills and accomplishments, the results of performance appraisals, and management philosophy. In general management positions, I probe the extent of marketing, manufacturing, financial, and administrative experience as well as the achievements over a period of time in terms of financial results and the steps taken to bring those about. I am particularly interested in the reasons behind job changes and who initiated the change or termination and for what reasons. In the last analysis, I am looking for individuals with a proven record of performance in jobs matching the position requirements.

MINIMUM SALARY LEVEL AT WHICH I WORK:
$150,000

GEOGRAPHIC SCOPE OF RECRUITING ACTIVITIES:
Clients nationwide and in Europe, the Far East, and Latin America

TOTAL YEARS OF RETAINER-TYPE RECRUITING EXPERIENCE:
20 years

GARDNER W. HEIDRICK
Chairman
The Heidrick Partners, Inc.
20 North Wacker Drive, Suite
  4000
Chicago, IL 60606
Telephone: (312) 845-9700

Date of birth: October 7, 1911
Grew up in: Peoria, IL

HIGHER EDUCATION:
University of Illinois,
  B.S. degree, banking and finance, 1935

Photo courtesy of The Heidrick Partners, Inc.

MILITARY:
United States Naval Reserve, 1945 to 1946

EMPLOYMENT HISTORY:
1982 to present: The Heidrick Partners, Inc.
1953 to 1982: Cofounder, Heidrick & Struggles, Inc.
1951 to 1953: Associate, Booz, Allen & Hamilton
1942 to 1951: Director of Personnel, Farmland Industries
1935 to 1942: Industrial District Manager, Scott Paper Company

PRIVATE CLUBS:
Hinsdale Golf Club
The Chicago Club
Tower Club
University Club, NY
Country Club of Florida
The Ocean Club
The Little Club

SPECIAL INTERESTS AND HOBBIES:
Golf, coin collecting

REPRESENTATIVE AND SIGNIFICANT PLACEMENTS:
Chief Executive Officer
  Major diversified cultural not-for-profit organization
Director
  One of *Fortune*'s top ten industrial organizations

Directors
  Major Southwestern telecommunications company
Director
  One of the top Eastern mutual life insurance companies
Director
  Pacific Northwest high-tech company

WHAT I LOOK FOR IN GENERAL IN A CANDIDATE:

In corporate director assignments: what the candidate will bring to the board and his or her visibility. Generally, this is a Chairman or a President. Overall, it is compatibility.

Targeted are: industries, functional position, geography (ability to attend meetings), minorities, and women.

In general management executives, it is primarily the same. The pattern of the past indicates the pattern of the future.

MINIMUM SALARY LEVEL AT WHICH I WORK:
  $200,000

GEOGRAPHIC SCOPE OF RECRUITING ACTIVITIES:
  Clients nationwide and internationally for director positions

TOTAL YEARS OF RETAINER-TYPE RECRUITING EXPERIENCE:
  38 years

ROBERT L. HEIDRICK
President
The Heidrick Partners, Inc.
20 North Wacker Drive, Suite
  4000
Chicago, IL 60606
Telephone: (312) 845-9700

Date of birth: June 8, 1941
Grew up in: Hinsdale, IL

Photo courtesy of The Heidrick Partners, Inc.

HIGHER EDUCATION:
Duke University
  B.A. degree, economics, 1963
University of Chicago
  M.B.A. degree, 1971

EMPLOYMENT HISTORY:
1982 to present: The Heidrick Partners, Inc.
1977 to 1982: President, Robert Heidrick Associates, Inc.
1975 to 1977: Vice President, Spriggs & Company
1963 to 1975: Division Vice President–Marketing, American Hospital Supply Corp.

PRIVATE CLUBS:
Glen View Club
The Chicago Club
The Racquet Club
The Tower Club

SPECIAL INTERESTS AND HOBBIES:
Golf, numismatics

REPRESENTATIVE AND SIGNIFICANT PLACEMENTS:
President, Chairman and Chief Executive Officer
  Electric and gas utility company
Head of Research and Development Center
  Packaged goods company
Head of Manufacturing Technology
  Industrial products company
Chief Executive Officer
  Chain of five bookstores
Head of Marketing Function
  Multibillion dollar packaged goods company

WHAT I LOOK FOR IN GENERAL IN A CANDIDATE:

First, is the executive's image: How well groomed? The person's presentability: assertive/retiring, etc.? In short, the individual's executive presence?

Second, education and compensation are a strong consideration. In most instances, it is important that the individual have a college degree, with graduate work a plus. In terms of compensation, there should be a pattern of good upward progression. For younger people, earnings should be three or four times the person's age. However, for older and more experienced executives, the age/salary ratio is less important.

Ultimately the compatibility of the candidate with the client and the client organization is important. The individual should have street smarts along with leadership skills.

Third is the background and experience. Does the person have a track record of success? Is he or she able to articulate accomplishments without overstating or taking too much personal credit? Is there humility? Does the career progress in a logical fashion?

MINIMUM SALARY LEVEL AT WHICH I WORK:
$100,000

GEOGRAPHIC SCOPE OF RECRUITING ACTIVITIES:
Clients nationwide

TOTAL YEARS OF RETAINER-TYPE RECRUITING EXPERIENCE:
14 years

GEORGE W. HENN, JR.
President
G.W. Henn & Company
85 East Gay Street, Suite 1007
Columbus, OH 43215
Telephone: **(614) 469-9666**

Date of birth: **November 13, 1936**
Grew up in: **Spring Lake, NJ**

Photo courtesy of G. W. Henn & Company

HIGHER EDUCATION:
Rutgers University
B.A. degree, American civilization, 1958

MILITARY:
Specialist Fourth Class (Reserve), United States Army, 1959

EMPLOYMENT HISTORY:
1987 to present: G.W. Henn & Company
1980 to 1987: Managing Director, Cleveland, SpencerStuart Associates
1971 to 1980: Partner, Booz, Allen & Hamilton Inc.
1969 to 1971: Associate, David North & Associates
1958 to 1969: Personnel Director, Great American Insurance Co.

PRIVATE CLUBS:
Cleveland Athletic Club
University Club of Columbus

SPECIAL INTERESTS AND HOBBIES:
Breed and exhibit American Saddlebred horses

REPRESENTATIVE AND SIGNIFICANT PLACEMENTS:
President
Major international materials handling manufacturing company
President and Chief Executive Officer
Large recreational vehicle manufacturer
Chief Information Officers (5)
Recruited for *Fortune* 100 companies
President and Chief Operating Officer
Major regional bank
Executive Vice President–Commercial Lending
Major U.S. bank

WHAT I LOOK FOR IN GENERAL IN A CANDIDATE:

Our objective in all client assignments is to recruit the best possible candidate for the position—the candidate who can best contribute to the client organization—in the short and long terms.

Leading candidates have a record of significant progression through larger well-managed companies. In addition to functional skills, candidates have demonstrated the personal dimension to work effectively in a corporate setting while aggressively and energetically pursuing business goals and objectives.

Successful candidates consistently demonstrate leadership skills and the strategic understanding of key business issues. They are also known and regarded within their industry.

MINIMUM SALARY LEVEL AT WHICH I WORK:
$100,000

GEOGRAPHIC SCOPE OF RECRUITING ACTIVITIES:
Clients nationwide and in Canada

TOTAL YEARS OF RETAINER-TYPE RECRUITING EXPERIENCE:
20 years

WILLIAM A. HERTAN
Chairman and Chief Executive Officer
Executive Manning Corp.
3000 Northeast 30th Place, Suite 402
Fort Lauderdale, FL 33306
Telephone: (305) 561-5100

Date of birth: July 15, 1921
Grew up in: Ridgewood, NJ

Photo by Blackstone-Shelburne New York

HIGHER EDUCATION:
University of Michigan
    B.A. degree, psychology, 1941
New York University
    B.S. degree, industrial relations, 1943

MILITARY:
Lieutenant Commander, United States Navy, 1941 to 1957

EMPLOYMENT HISTORY:
1956 to present: Executive Manning Corp.

PRIVATE CLUBS:
Boca Raton Country Club

SPECIAL INTERESTS AND HOBBIES:
Fishing, boating, outdoor activities

REPRESENTATIVE AND SIGNIFICANT PLACEMENTS:
President to Chairman
    Major automotive firm
Division President to Executive Vice President of a multinational
    corporation
    Electronics corporation
President
    Major aerospace corporation
President
    International business equipment firm
Group Executive
    International chemical firm

WHAT I LOOK FOR IN GENERAL IN A CANDIDATE:

Openness

Communications ability

Technical experience in his or her given field

Stability of employment

Loyalty

Family stability

General well-rounded experience in his or her chosen
field of endeavor

An ability to understand corporate politics and the ability
to achieve promotions without an apparent need of the
use of politics

MINIMUM SALARY LEVEL AT WHICH I WORK:
$100,000

GEOGRAPHIC SCOPE OF RECRUITING ACTIVITIES:
Clients nationwide and in Europe

TOTAL YEARS OF RETAINER-TYPE RECRUITING EXPERIENCE:
33 years

JAMES N. HEUERMAN
Vice President
Korn/Ferry International
600 Montgomery Street
San Francisco, CA 94111
Telephone: (415) 956-1834

Date of birth: August 9, 1940
Grew up in: St. Cloud, MN

Photo by Gabriel Moulin Studios

HIGHER EDUCATION:
University of Minnesota
   B.S. degree, business, 1965
   M.A. degree, hospital and health care administration, 1971

MILITARY:
Specialist Fourth Class, United States Army, 1960 to 1962

EMPLOYMENT HISTORY:
1983 to present: Korn/Ferry International
1977 to 1983: Vice President, Booz, Allen & Hamilton Inc.
1972 to 1977: Principal, Arthur Young & Company
1971 to 1972: Assistant Administrator, Evanston Hospital, Illinois
1965 to 1970: Marketing Representative, IBM

SPECIAL INTERESTS AND HOBBIES:
Tennis, running, cycling, reading

REPRESENTATIVE AND SIGNIFICANT PLACEMENTS:
Dr. Monroe Trout, President and Chief Executive Officer
   American Healthcare Systems
Sheldon King, President and Chief Executive Officer
   Cedars Sinai Medical Center, Los Angeles
Steven Ummel, President and Chief Executive Officer
   Memorial Health System, Long Beach
Duane Dauner, President
   California Hospital Association
Robert Montgomery, President
   Alta Bates Corporation

WHAT I LOOK FOR IN GENERAL IN A CANDIDATE:
A series of milestones over time that include
Work ethic, usually developed at a young age

Solid education, good schools, and accomplishment
Early jobs that refine analytical skills
Mentors that contribute to style and character
Employer organizations of quality and reputation
Demonstrated profit and loss responsibility and results
A well-developed management philosophy and style
A vision of one's industry that demonstrates depth of
   thinking
An ability to communicate in a clear and meaningful
   fashion
   In addition a solid family and personal life-style that
supports an ambitious executive. Finally a level of health
and fitness to be productive over time.

MINIMUM SALARY LEVEL AT WHICH I WORK:
$75,000

GEOGRAPHIC SCOPE OF RECRUITING ACTIVITIES:
Clients nationwide with a strong concentration on the West

TOTAL YEARS OF RETAINER-TYPE RECRUITING EXPERIENCE:
6 years

HENRY G. HIGDON
Managing Director
Higdon, Joys & Mingle, Inc.
375 Park Avenue, Suite 3008
New York, NY 10152
Telephone: (212) 752-9780

Date of birth: June 1, 1941
Grew up in: Shaker Heights OH
  and Greenwich, CT

HIGHER EDUCATION:
Yale University
  B.A. degree, American studies, 1964

Photo courtesy of Higdon, Joys &
Mingle

MILITARY:
Staff Sergeant, United States Marine Corps Reserve, 1964 to 1970

EMPLOYMENT HISTORY:
1986 to present: Higdon, Joys & Mingle, Inc.
1971 to 1986: Executive Vice President, Russell Reynolds Associates, Inc.
1964 to 1971: Associate, Massachusetts Mutual Life Insurance Co.

PRIVATE CLUBS:
Yale Club of New York City
Greenwich Country Club
California Club

SPECIAL INTERESTS AND HOBBIES:
Skiing, running, squash, rugby, coaching Little League Baseball, church, alumni affairs of Andover and Yale

REPRESENTATIVE AND SIGNIFICANT PLACEMENTS:
Stephen M. Wolf, President and Chief Operating Officer
  Continental Airlines
Ralph S. Cunningham, President and Chief Executive Officer
  Apex Oil Company
E.L. "Ed" Sambuchi, President and Chief Executive Officer
  McLouth Steel Products Corp.
Warren E. Bartel, Executive Vice President and Chief Operating Officer
  Weirton Steel Corporation

Burton J. Megargel, Managing Director–Head of Mergers and Acquisitions Department
Kidder, Peabody and Company, Inc.

WHAT I LOOK FOR IN GENERAL IN A CANDIDATE:

In general, I look for the following characteristics in candidates:

Integrity. This would appear to go without saying, but it can never be assumed and is the single most important characteristic for any candidate.

Intelligence. Although a high level of intellect is preferred, basic street smarts, savvy, and instincts are as important.

High level of energy. Energy is critically important and assumes great stamina and endurance and even physical fitness.

Team leadership. Most people look for team players, which is important, but I believe it is more important for someone to be a team builder and a team leader.

Self-confidence and inner security. I look for self-confidence, which also means than an individual can admit mistakes.

Communications ability. People who are organized in their thought process and can present ideas with clarity and brevity.

A sense of humor. A sense of humor is absolutely essential because it enables people to not take themselves too seriously, to have some grace under pressure, and to laugh at themselves.

Humility. Self-effacement can be an important characteristic, especially in today's world of occasionally superarrogant CEOs who may feel they can do absolutely no wrong.

Balance. I look for people who have their lives in balance, meaning that their personal, family, business, intellectual, and even spiritual existences blend well together. I am not impressed with people who are single dimensional or monomaniacal.

MINIMUM SALARY LEVEL AT WHICH I WORK:
$150,000–$200,000

GEOGRAPHIC SCOPE OF RECRUITING ACTIVITIES:
Clients nationwide and internationally through affiliates

TOTAL YEARS OF RETAINER-TYPE RECRUITING EXPERIENCE:
18 years

MICHAEL J. HOEVEL
Partner
Poirier, Hoevel & Company
12400 Wilshire Boulevard, Suite
1250
Los Angeles, CA 90025
Telephone: (213) 207-3427

Date of birth: September 16, 1944
Grew up in: Pasadena, CA

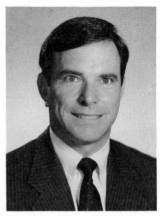

HIGHER EDUCATION:
California State University
B.S. degree, 1967

Photo courtesy of Poirier, Hoevel & Company

EMPLOYMENT HISTORY:
1975 to present: Poirier, Hoevel & Co.
1972 to 1975: Consultant–Executive Search, Peat Marwick Main & Co.
1967 to 1972: Manager of Recruiting, City of Los Angeles
1967: Management Trainee, Shell Oil Company

SPECIAL INTERESTS AND HOBBIES:
Family, travel, river rafting, scuba diving, snow skiing

REPRESENTATIVE AND SIGNIFICANT PLACEMENTS:
Chief Financial Officer
$700 million retail holding company
Chief Executive Officer
$6.5 billion asset management company
Executive Vice President, Marketing
Top-ten U.S. financial institution
Critical Tax Management Positions (5)
Major multinational subsidiary of a *Fortune* 10 company
Senior Vice President and Chief Operating Officer
Major nonprofit business, economic, and technical research organization

WHAT I LOOK FOR IN GENERAL IN A CANDIDATE?

A solid employment history with excellent progression. Good articulation, an easy but slightly aggressive manner, intelligent, a sense of humor, a life outside of business, and honesty.

Couple the above with experience that meets or exceeds what my client is looking for.

MINIMUM SALARY LEVEL AT WHICH I WORK:
$75,000

GEOGRAPHIC SCOPE OF RECRUITING ACTIVITIES:
Clients nationwide and in Europe and Latin America

TOTAL YEARS OF RETAINER-TYPE RECRUITING EXPERIENCE:
17 years

DAVID H. HOFFMANN
President
DHR International, Inc.
10 South Riverside Plaza, Suite
    1650
Chicago, IL 60606
Telephone: (312) 782-1581

Date of birth: August 7, 1952
Grew up in: Washington, MO

HIGHER EDUCATION:
Central Missouri State University
    B.S. degree, 1974

Photo courtesy of DHR International, Inc.

EMPLOYMENT HISTORY:
1989 to present: DHR International
1985 to 1989: Senior Vice President/Managing Partner, Boyden
    International
1983 to 1985: Vice President/Partner, Korn/Ferry International
1977 to 1983: Director of Employee Relations, GATX Corporation
1975 to 1977: Various Human Resource Positions, Pullman Inc.
1974 to 1975: Various Human Resource Positions, Clark Equipment
    Co.

SPECIAL INTERESTS AND HOBBIES:
Lawrence Hall School for Boys, board member; coaching various
    Little League organizations

REPRESENTATIVE AND SIGNIFICANT PLACEMENTS:
Vice President Marketing to President
    Major *Fortune* 500 consumer packaged goods company
Controller to Chief Financial Officer
    Fortune 500 company
Chief Financial Officer to President of company's largest division
    Multibillion dollar financial services company
Vice President–Research and Development to President
    Pharmaceutical company
Division Vice President–Human Resources to Senior Vice Presi-
    dent–Corporate Human Resources

WHAT I LOOK FOR IN GENERAL IN A CANDIDATE:

An individual who can effect change and be perceived as a
change agent. A charismatic leader who achieves results. Excep-

tional track record of accomplishment. Exceptional communication skills both orally and written. Strong people skills—a total business acumen. A career orientation. Interests outside the job—family, civic, philanthropic, etc. A well-rounded and grounded individual. A visionary.

MINIMUM SALARY LEVEL AT WHICH I WORK:
$60,000

GEOGRAPHIC SCOPE OF RECRUITING ACTIVITIES:
Clients nationwide and internationally

TOTAL YEARS OF RETAINER-TYPE RECRUITING EXPERIENCE:
7 years

LAWRENCE J. HOLMES
President
Consulting Associates, Inc.
5525 Twin Knolls Road, #326
Columbia, MD 21045
Telephone: (301) 997-5800

Date of birth: December 19, 1941
Grew up in: Tidewater, VA

HIGHER EDUCATION:
Old Dominion University
B.S. degree, science/education, 1964

Photo by James Ferry Photography

EMPLOYMENT HISTORY:
1978 to present: HGPL, Inc. d/b/a Consulting Associates
1977 to 1978: Partner, Harold Denton Associates
1973 to 1977: President, Cantrell Associates
1969 to 1973: Director of Training and Development, Maryland Casualty Company
1966 to 1969: Loss Control Engineer, Aetna Life & Casualty
1965 to 1966: Science Teacher, Norfolk School System

PRIVATE CLUBS:
New York Athletic Club
Turf Valley Country Club

SPECIAL INTERESTS AND HOBBIES:
Sports, reading, Key West

REPRESENTATIVE AND SIGNIFICANT PLACEMENTS:
Milton Adair, President
Mountain Medical Corp.
Steven Stepnes, Senior Vice President
RCA Consumer Electronics
James O'Connor, President
Kores-Nordic USA Corp.
Joseph Johnson, Senior Vice President
New York Stock Exchange
Michael Repoli, President
Maryland Casualty Company

WHAT I LOOK FOR IN GENERAL IN A CANDIDATE:

The primary traits and characteristics I look for in an individual are

A successful track record

The ability to listen

The quality of questions the individual asks

The direct related experience that the client wants

A sense of humor and a personality

An independent and competitive nature

The technical and educational experience as it relates to
the opportunity

MINIMUM SALARY LEVEL AT WHICH I WORK:
$75,000

GEOGRAPHIC SCOPE OF RECRUITING ACTIVITIES:
Clients nationwide and through international affiliates

TOTAL YEARS OF RETAINER-TYPE RECRUITING EXPERIENCE:
16 years

EDWARD R. HOWE, JR.
Partner
Diversified Search Inc.
One Commerce Square
2005 Market Street, Suite 3300
Philadelphia, PA 19103
Telephone: (215) 732-6666

Date of birth: March 13, 1947
Grew up in: Hartford, CT

Photo by Bachrach

HIGHER EDUCATION:
University of Denver
B.S. degree, marketing, 1970

EMPLOYMENT HISTORY:
1981 to present: Diversified Search Inc.
1979 to 1981: Chief Operating Officer, United Nesco Steel
1974 to 1979: Sales Manager, Polaroid Corp.
1970 to 1974: National Sales Manager, Burlington Industries

PRIVATE CLUBS:
Fishers Island Country Club, NY
Pennsylvania:
Merion Cricket Club
Gulph Mills Golf Club
The Courts

SPECIAL INTERESTS AND HOBBIES:
Sports, fishing, hiking

REPRESENTATIVE AND SIGNIFICANT PLACEMENTS:
Bill Cuff, President
Bachman Pretzels
John Henning, Senior Vice President, Mergers and Acquisitions
Shawmut National Corp.
Jim W. Oddall, Senior Vice President
Fred S. James Co.
Al Clay, Director of Taxes
Pitcairn Financial Group
Warren Weigand, Senior Vice President
Connecticut National Bank

WHAT I LOOK FOR IN GENERAL IN A CANDIDATE:
At the top-level search work that I do I look for
Candidate's ability to make a decision that would effect
  his or her company's bottom line
Chemistry with my client
Leadership abilities
Sense of humor, intellect, family values
People skills, listening ability, comprehension
Personality traits
Ability to answer a tough question regarding his failures,
  problems in both work and social worlds
    I do not spend time (in great detail) exploring a
candidate's technical knowledge of his job. When he
becomes a top executive—Senior Vice President or
higher—he has the technical ability. I find out about
personal and management and worldly aspects.

MINIMUM SALARY LEVEL AT WHICH I WORK:
$60,000

GEOGRAPHIC SCOPE OF RECRUITING ACTIVITIES:
Clients nationwide

TOTAL YEARS OF RETAINER-TYPE RECRUITING EXPERIENCE:
8 years

D. JOHN INGRAM
Partner
Ingram Inc.
350 Park Avenue, Suite 900
New York, NY 10022
Telephone: (212) 319-7777

Date of birth: May 15, 1939
Grew up in: Detroit, MI

Photo by Bachrach

HIGHER EDUCATION:
Michigan State University
B.S. degree, 1964
M.S. degree, 1965

MILITARY:
Lance Corporal, United States Marines, 1958 to 1964

EMPLOYMENT HISTORY:
1984 to present: Ingram Incorporated
1980 to 1984: Partner, Heidrick and Struggles, Inc.
1969 to 1980: Senior Vice President, American Express Co. (Fireman's Fund)
1965 to 1969: Supervisor, Bell Telephone Laboratories
1965 to 1966: Industrial Relations Analyst, Ford Motor Co.

PRIVATE CLUBS:
New York Yacht Club
Belle Haven Club

REPRESENTATIVE AND SIGNIFICANT PLACEMENTS:
Andrew L. Lewis, Jr., Chairman and Chief Executive Officer
Union Pacific Corporation
Michael H. Walsh, Chairman and Chief Executive Officer
Union Pacific Railroad
Thomas C. Barry, President and Chief Executive Officer
Rockefeller & Co.
Howard L. Clark, Jr., Executive Vice President and Chief Financial
Officer
American Express Company
Morgan Davis, President–Commercial Lines
Fireman's Fund Insurance Company

WHAT I LOOK FOR IN GENERAL IN A CANDIDATE:

We seek to be the best. Therefore, we are committed to recruiting the best candidates for our client's needs. We listen carefully to what our clients intend to accomplish; we strive for excellence in everything we do; our clients' needs always come first.

Moreover, we believe each search is our most important goal; therefore, each search deserves direct intense involvement with a partner. Our clients deserve and pay for the very best effort and experience we offer.

Further, our goal is to develop a partnership with our clients. We expect our clients to listen to our views, and we, in turn, value their trust. Our goal is to help our clients recruit the very best executives for their positions.

MINIMUM SALARY LEVEL AT WHICH I WORK:
$100,000

GEOGRAPHIC SCOPE OF RECRUITING ACTIVITIES:
Clients nationwide and in Europe and the Far East

TOTAL YEARS OF RETAINER-TYPE RECRUITING EXPERIENCE:
10 years

RICHARD K. IVES
Partner
Wilkinson & Ives
601 California Street, Suite 502
San Francisco, CA 94108
Telephone: (415) 433-2155

Date of birth: October 22, 1929
Grew up in: Southern California

Photo courtesy of Wilkinson & Ives

HIGHER EDUCATION:
University of Southern California
    B.S. degree, commerce, 1952
Stanford University Graduate School of Business
    M.B.A. degree, marketing/finance, 1954

MILITARY:
Lieutenant, United States Navy, 1954 to 1957

EMPLOYMENT HISTORY:
1984 to present: Wilkinson & Ives
1975 to 1984: Principal, Richard K. Ives & Company
1972 to 1975: Partner, Bacchi, Bentley, Evans & Gould
1970 to 1972: Western Regional Manager, DPF&G
1957 to 1970: Various Sales and Marketing Management Positions,
    IBM Corp.

PRIVATE CLUBS:
Jonathan Club
Merchants Exchange Club
Meadow Club

SPECIAL INTERESTS AND HOBBIES:
Golf, travel, reading, cooking

REPRESENTATIVE AND SIGNIFICANT PLACEMENTS:
Vice President, Chief Financial Officer, and Board Member
    $1.5 billion West Coast high-technology company
Director of the Ocean Mining Laboratory
    One of the world's largest copper and nickel mining companies
President of the U.S. Information Processing Subsidiary
    N.V. Philips, one of The Netherlands' largest multinational cor-
    porations

Senior Vice President, International Operations
  Large New York–based property and casualty insurance firm
Chairman and Chief Executive Officer
  Privately held Southern California software firm

WHAT I LOOK FOR IN GENERAL IN A CANDIDATE:

I look for a balance between a candidate's professional accomplishments and his or her personal qualities. Both are extremely important to the successful conclusion of a search assignment.

Of course, each client is different, as is each search assignment. The more time one can spend with his or her client to better understand the company, the industry, the position, and the culture in which all revolve, the more promising the prospects will be for the search assignment itself.

The professional background evaluated includes the obvious—education, achievements in his or her specific field, breadth of experience, record of success, personal reputation, professional stability and maturity, etc. Does the prospective candidate have a career vision or objective, or is he or she a professional wanderer?

Personal qualities are subjective but, as stated earlier, of equal significance. Intelligence, creativity, judgment, personal self-discipline, leadership ability, motivational skills, personal confidence, and personal appearance are all important.

In summary, each search assignment is unique; the blend of personal qualities and professional skills possessed by the successful candidate must be regarded as essential to the longer term impact he or she will have on the client organization.

MINIMUM SALARY LEVEL AT WHICH I WORK:
  $120,000

GEOGRAPHIC SCOPE OF RECRUITING ACTIVITIES:
  Clients nationwide and in Canada, the United Kingdom, Germany, the Netherlands

TOTAL YEARS OF RETAINER-TYPE RECRUITING EXPERIENCE:
  18 years

MIKE JACOBS
President
Thorne, Brieger Associates Inc.
11 East 44th Street
New York, NY 10017
Telephone: (212) 682-5424

Date of birth: June 6, 1932
Grew up in: Brooklyn, NY

HIGHER EDUCATION:
Brooklyn College
B.A. degree, psychology, 1953

Photo courtesy of Thorne, Brieger Associates, Inc.

MILITARY:
Corporal, United States Army, 1953 to 1955

EMPLOYMENT HISTORY:
1989 to present: Thorne, Brieger Associates
1975 to 1989: President, The Thorne Group
1979 to 1981: Chairman, Kien, Jacobs Associates
1960 to 1975: President, Garnet Associates
1957 to 1960: Counsellor, Allen Employment
1955 to 1957: Personnel Assistant, Rotobroil Corp. of America

SPECIAL INTERESTS AND HOBBIES:
Tennis

REPRESENTATIVE AND SIGNIFICANT PLACEMENTS:
Milt Oliviera, President
  Haskon Corp.
Charles Saldarini, Senior Vice President–Head of Corporate Banking
  First Union National Bank
Henry Glass, Division Vice President–Operations
  Lightolier
Richard Morrison, Vice President–Sales and Marketing
  Maine Rubber
Charles Naff, Vice President–Stores and Operations
  Today's Man

WHAT I LOOK FOR IN GENERAL IN A CANDIDATE:
I look for candidates who are strong enough and smart enough not to be intimidated by the search process or by me.

I look for people who bring the same objectivity to our discussions that I do. They know how to listen. They focus on what is important and ask good questions. They are not turned off by negatives but instead put them in perspective.

I look for individuals who will try to manage me . . . people who will come to the interview prepared . . . who know what they want me to discover about them and what they want to learn about the position . . . and who, before the meeting is over, will find a way to accomplish their agenda.

I look for people with a sense of humor who can laugh at themselves but still take their work seriously.

Ultimately, what I always look for in a candidate is someone who not only meets the needs of my client but whose own needs will be equally satisfied by the new position.

MINIMUM SALARY LEVEL AT WHICH I WORK:
$70,000

GEOGRAPHIC SCOPE OF RECRUITING ACTIVITIES:
Clients nationwide

TOTAL YEARS OF RETAINER-TYPE RECRUITING EXPERIENCE:
14 years

THEODORE JADICK
Partner and Member of Executive Committee
Heidrick & Struggles, Inc.
245 Park Avenue
New York, NY 10167
Telephone: (212) 867-9876

Date of birth: July 16, 1939
Grew up in: Scranton, PA

HIGHER EDUCATION:
University of Scranton

Photo by Bachrach

B.S. degree, business administration/accounting, 1961

MILITARY:
Specialist Fourth Class, United States Army, 1962 to 1968

EMPLOYMENT HISTORY:
1975 to present: Heidrick & Struggles, Inc.
1965 to 1975: Senior Vice President, F.W. Hastings Associates
1962 to 1965: Senior Accountant, Deloitte Haskins & Sells

PRIVATE CLUBS:
New York:
Sky Club
Union League Club
Sleepy Hollow Country Club
Melrose Club, SC

SPECIAL INTERESTS AND HOBBIES:
Squash, tennis, golf

REPRESENTATIVE AND SIGNIFICANT PLACEMENTS:
Timm Crull, President
Norton Simon, Inc. (currently Chief Executive Officer, Carnation, Inc.)
Frederick Rentschler, Chief Executive Officer
Hunt-Wesson, Inc. (currently Chief Executive Officer, Beatrice Companies)
James Osterhoff, Chief Financial Officer
Digital Equipment Corp.

Edwin P. Hoffman, Executive Vice President and Group Executive
  Citibank, New York
Bill White, President
  National Baseball League

WHAT I LOOK FOR IN GENERAL IN A CANDIDATE:

As I address potential candidates against predetermined search criteria, my prime concern centers around specific, direct, and quantifiable accomplishments. All of us live and function in a competitive marketplace. What sets some individuals apart are their accomplishments and the environment in which these results are produced. Personal characteristics also play a major role in my evaluation. Much attention is given to integrity, values, people skills, creativity, drive, and initiative. Obviously the ability to get the job done through and with people is an important measure of success. These qualities are certainly tested in flat organizations where the best thinking by a group of people working together in a positive fashion can result in a well-defined team effort. Today's shrinking world also places a premium on a global outlook and candidates with international expertise. More and more the international thread is woven into the fabric of many of our position specifications.

MINIMUM SALARY LEVEL AT WHICH I WORK:
  $150,000

GEOGRAPHIC SCOPE OF RECRUITING ACTIVITIES:
  Clients nationwide and in Europe

TOTAL YEARS OF RETAINER-TYPE RECRUITING EXPERIENCE:
  14 years

E. PENDLETON JAMES
Chairman
Pendleton James and Associates, Inc.
200 Park Avenue, Suite 3706
New York, NY 10166
Telephone: (212) 557-1599

Date of birth: October 23, 1929
Grew up in: Midwest and California

Photo by The White House

HIGHER EDUCATION:
University of the Pacific
B.A. degree, 1954

MILITARY:
United States Army, 1950 to 1962

EMPLOYMENT HISTORY:
1978 to present: Pendleton James and Associates, Inc.
Prior employment: Heidrick and Struggles, Inc.
Russell Reynolds Associates

PRIVATE CLUBS:
New York:
The River Club
The Economic Club
Sky Club
Union League Club
The Metropolitan Club, Washington, DC
Round Hill Club, Greenwich, CT
The California Club, Los Angeles

SPECIAL INTERESTS AND HOBBIES:
Tennis, skiing, reading

REPRESENTATIVE AND SIGNIFICANT PLACEMENTS:
President and Chief Executive Officer
Major retailing organization
Member of the Board of Directors
Multibillion dollar diversified transportation company

Chief Financial Officer
  Multibillion dollar food company
General Counsel
  One of America's five largest public companies
White House recruiting–Reagan Administration
  Cabinet and sub-Cabinet positions, regulatory agencies, boards, commissions, ambassadorships

WHAT I LOOK FOR IN GENERAL IN A CANDIDATE:

Initial overall appearance—both physical and verbal. How well does candidate present himself or herself? His or her background, experience, career goals, outside interests. Is his or her personal life stable? Is he or she smart in life? Can he or she handle himself or herself at all levels and in all situations? Is the candidate flexible? Does the candidate respond well to change (not job-hopping change but changes within his or her environment)? Does he or she have a stable work background?

MINIMUM SALARY LEVEL AT WHICH I WORK:
  $100,000

GEOGRAPHIC SCOPE OF RECRUITING ACTIVITIES:
  Clients nationwide

TOTAL YEARS OF RETAINER-TYPE RECRUITING EXPERIENCE:
  22 years

JOHN F. JOHNSON
President and Chief Executive Officer
Lamalie Associates, Inc.
One Cleveland Center
1375 East Ninth Street
Cleveland, OH 44114
Telephone: (216) 694-3000

Date of birth: April 23, 1942
Grew up in: Brooklyn, NY

Photo by Stuart-Rodgers-Reilly Photography

HIGHER EDUCATION:
Tufts University
B.A. degree, economics, 1963
Columbia University
M.B.A. degree, industrial relations, 1964

EMPLOYMENT HISTORY:
1976 to present: Lamalie Associates, Inc.
1967 to 1976: Various Human Resource Positions, General Electric Co.
1964 to 1967: Industrial Relations Analyst, Ford Motor Company

PRIVATE CLUBS:
Union Club

SPECIAL INTERESTS AND HOBBIES:
Wine collecting, big-game fishing, sports in general

REPRESENTATIVE AND SIGNIFICANT PLACEMENTS:
Roger T. Fridholm, President and Chief Operating Officer
The Stroh Brewery Company
Michael A. Wolf, Executive Vice President and General Manager, Worldwide Agricultural Equipment
J. I. Case Company/Tenneco Inc.
Wallace B. Askins, Executive Vice President and Chief Financial Officer (and Director)
Armco Inc.
Joyce E. Hergenhan, Vice President–Corporate Public Relations
General Electric Company

Jay T. Holmes, Senior Vice President–Corporate Affairs and Secretary (and Director)
Bausch & Lomb Inc.

WHAT I LOOK FOR IN GENERAL IN A CANDIDATE:

When evaluating candidates for a senior search assignment, I believe that there are four areas that must be explored in detail:

1. Intellectual capability
2. Functional/technical/industry experience
3. Values
4. Management/leadership style

Each of these factors must be evaluated against both the specification that I develop with my client and my knowledge of the hiring manager and the organization.

Based on prior work history, intellect and experience are easier to assess. Values and management/leadership capabilities are harder to evaluate and must be sorted out over the course of a two- to three-hour interview. The candidate's value system needs to be compatible with that of the organization, and his or her management/leadership style must enable the individual to function effectively not only in the immediate role but also in broader responsibilities as the individual moves higher in the organization.

Poor management and leadership skills become the Achilles' heel of too many executives as they rise through an organization. They are the toughest issues to quantify in an interview; and therefore I address them in detail when referencing finalist candidates.

MINIMUM SALARY LEVEL AT WHICH I WORK:
$150,000

GEOGRAPHIC SCOPE OF RECRUITING ACTIVITIES:
Clients nationwide

TOTAL YEARS OF RETAINER-TYPE RECRUITING EXPERIENCE:
13 years

NANCY F. KEITHLEY
Senior Manager
Ernst & Young
1300 Huntington Building
Cleveland, OH 44115
Telephone: (216) 861-5000

Date of birth: August 8, 1946
Grew up in: Massachusetts

HIGHER EDUCATION:
Northeastern University, MA
    B.S. degree, 1969
University of Pennsylvania
    M.S. degree, 1971

Photo by Paul's Studios, Inc.

EMPLOYMENT HISTORY:
1980 to present: Ernst & Young (formerly Ernst & Whinney)
1978 to 1979: Research Analyst, Booz, Allen & Hamilton, Inc.

PRIVATE CLUBS:
Cleveland Skating Club
Intown Club

SPECIAL INTERESTS AND HOBBIES:
Tennis, hiking, performing arts

REPRESENTATIVE AND SIGNIFICANT PLACEMENTS:
Since 1980, Mrs. Keithley has been responsible for conducting searches for senior management positions for large multinational companies, health care organizations, closely held companies, and not-for-profit organizations.

WHAT I LOOK FOR IN GENERAL IN A CANDIDATE:
I look for an individual who is articulate and can conceptualize about his or her career to date. Telling events are the attention the individuals pay to business and personal relationships: Are these long-standing and based on respect? The degree to which a candidate can explain how he or she got where he is and infuse humor into this explanation is a good measure of how seriously he or she takes himself or herself.

Integrity and compassion are two qualities that wear well. Prudence and tact are essential. Platform skills based on the four characteristics just mentioned in combination with technical competence make a very appealing person. Image that is appropriate and this takes many forms, but is generally based on hygiene and a concern for personal health.

A sense of adventure, a willingness to consider, and the openness to reconsider all cause me to want to take a person seriously and see his or her point of view. When this is reciprocated in a candidate, both he or she and the potential employer are well-served. Straight talk and courtesy above all.

MINIMUM SALARY LEVEL AT WHICH I WORK:
$50,000

GEOGRAPHIC SCOPE OF RECRUITING ACTIVITIES:
Clients nationwide and in the United Kingdom and Continental Europe

TOTAL YEARS OF RETAINER-TYPE RECRUITING EXPERIENCE:
10 years

ROGER M. KENNY
Partner
Kenny, Kindler, Hunt & Howe
780 Third Avenue, Suite 2202
New York, NY 10017
Telephone: (212) 355-5560

Date of birth: October 3, 1938
Grew up in: New York, NY

HIGHER EDUCATION:
Manhattan College

Photo courtesy of Kenny, Kindler, Hunt & Howe

B.B.A. degree, 1959
New York University Graduate School of Business
M.B.A. degree, 1961

MILITARY:
Specialist Fourth Class, United States Army/National Guard, 1962 to
1968

EMPLOYMENT HISTORY:
1982 to present: Kenny, Kindler, Hunt & Howe
1967 to 1982: Senior Vice President and Partner, SpencerStuart &
Associates
1959 to 1967: Manager–Operations, Port Authority of New York and
New Jersey

PRIVATE CLUBS:
Westchester Country Club
The Board Room

SPECIAL INTERESTS AND HOBBIES:
Hiking, sports, reading

REPRESENTATIVE AND SIGNIFICANT PLACEMENTS:
President
International bank
President
Major international advertising agency
President–North America
European pharmaceutical company
Chief of Staff–Human Resources
Major international consulting firm

Executive Vice President–Marketing
Multinational information services institution

WHAT I LOOK FOR IN GENERAL IN A CANDIDATE:

Track record as perceived by subordinates as well as superiors; multiple questions related to leadership. How a person handles adversity; willingness to experiment, etc.

Since we are dealing with the 95 percentile of corporate executives, we insist on intelligent contribution as well, so we request speeches, articles. We challenge candidates as to their thinking on current issues. One typical question: What subject would you select that would enable us to determine what is special about you as a business person, a marketer, a financial person, etc.?

We insist on getting a special handle on each candidate.

What would the candidate have done differently during his or her career?

MINIMUM SALARY LEVEL AT WHICH I WORK:
$100,000

GEOGRAPHIC SCOPE OF RECRUITING ACTIVITIES:
Clients nationwide and in Europe, the Middle East, and Far East

TOTAL YEARS OF RETAINER-TYPE RECRUITING EXPERIENCE:
22 years

MICHAEL C. KIEFFER
President
Kieffer, Ford & Associates, Inc.
2015 Spring Road, Suite 510
Oak Brook, IL 60521
Telephone: (312) 990-1370

Date of birth: December 23, 1942
Grew up in: Kingston, NY

HIGHER EDUCATION:
Marist College, NY
    B.A. degree, liberal arts, 1969
Central Michigan University

Photo by Robert Brandt & Associates

    M.A. degree, management (health care concentration), 1979

MILITARY:
Staff Sergeant, United States Air Force, 1963 to 1967

EMPLOYMENT HISTORY:
1983 to present: Kieffer, Ford & Associates
1977 to 1983: Regional Vice President, Witt Associates
1975 to 1977: Vice President–Human Resources, Geneva General
    Hospital
1970 to 1975: Vice President–Human Resources, St. Francis Hospital
1969 to 1970: Assistant Director, Mid Hudson Career Development
    Center

PRIVATE CLUBS:
Aurora Country Club
DuPage Club
Carlton Club

SPECIAL INTERESTS AND HOBBIES:
Golf, sailing, international travel, skiing, tennis

REPRESENTATIVE AND SIGNIFICANT PLACEMENTS:
Ronald Aldrich, President and Chief Executive Officer
    Franciscan Health Systems
Thomas Rockers, President and Chief Executive Officer
    Santa Rosa Health Care Corporation
John Johnson, President and Chief Executive Officer
    Berkshire Health System

Jan Jennings, President and Chief Executive Officer
  Millard Fillmore System
Paul Tejada, President and Chief Executive Officer
  Foote Memorial Hospital

WHAT I LOOK FOR IN GENERAL IN A CANDIDATE:

General intelligence and broad-based knowledge (i.e., over and beyond the candidate's own industry). Sense of vision for his or her industry. Intelligence, relational skills, articulate. Well balanced in his or her life; combining leisure time with work time, and compassion with business drive. Executive poise and presence. Quick thinker, i.e., good on his or her feet. Sense of wit and humor—doesn't take oneself too seriously. Ability to deal with multiple issues simultaneously. Ability to educate and lead boards. Strong business skills. Understanding of marketing. A leader! Politically astute, socially adept. Ability to establish quick trust and high credibility. Because our industry is one of healing and caring for people, a strong sense of commitment to the healing mission of the organization. Ability to form partnership attitudes with physicians, in which both sides perceive themselves to have a real stake in the success or failure of the organization.

MINIMUM SALARY LEVEL AT WHICH I WORK:
  $150,000

GEOGRAPHIC SCOPE OF RECRUITING ACTIVITIES:
  Serve clients nationwide

TOTAL YEARS OF RETAINER-TYPE RECRUITING EXPERIENCE:
  12 years

R. PAUL KORS
Partner
Kors Montgomery International
1980 Post Oak Boulevard, Suite 2280
Houston, TX 77056
Telephone: (713) 840-7101

Date of birth: June 12, 1935
Grew up in: Pontiac, MI

Photo by Kaye Marvins Photography, Inc.

HIGHER EDUCATION:
University of Michigan
   B.B.A. degree, 1958
University of Southern California
   M.B.A. degree, marketing and finance, 1965

MILITARY:
First Lieutenant, United States Army Reserve, 1958 to 1966

EMPLOYMENT HISTORY:
1978 to present: Kors Montgomery International
1973 to 1978: Managing Partner, Korn/Ferry International
1966 to 1973: Account Manager, Dean Witter & Company
1958 to 1966: Salesman, Nalco Chemical Company

PRIVATE CLUBS:
Houston Racquet Club
Palmas Del Mar Country Club

SPECIAL INTERESTS AND HOBBIES:
Skiing, mountain climbing, tennis, golf, classic films

REPRESENTATIVE AND SIGNIFICANT PLACEMENTS:
Richard A. Bray, Executive Vice President–Board of Directors
   BP America
Paul G. Fusco, Vice President–Information Services
   Bertelsmann Music Group
C. Russell Luigs, Chairman and Chief Executive Officer
   Global Marine Corporation
Robert L. Mandeville, Director of Operations
   King Khaled International Airport

Paul J. Norris, President–Chemicals and Catalyst Division
Engelhard Corporation

WHAT I LOOK FOR IN GENERAL IN A CANDIDATE:

My objectives in evaluating candidates are usually threefold. The first is to gain enough insight to be able to predict whether or not that candidate will be successful at our client company. The key here is to look beyond the candidate's experience and qualifications—better to try to understand his accomplishments. My prime criterion for recommending a candidate is to look in depth at how the candidate handled responsibilities similar to those he will have in his new position.

Second is to measure the candidate's own interpretation of the challenges and opportunities of the new position and his ability to work with the person he will be reporting to. This is a good time to verify his accomplishments by discussing the responsibilities and the tasks of the new position. A candidate who can demonstrate to me that he grasps the issues involved and can articulate how his past accomplishments will enable him to be successful in his new position is usually someone whom makes our short list.

The third objective is to determine how strong a hold his current company and environment have on him. Getting somebody to move becomes more difficult every year. This can best be determined by learning more about the candidate's career aspirations and then making a judgment as to whether or not they are consistent with the parameters of the opportunity at our client organization.

MINIMUM SALARY LEVEL AT WHICH I WORK:
$100,000

GEOGRAPHIC SCOPE OF RECRUITING ACTIVITIES:
Clients 50 percent in the United States and 50 percent internationally in Western Europe, Japan, Australia, Brazil, Argentina, and People's Republic of China

TOTAL YEARS OF RETAINER-TYPE RECRUITING EXPERIENCE:
16 years

ROBERT E. LAMALIE
President
Robert Lamalie Inc.
317 North Collier Boulevard
Marco Island, FL 33937
Telephone: (813) 642-8588

Date of birth: June 3, 1931
Grew up in: Fremont, OH

HIGHER EDUCATION:
Capital University, Ohio
B.A. degree, psychology, 1954

Photo by Allan C. Moberg

MILITARY:
Specialist Third Class, United States Army, 1954 to 1956

EMPLOYMENT HISTORY:
1988 to present: Robert Lamalie Inc.
1967 to 1988: Chairman and Chief Executive Officer, Lamalie Associates, Inc.
1965 to 1967: Search Consultant, Booz, Allen & Hamilton, Inc.
1962 to 1965: Manager, Organizational Planning and Professional Recruiting, Glidden Co.
1959 to 1962: Director–Recruiting, Xerox Corp.
1956 to 1959: Personnel Manager, American Greetings Corp.

SPECIAL INTERESTS AND HOBBIES:
Tennis, scuba diving, fishing

REPRESENTATIVE AND SIGNIFICANT PLACEMENTS:
President and Chief Operating Officer
$2.5 billion diversified manufacturer
President and Chief Operating Officer
$6 billion automotive manufacturer
President and Chief Operating Officer
$10 billion food company
Executive Vice President and Chief Financial Officer
$5 billion computer manufacturer
President and Chief Executive Officer
$800 million manufacturer of computer peripherals

WHAT I LOOK FOR IN GENERAL IN A CANDIDATE:

Although the specific requirements such as industry and functional experience vary with each assignment and cannot be minimized, I concentrate a great deal of attention on understanding the pattern of each potential candidate's life. Some of the things I look for in establishing an individual's pattern are

Initial impression—dress, physical package, and demeanor.

Motivators—what drives the person?

Objectives—what are they? Is there a sense of purpose and direction?

What values are important to the person? Is there a sense of honesty and integrity?

Personality characteristics—overtly aggressive or more laid back? How big an ego? A team player or a loner? Degree of flexibility.

Speech—use of slang and profanity.

Sense of humor.

Well organized—does the individual develop a logical, complete but succinct story or get off on irrelevant tangents?

Depth of thinking—does the person develop enough detail or superficially skim the surface?

Level of accomplishments—are they significant to the client's needs?

Style of management—driver versus leader versus coordinator.

What kind of cultures has the individual worked in and how do they relate to the client's culture? Is the individual flexible and adaptable?

How sincere is the individual in considering the client situation and what will attract the individual?

MINIMUM SALARY LEVEL AT WHICH I WORK:

$300,000 (base plus first-year bonus)

GEOGRAPHIC SCOPE OF RECRUITING ACTIVITIES:

Clients nationwide

TOTAL YEARS OF RETAINER-TYPE RECRUITING EXPERIENCE:

34 years

JOHN S. LLOYD
President
Witt Associates Inc.
1211 W. 22nd Street
Oak Brook, IL 60521
Telephone: (312) 574-5070

Date of birth: February 18, 1946
Grew up in: Jefferson City, MO

Photo courtesy of Witt Associates Inc.

HIGHER EDUCATION:
University of Missouri
B.S. degree, business administration, 1968
M.B.A. and M.S.P.H., health care management, 1970

EMPLOYMENT HISTORY:
1973 to present: Witt Associates, Inc.
1970 to 1972: Associate, A.T. Kearney

SPECIAL INTERESTS AND HOBBIES:
Bicycling, aerobics, video production

REPRESENTATIVE AND SIGNIFICANT PLACEMENTS:
Knox Singleton, President
Inova Health System
Rod Wolford, President
Norton Childrens & Methodist Hospital
Robert Ambrose, M.D., Senior Vice President of Medical Affairs
Atlantic Health System
Richard Clarke, President
Healthcare Financial Management Association
Don Brennan, President
Sisters of Providence Health System

WHAT I LOOK FOR IN GENERAL IN A CANDIDATE:

I exclusively search for candidates who comprehend the complexities of the one industry served by Witt Associates—that being health care. Our industry is in a great transition—it is very expensive, the aging population is growing, and there is professional unrest. Internationally, as well as domestically, people want better health services and health and medical products.

Successful candidates must have displayed leadership traits since their youngest years. Candidates must be intelligent and show interest in continuing to pursue personal education. The successful candidate must be able to formulate and clearly express his or her ideas on corporate mission, goals, and objectives. A sense of humor is absolute. A balance must exist between bottom line focus and people motivational skills. The person must not be afraid to change to be successful in the 1990s.

MINIMUM SALARY LEVEL AT WHICH I WORK:
$100,000

GEOGRAPHIC SCOPE OF RECRUITING ACTIVITIES:
Clients nationwide and in Europe, Africa, and Asia

TOTAL YEARS OF RETAINER-TYPE RECRUITING EXPERIENCE:
17 years

JOHN LUCHT
President
The John Lucht Consultancy Inc.
641 Fifth Avenue
New York, NY 10022
Telephone: (212) 935-4660

Date of birth: June 1, 1933
Grew up in: Reedsburg, WI

Photo by Hugh Williams

HIGHER EDUCATION:
University of Wisconsin
B.S. degree, 1955
University of Wisconsin Law School
L.L.B. degree, 1960

EMPLOYMENT HISTORY:
1977 to present: The John Lucht Consultancy Inc.
1971 to 1977: Vice President, Heidrick and Struggles Inc.
1970 to 1971: General Manager, Tetley Tea Division (Squibb Beech-Nut Inc.)
1969 to 1970: Director of Marketing, W.A. Sheaffer Pen Co.
1964 to 1969: Director of New Product Marketing, Bristol-Myers Co.
1960 to 1964: Account Executive, J. Walter Thompson Co.
1959 to 1960: Instructor, University of Wisconsin Law School

PRIVATE CLUBS:
Metropolitan Club of New York
Canadian Club of New York

SPECIAL INTERESTS AND HOBBIES:
Writing and lecturing. Author of the best-seller *Rites of Passage at $100,000+ . . . The Insider's Guide to Executive Job Changing*

REPRESENTATIVE AND SIGNIFICANT PLACEMENTS:
John Backe, President and Chief Executive Officer
CBS Inc.
Patrick Donaghy, President–Silver Burdett & Ginn
SFN Corporation
Richard Casabonne, President–Franklin Watts Inc.
Grolier Inc.
James Knabe, President
Associated Merchandising Corporation

Erna Zint, Regional Vice President–Far East (recruited and stationed in Hong Kong)
Associated Merchandising Corporation

WHAT I LOOK FOR IN GENERAL IN A CANDIDATE:

For almost every high-level position in almost every industry, a rare few executives stand out. Their leadership, creativity, expertise, and fine personal characteristics produce an outstanding performance and reputation, which are observable both outside and inside their organization.

So in evaluating every candidate, I always look for the person my client will be most strengthened to gain and, unfortunately, a competitive organization will be weakened to lose. And sometimes, of course, that person is junior and rising, rather than flying high.

Practicing independently, I have only my own clients' employees off limits. Therefore, my central criterion is "who will strengthen this client most?" rather than "who is within the specifications?"

MINIMUM SALARY LEVEL AT WHICH I WORK:
$120,000

GEOGRAPHIC SCOPE OF RECRUITING ACTIVITIES:
Clients nationwide and in Canada, Europe, and Asia

TOTAL YEARS OF RETAINER-TYPE RECRUITING EXPERIENCE:
18 years

JONATHAN E. McBRIDE
President
McBride Associates, Inc.
1511 K Street, NW
Washington, DC 20005
Telephone: (202) 638-1150

Date of birth: June 16, 1942
Grew up in: Washington, DC

HIGHER EDUCATION:
Yale University
B.A. degree, American studies, 1964

Photo courtesy of McBride Associates, Inc.

MILITARY:
Lieutenant, United States Naval Reserve, 1964 to 1968

EMPLOYMENT HISTORY:
1979 to present: McBride Associates, Inc.
1976 to 1979: Vice President, Simmons Associates, Inc.
1972 to 1976: Vice President, Lionel D. Edie & Co.
1968 to 1972: Account Executive, Merrill Lynch, Pierce, Fenner & Smith, Inc.

PRIVATE CLUBS:
Metropolitan Club of Washington, DC
Chevy Chase Club
Yale Club of New York City

REPRESENTATIVE AND SIGNIFICANT PLACEMENTS:
Vice President–Corporate Communications
    Major NYSE listed drug company
Senior Vice President/Managing Director–Equity Investments
    NYSE buy-side institutional financial services company
President and Chief Executive Officer
    Technical/trade association
President and Chief Executive Officer
    Privately held, wholesale distribution company
Vice President–Marketing and Sales
    ASE listed, specialty manufacturing firm

WHAT I LOOK FOR IN GENERAL IN A CANDIDATE:

It seems to me a hiring manager working with a corporate headhunter will be more successful by hunting for hearts not just heads. Same goes for the headhunter, or perhaps better said, the hearthunter.

I see myself as a hearthunter. I seek personal as well as professional commitment—a synthesis of emotional and rational considerations—in favor of my clients' needs. I also seek integrity—not just honesty, but a sense of wholeness—in those candidates I elect to pursue for clients.

Circumstances will arise in a job that neither client nor candidate can anticipate while still in the recruiting process. A candidate who accepts and takes on a new job because it is a natural expression of who she or he *is,* is much more likely to meet the challenges successfully than is one who changes jobs because it "looks good" or just "makes sense."

MINIMUM SALARY LEVEL AT WHICH I WORK:
  $100,000

GEOGRAPHIC SCOPE OF RECRUITING ACTIVITIES:
  Clients nationwide

TOTAL YEARS OF RETAINER-TYPE RECRUITING EXPERIENCE:
  13 years

MILLINGTON F. McCOY
Managing Director
Gould & McCoy, Inc.
551 Madison Avenue
New York, NY 10022
Telephone: (212) 688-8671

Date of birth: January 22, 1941
Grew up in: Cape Girardeau, MO

Photo by Bachrach

HIGHER EDUCATION:
University of Missouri
  B.A. degree, 1962
Harvard-Radcliffe Program in Business Administration
  Certificate, 1963

EMPLOYMENT HISTORY:
1977 to present: Gould & McCoy, Inc.
1966 to 1977: Vice President, Handy Associates
1965 to 1966: Advertising and Market Research Analyst, Gardner
  Advertising Agency
1964 to 1965: Field Market Researcher, Procter & Gamble Co.

PRIVATE CLUBS:
Harvard Club

SPECIAL INTERESTS AND HOBBIES:
Committee of 200 (founding member), (horses) cross-country jump-
  ing and dressage, gardening, study of the Enneagram

REPRESENTATIVE AND SIGNIFICANT PLACEMENTS:
A. Donald McCulloch, Jr.
  Placed as President, Hathaway Brand Division of Warnaco, Inc.
  (now President and Chief Executive Officer of Nutri/System, Inc.)
Clifford Drake, Jr.
  President–Avant Petroleum, division of Mitsui & Co. (U.S.A.), Inc.
John W. Argabright
  President, International Division, Campbell Soup Company
Ronald D. Glosser
  President, Hershey Trust Company
Senior Vice Presidents (9)
  Chemical Bank (four have had promotions in last three years)

WHAT I LOOK FOR IN GENERAL IN A CANDIDATE:

Gaining an understanding of the client culture and its requirements for success is the first step in determining what I look for in a candidate. My key to the successful search assignment is the right cultural fit.

For example, in some companies, diplomacy, well-developed interpersonal skills, and a nonconfrontational approach are essential. Other environments may require political skills or the ability to be confrontational for the candidate to be successful. Candidates must have the appropriate orientation for the culture.

After determining cultural fit, the most important part of the assessment process is to figure out whether the candidate is on a positive, upward trend in his or her life and career. I have found that the best way to predict future success is to look for a solid and consistent record of past success, going back to the person's early formative years. Critical qualities I seek in an individual are warmth, a good sense of humor, integrity, strong values, and adaptability. I always look for self-knowledge and awareness including personal strategy and direction.

Relative to the client organization and its needs, the other things I look for in a candidate include the requisite level of intelligence, emotional maturity, drive, vision, risk-orientation, personality type, and skill fit with the position requirements.

Unfortunately, there are no short cuts to the assessment process. It takes an assessor who is self-aware, mature, and seasoned. Like the best candidates, those of us who learn by our experiences are the ones who get ahead.

MINIMUM SALARY LEVEL AT WHICH I WORK:
$150,000

GEOGRAPHIC SCOPE OF RECRUITING ACTIVITIES:
Clients nationwide and in Europe, the Far East, and South America

TOTAL YEARS OF RETAINER-TYPE RECRUITING EXPERIENCE:
23 years

RICHARD M. McFARLAND
President
Brissenden, McFarland, Wagoner
& Fuccella, Inc.
One Canterbury Green
Stamford, CT 06901
Telephone: (203) 324-1598

Date of birth: September 10, 1923
Grew up in: Portland, ME

HIGHER EDUCATION:

Rensselaer Polytechnic Institute

Photo courtesy of Brissenden, McFarland, Wagoner & Fuccella, Inc.

   B.A. degree, chemical engineering, 1944

MILITARY:

Lieutenant Commander, United States Navy, 1943–46 and 1951–53

EMPLOYMENT HISTORY:

1981 to present: Brissenden, McFarland, Wagoner & Fuccella, Inc.

1969 to 1981: Senior Vice President, Heidrick & Struggles, Inc.

1967 to 1969: Vice President and General Manager, Inorganic Div., Wyandotte Chemical Co.

1961 to 1967: President, Cumberland Chemical Company

1959 to 1961: Manager, Marketing Development and Application Research, Texas Butadiene & Chemical

1955 to 1959: Product Manager, FMC Corporation

1953 to 1955: Manager Market Research, Brea Chemical Company

PRIVATE CLUBS:

Landmark Club

Cedar Point Yacht Club

SPECIAL INTERESTS AND HOBBIES:

Sailing, skiing, golf, history (ancient and American)

REPRESENTATIVE AND SIGNIFICANT PLACEMENTS:

Brian M. Rushton, Vice President Research to Vice President Research and Development

Air Products and Chemicals

Robert A. Roland, President and Chief Executive Officer

Chemical Manufacturers Association

Corbin J. McNeill, Executive Vice President (Nuclear)
  Philadelphia Electric
E. James Ferland, Chairman and Chief Executive Officer
  Public Service Electric and Gas
Standley H. Hoch, Chairman and Chief Executive Officer
  General Public Utilities

WHAT I LOOK FOR IN GENERAL IN A CANDIDATE:

Before a prospect becomes a candidate, he or she is screened by telephone. At this time pertinent facts are obtained directed toward the requirements of the job and the specification developed with the client. Having passed that screen, next comes the face-to-face, in-depth interview, at which time the highly critical first impressions are observed—physical appearance, speech, bearing, credibility, humor, enthusiasm, charisma. Next comes a detailed questioning of early background, education, service time, if any, family, and professional career. Each job is explored, as to responsibilities, reporting relationships, accomplishments, and how these were achieved. Emphasis here is on style, managerial skill, leadership, and knowledge. All during this phase, I test for accuracy, truthfulness, communicating skills, and personal stimulus value. At the conclusion of two to three hours of conversation I decide whether the candidate has the requisite knowledge, the desired potential for growth, and the right personal chemistry to fit the client's environment.

MINIMUM SALARY LEVEL AT WHICH I WORK:
$100,000

GEOGRAPHIC SCOPE OF RECRUITING ACTIVITIES:
Clients nationwide

TOTAL YEARS OF RETAINER-TYPE RECRUITING EXPERIENCE:
20 years

CLARENCE E. McFEELY
Partner
McFeely Wackerle Jett
20 North Wacker Drive
  Suite 3110
Chicago, IL 60606
Telephone: (312) 641-2977

Date of birth: May 12, 1929
Grew up in: Chicago, IL

HIGHER EDUCATION:
  Bradley University, IL
    B.S. degree, 1951

Photo by Stuart-Rodgers-Reilly Photography

MILITARY:
  First Lieutenant, United States Marine Corps, 1951 to 1953

EMPLOYMENT HISTORY:
  1969 to present: McFeely Wackerle Jett
  1969: Managing Partner, William H. Clark & Associates
  1960 to 1969: Principal, A.T. Kearney & Company
  1959 to 1960: Representative, Dansk Designs, Inc.
  1955 to 1959: Employee Relations Manager, The Budd Company
  (C.D.F.)
  1953 to 1955: Personnel Supervisor, Campbell Soup Company

PRIVATE CLUBS:
  Barrington Hills Country Club
  Moss Creek Golf Club
  Tower Club
  East Bank Club

SPECIAL INTERESTS AND HOBBIES:
  Golf, classical music, theatre, travel

REPRESENTATIVE AND SIGNIFICANT PLACEMENTS:
  President and Chief Executive Officer
    North American subsidiary of a major U.K. medical and research
    products company
  President and Chief Executive Officer
    Independent major market television broadcasting company
  President and Chief Executive Officer
    Fortune 500 holding company–hotel, gaming, and entertainment

President and Chief Operating Officer
Start-up software application development company
President and Chief Executive Officer
Fortune 500 holding company–medical products group

WHAT I LOOK FOR IN GENERAL IN A CANDIDATE:

A high level of personal and professional value standards;
  integrity and ethics
Perception, intuitiveness, and insight to understanding
  people
Ability to lead and motivate others
Decisiveness and courage to solve difficult problems
Ability to plan, organize, and set priorities
A high energy level and commitment to excel
Good intellectual, educational, and cultural background
Healthy balance between personal and professional life
Community commitment and social awareness
Can handle both success and adversity
Good health, fitness, and grooming

MINIMUM SALARY LEVEL AT WHICH I WORK:
$150,000

GEOGRAPHIC SCOPE OF RECRUITING ACTIVITIES:
Clients nationwide and in Hong Kong and the United Kingdom

TOTAL YEARS OF RETAINER-TYPE RECRUITING EXPERIENCE:
29 years

JOSEPH P. McGINLEY
Senior Director
SpencerStuart
55 East 52nd Street
New York, NY 10055
Telephone: (212) 407-0200

Date of birth: October 11, 1932
Grew up in: Brooklyn, NY

Photo courtesy of SpencerStuart

HIGHER EDUCATION:
St. John's University
B.B.A. degree, industrial relations, 1960

MILITARY:
Second-Class Petty Officer, United States Coast Guard, 1952 to 1955

EMPLOYMENT HISTORY:
1980 to present: SpencerStuart Associates
1973 to 1980: Partner, Booz, Allen & Hamilton, Inc.
1969 to 1973: Executive Vice President, David North
1966 to 1969: Director of Recruiting, Atlantic Richfield
1955 to 1966: Various Personnel and Sales positions, Sinclair Oil

PRIVATE CLUBS:
University Club, New York
Cherry Valley Country Club

SPECIAL INTERESTS AND HOBBIES:
Golf, tennis, boating

REPRESENTATIVE AND SIGNIFICANT PLACEMENTS:
Ralph Reins, President and Chief Operating Officer
Mack Truck
John Rowe, President and Chief Executive Officer
New England Electric
Richard Kral, Chairman and Chief Executive Officer
Crystal Brands
George Kimmel, President and Chief Operating Officer
Combustion Engineering
Michael Roth, Executive Vice President and Chief Financial Officer
Mony Financial Services

WHAT I LOOK FOR IN GENERAL IN A CANDIDATE:

Leadership

Intelligence

Strong personal and professional integrity

Self-confidence

A desire to be successful

A successful track record of accomplishments

MINIMUM SALARY LEVEL AT WHICH I WORK:

$150,000

GEOGRAPHIC SCOPE OF RECRUITING ACTIVITIES:

Clients nationwide

TOTAL YEARS OF RETAINER-TYPE RECRUITING EXPERIENCE:

19 years

CARL W. MENK
Chairman
Canny, Bowen Inc.
425 Park Avenue
New York, NY 10022
Telephone: (212) 758-3400

Date of birth: October 19, 1921
Grew up in: Montclair, NJ

HIGHER EDUCATION:
Seton Hall University

Photo by Bachrach

B.S. degree, business administration, 1943
Columbia University
M.A. degree, 1950

MILITARY:
Second Lieutenant, United States Army Air Force, 1943 to 1946

EMPLOYMENT HISTORY:
1984 to present: Canny, Bowen Inc.
1969 to 1984: President, Boyden Associates, Inc.
1946 to 1969: Senior Vice President, P. Ballantine & Sons

PRIVATE CLUBS:
New Jersey:
Spring Lake Golf Club
Montclair Golf Club
Glen Ridge Country Club
New York:
Union League Club
Columbia Club
Johns Island, FL

SPECIAL INTERESTS AND HOBBIES:
Golf, swimming, oil painting

REPRESENTATIVE AND SIGNIFICANT PLACEMENTS:
Ray C. Adam, Chairman and Chief Executive Officer
NL Industries
Edward A. Fox, President and Chief Executive Officer
Student Loan Marketing Association (Sallie Mae)

John T. Lundegard, Chairman and Chief Executive Officer
  Western Auto Supply Co.
John J. Shea, President and Chief Executive Officer
  Spiegel, Inc.
James L. Vincent, Chairman and Chief Executive Officer
  Biogen Inc.

WHAT I LOOK FOR IN GENERAL IN A CANDIDATE:

Stature
Intelligence
Motivation
Problem-solving ability
Interpersonal skills
Communication skills
Leadership skills in stress situations

MINIMUM SALARY LEVEL AT WHICH I WORK:
$200,000

GEOGRAPHIC SCOPE OF RECRUITING ACTIVITIES:
Clients nationwide and in Europe, Latin America, the Pacific Basin

TOTAL YEARS OF RETAINER-TYPE RECRUITING EXPERIENCE:
20 years

HERBERT T. MINES
President and Chief Executive Officer
Herbert Mines Associates, Inc.
780 Third Avenue
New York, NY 10017
Telephone: (212) 355-0909

Date of birth: January 30, 1929
Grew up in: West Hartford, CT

HIGHER EDUCATION:
Babson College, MA
B.S. degree, economics, 1949
Cornell University
M.I.L.R. degree, industrial relations, 1954

Photo courtesy of Herbert Mines Associates, Inc.

EMPLOYMENT HISTORY:
1981 to present: Herbert Mines Associates
1972 to 1981: Chairman, Search Division, Wells Management Corp.
1970 to 1972: Vice President Human Resources, Revlon
1966 to 1970: Senior Vice President Human Resources, Neiman Marcus
1954 to 1966: Administrator–Training and Organizational Development, Macy's

PRIVATE CLUBS:
Beach Point Club

SPECIAL INTERESTS AND HOBBIES:
Tennis, reading

REPRESENTATIVE AND SIGNIFICANT PLACEMENTS:
Robert Suslow, President and Chief Executive Officer (Chairman, Batus Retail Group)
Saks Fifth Avenue
David Fuente, President and Chief Executive Officer
Office Depot
Peter Hayes, President and Chief Executive Officer
Gold Circle Stores
John Eyler, President and Chief Executive Officer–Retail Division
Hartmarx
Phil Miller, Chairman and Chief Executive Officer
Marshall Fields

WHAT I LOOK FOR IN GENERAL IN A CANDIDATE:

General appearance, dress, manner, stature, and verbal presentation

The ability to express themselves clearly and concisely and know when they have completed their thought

The willingness to discuss subjects that are embarrassing or failures in their career and to deal with them in a practical, understandable way without blaming others. Self-knowledge and a sense of self-worth make it possible for them to discuss their strengths and weaknesses dispassionately

An understanding of their own personal psychological profile so they can relate their experiences realistically, particularly where these involve other personalities with whom they were uncomfortable or work situations that did not fit

Energy, a sense of humor, consistency, and clarity in their description of past activities and future objectives

The understanding of why they made mistakes in the past and how they can be avoided in the future. The perception of how to avoid situations where they are likely to fail and to seek those where their strengths can be best utilized

The ability to formulate a clear response to the position being discussed and if both sides are interested, to pursue the project with consistency but without being overly aggressive

MINIMUM SALARY LEVEL AT WHICH I WORK:
$200,000

GEOGRAPHIC SCOPE OF RECRUITING ACTIVITIES:
Serve clients nationwide and in England, France, and Canada

TOTAL YEARS OF RETAINER-TYPE RECRUITING EXPERIENCE:
17 years

JAMES M. MONTGOMERY
President
Houze, Shourds & Montgomery, Inc.
Greater Los Angeles Trade Center
One World Trade
Long Beach, CA 90831
Telephone: (213) 495-6495

Date of birth: May 5, 1939
Grew up in: Southern California

Photo courtesy of Houze, Shourds & Montgomer, Inc.

MILITARY:
Private First Class, United States Marine Corps, 1957 to 1960

EMPLOYMENT HISTORY:
1978 to present: Houze, Shourds & Montgomery, Inc.
1973 to 1978: Director, Industrial Relations, Rohr Industries
1962 to 1973: Director–Personnel, Corporate, Rockwell International

PRIVATE CLUBS:
Long Beach Yacht Club
Old Ranch Tennis Club
World Trade Association

SPECIAL INTERESTS AND HOBBIES:
Tennis, sailing, running, collecting Southwestern art

REPRESENTATIVE AND SIGNIFICANT PLACEMENTS:
Senior Vice President–Operations to President, Chairman and Chief Executive Officer
$1 billion company
President and Chief Operating Officer (troubled $500 million company) to Chairman and Chief Executive Officer
$1 billion company
Vice President–Operations
Major aerospace company who successfully produced a complex, state-of-the-art multibillion dollar weapon system
Vice President and General Manager
$9 million dollar information services start-up (now a $100 million multiproduct business)

Group Human Resources Director to Vice President–Human Resources
$1 billion corporation

WHAT I LOOK FOR IN GENERAL IN A CANDIDATE:

Candor, self-confidence, and substance; coupled with intellectual capacity, an apparent willingness to work hard, and a sense of humor.

MINIMUM SALARY LEVEL AT WHICH I WORK:
$75,000

GEOGRAPHIC SCOPE OF RECRUITING ACTIVITIES:
Clients nationwide and in Europe

TOTAL YEARS OF RETAINER-TYPE RECRUITING EXPERIENCE:
11 years

FERDINAND NADHERNY
Vice Chairman
Russell Reynolds Associates, Inc.
200 South Wacker Drive, Suite 3600
Chicago, IL 60606
Telephone: (312) 993-9696

Date of birth: December 12, 1926
Grew up in: Berwyn, IL

HIGHER EDUCATION:
Yale University
A.B. degree, economics, 1950
Harvard University Graduate School of Business
M.B.A. degree, 1952

Photo courtesy of Russell Reynolds Associates, Inc.

MILITARY:
Specialist Second Class, United States Navy, 1945 to 1946

EMPLOYMENT HISTORY:
1974 to present: Russell Reynolds Associates
1972 to 1974: Vice President, Boyden Associates
1969 to 1972: Executive Vice President, Combined Motivation Education Systems, Inc.
1968 to 1969: Group Vice President, Nationwide Industries
1966 to 1968: Assistant to the President, Science Research Associates
1964 to 1966: Executive Secretary, Office of Economic Opportunity
1952 to 1964: General Manager, Cabot Corporation

PRIVATE CLUBS:
Illinois:
Glen View Club
Indian Hill Country Club
Chicago Club
University Club
Yale Club of New York City

SPECIAL INTERESTS AND HOBBIES:
International travel, reading, education, golf

REPRESENTATIVE AND SIGNIFICANT PLACEMENTS:
Barry Sullivan, Chairman and Chief Executive Officer
First National Bank of Chicago

William Goessel, President and Chief Operating Officer to Chairman and Chief Executive Officer
Harnischfeger Industries, Inc.

Nolan D. Archibald, President and Chief Operating Officer to Chairman and Chief Executive Officer
The Black & Decker Corporation

Alger B. Chapman, Chairman and Chief Executive Officer
Chicago Board of Options Exchange

Ralph Guthrie, Chairman and Chief Executive Officer
Urban Investment and Development Company

WHAT I LOOK FOR IN GENERAL IN A CANDIDATE:

In general, what I look for in a candidate is someone who has had an extremely successful career, who has reached a point where it is timely to make a job change and preferably a change in company. I tend to look for people who are bright and have high energy levels. Good people skills are also extremely important since most people who are successful are able to motivate and relate well to others. They must also be good communicators. Integrity and honesty are a must. Attempting to make sure that an individual candidate would fit well into a company's culture, share a similar business philosophy, and especially have a good chemistry with the Board of Directors or person to whom one is reporting is also important. I like to present candidates who have interests outside of business and are happily married.

MINIMUM SALARY LEVEL AT WHICH I WORK:
Depends on the position

GEOGRAPHIC SCOPE OF RECRUITING ACTIVITIES:
Serve clients nationwide and in Western Europe

TOTAL YEARS OF RETAINER-TYPE RECRUITING EXPERIENCE:
17 years

THOMAS J. NEFF
President
SpencerStuart
55 East 52nd Street
New York, NY 10055
Telephone: (212) 407-0200

Date of birth: October 2, 1937
Grew up in: Easton, PA

HIGHER EDUCATION:
Lafayette College, Pennsylvania

Photo courtesy of SpencerStuart

B.S. degree, industrial engineering, 1959
Lehigh University, Pennsylvania
M.B.A. degree, marketing and finance, 1961

MILITARY:
First Lieutenant, United States Army, 1961 to 1963

EMPLOYMENT HISTORY:
1976 to present: SpencerStuart
1974 to 1976: Principal, Booz, Allen & Hamilton, Inc.
1969 to 1974: President, Hospital Data Sciences, Inc.
1966 to 1969: Director of Marketing Planning, TWA, Inc.
1963 to 1966: Associate, McKinsey & Company

PRIVATE CLUBS:
Blind Brook Club
The Links
Racquet & Tennis
Round Hill Field Club
Sky Club
Yale Club
Quogue Field Club
Quogue Beach Club

REPRESENTATIVE AND SIGNIFICANT PLACEMENTS:
Edmund M. Carpenter, Chief Executive Officer
General Signal
James B. Farley, President
Mony Financial Services
Peter C. Goldmark, Jr., Chief Executive Officer
Rockefeller Foundation

Lou Gerstner, Chairman
   RJR Nabisco
Richard Miller, President
   Wang Laboratories

WHAT I LOOK FOR IN GENERAL IN A CANDIDATE:

Each client and each assignment is unique, and it is essential to understand this to ensure that we are recruiting a tailor-made executive and not a generic solution.

MINIMUM SALARY LEVEL AT WHICH I WORK:
No minimum

GEOGRAPHIC SCOPE OF RECRUITING ACTIVITIES:
Clients nationwide and internationally through their overseas offices

TOTAL YEARS OF RETAINER-TYPE RECRUITING EXPERIENCE:
15 years

LAWRENCE F. NEIN
Managing Partner
Nordeman Grimm, Inc.
150 North Michigan Avenue
Chicago, IL 60601
Telephone: (312) 332-0088

Date of birth: April 2, 1936
Grew up in: Ohio

Photo courtesy of Nordeman Grimm, Inc.

HIGHER EDUCATION:
Miami University of Ohio
   B.S. degree, 1958
Wharton School, University of Pennsylvania
   M.B.A. degree, 1963

MILITARY:
Lieutenant Junior Grade, United States Navy, 1958 to 1962

EMPLOYMENT HISTORY:
1984 to present: Nordeman Grimm, Inc.
1982 to 1984: President, Education & Information Systems, Inc.
1976 to 1982: President, Sargent-Welch Scientific Company
1973 to 1976: President, Hartmarx Corporation–Gleneagles Division
1970 to 1973: President, The House Stores, Inc.
1963 to 1970: Management Consultant, McKinsey & Company, Inc.

PRIVATE CLUBS:
The Chicago Club
Sunset Ridge Country Club

SPECIAL INTERESTS AND HOBBIES:
Real estate investment, golf

REPRESENTATIVE AND SIGNIFICANT PLACEMENTS:
Richard Sim, President and Chief Operating Officer to Chief Executive Officer
   Applied Power Corporation
Melody Camp, Vice President and Treasurer
   Coldwell Banker Real Estate Group
Charles Fink, Vice President and General Manager, Defense Systems Group
   FMC Corporation

John Struck, Vice President
  Pru Bache Capital Funding
Howard Larsen, General Manager, Minnetonka Medical
  Minnetonka Corporation

WHAT I LOOK FOR IN GENERAL IN A CANDIDATE:

I look at all candidates with a few key thoughts in mind.

First, what are his or her achievements versus the critical needs of the position I am recruiting for? That is, how do this person's accomplishments match up against the (two or three) things that need to be done really well in the position to get exceptional results?

The second thing I look for is cultural fit. Some organizations and positions call for dashing, aggressive, flamboyant, risk-taking personalities. In others, such a person would fall flat on his face.

In all cases, I look for fervor, energy, and leadership in the sense of letting others shine and not having to take all the credit personally. These are key elements in a true leader at any level, I believe, and are "must haves" in my personal screen.

MINIMUM SALARY LEVEL AT WHICH I WORK:
$100,000

GEOGRAPHIC SCOPE OF RECRUITING ACTIVITIES:
Clients nationwide

TOTAL YEARS OF RETAINER-TYPE RECRUITING EXPERIENCE:
5 years

JACQUES C. NORDEMAN
Chairman
Nordeman Grimm, Inc.
717 Fifth Avenue
New York, NY 10022
Telephone: (212) 935-1000

Date of birth: March 24, 1937
Grew up in: New York, NY

Photo courtesy of Nordeman Grimm, Inc.

HIGHER EDUCATION:
Colgate University
B.A. degree, fine arts, 1958
Harvard University Graduate School of Business
M.B.A. degree, 1964

MILITARY:
Lieutenant Junior Grade, United States Navy, 1959 to 1962

EMPLOYMENT HISTORY:
1969 to present: Nordeman Grimm, Inc.
1968 to 1969: Partner, Parker Nordeman
1964 to 1968: Account Management, Benton & Bowles

PRIVATE CLUBS:
Shinnecock Hills Golf Club
National Golf Links of America
University Club

SPECIAL INTERESTS AND HOBBIES:
Golf, skiing, Dixieland music (drummer), photography, theatre, travel
Cancer Research Institute (President); Union Theological Seminary
(Board Member); Metropolitan Museum of Art (Vice Chairman,
Business Committee)

REPRESENTATIVE AND SIGNIFICANT PLACEMENTS:
Michael Ainslie, Chief Executive Officer
Sotheby's Holdings Inc.
William Grimes, Chief Executive Officer
ESPN
John Whitman, Chief Executive Officer
Prudential Bache Interfunding
Duwayne Peterson, Executive Vice President and Chief Information
Officer
Merrill Lynch & Company

Adrian Belamy, Chief Executive Officer
DFS Group Limited

WHAT I LOOK FOR IN GENERAL IN A CANDIDATE:

People who are real. They are down-to-earth and without pretension. Individuals with the highest personal standards of honesty, integrity, and trust.

"Smarts." I am intrigued with a person's intelligence and thought processes and am attracted to (1) individuals who are quick and able to cut through to the heart of an issue and (2) individuals with sound judgment.

A strong sense of self, combined with a sensitivity to others. I am attracted to individuals with an understated confidence and humility. Individuals who are good listeners and, through their interpretive skills, can inspire and motivate those around them.

A sense of balance—between family, professional life, and outside interests. More often than not they are multidimensional and bring a diverse range of involvements and interests.

A strong sense of purpose, combined with creativity, energy, and often a flare or passion for whatever they do.

Good communicators who express ideas in a logical, forthright, and direct manner. A sense of humor.

Leadership—usually evident throughout every stage of an exceptional career.

MINIMUM SALARY LEVEL AT WHICH I WORK:
$200,000

GEOGRAPHIC SCOPE OF RECRUITING ACTIVITIES:
Clients nationwide and internationally

TOTAL YEARS OF RETAINER-TYPE RECRUITING EXPERIENCE:
20 years

DAYTON OGDEN
Chief Executive Officer
SpencerStuart
55 East 52nd Street
New York, NY 10055
Telephone: (212) 407-0200

Date of birth: January 11, 1945
Grew up in: New Canaan, CT

HIGHER EDUCATION:
Yale University
B.A. degree, American studies, 1967

Photo courtesy of SpencerStuart

MILITARY:
Lieutenant Junior Grade, United States Navy, 1968 to 1971

EMPLOYMENT HISTORY:
1979 to present: SpencerStuart Associates
1975 to 1979: Vice President, Simmons Associates
1973 to 1975: Personnel Director, Dunham and Smith Agencies
1967 to 1973: Assistant to Personnel Director, Port Authority of NY
& NJ

PRIVATE CLUBS:
Woodway Country Club, CT
Racquet and Tennis Club, NY

SPECIAL INTERESTS AND HOBBIES:
Fishing, skiing, sailing, reading, tennis

REPRESENTATIVE AND SIGNIFICANT PLACEMENTS:
Gerrit Venema, Chief Executive Officer
National Bank of Kuwait
Steve Wheeler, Chief Executive Officer
First Winthrop Corporation
Paul Karas, Chief Executive Officer, JFK 2000
Port Authority of NY & NJ
Robin Wilson, President
Long Island Railroad
James Bigham, Executive Vice President/Chief Financial Officer
Continental Grain Company

WHAT I LOOK FOR IN GENERAL IN A CANDIDATE:

Strong record of achievement—is there a pattern of success in early life, i.e., education, military, business?

Sense of humor—can the candidate view himself or herself with perspective?

Vision—the ability to see ideas and outcomes that others don't, to bring creative ways of doing things to fruition.

Strong intellectual dimension—the ability to associate, adapt, and move between conceptual benchmarks.

An international perspective—the capacity to operate across geographic boundaries and deal with global markets.

Leadership skills—the ability to persuade and motivate others.

Toughness—is the candidate resilient and equipped to deal with difficult people issues?

Honesty—is the candidate honest with himself or herself and with others?

Communications—can the candidate articulate ideas verbally and in writing?

Salesmanship—can the candidate sell ideas, solutions, products, etc.?

MINIMUM SALARY LEVEL AT WHICH I WORK:
$150,000

GEOGRAPHIC SCOPE OF RECRUITING ACTIVITIES:
Clients nationwide and in the United Kingdom, Soviet Union, Hong Kong, Japan, Kuwait, Brazil

TOTAL YEARS OF RETAINER-TYPE RECRUITING EXPERIENCE:
11 years

THOMAS H. OGDON
President
The Ogdon Partnership
375 Park Avenue
New York, NY 10152
Telephone: (212) 308-1600

Date of birth: April 16, 1935
Grew up in: Tarrytown, NY, and
   Greenwich, CT

HIGHER EDUCATION:
Amherst College
   B.A. degree, English, 1957

Photo courtesy of The Ogdon Partnership

EMPLOYMENT HISTORY:
1987 to present: The Ogdon Partnership
1980 to 1987: Executive Vice President/Chief Operating Officer,
   Haley Associates
1979: Vice President, Russell Reynolds Associates
1975 to 1978: Senior Vice President, Needham Harper & Steers
1961 to 1975: Senior Vice President, Management Supervisor, Benton & Bowles
1959 to 1961: Copywriter, Grey Advertising
1958: Trainee, Ted Bates Advertising

PRIVATE CLUBS:
Union Club
Indian Harbor Yacht Club
Brook Club

SPECIAL INTERESTS AND HOBBIES:
Fishing, tennis, squash, gardening, golf

REPRESENTATIVE AND SIGNIFICANT PLACEMENTS:
Peter Brinckerhoff, Managing Director of High Yield and LBO
   Departments
   Paine Webber
Ronald David, Chief Executive Officer
   Perrier
Gene Bedell, Managing Director of MIS/EDP
   First Boston Corporation

Charles Townsend, President and Publisher, *Family Circle* Magazine
   The New York Times Magazine Group
Robert Davies, President and Chief Executive Officer
   CHB Foods (at the time of LBO)

WHAT I LOOK FOR IN GENERAL IN A CANDIDATE:

The first thing I look for is the degree to which a candidate is truly comfortable with himself or herself. It's a kissing cousin to self-confidence—but different. Other things we all look for—leadership abilities, a sense of humor, the ability to move all the way to an important decision, and handling difficult interpersonal situations all come naturally to someone with this sense of self. That a person have the proper technical qualifications for the position is, of course, a given.

MINIMUM SALARY LEVEL AT WHICH I WORK:
   $100,000

GEOGRAPHIC SCOPE OF RECRUITING ACTIVITIES:
   Clients nationwide and in England, Hong Kong, France, Canada

TOTAL YEARS OF RETAINER-TYPE RECRUITING EXPERIENCE:
   11 years

DAVID R. PEASBACK
President and Chief Executive Officer
Canny, Bowen Inc.
425 Park Avenue
New York, NY 10022
Telephone: (212) 758-3400

Date of birth: March 15, 1933
Grew up in: Mt. Lakes, NJ

Photo by Bachrach

HIGHER EDUCATION:
Colgate University
B.A. degree, economics, 1955
University of Virginia Law School
L.L.B. degree, 1961

MILITARY:
Sergeant, United States Marine Corps, 1956 to 1958

EMPLOYMENT HISTORY:
1988 to present: Canny, Bowen Inc.
1972 to 1988: President and Chief Executive Officer, Heidrick & Struggles, Inc.
1968 to 1972: Vice President of Subsidiary, Bangor Punta Corp.
1965 to 1968: Litigation Attorney, Litton Industries Inc.
1961 to 1965: Associate, Covington & Burling Law Firm
1955 to 1956 and 1958: Salesman, Case Soap, Procter & Gamble

PRIVATE CLUBS:
Racquet & Tennis Club, NY
Belle Haven Club, Greenwich, CT

SPECIAL INTERESTS AND HOBBIES:
Skiing, tennis, paddle tennis, swimming

REPRESENTATIVE AND SIGNIFICANT PLACEMENTS:
Edward Gee, Chairman, President and Chief Executive Officer
International Paper Company
Thomas C. McDermott, President and Chief Operating Officer
Bausch & Lomb Inc.
Martin R. Hoffmann, Vice President and General Counsel
Digital Equipment Corporation

John P. Frestel, Jr., Senior Vice President–Human Resources
USAir, Inc.
Robert C. Butler, Senior Vice President and Chief Financial Officer
International Paper Company

WHAT I LOOK FOR IN GENERAL IN A CANDIDATE:

I think it is a mistake to evaluate a candidate in a vacuum. The executive must be evaluated on how he or she could be expected to perform for a specific client. Accordingly, once it is determined that the candidate has the requisite function and industry experience, *personal impact* becomes a pivotal issue. I define this as a combination of personality, appearance, and management style that forms the cornerstone for building acceptance in the new environment. It enables the individual to gain the trust and respect throughout the client organization that is essential for achieving outstanding performance. Every organization has a culture unique unto itself and the candidate must be comfortable with it and vice versa. The absence of this "fit" explains why an executive with an unblemished record of success sometimes fails when he changes jobs. Personal chemistry also must be considered. Although it is related to what I labeled personal impact, personal chemistry is more individualized; e.g., will the new Chief Financial Officer or Senior Vice President Human Resources get along with the Chief Executive Officer?

MINIMUM SALARY LEVEL AT WHICH I WORK:
$100,000

GEOGRAPHIC SCOPE OF RECRUITING ACTIVITIES:
Clients nationwide and in Europe and Canada

TOTAL YEARS OF RETAINER-TYPE RECRUITING EXPERIENCE:
17 years

P. ANTHONY PRICE
Managing Director
Russell Reynolds Associates, Inc.
101 California Street, Suite 3140
San Francisco, CA 94111
Telephone: (415) 392-3130

Date of birth: January 5, 1941
Grew up in: San Francisco, CA

Photo courtesy of Russell Reynolds Associates, Inc.

HIGHER EDUCATION:
University of California–Berkeley
B.S. degree, mechanical engineering, 1963
Harvard University Graduate School of Business
M.B.A. degree, 1965

EMPLOYMENT HISTORY:
1978 to present: Russell Reynolds Associates, Inc.
1974 to 1978: Vice President–Finance to Executive Vice President
and Chief Operating Officer, MacLean-Fogg Company
1965 to 1974: Various Positions to Manager, Planning–Mergers and
Acquisitions, FMC Corp.

PRIVATE CLUBS:
Bohemian Club
Harvard Business School Club of Northern California
Bay Area International Forum
Lake Geneva Country Club
University of California–Berkeley Alumni Association
San Francisco Grid Club
Bay Area Council
Walter Hass School of Business Development Council
Board of California Executive Recruiters Association

SPECIAL INTERESTS AND HOBBIES:
Running, tennis, golf, piano

REPRESENTATIVE AND SIGNIFICANT PLACEMENTS:
Paul C. Ely, Jr., Chairman and Chief Executive Officer
Convergent Technologies, Inc.
Mellon C. Baird, President–Defense and Electronics Group
Eaton Corporation

Frank N. Newman, Vice Chairman and Chief Financial Officer
Bank of America

Edward M. Davis, President and Chief Executive Officer
Raynet, Inc.

Thomas S. Stevens, Executive Vice President and Chief Financial
Officer
Duty Free Shoppers Limited

WHAT I LOOK FOR IN GENERAL IN A CANDIDATE:

When looking for and evaluating candidates, I pay particular attention to depth of character and experience. In this day and age of talented executives crossing industries, I am interested in the candidate's ability to understand the client's business. Therefore, I look beyond whether a candidate actually has experience in the industry and instead review closely a candidate's motivation and leadership and interpersonal skills. Of course a candidate should fit in with the company's culture and have a good chemistry, particularly with the person to whom he or she reports. International experience is a valuable plus in today's business world.

MINIMUM SALARY LEVEL AT WHICH I WORK:
Open. Depends on level of position.

GEOGRAPHIC SCOPE OF RECRUITING ACTIVITIES:
Clients nationwide and internationally through the firm's offices worldwide

TOTAL YEARS OF RETAINER-TYPE RECRUITING EXPERIENCE:
11 years

WINDLE B. PRIEM
Managing Director
Korn/Ferry International
237 Park Avenue
New York, NY 10017
Telephone: (212) 687-1834

Date of birth: October 17, 1937
Grew up in: Wellesley, MA

HIGHER EDUCATION:
Worchester Polytechnic Institute
B.S. degree, mechanical engineering, 1959
Babson College
M.B.A. degree, finance, 1964

Photo by Pach Bros., N.Y.

MILITARY:
Lieutenant Junior Grade, United States Navy, 1959 to 1962

EMPLOYMENT HISTORY:
1976 to present: Korn/Ferry International
1972 to 1976: Regional Director, U.S. Small Business Administration
1964 to 1972: Vice President, Marine Midland Bank

PRIVATE CLUBS:
Harvard Club of New York
New York Athletic Club

SPECIAL INTERESTS AND HOBBIES:
Running, power boating

REPRESENTATIVE AND SIGNIFICANT PLACEMENTS:
Thomas Donovan, Chairman and Chief Executive Officer
Mellon Bank (East), Philadelphia
Raymond Dempsey, Chairman and Chief Executive Officer
European American Bank, New York
Robert Horner, President
Citicorp Mortgage Bank
John Cook, President
Fidelity Trust Company, Boston
Richard Cooley, Chairman and Chief Executive Officer
Seafirst, Seattle

WHAT I LOOK FOR IN GENERAL IN A CANDIDATE:

I take a businessman's approach to search, meaning I always have my eye on the bottom line. This is true whether I'm recruiting for a general management position, such as a CEO, or looking for someone who's transaction oriented, such as a head of mergers and acquisitions. Whatever the position, I ask myself: "Will this candidate make a difference? Will this individual bring added value to the company?" I'm always looking for people who can take the job one step further and grow with the organization. I want people who are more than their resumes.

MINIMUM SALARY LEVEL AT WHICH I WORK:
$150,000

GEOGRAPHIC SCOPE OF RECRUITING ACTIVITIES:
Clients nationwide and in the United Kingdom

TOTAL YEARS OF RETAINER-TYPE RECRUITING EXPERIENCE:
13 years

BARBARA L. PROVUS
Principal
**Sweeney Shepherd Bueschel
Provus Harbert & Mummert
Inc.**
**One South Wacker Drive, Suite
2740**
Chicago, IL 60606
Telephone: (312) 372-1142

Date of birth: November 20, 1949
Grew up in: Evanston, IL

Photo by Stuart-Rodgers-Reilly Photography

HIGHER EDUCATION:
Russell Sage College, New York
  B.A. degree, sociology, 1971
Loyola University
  M.S. degree, industrial relations, 1978

EMPLOYMENT HISTORY:
1986 to present: Sweeney Shepherd Bueschel Provus Harbert &
  Mummert Inc.
1982 to 1986: Vice President, Lamalie Associates
1980 to 1982: Manager, Management Development, Federated Department Stores
1973 to 1980: Secretary to Consultant–Executive Search, Booz, Allen
  & Hamilton, Inc.

PRIVATE CLUBS:
Executives Club of Chicago

SPECIAL INTERESTS AND HOBBIES:
Board member of the Anti-Cruelty Society, Illinois Cancer Council,
  Association of Executive Search Consultants, and Chicago Finance
  Exchange

REPRESENTATIVE AND SIGNIFICANT PLACEMENTS:
William H. Clover, Ph.D., Director, Executive Education and Lead-
  ership Development
  TRW Inc.
Matthew P. Gonring, Director Public Relations
  USG Corporation

James R. Koehn, Director, Strategic Account Marketing
Tektronix, Inc.
Mary C. Moster, Vice President, Communications
Navistar International Transportation Corp.
Thomas Smallwood, Vice President, Director Creative
Marshall Field and Company

WHAT I LOOK FOR IN GENERAL IN A CANDIDATE:

In addition to the predefined requirements of the position
(i.e., education, industry experience, functional skills, management ability, etc.), I believe there are several additional components the successful candidate should have:

1. The ability to stretch and challenge the organization. Will
    this candidate simply fill a functional void—or will he or she
    bring additional value to the equation? Can he or she be a
    catalyst to drive the organization beyond the status quo in
    a positive, productive manner?
2. Also, the candidate must be recruitable—and for the right
    reasons. If there's no acceptable reason for the candidate to
    leave his or her current job, you may be going after the
    wrong candidate. However, part of my role is to *help* the
    candidate assess his or her current situation and to try to
    find a reason they should be attracted to my client's oppor-
    tunity.
3. Third, I look for humanness. What kind of person is he or
    she—and will they, in some small way, be able to bring good
    values and people skills to my client, beyond their technical
    abilities?

MINIMUM SALARY LEVEL AT WHICH I WORK:
$75,000

GEOGRAPHIC SCOPE OF RECRUITING ACTIVITIES:
Clients nationwide

TOTAL YEARS OF RETAINER-TYPE RECRUITING EXPERIENCE:
10 years

EDWARD A. RAISBECK, JR.
Partner
Thorndike Deland Associates
275 Madison Avenue
New York, NY 10016
Telephone: (212) 661-6200

Date of birth: December 15, 1904
Grew up in: New Jersey and
** Connecticut**

HIGHER EDUCATION:
  Dartmouth College
    B.S. degree, sociology, 1926

Photo courtesy of Thorndike Deland Associates

MILITARY:
  United States Army, 1942 to 1945:
    Colonel–Assistant to Director of Personnel, Army Service Forces,
      recruiting and commissioning civilian executives for Army Ser-
      vice Forces
    Legion of Merit

EMPLOYMENT HISTORY:
  1927 to present: Thorndike Deland Associates

PRIVATE CLUBS:
  University Club of New York
  Wee Burn Country Club, CT

SPECIAL INTERESTS AND HOBBIES:
  World War II history, photography, freshwater fishing

REPRESENTATIVE AND SIGNIFICANT PLACEMENTS:
  Chairman and Chief Executive Officer
    National department store chain
  President
    Men's specialty store chain
  Chairman and Chief Executive Officer
    Large textile corporation
  Vice Chairman
    International travel and banking company
  Chairman and Chief Executive Officer
    Mass merchandising chain

WHAT I LOOK FOR IN GENERAL IN A CANDIDATE:

To be worth hiring, an executive must excel in five qualities:
Integrity
Knowledge of the field
People skills
Energy
Dedication
Lacking any, he or she probably is a poor risk.

MINIMUM SALARY LEVEL AT WHICH I WORK:
$100,000

GEOGRAPHIC SCOPE OF RECRUITING ACTIVITIES:
Clients nationwide and in Europe, Asia, and the Caribbean

TOTAL YEARS OF RETAINER-TYPE RECRUITING EXPERIENCE:
62 years

PAUL R. RAY, JR.
President and Chief Executive Officer
Paul R. Ray & Company, Inc.
301 Commerce Street, Suite 2300
Fort Worth, TX 76102
Telephone: (817) 334-0500

Date of birth: November 6, 1943
Grew up in: Fort Worth, TX

Photo courtesy of Paul R. Ray & Company Inc.

HIGHER EDUCATION:
University of Arkansas
B.S. degree, business administration, 1966
University of Texas
J.D., 1970

EMPLOYMENT HISTORY:
1978 to present: Paul R. Ray & Company
1969 to 1978: Various Marketing and Management Positions, R.J. Reynolds Tobacco Co.

PRIVATE CLUBS:
River Crest Country Club
Fort Worth City Club
Fort Worth Club

SPECIAL INTERESTS AND HOBBIES:
Community activities specifically related to education and substance abuse

REPRESENTATIVE AND SIGNIFICANT PLACEMENTS:
Philip B. Fletcher, President and Chief Operating Officer
ConAgra, Inc.
John B. Phillips, President of Banquet Foods
ConAgra, Inc. (currently Assistant to the Chairman of ConAgra, Inc.)
Roy Satchell, President and Chief Executive Officer
Diamond Crystal Salt Company
Ronald Brinson, President and Chief Executive Officer (1988 New Orleans Businessman of the Year)
Port of New Orleans
Raymond Trapp, President–Keller Crescent Southwest
American Standard

WHAT I LOOK FOR IN GENERAL IN A CANDIDATE:

The following are the attributes I look for in candidates:

Track record of accomplishment through direct personal involvement or supervision

Upward career progression

Self-confidence, high integrity

Creativity

Personal warmth (charisma)

Analytical skills

Strategic vision

Strong indication of good communication skills from both track record and personal interview

Indication of good people skills

Stability in career and tenure with prior employers

Good appearance and stature

MINIMUM SALARY LEVEL AT WHICH I WORK:
$90,000

GEOGRAPHIC SCOPE OF RECRUITING ACTIVITIES:
Clients nationwide and in Europe and Great Britain

TOTAL YEARS OF RETAINER-TYPE RECRUITING EXPERIENCE:
11 years

PAUL R. RAY, SR.
Chairman and Founder
Paul R. Ray & Company Inc.
301 Commerce Street, Suite 2300
Ft. Worth, TX 76102
Telephone: (817) 334-0500

Date of birth: April 27, 1918
Grew up in: Minneapolis, MN

Photo courtesy of Paul R. Ray & Company Inc.

MILITARY:
Major, United States Army, 1941 to 1945

EMPLOYMENT HISTORY:
1965 to present: Paul R. Ray & Company, Inc.
1961 to 1965: Vice President, Boyden Associates Dallas
1952 to 1961: Vice President and General Manager, Burrus Mills
1948 to 1952: General Manager–Soybean Division, A.E. Staley Manufacturing Co.
1945 to 1948 & 1939 to 1941: Vice President and General Manager, Doughboy Industries
1937 to 1939: Finance Department Trainee, Cargill Inc.

PRIVATE CLUBS:
Eldorado Country Club, Palm Springs
Union League New York
Minneapolis Club
Fort Worth:
River Crest Country Club
Shady Oaks Country Club
Fort Worth City Club

SPECIAL INTERESTS AND HOBBIES:
Golf (member, United States Seniors Golf Association)

REPRESENTATIVE AND SIGNIFICANT PLACEMENTS:
Stan Pace, Chairman and Chief Executive Officer
General Dynamics
Vic Bonomo, Vice Chairman
Pepsico, Inc.
Bill Boyd, Chairman, President and Chief Executive Officer
American Standard
Tom Racciatti, President–ConAgra Grain Companies
ConAgra, Inc.

Chris Steffen, Vice President Finance (Chief Financial Officer)
Honeywell, Inc.

WHAT I LOOK FOR IN GENERAL IN A CANDIDATE:

What I look for in a candidate:

Consistent record of achievement

Verified integrity

Mandatory potential to move upward

Strong leadership qualities

Manages in an atmosphere of openness that encourages people to achieve results

Good personal communicator who insists on that from subordinates

A builder—not a caretaker—who has the necessary toughness and discipline

A risk taker who provides entrepreneurial leadership

A good delegator

A good business strategist

Someone who surrounds himself with competent, successful people

Is self-reliant and is capable of operating with independence

Has courage to be open with others and to be flexible

The word "commitment" has a special meaning to him

Puts family and friends high on his list of priorities

MINIMUM SALARY LEVEL AT WHICH I WORK:
$150,000

GEOGRAPHIC SCOPE OF RECRUITING ACTIVITIES:
Clients nationwide and in Europe, Asia, and South America

TOTAL YEARS OF RETAINER-TYPE RECRUITING EXPERIENCE:
27 years

RUSSELL S. REYNOLDS, JR.
Chairman
Russell Reynolds Associates, Inc.
200 Park Avenue
New York, NY 10166
Telephone: (212) 351-2000

Date of birth: December 14, 1931
Grew up in: Greenwich, CT

Photo by Stanford Golob

HIGHER EDUCATION:
Yale University
    B.A. degree, history, 1954

EMPLOYMENT HISTORY:
    1969 to present: Russell Reynolds Associates, Inc.
    1966 to 1969: Partner, William H. Clark Associates, Inc.
    1957 to 1966: Commercial Lending Officer–National Division, Morgan Guaranty Trust Company

SPECIAL INTERESTS AND HOBBIES:
    Director of Oppenheimer Management Corporation, Director of the Foreign Policy Association. Trustee of International House, the Greenwich Historical Society, and the Naval War College Foundation, Inc. Served as a Board member of the Greater New York Advisory Board of the Salvation Army. Former officer and director of the Association of Executive Recruiting Consultants, Inc. Also a member of the English-Speaking Union, the Pilgrims, the Society of Colonial Wars, and the Advisory Board of "Up With People." Founding President of the Society for the Archaeological Study of the Mary Rose, Inc., a fund-raising organization involved in the raising of the Mary Rose, the flagship of the English fleet, which sank in 1545.
    Sailing, skiing, squash, tennis

REPRESENTATIVE AND SIGNIFICANT PLACEMENTS:
    Barry Sullivan, Chairman and Chief Executive Officer
        First National Bank of Chicago
    William M. Agee, Executive Vice President and Chief Financial Officer to Chairman, President and Chief Executive Officer
        Bendix Corp.
    Robert P. Bauman, Chairman
        Beecham Group Plc

Jeffrey C. Tarr, Managing Partner
Odyssey Partners

WHAT I LOOK FOR IN GENERAL IN A CANDIDATE:

In general, I look for character and commitment in a candidate. I certainly want to be sure of a person's honesty and ethics. But I look for intangible qualities such as naturalness and comfortableness, an interest in people, a sense of humor, and even a nice smile. Character is an indication of a candidate's leadership potential—how well he can get along with, communicate with, and motivate people.

Commitment and performance are inextricably linked. I look for dedication, perseverance, and proven results in a candidate's previous positions. I want a person who is steady and focused. In addition, commitment to family, career, and community show a healthy balance of priorities.

MINIMUM SALARY LEVEL AT WHICH I WORK:
Varies with position

GEOGRAPHIC SCOPE OF RECRUITING ACTIVITIES:
Clients nationwide and internationally through the firm's offices worldwide

TOTAL YEARS OF RETAINER-TYPE RECRUITING EXPERIENCE:
23 years

JOHN H. ROBISON
President
Robison & McAulay
1350 First Citizens Plaza
128 South Tryon Street
Charlotte, NC 28202
Telephone: (704) 376-0059

Date of birth: September 25, 1930
Grew up in Salisbury, NC

Photo courtesy of Robison & McAulay

HIGHER EDUCATION:
University of North Carolina, Chapel Hill
    B.S. degree, business administration, 1952
Rutgers University
    Stonier Graduate School of Banking, 1964

MILITARY:
Captain, United States Army, 1952 to 1955

EMPLOYMENT HISTORY:
1979 to present: Robison & McAulay
1975 to 1979: President, Locke & Robison
1973 to 1975: Principal, Woodward, Harris, Robison & Associates
1967 to 1973: Executive Vice President, Bankers Trust of South Carolina (now NCNB)
1952 to 1967: Senior Vice President, NCNB National Bank

PRIVATE CLUBS:
Charlotte Country Club
Charlotte City Club

REPRESENTATIVE AND SIGNIFICANT PLACEMENTS:
E. P. Wilkinson (Vice Admiral Retired), President
    Institute of Nuclear Power Operations (INPO)
Theodore E. Darling, President
    Rex-Rosenlew
William F. Malec, Chief Financial Officer
    Tennessee Valley Authority (TVA)
Artur C. Marquardt, President
    Pacific Nuclear Corporation
Dr. C. Brent DeVore, President
    Otterbein College

WHAT I LOOK FOR IN GENERAL IN A CANDIDATE:

My philosophical position on selecting candidates encompasses three major elements:

The first and most critical, although the least difficult, is the assessment of technical competence. If a prospect cannot meet the level of technical competence that the position requires, his or her other qualifications, regardless of how strong, cannot compensate for this basic requirement.

The second, and most difficult, element of candidate selection falls under the category of what might be called "chemistry." This simply is matching the personal characteristics of the candidate with the client's culture. This is difficult because every client has an entirely different culture and one that is constantly subject to change by those factors which influence its corporate personality and its reason for existence. This initially requires the most complete understanding of the client culture that we can attain. It requires intensive investigation directly and then incisive interpretation of what we learned and perceive.

The final element of candidate selection is the appropriate evaluation of potential. We do not loudly protest the accusation that we are always searching for the next President of General Motors. With due regard to appropriateness, our bent is always toward the selection of middle-management candidates who can fill the position in question and also have the potential to achieve higher levels of responsibility.

The successes of our clients as measured by their long-term effectiveness in achieving their objectives is the legacy we aspire to through our recruiting philosophy and efforts.

MINIMUM SALARY LEVEL AT WHICH I WORK:
$40,000, if situation warrants it

GEOGRAPHIC SCOPE OF RECRUITING ACTIVITIES:
Clients nationwide and in England, Germany, Switzerland, Finland, and France

TOTAL YEARS OF RETAINER-TYPE RECRUITING EXPERIENCE:
16+ years

GERARD R. ROCHE
Chairman
Heidrick & Struggles, Inc.
245 Park Avenue, Suite 3230
New York, NY 10167-0152
Telephone: (212) 867-9876

Date of birth: July 27, 1931
Grew up in: Scranton, PA

HIGHER EDUCATION:
University of Scranton,
   B.S. degree, accounting, 1953
New York University,
   M.B.A. degree, 1958
University of Scranton
   Honorary Doctor of Laws, 1982

Photo courtesy of Heidrick & Struggles, Inc.

MILITARY:
Lieutenant, Junior Grade, United States Navy, Mediterranean, 1953
   to 1955

EMPLOYMENT HISTORY:
1964 to present: Heidrick & Struggles, Inc.
1959 to 1963: Marketing Director–Kordite, Mobil Oil Company
1956 to 1958: Account Executive, American Broadcasting Company
1955 to 1956: Management Trainee, American Telephone and Tel-
   egraph

PRIVATE CLUBS:
University Club
Sky Club
Yale Club
Blind Brook Country Club
Sleepy Hollow Country Club
The Loxahatchee Club
Member of the Knights of Malta

REPRESENTATIVE AND SIGNIFICANT PLACEMENTS:
John Sculley, Chairman, President and Chief Executive Officer
   Apple Computer, Inc.
Paul G. Stern, Vice Chairman and Chief Executive Officer
   Northern Telecom, Ltd.

Frank V. Cahouet, Chairman and Chief Executive Officer
  Mellon Bank Corporation
Stephen M. Wolf, Chairman and Chief Executive Officer
  UAL Corporation
C. Joseph LaBonte, President and Chief Operating Officer
  Reebok International Ltd.

WHAT I LOOK FOR IN GENERAL IN A CANDIDATE:

Energy, drive, common sense, judgment, tact, values, innovativeness, enthusiasm, creativity and balance . . . These are key elements that I look for in a candidate's personal characteristics.

Equally important are interpersonal skills of the candidates.

MINIMUM SALARY LEVEL AT WHICH I WORK:
$250,000

GEOGRAPHIC SCOPE OF RECRUITING ACTIVITIES:
Clients nationwide and in Europe and Asia

TOTAL YEARS OF RETAINER-TYPE RECRUITING EXPERIENCE:
25 years

BRENDA L. RUELLO
Partner
Heidrick and Struggles, Inc.
245 Park Avenue
New York, NY 10167
Telephone: (212) 867-9876

Date of birth: December 22, 1937
Grew up in: Florence, SC

HIGHER EDUCATION:
Syracuse University
B.A. degree, fine arts, 1959

Photo courtesy of Heidrick & Struggles, Inc.

EMPLOYMENT HISTORY:
1977 to present: Heidrick and Struggles, Inc.
1975 to 1977: Manager–Executive Search, Peat, Marwick, Mitchell & Co.
1970 to 1975: Consultant/Recruiter, Booz, Allen & Hamilton, Inc.
1964 to 1966: Consultant–Executive Search, Kiernan & Company
1959 to 1964: Personnel Training, Bloomingdale's

PRIVATE CLUBS:
The Metropolitan Club
The Board Room

SPECIAL INTERESTS AND HOBBIES:
Photography, gardening, landscaping

REPRESENTATIVE AND SIGNIFICANT PLACEMENTS:
Floyd Hall, Chief Executive Officer
Grand Union
Al Dunlap, Partner with Sir James Goldsmith and Jacob Rothschild
Hoylake Investments Ltd.
Ronald L. Ziegler, President and Chief Executive Officer
National Association of Chain Drug Stores
Ken Riedlinger, President and Chief Executive Officer
Applied Learning International, Inc. (Div. of N.E.C.)
Malcolm Schwartz, Partner-in-Charge–Financial Services Consulting, New York
Coopers & Lybrand

WHAT I LOOK FOR IN GENERAL IN A CANDIDATE:

A results-oriented leader with progressive experience in managing difficult and challenging businesses . . . The ability to generate profits in high pressure situations with diverse requirements . . . Above all, a professional manager with sound business judgment, maturity, ego under control, and the motivation and desire to not only meet but exceed corporate objectives . . . Entrepreneurial spirit, drive, and tenacity plus the acknowledgment by peers and superiors that he or she is a team player and a skilled developer of people . . . That he or she has both the professional and personal qualifications necessary to gain immediate credibility.

MINIMUM SALARY LEVEL AT WHICH I WORK:
$100,000

GEOGRAPHIC SCOPE OF RECRUITING ACTIVITIES:
Clients nationwide and in London, Paris, and Holland

TOTAL YEARS OF RETAINER-TYPE RECRUITING EXPERIENCE:
14 years

ANDREW SHERWOOD
Chairman and Chief Executive
Officer
Goodrich & Sherwood Company
521 Fifth Avenue
New York, NY 10175
Telephone: (212) 697-4131

Date of birth: January 8, 1942
Grew up in: New Jersey

Photo by Bachrach

HIGHER EDUCATION:
Nichols College
B.B.A. degree (with honors), marketing/management, 1964

EMPLOYMENT HISTORY:
1971 to present: Goodrich & Sherwood Company
1967 to 1971: Executive Vice President, Ward Clancy Associates
1965 to 1967: Director, Gilbert Lane

PRIVATE CLUBS:
Explorer's Club
University Club
Rolling Rock Club
Safari Club
Young Presidents' Organization
Economic Club
Greenwich Polo Club

SPECIAL INTERESTS AND HOBBIES:
Member National Ski Patrol, restoring vintage race cars, tennis, hunting, fishing

REPRESENTATIVE AND SIGNIFICANT PLACEMENTS:
President
Major food and consumer products company
Executive Vice President
International industrial company
Director
Board of *Fortune* 100 company
Chief Executive Officer
Major U.S. charitable service organization
Vice President
Major electronics conglomerate

WHAT I LOOK FOR IN GENERAL IN A CANDIDATE:

When interviewing a top-level candidate I look for balance and ability to communicate appropriately to the situation.

Integrity, strength of character, a good role model.

Results oriented. What has the person accomplished?

Sense of humor. Do people enjoy interacting with this person? Have they in the past?

Presence. Will this person represent the company well?

Energy. A sense of urgency, enough to do the job and motivate others without intimidating.

Vision. Will this person build for the future or just maintain?

Stamina. Enough to handle tough decisions without getting bogged down, sick, or exhausted.

Communicator. Leads by communicating and encouraging.

Loyalty. To the company, staff, customers, stockholders, and family.

Well organized. Does the individual organize thoughts and work and work well?

Leadership. A person others seek out and follow willingly.

High frustration level.

Open. To new ideas that others sponsor.

Secure. With superiors, subordinates alike.

MINIMUM SALARY LEVEL AT WHICH I WORK:
Depends on client—new client $125,000

GEOGRAPHIC SCOPE OF RECRUITING ACTIVITIES:
Clients nationwide and in Holland, Canada, the United Kingdom, and Germany

TOTAL YEARS OF RETAINER-TYPE RECRUITING EXPERIENCE:
22 years

MARY E. SHOURDS
Executive Vice President
Houze, Shourds & Montgomery, Inc.
Greater Los Angeles World Trade Center
One World Trade
Long Beach, CA 90831
Telephone: (213) 495-6495

Date of birth: November 7, 1942
Grew up in: Turtle Creek, PA

Photo courtesy of Houze, Shourds & Montgomery, Inc.

HIGHER EDUCATION:
Pepperdine University
B.S. degree, 1974
University of California, Los Angeles
M.B.A. degree, 1983

EMPLOYMENT HISTORY:
1977 to present: Houze, Shourds & Montgomery
1975 to 1977: Vice President, Hergenrather & Company
1964 to 1975: Various Human Resources Positions to Director–Human Resources Information Systems, Organization and Corporate Offices, Rockwell International

SPECIAL INTERESTS AND HOBBIES:
Founding member of the Board of Directors for the Center for Telecommunications Management at the University of Southern California and a past member of the Board of Directors of the JIA Management Group, a nationally recognized information systems consulting firm (recently acquired by A.T. Kearney)
Sailing, reading, cooking

REPRESENTATIVE AND SIGNIFICANT PLACEMENTS:
President and Chief Operating Officer
Well-established $300 million computer company
President
Newly formed business within a successful company
Vice President–Human Resources
Well-established company implementing sweeping changes in its organization

WHAT I LOOK FOR IN GENERAL IN A CANDIDATE:

Real people aren't perfect—and thus neither are real candidates. However, traits I find most important in evaluating candidates for all positions include:

A well-seasoned value system, for which there is ample evidence of having been tested successfully. I look for high standards; how (and when) a person struggles with gray areas; intellectual integrity.

A good sense of humor; that is, someone who doesn't take himself too seriously; and, along with good humor, the good judgment to know how to inject humor appropriate to the place and time.

Vision—but especially how well it is balanced by personal organization and a sense of follow-through. There is an old Zen saying that goes something like, "first enlightenment, then the laundry" which makes the point that vision, without at least the sense of what it takes to implement that vision, has limited value.

A healthy tolerance for ambiguity coupled with the ability to adapt and respond to unforeseen changes in organization, customers, markets, etc.

Self-assured and people-oriented. By this I mean that the candidate is capable of standing on his own, but at the same time, he elicits information, involvement, even criticism, from coworkers and subordinates.

Good balance—a dedication to family; a commitment to the company; and a sense of responsibility to the society at large.

MINIMUM SALARY LEVEL AT WHICH I WORK:

It varies depending on the assignment, but our minimum fee is $25,000

GEOGRAPHIC SCOPE OF RECRUITING ACTIVITIES:

Clients nationwide

TOTAL YEARS OF RETAINER-TYPE RECRUITING EXPERIENCE:

14 years

J. GERALD SIMMONS
President
Handy Associates
250 Park Avenue
New York, NY 10177
Telephone: (212) 692-2222

Date of birth: September 17, 1929
Grew up in: Miami, FL

Photo courtesy of Handy Associates

HIGHER EDUCATION:
University of Miami
B.S. degree, marketing, 1956

MILITARY:
Special Agent, United States Army (Counter Intelligence Corps),
1951 to 1953

EMPLOYMENT HISTORY:
1976 to present: Handy Associates
1973 to 1976: Vice President Marketing, Wiltek
1971 to 1973: Vice President and General Manager–Department and
Specialty Store Division, Revlon
1956 to 1971: Director of Marketing, IBM

PRIVATE CLUBS:
University Club
Sky Club
Greenwich Country Club

REPRESENTATIVE AND SIGNIFICANT PLACEMENTS:
President and Chief Executive Officer
A leading mini-computer organization
President–International
One of the country's top computer organizations
Chief Information Officer
Major commercial bank
Outside Director
Major Midwest insurance company
Outside Director
Major electrical appliance company

WHAT I LOOK FOR IN GENERAL IN A CANDIDATE:

In general, I consider three distinct areas to be important to understanding and evaluating a candidate for a senior-level position:

1. Personal attributes. This wide-ranging subject involves such things as appearance, personality, ability to communicate, initiative, intuitiveness, intelligence, and ability to react to change.
2. Personal values. This would include such important items as integrity, loyalty (up, down, and sideways), honesty and the willingness to admit when a mistake has been made—pick up the pieces and move on.
3. Professional experience. The more senior the executive position, the less important are the technical skills that may have launched someone on to a business career. It is of vital importance to understand from the candidate and from intensive reference checks his past work experiences, failures, and successes. Too many times we focus on what someone has accomplished and not how they accomplished it. In speaking with candidates and references we must sort out the contributions made by the individual versus the contributions made by others and understand what, if any, real impact the individual had on a particular event, project, or organization.

MINIMUM SALARY LEVEL AT WHICH I WORK:
$250,000

GEOGRAPHIC SCOPE OF RECRUITING ACTIVITIES:
Clients nationwide

TOTAL YEARS OF RETAINER-TYPE RECRUITING EXPERIENCE:
13 years

ROBERT W. SLATER
Managing Director/North America
Korn/Ferry International
3950 Lincoln Plaza
Dallas, TX 75201
Telephone: (214) 954-1834

Date of birth: April 18, 1938
Grew up in: Chicago, IL

HIGHER EDUCATION:
Cornell College of Iowa
Photo by Gittings
   B.A. degree, history and political science, 1960

MILITARY:
Corporal, United States National Guard, 1961 to 1965

EMPLOYMENT HISTORY:
1989 to present: Korn/Ferry International
1979 to 1989: Managing Director/N.A., SpencerStuart
1969 to 1979: Partner–Management Services, Arthur Young & Co.
1962 to 1969: Regional Personnel Manager, Allstate Insurance
1960 to 1962: Admissions Representative, Cornell College (Iowa)

PRIVATE CLUBS:
The Dallas Club

SPECIAL INTERESTS AND HOBBIES:
Tennis, fine art, history

REPRESENTATIVE AND SIGNIFICANT PLACEMENTS:
Dick Rivera, President and Chief Operating Officer
   El Chico
Clint Alston, Vice President and Director of IS Training and Development
   Philips N.V.
Jack Bell, Chief Financial Officer
   Burlington Northern
E.H. Clark, Jr., Board Member
   Kerr McGee
Phil Yarbrough, Chief Operating Officer
   CompuTrac

WHAT I LOOK FOR IN GENERAL IN A CANDIDATE:

I seek candidates with the following:

A record of accomplishment/success as well as the demonstrated ability to function effectively under both ideal and adverse conditions.

General management skills developed through leadership of a staff of people on a profit and loss/functional basis.

Functional/technical knowledge seasoned by overall experience.

Interpersonal/presentation skills, especially the ability to communicate effectively and listen well.

In addition to all of this, you've got to look at personal chemistry and how an individual will match up with the hiring executive.

MINIMUM SALARY LEVEL AT WHICH I WORK:
$100,000

GEOGRAPHIC SCOPE OF RECRUITING ACTIVITIES:
Clients nationwide

TOTAL YEARS OF RETAINER-TYPE RECRUITING EXPERIENCE:
20 years

RICHARD C. SLAYTON
President
Slayton International, Inc.
10 South Riverside Plaza, Suite
   312
Chicago, IL 60606
Telephone: (312) 648-0056

Date of birth: April 3, 1937
Grew up in: Toledo, OH

HIGHER EDUCATION:

Photo courtesy of Slayton International, Inc.

University of Michigan
   B.S. degree, industrial engineering, 1960
University of Michigan
   M.B.A. degree, 1965

MILITARY:
Rated, United States Navy, 1954 to 1965

EMPLOYMENT HISTORY:
1985 to present: Slayton International
1976 to 1985: Boyden International
   1983 to 1985: Senior Vice President and Manager Midwest Operations
   1982 to 1983: Vice President and Manager Toledo Office
   1976 to 1982: Vice President
1970 to 1976: President, Business Technology Associates
1967 to 1970: Associate Director Consulting, K.W. Tennell
1960 to 1967: Manufacturing Training Program, General Electric Company

PRIVATE CLUBS:
Metropolitan Club of Chicago
Toledo Club
Executives Club of Chicago

SPECIAL INTERESTS AND HOBBIES:
Fly fishing, skeet, bird hunting

REPRESENTATIVE AND SIGNIFICANT PLACEMENTS:
O. Lee Henry, President and Chief Executive Officer
Champion Sparkplug Company

Ronald W. Skeddle, President and Chief Executive Officer
Libbey-Owens Ford
John C. Dendy, President and Chief Executive Officer
Aerospatiale Helicopter Company
Paul S. Rappaport, Vice President, Tax Counsel
Guardian Industries, Inc.
Benjamin R. Yorks, President Mobile Hydraulics Division
Blount, Inc.

WHAT I LOOK FOR IN GENERAL IN A CANDIDATE:

Each professional is endowed at birth with certain qualities common to all—namely intelligence, energy level, appearance, common sense, and feelings. As a professional develops, other qualities are developed—namely knowledge in one's chosen field, integrity, aggressiveness, organization, written and verbal skills, decision-making ability, interpersonal relations, personality, and overall executive stature.

All of the above comprise a total composite of a candidate that, with career accomplishments, must be evaluated and matched with the particular requirements of a client.

MINIMUM SALARY LEVEL AT WHICH I WORK:
$85,000

GEOGRAPHIC SCOPE OF RECRUITING ACTIVITIES:
Clients nationwide and in Europe and the Far East

TOTAL YEARS OF RETAINER-TYPE RECRUITING EXPERIENCE:
16 years

DAVID F. SMITH
Managing Director–Northeast
  Region
Korn/Ferry International
237 Park Avenue
New York, NY 10017
Telephone: (212) 687-1834

Date of birth: July 12, 1931
Grew up in: Boston MA, and
  Providence, RI

HIGHER EDUCATION:
  Bryant College, Rhode Island
    B.S. B.A. degree, accounting, 1956

Photo courtesy of Korn/Ferry International

MILITARY:
  Staff Sergeant, United States Army, 1952 to 1953

EMPLOYMENT HISTORY:
  1979 to present: Korn/Ferry International
  1967 to 1979: Principal, Peat, Marwick, Mitchell & Co.
  1965 to 1967: Controller, Affiliated FM Insurance Co.
  1958 to 1964: Regional Accounting Manager, Allstate Insurance Co.
  1956 to 1958: Agent, Metropolitan Insurance Co.

PRIVATE CLUBS:
  Wykagyl Country Club
  Pelican Bay Country Club
  Ballymead Country Club
  New Seabury Country Club
  Union League Club

SPECIAL INTERESTS AND HOBBIES:
  Golf, travel, reading (Civil War buff)

REPRESENTATIVE AND SIGNIFICANT PLACEMENTS:
  William Waltrip, President and Chief Executive Officer
    Purolator, Inc.
  Robert E. Fowler, President and Chief Executive Officer
    Josephson International Inc.
  John W. Adamson, President
    The New York Blood Center

Thomas Steckbeck, Executive Vice President
  Toshiba America, Inc.
Claude Feninger, President–International
  ARA Services, Inc.

WHAT I LOOK FOR IN GENERAL IN A CANDIDATE:

Every executive search assignment should start with the structuring of a job specification against which subsequent selection decisions will be made. This is a dynamic document that changes frequently during the search. The successful candidate will many times not resemble the original profile. However, candidates must be measured against something, and it has to be against the profile of the executive as described by the client. The experience requirements of a position are easy to define and document. It therefore is not difficult to compare an executive's experience to that which a client needs. The experience is either there or not—of course it is always a matter of degree.

I personally spend most of my time during a search with softer issues. Will this candidate fit the culture of my client organization? What types of executives work for my client? Will this candidate fit with them? Most executives lose their positions because their style simply is wrong, not because of technical or management deficiencies.

MINIMUM SALARY LEVEL AT WHICH I WORK:
  $100,000

GEOGRAPHIC SCOPE OF RECRUITING ACTIVITIES:
  Clients nationwide

TOTAL YEARS OF RETAINER-TYPE RECRUITING EXPERIENCE:
  22+ years

ROBERT D. SPRIGGS
Chairman
Spriggs & Company Inc.
175 North Franklin Street
Chicago, IL 60606
Telephone: (312) 372-7999

Date of birth: September 10, 1929
Grew up in: Villa Grove, IL

HIGHER EDUCATION:
University of Illinois
B.S. degree, 1955
J.D., 1957

Photo by Evanston Photo Studios Inc.

MILITARY:
Communications Technician, Grade 3, United States Navy, 1951 to 1954

EMPLOYMENT HISTORY:
1967 to present: Chairman, Spriggs & Company Inc.
1964 to 1967: Vice President, Johnson & Associates, Inc.
1963 to 1964: Consultant, McKinsey & Company Inc.
1959 to 1962: Director, Industrial Relations, Robertshaw Corporation
1958 to 1959: Manager, Salaried Employment, Brunswick Corporation
1957 to 1958: Labor Relations Staff Assistant, Caterpillar Tractor

PRIVATE CLUBS:
Saddle & Cycle Club
Carlton Club
Metropolitan Club

REPRESENTATIVE AND SIGNIFICANT PLACEMENTS:
Wayne Matschullat, Chairman
Gamble Skogmo
Bruce Gescheider, President
Beatrice Meats
Robert Weisman, Vice President Marketing
Tropicana
Donald McCarthy, President
Beatrice Canada

Mark de Naray, President
Magic Pantry

WHAT I LOOK FOR IN GENERAL IN A CANDIDATE:

Beyond the usual need to determine whether a candidate has already successfully solved problems similar to the ones my client is plagued with, I concentrate principally on the "Tom Sawyer" quotient—that is to say, how effective one is in getting others to help paint the fence instead of heading for the old swimmin' hole. In the corporate world, nothing of significance is accomplished singlehandedly. The true corporate superstar has the ability to recruit willing and dedicated hands for his projects from the ranks of those whose bosses don't have to and probably won't either reward them for their efforts nor punish them if they decline to help. The ability to engender interfunctional cooperation is the very essence of the superstar. Knowing how to solve problems ranks second in importance because most failures are not rooted in esoteric miscalculations. Getting willing hands behind a solution produces the home runs for a company and a satisfied client for the search firm.

MINIMUM SALARY LEVEL AT WHICH I WORK:
$100,000

GEOGRAPHIC SCOPE OF RECRUITING ACTIVITIES:
Clients nationwide and in Canada, England, and South Africa

TOTAL YEARS OF RETAINER-TYPE RECRUITING EXPERIENCE:
25+ years

ROBERT A. STAUB
President
Staub, Warmbold & Associates,
Inc.
655 Third Avenue
New York, NY 10017
Telephone: (212) 599-4100

Date of birth: April 4, 1934
Grew up in: Scarsdale, NY

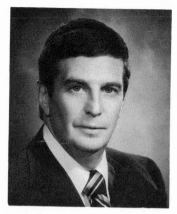

Photo by Fabian Bachrach

HIGHER EDUCATION:
University of Miami
B. B. A. degree, economics, 1956

EMPLOYMENT HISTORY:
1962 to present: Staub, Warmbold & Associates, Inc.
1960 to 1962: Associate, Burke & O'Brien
1959 to 1960: Personnel Manager, Allstate Insurance Company
1956 to 1959: Various positions in Sales, Marketing and Personnel,
Ford Motor Co.

PRIVATE CLUBS:
Metropolitan Club
Royal Cercle Gaulois
New York Athletic Club
La Gorce Country Club
Doubles

REPRESENTATIVE AND SIGNIFICANT PLACEMENTS:
Jack Hatcher, Chairman and Chief Executive Officer
H. H. Robertson Company
Ben Craig, Chairman and Chief Executive Officer
Northwestern Financial Corporation
Don Smith, President, Food Service Group
Pepsico, Inc.
Pierce Smith, Executive Vice President and Treasurer
Paine Webber, Inc.
N. Paul Masturzo, President
Max Factor

WHAT I LOOK FOR IN GENERAL IN A CANDIDATE:

In general, certain elements are critical in the evaluation of senior management candidates. I look at each prospective candidate in terms of the following:

How strong a businessman is the candidate?

How will the candidate's personality and style fit into the client organization?

How substantial is the candidate's intellect?

How do I rate the candidate's managerial capabilities?

How qualified is the candidate functionally?

How stable is the candidate's family environment?

Will the candidate's family be able to adjust to the location of his or her new position?

MINIMUM SALARY LEVEL AT WHICH I WORK:
$125,000

GEOGRAPHIC SCOPE OF RECRUITING ACTIVITIES:
Clients nationwide and in Europe and Asia

TOTAL YEARS OF RETAINER-TYPE RECRUITING EXPERIENCE:
27 years

ALLAN D. R. STERN
Managing Director
Haskell & Stern Associates Inc.
529 Fifth Avenue
New York, NY 10017
Telephone: (212) 687-7292

Date of birth: April 10, 1932
Grew up in: New York, NY

Photo courtesy of Haskell & Stern Associates Inc.

EMPLOYMENT HISTORY:
1977 to present: Haskell & Stern Associates
1968 to 1977: Vice President, Bankers Trust Company
1963 to 1968: Partner, Coleman & Company
1958 to 1963: Business Manager, Lennen & Newell
1955 to 1958: Television Account Executive, Young & Rubicam

PRIVATE CLUBS:
Century Country Club
Sunningdale Country Club

SPECIAL INTERESTS AND HOBBIES:
Golf

REPRESENTATIVE AND SIGNIFICANT PLACEMENTS:
Roger Corbett, President
  Giltspur
Ted Pappit, President
  Unigate Restaurants
Edward Legard, Managing Director
  EM Warburg Pincus
John Amerman, Chairman and Chief Executive Officer
  Mattel Inc.
James McDermott, President
  Lion Ribbon

WHAT I LOOK FOR IN GENERAL IN A CANDIDATE:

Since most of the assignments I handle are general management positions in a wide variety of industries, I look for the most important ingredients that make a good general manager. These are

Exceptional leadership and interpersonal skills

Common sense
A tangible record of accomplishments
A clear thought process
The ability to function well in crisis situations
Ability to adapt to new and unexpected situations
Promotability
Presentation skills and overall demeanor

MINIMUM SALARY LEVEL AT WHICH I WORK:
  $90,000

GEOGRAPHIC SCOPE OF RECRUITING ACTIVITIES:
  Clients nationwide and in Europe and the United Kingdom

TOTAL YEARS OF RETAINER-TYPE RECRUITING EXPERIENCE:
  12 years

CARLTON "TONY" W. THOMPSON
Senior Director
SpencerStuart
695 East Main Street
Stamford, CT 06904
Telephone: (203) 324-6333

Date of birth: November 8, 1933
Grew up in: Los Angeles

HIGHER EDUCATION:
Stanford University
B.A. degree, English, 1955

Photo by Bachrach

MILITARY:
First Lieutenant, United States Air Force, 1956 to 1959

EMPLOYMENT HISTORY:
1983 to present: SpencerStuart
1973 to 1983: Senior Vice President, Russell Reynolds Associates
1959 to 1973: Time Inc.
   1972 to 1973: Vice President Marketing, HBO
   1970 to 1972: Southern Pacific Publishing Division, Time-Life Books
   1969 to 1970: Associate Publisher Life En Espanol
   1968 to 1969: Division Manager, Time Inc.
   1966 to 1968: Division Manager, Time International
   1959 to 1966: Various sales and promotion assignments

PRIVATE CLUBS:
University Club of New York City
Country Club of New Canaan, CT

SPECIAL INTERESTS AND HOBBIES:
Fitness, tennis, reading

REPRESENTATIVE AND SIGNIFICANT PLACEMENTS:
Joe Neubauer, Chief Financial Officer to Chief Executive Officer
ARA Services
Trygve Myhron, Vice President Marketing to Chief Executive Officer
AmerTelevision Communication (Time Inc.)
Gerry Smith, Associate Publisher to Publisher
Newsweek

Bruce Aray, Publisher *Publishers Weekly* to President RR Bowker
Xerox Publishing

Terrance McGarty, Vice President Engineering Warner/American
Cable to President, Warner Electronic Home Services
Warner Communications

WHAT I LOOK FOR IN GENERAL IN A CANDIDATE:

Intelligence

Excellent interpersonal skills

Sense of humor

High energy level

Good communicator

Well groomed

MINIMUM SALARY LEVEL AT WHICH I WORK:

No minimum salary—minimum fee

GEOGRAPHIC SCOPE OF RECRUITING ACTIVITIES:

Clients nationwide and in the United Kingdom, Japan, Hong Kong,
and Mexico

TOTAL YEARS OF RETAINER-TYPE RECRUITING EXPERIENCE:

16 years

MAX M. ULRICH
President
Ward Howell International Group
  Inc.
99 Park Avenue, Suite 2000
New York, NY 10016
Telephone: (212) 697-3730

Date of birth: March 21, 1925
Grew up in: St. Petersburg, FL

Photo courtesy of Ward Howl
International Group, Inc.

HIGHER EDUCATION:
  U.S. Military Academy, West Point, New York
    B.S. degree, general engineering, 1946
  Massachusetts Institute of Technology
    M.S. degree, civil engineering, 1951

MILITARY:
  Captain, United States Army Corps of Engineers, 1946 to 1954

EMPLOYMENT HISTORY:
  1971 to present: Ward Howell International, Inc.
  1958 to 1971: Corporate Vice President, Consolidated Edison Company of New York
  1954 to 1958: Assistant to Managing Director, Edison Electric Institute

PRIVATE CLUBS:
  University Club
  Sky Club
  Rockland Country Club

SPECIAL INTERESTS AND HOBBIES:
  Golf, fishing, gardening, landscaping, reading

REPRESENTATIVE AND SIGNIFICANT PLACEMENTS:
  Chairman and Chief Executive Officer
    $9 billion insurance company
  President and Chief Executive Officer
    One of the nation's largest financial services company
  President and Chief Operating Officer
    $2 billion natural gas exploration and drilling company

President and Chief Operating Officer designate
Multibillion dollar major chemical company
President and Chief Executive Officer
Major research and engineering company

WHAT I LOOK FOR IN GENERAL IN A CANDIDATE:

In general, I look for those characteristics that are common to most successful executives. These include such things as intelligence, education, articulateness, mental toughness, aggressiveness, initiative, appearance, personality, and self-assurance.

There are five things I consider of particular importance in the evaluation of a candidate:

1. Integrity—This is of prime significance. It can be sensed in interviews but is best determined by careful referencing. I seek people whose word is their bond.
2. Leadership—Too often people confuse management with leadership. Leadership takes many forms, but to be a successful top executive requires one who is not only a good manager but also a good leader.
3. Business abilities—This is a quality that all too few executives have. Many are administrators and managers, but relatively few know how to run a business over the long term and make money.
4. Listener—The ability to listen is a key quality in an executive. One seldom learns anything while talking.
5. A failure in one's background. I personally am leery of an executive who has never experienced a failure or serious setback in his or her career. I look for people who have experienced and overcome adversity. It tells a lot about their moral fiber and helps predict their ability to handle tough problems.

MINIMUM SALARY LEVEL AT WHICH I WORK:
$100,000

GEOGRAPHIC SCOPE OF RECRUITING ACTIVITIES:
Clients nationwide and through international affiliates

TOTAL YEARS OF RETAINER-TYPE RECRUITING EXPERIENCE:
18 years

JUDITH M. VON SELDENECK
President
Diversified Search Inc.
One Commerce Square
2005 Market Street, Suite 3300
Philadelphia, PA 19103
Telephone: (215) 732-6666

Date of birth: June 6, 1940
Grew up in: High Point, NC

Photo courtesy of Diversified Search Inc.

HIGHER EDUCATION:
University of North Carolina
    B.A. degree, political science, 1962
St. Mary's Junior College
    A.A., 1960

EMPLOYMENT HISTORY:
1973 to present: Diversified Search Inc.
1963 to 1972: Executive Assistant, Vice President Walter F. Mondale

PRIVATE CLUBS:
Union League of Philadelphia
Racquet Club of Philadelphia
Philadelphia Cricket Club
Sunneybrook Golf Club
Cape May Cottagers and Beach Club

SPECIAL INTERESTS AND HOBBIES:
Golf, fishing, reading

REPRESENTATIVE AND SIGNIFICANT PLACEMENTS:
Richard Greenawalt, President
    Advanta Corporation
Ralph Thurman, President
    Rorer Pharmaceutical Company
Dr. Brenden Riley, Chairman, Department of Medicine
    St. Marys Hospital
James Malloy, Chief Executive Officer
    St. Dominics
David Lacey, President
    Philadelphia Private Industry Council

WHAT I LOOK FOR IN GENERAL IN A CANDIDATE:

I rely a lot on my first impressions and gut instincts about people, in both my professional and personal life, in things such as how they handle themselves, their appearance, demeanor, preparedness, and approach to me at our first meeting.

I think clients hiring search firms have high expectations in terms of the quality of candidates they expect to be presented with and will judge firms and recruiters on this basis. Assuming that the technical, academic, and professional qualifications meet the requirements, the trick is to sort out the winners who have the added ingredients that make them a good bet to be successful. For this added dimension, I look at how balanced their lives are. I like to see successful people who have other outside interests, whether it's family, sports, or some other success endeavor that they feel fervently about. People who have achieved success in sports while maintaining a happy family life and business success impress me. I think competitive sports is a great teacher about life and business success. I also like people who admit they go to church along with everything else in their busy life. Integrity and the highest moral standards are critical ingredients and often the hardest to verify, but in the end I have to be most comfortable with these in the candidates I present to my clients.

MINIMUM SALARY LEVEL AT WHICH I WORK:
$100,000

GEOGRAPHIC SCOPE OF RECRUITING ACTIVITIES:
Clients nationwide

TOTAL YEARS OF RETAINER-TYPE RECRUITING EXPERIENCE:
10 years

FREDERICK W. WACKERLE
Partner
McFeely Wackerle Jett
20 North Wacker Drive
Chicago, IL 60606
Telephone: (312) 641-2977

Date of birth: June 25, 1939
Grew up in: Chicago, IL

HIGHER EDUCATION:
Monmouth College, Illinois,
B.A. degree, 1961

Photo by Stuart-Rodgers-Reilly Photography

EMPLOYMENT HISTORY:
1970 to present: McFeely Wackerle Jett
1968 to 1970: Vice President, R.M. Schmitz
1966 to 1968: Partner, Berry Henderson & Aberlin
1964 to 1966: Associate, A.T. Kearney Search
1962 to 1964: Assistant Personnel Director, Stewart Warner Corp.
1961 to 1962: Operations Manager, Ball Brothers Co.

PRIVATE CLUBS:
Bob O'Link Golf Club
Moss Creek Golf Club

SPECIAL INTERESTS AND HOBBIES:
Playing tuba in a Dixieland band, collecting erotic art

REPRESENTATIVE AND SIGNIFICANT PLACEMENTS:
President, Chief Operating Officer
Fortune 500 medical equipment manufacturer
President, Chief Operating Officer
Fortune 75 conglomerate
Group Chief Executive
Fortune 100 transportation equipment manufacturer
Vice President General Manager
$300 million defense product manufacturer
President
$150 million food products manufacturer

WHAT I LOOK FOR IN GENERAL IN A CANDIDATE:
Unquestioned integrity
High work ethic

Ability to handle failure
Leadership/motivational skill
High personal values
Appropriate balance between business and family
Ability to separate and prioritize
High self-confidence
Earnest and truthful
Willingness to make a tough, or unpopular, decision

MINIMUM SALARY LEVEL AT WHICH I WORK:
$200,000

GEOGRAPHIC SCOPE OF RECRUITING ACTIVITIES:
Clients nationwide

TOTAL YEARS OF RETAINER-TYPE RECRUITING EXPERIENCE:
26 years

J. ALVIN WAKEFIELD
Managing Director
Gilbert Tweed Associates
630 Third Avenue
New York, NY 10017
Telephone: (212) 697-4260

Date of birth: July 25, 1938
Grew up in: Columbia, SC

HIGHER EDUCATION:
New York University
    B.A. degree, English literature, 1960

Photo courtesy of Gilbert Tweed Associates

MILITARY:
Captain, United States Air Force, 1961 to 1966

EMPLOYMENT HISTORY:
1986 to present: Gilbert Tweed Associates
1984 to 1986: President, Wakefield Enterprises, Inc./Wil-ern, Inc.
1981 to 1983: Vice President/Partner, Korn/Ferry International
1973 to 1981: Vice President Personnel Worldwide, Avon Products, Inc.
1970 to 1972: Manager Recruiting, Singer Company
1968 to 1970: Supervisor Employee Relations, Celanese Corporation
1966 to 1968: Employee Relations Assistant, Mobil Oil Corporation

SPECIAL INTERESTS AND HOBBIES:
Classical/jazz flute, Alpine skiing, sports cars

REPRESENTATIVE AND SIGNIFICANT PLACEMENTS:
Jack R. Plaxe, Chief Financial Officer
    City Investing Corporation (Home Insurance Company)
John Roberts, President–Canada
    National Safety Associates
Robert Young, Chief Financial Officer
    Central Vermont Public Service Corporation
Dennis DeLeon, Deputy Manhattan (NYC) Borough President
    Manhattan Borough President, City of New York
Andy Noble, Vice President Commercial Development–International
    Mary Kay Cosmetics

WHAT I LOOK FOR IN GENERAL IN A CANDIDATE:

The selection of the most appropriate executive leadership for an organization is the first, most important decision the enterprise will make—bar none.

The role of the executive recruiter then is that of a significant *partner* with the client in providing it with the best alternatives available from which to make this important selection decision. The most important criteria that I use in evaluating a candidate for my client are first, what are the specific candidate *skills* (not experience) required by the client in defining the position. Second, how do the candidate's skills compare with the specific requirements of the position. In other words, what is the competence level of each skill when matched against the skill level of the responsibility?

Once skill level and experience have been ascertained, I look for other skills: How effective a leader is this person? What are her or his management skills and experience? How creative is the person? What is the level of that creativity when measured against the pragmatic aspects of the environment the person will be working in? How strategically does the person think? Is he or she a person of the moment or has the person an ability to stretch himself or herself and those around him? Just as important as each of the above in a management role is the concept of the team player.

Finally, is this a person of honesty and integrity. Do I believe him? Will my client? Should he be believed? Finally, assessing and summarizing all of the above, how does this person measure up against the perfect 10? Although a 10 may be difficult to find in every case, my goal is to come as close to a 10 as possible in considering each candidate. Having been myself a client for over twenty years, I know that my client expects no less.

MINIMUM SALARY LEVEL AT WHICH I WORK:
$60,000

GEOGRAPHIC SCOPE OF RECRUITING ACTIVITIES:
Clients nationwide and in Europe

TOTAL YEARS OF RETAINER-TYPE RECRUITING EXPERIENCE:
6 years

PUTNEY WESTERFIELD
President
Boyden International
260 Madison Avenue
New York, NY 10016
Telephone: (212) 685-3400

Date of birth: February 9, 1930
Grew up in: New Haven, CT

HIGHER EDUCATION:
   Yale University
      B.A. degree, 1951

Photo courtesy of Boyden International

EMPLOYMENT HISTORY:
   1976 to present: Boyden International
   1973 to 1975: President, Chase World Information Corp., Chase-Manhattan
   1957 to 1973: Time Inc.
      1968 to 1973: Publisher, *Fortune*
      1966 to 1967: Assistant Publisher, *Life*
      1965 to 1967: Assistant Publisher, *Time*
      1960 to 1965: Circulation Director
   1952 to 1957: Political Officer, Department of State

PRIVATE CLUBS:
   Yale Club
   Links Club
   Union League Club of New York
   Bohemian Club
   Pacific Union
   Burlingame Club (San Francisco)
   California Club (Los Angeles)

SPECIAL INTERESTS AND HOBBIES:
   Reading, international affairs, piano, nature

REPRESENTATIVE AND SIGNIFICANT PLACEMENTS:
   President
      Apparel company
   President
      Cable television company

President
  Conglomerate
Presidents
  Alaskan Native corporations
Publisher
  Magazine company

WHAT I LOOK FOR IN GENERAL IN A CANDIDATE:

I look for evidence about a candidate in these five areas:

1. Problem solving
   Problem analysis—grasps the source of a problem
   Judgment—reaches appropriate conclusions
2. Communication
   Dialogue skills—effectiveness of discussion and expression
   Listening skills—attends to what others are saying
   Presentation skills—expresses ideas effectively
   Writing skills
3. Motivation
   Initiative—self-starting behavior
   Drive—sustained energy in accomplishing objectives
   Reaction to pressure—effective under stress
   Commitment to excellence—determination that task will
   be done well; sets high standards
4. Interpersonal
   Leadership—directs behavior of others toward achieve-
   ment of common goals by charisma, insights, or of will
   Sensitivity—demonstrates due consideration for the needs
   and feelings of others
   Impact—creates positive impression of self-assurance
5. Administrative
   Planning and organization—anticipates situations
   Delegation—assigns work and responsibility effectively

MINIMUM SALARY LEVEL AT WHICH I WORK:
$200,000

GEOGRAPHIC SCOPE OF RECRUITING ACTIVITIES:
Clients nationwide and internationally through firm's offices

TOTAL YEARS OF RETAINER-TYPE RECRUITING EXPERIENCE:
13 years

WILLIAM R. WILKINSON
Partner
Wilkinson & Ives
601 California Street, Suite 502
San Francisco, CA 94108
Telephone: (415) 433-2155

Date of birth: February 5, 1932
Grew up in: Upstate New York

HIGHER EDUCATION:
St. Lawrence University, New York
B.A. degree, sociology, 1953

Photo courtesy of Wilkinson & Ives

MILITARY:
Sergeant, United States Army, 1953 to 1955

EMPLOYMENT HISTORY:
1984 to present: Wilkinson & Ives
1971 to 1984: President, William R. Wilkinson & Company, Inc.
1961 to 1971: President (Founder), Wilkinson, Sedwick & Yelverton, Inc.
1956 to 1961: Vice President, McMurry, Hamstra & Company

PRIVATE CLUBS:
Orinda Country Club
World Trade Club
Lakeview Club

SPECIAL INTERESTS AND HOBBIES:
Author, *Executive Musical Chairs;* Association of Executive Search Consultants; California Executive Recruiters Association (Past President and Past Director); Director for three client companies
Tennis, bicycling, reading, family activities

REPRESENTATIVE AND SIGNIFICANT PLACEMENTS:
The most unusually representative and significant work I have personally handled has been conducted for one large international food and beverage products company. Since 1973 I have brought over thirty executives into the company as it has grown from $1 million to over $700 million in sales. *All* executives recruited are still employed there; almost all have had at least one promotion;

several have grown into business unit presidencies, and others have advanced to senior corporate positions.

WHAT I LOOK FOR IN GENERAL IN A CANDIDATE:

It is always our practice to spend considerable time with client executives at the outset of each new search engagement. It is important that we get to know that client well and that we become acquainted with the culture of the company.

In general, what I both look and probe for in a candidate is information that will enable me to get to know the individual and his or her background well. In this manner I can ascertain the "rightness" of the "fit" with the position and in the culture. In virtually every candidate investigation I look at characteristics such as intellect, job stability, emotional maturity, industriousness, perseverance, and the ability to get the job done with and through others. There must be a strong motivation to succeed.

If the position is Chief Executive, I superimpose on the above the following: experience and characteristics that demonstrate an ability to attain any mandate that has been established by the board; the competence to bring to the position leadership behavior, ethical values, and the sound business knowledge to encourage performance at a high level; the ability to think conceptually, plan strategically, set the pace and priorities, to focus on critical issues, and to make hard decisions; the talent to motivate others to perform at a high level; and the expertise to manage the Board. Each search may require determination of additional characteristics.

MINIMUM SALARY LEVEL AT WHICH I WORK:
$80,000

GEOGRAPHIC SCOPE OF RECRUITING ACTIVITIES:
Clients nationwide and in the United Kingdom, Italy, Norway, and Sweden

TOTAL YEARS OF RETAINER-TYPE RECRUITING EXPERIENCE:
32 years

WILLIAM H. WILLIS, JR.
President
William H. Willis, Inc.
164 Mason Street
Greenwich, CT 06830
Telephone: (203) 661-4500

Date of birth: December 19, 1927
Grew up in: Washington, DC,
    Miami Beach, FL, and
    Greenwich, CT

HIGHER EDUCATION:
    Yale University
        B.A. degree, sociology, 1949   *Photo by Gretchen Tatje*

MILITARY:
    Sergeant First Class, United States Army, 1950 to 1952

EMPLOYMENT HISTORY:
    1970 to present: William H. Willis, Inc.
    1965 to 1970: Partner, Devine, Baldwin & Willis
    1962 to 1965: Manager, Food Processing Equipment Business, AMF
    1956 to 1962: Marketing Manager, Owens-Corning Fiberglas Corpo-
        ration
    1953 to 1956: Assistant to Executive Vice President, Heidelberg East-
        ern, Inc.
    1952 to 1953: Expedition Leader, American Museum of Natural His-
        tory
    1949 to 1950: Registered Representative, Gordon Graves & Co., Inc.

PRIVATE CLUBS:
    Yale Club of New York
    Racquet and Tennis Club of New York
    The Field Club of Greenwich

SPECIAL INTERESTS AND HOBBIES:
    Tennis, squash, sailing, and travel

REPRESENTATIVE AND SIGNIFICANT PLACEMENTS:
    John Burke, President and Chief Executive Officer
        Automation Industries, Inc.

Chairman
  Christies (Christie, Manson & Woods International, Inc.)
Kay K. Clarke, Vice President–Communications
  Connecticut General Life Insurance Company
Darrell G. Medcalf, Ph.D., Vice President–Basic Sciences
  Kraft/General Foods Corporation
Edith Phelps, National Executive Director
  Girls Clubs of America, Inc.

WHAT I LOOK FOR IN GENERAL IN A CANDIDATE:

In assessing a candidate, the number one requirement I seek is integrity. Then the critical judgment has to be "Do this candidate's qualifications match the requirements of the position?" Key elements I look for include

Management and leadership skills

A record of significant and relevant accomplishments

Appropriate education

Effective communication skills

Technical qualifications and industry knowledge

Sufficient drive

A personal chemistry match with the hiring manager

A fit between the candidate and the client's corporate culture

I see effective search consultants as true matchmakers.

MINIMUM SALARY LEVEL AT WHICH I WORK:
  $75,000

GEOGRAPHIC SCOPE OF RECRUITING ACTIVITIES:
  Clients nationwide and internationally through affiliates

TOTAL YEARS OF RETAINER-TYPE RECRUITING EXPERIENCE:
  22 years

JANIS M. ZIVIC
President
The Zivic Group, Inc.
611 Washington Street, Suite 2505
San Francisco, CA 94111
Telephone: (415) 421-2325

Date of birth: July 17, 1942
Grew up in: Mt. Lebanon,
  Pittsburgh, PA

HIGHER EDUCATION:
California State College
  B.S. degree, education, 1964
University of Pittsburgh
  M.A. degree, teaching, 1967

Photo courtesy of The Zivic Group, Inc.

EMPLOYMENT HISTORY:
1983 to present: The Zivic Group, Inc.
1982 to 1983: Vice President and Managing Director, William H. Clark Associates
1978 to 1982: Vice President and Partner, Heidrick and Struggles, Inc.
1974 to 1978: Manager, Professional Recruitment, Castle & Cooke, Inc.
1973 to 1974: Placement Coordinator, Crown Zellerbach
1967 to 1972: English Teacher, Upper St. Clair High School, Pittsburgh
1964 to 1966: English Teacher, Bay Village High School, Ohio

SPECIAL INTERESTS AND HOBBIES:
Writing

REPRESENTATIVE AND SIGNIFICANT PLACEMENTS:
Representative clients:
  One of the two leading U.S. biotechnology firms
  Four of five of California's largest to most prestigious medical centers
  One of the top three world-ranked golf resorts
  One of the world's largest and oldest environmental organizations
  One of the top five private universities in the United States

WHAT I LOOK FOR IN GENERAL IN A CANDIDATE:

What I look for in a candidate is the same as what I look for in a client, because when we succeed, our candidates become our clients; therefore, we try to identify them and treat them in much the same way. That may sound simple, but I don't believe it is a standard in executive search; in trying to develop a relationship with the client, ironically, we too often short-change the candidate. Although other search firms use the same language as we do to describe their approach, the clients and competitors who know us describe the level of and equality of service we give both our candidates and our clients as unique. We actually believe that the foundation for good business is people; product, profit, strategy, business practices—they are all secondary. It is not good enough for a client to say the basis for his or her business is the people, the question is, does the practical and operational way the business is managed demonstrate that belief? I look for examples of congruence between stated values and demonstrated behavior in the client as well as the candidate. What do we look for? Integrity, appropriate technical competence, honest communication, and a team (client-candidate-consultant) approach to problem solving.

MINIMUM SALARY LEVEL AT WHICH I WORK:
$60,000

GEOGRAPHIC SCOPE OF RECRUITING ACTIVITIES:
Clients nationwide and in Europe, Japan, and Australia

TOTAL YEARS OF RETAINER-TYPE RECRUITING EXPERIENCE:
11 years

6

The Top 2 Percenters:
Who They Are

The 100 women and men who make up what we have called the Top 2 Percenters are exceptional recruiters. Many missed making the Top 100 group by only a nomination or two. They are listed alphabetically in the pages that follow.

In Chapter 7, Areas of Recruiter Specialization, the Top 2 Percenters are ranked by category along with those from the Top 100. In numerous instances, they stand higher in certain functional or organizational categories than recruiters from the Top 100. In a few categories, individuals from the Top 2 Percenter group actually lead all others in the rankings. For these reasons, employers and job seekers alike should make no distinctions in choosing between the two groups. As noted in an earlier chapter, it is nearly as likely that the right recruiter for an employer to turn to, or who presently is working on a search representing the perfect opportunity for a job seeker, is among those in the Top 2 Percenters instead of being one of the Top 100.

Akin, J.R.
President
J. R. Akin & Company
183 Sherman Street
Fairfield, CT 06430
(203) 259-0007

Arnold, William B.
President
William B. Arnold Associates, Inc.
Cherry Creek Plaza
600 South Cherry Street, Suite 1105

Denver, CO 80222
(303) 393-6662

Ballantine, Caroline
Partner
Heidrick and Struggles, Inc.
245 Park Avenue
New York, NY 10067
(212) 867-9876

Barton, Gary R.
Partner
Barton Raben, Inc.
Three Riverway, Suite 910
Houston, TX 77056
(713) 961-9111

Battalia, O. William
Chairman
Battalia & Associates, Inc.
275 Madison Avenue
New York, NY 10016
(212) 683-9440

Beall, Charles P.
Managing Partner
Beall & Company, Inc.
535 Colonial Park Drive
Roswell, GA 30075
(404) 992-0900

Beaudine, Frank R.
Chairman and Chief Executive
    Officer
Eastman & Beaudine, Inc.
1370 One Galleria Tower
13335 Noel Road
Dallas, TX 75240
(214) 661-5520

Beeson, William B.
Vice President
Lawrence-Leiter & Company
427 West 12th Street
Kansas City, MO 64105
(816) 474-8340

Berman, Frederic E.
Principal
The Berman Consulting Group
209 14th Street, Suite 307
Atlanta, GA 30309
(404) 875-8463

Bernard, Harry
Executive Vice President
Colton Bernard Inc.
417 Spruce Street
San Francisco, CA 94118
(415) 386-7400

Bishop, James F.
President
Burke, O'Brien & Bishop
    Associates, Inc.
100 Thanet Circle, Suite 108
Princeton, NJ 08540
(609) 921-3510

Bryza, Robert M.
President
Robert Lowell International, Inc.
12221 Merit Drive, Suite 1510
Dallas, TX 75251
(214) 233-2270

Clarey, Jack R.
President
Jack Clarey Associates, Inc.
1200 Shermer Road, Suite 108
Northbrook, IL 60062
(708) 498-2870

Clark, Leonard J., Jr.
Senior Vice President
Boyden International
260 Madison Avenue
New York, NY 10016
(212) 685-3400

Clovis, James R., Jr.
Vice President
Handy Associates

250 Park Avenue
New York, NY 10177
(212) 557-0400

Colton, W. Hoyt
President
W. Hoyt Colton Associates Inc.
67 Wall Street
New York, NY 10005
(212) 509-1800

Cox, Robert G.
Managing Director
A.T. Kearney, Inc.
875 Third Avenue
New York, NY 10022
(212) 980-5445

Crist, Peter D.
Managing Director and Co-Office
   Manager (Chicago)
Russell Reynolds Associates, Inc.
200 South Wacker Drive, Suite
   3600
Chicago, IL 60606
(312) 993-9696

Cronin, Richard J.
President
Hodge-Cronin & Associates, Inc.
9575 West Higgins Road, Suite 503
Rosemont, IL 60018
(708) 692-2041

Crowley, Lawrence P.
Vice President
Blendow, Crowley & Oliver, Inc.
767 Third Avenue
New York, NY 10017
(212) 838-7580

Crystal, Jonathan A.
Director
SpencerStuart
1111 Bagby Street, Suite 1616

Houston, TX 77002
(713) 225-1621

Danforth, W. Michael
Executive Vice President, Secretary,
   and Treasurer
Hyde Danforth & Co.
5950 Berkshire Lane, Suite 1600
Dallas, TX 75225
(214) 691-5966

Darter, Steven M.
Senior Vice President
People Management Inc.
10 Station Street
Simsbury, CT 06070
(203) 651-3581

Dukes, Ronald
Partner & Director
Heidrick and Struggles, Inc.
125 South Wacker Drive
Chicago, IL 60606
(312) 372-8811

Early, Bert H.
President
Bert H. Early Associates, Inc.
111 West Washington Street, Suite
   1421
Chicago, IL 60602
(312) 236-6868

Ferneborg, John R.
Partner
Smith, Goerss & Ferneborg
25 Ecker Street, Suite 600
San Francisco, CA 94105
(415) 543-4181

Finnegan, Richard G.
President and Chief Executive
   Officer
Finnegan & Associates, Inc.
36 Malago Cove Building

Palos Verdes Estates, CA 90274
(213) 337-1633

Franklin, John W., Jr.
Managing Director
Russell Reynolds Associates, Inc.
1850 K Street, NW, Suite 365
Washington, DC 20006
(202) 628-2150

Gardner, John T.
Managing Partner
Lamalie Associates, Inc.
123 North Wacker Drive
Chicago, IL 60606
(312) 782-3113

Gates, Douglas H.
Vice President
Haley BDC
500 Fifth Avenue, Suite 5416
New York, NY 10110
(212) 768-1610

Griesedieck, Joseph E., Jr.
Managing Director–U.S. Region
SpencerStuart
333 Bush Street
San Francisco, CA 94104
(415) 495-4141

Hayden, James A., Jr.
Chairman and President
Hayden Group, Inc.
10 High Street
Boston, MA 02110
(617) 482-2445

Henard, John "Jack" B., Jr.
President
Henard Associates
15303 Dallas Parkway
Dallas, TX 75248
(214) 991-7151

Hill, Lawrence "Larry" W.
Managing Director
Russell Reynolds Associates, Inc.

1000 Louisiana, Suite 4800
Houston, TX 77002
(713) 658-1776

Houze, William C.
Partner
William C. Houze & Co.
Del Amo Financial Center
21535 Hawthrone Boulevard, Suite
   209
Torrance, CA 90503
(213) 540-4442

Hunt, James E.
Partner
Kenny, Kindler, Hunt & Howe
780 Third Avenue, Suite 2202
New York, NY 10017
(212) 355-5560

Hunter, Durant "Andy"
Partner
Gardiner Stone Hunter
   International
800 Boylston Street, Suite 1580
Boston, MA 02199
(617) 338-5550

Hyde, W. Jerry
President
Hyde Danforth & Co.
5950 Berkshire Lane, Suite 1600
Dallas, TX 75225
(214) 691-5966

Iklé, A. Donald
Partner
Ward Howell International, Inc.
99 Park Avenue
New York, NY 10016
(212) 697-3730

Jeffers, Carol S.
Partner
John Sibbald Associates, Inc.
8725 West Higgins Road, Suite 575

Chicago, IL 60631
(312) 693-0575

Joys, David S.
Managing Director
Higdon, Joys & Mingle, Inc.
375 Park Avenue
New York, NY 10152
(212) 752-9780

Keating, Pierson
Partner
Nordeman Grimm
717 Fifth Avenue
New York, NY 10022
(212) 935-1000

Kepler, Charles W.
Managing Director
Russell Reynolds Associates, Inc.
200 South Wacker Drive, Suite
  3600
Chicago, IL 60606
(312) 993-9696

Kinser, Richard E.
President
Richard Kinser & Associates
405 Lexington Avenue, Suite 4515
New York, NY 10174
(212) 557-0225

Knisely, Gary
Managing Director
Johnson Smith & Knisely Inc.
475 Fifth Avenue
New York, NY 10017
(212) 686-9760

Kremple, Robert
Senior Partner
Kremple & Meade
23440 Civic Center Way, Suite 100
Malibu, CA 90265
(213) 456-6451

Krinsky, Ira
President
Ira Krinsky & Associates
2121 Avenue of the Stars, Suite 600
Los Angeles, CA 90067
(213) 551-6508

Long, Gretchen
Managing Director
Haskell & Stern Associates, Inc.
529 Fifth Avenue
New York, NY 10017
(212) 687-7292

Lorenzetti, Mark
Principal
Roberts, Ryan & Bentley
1099 Winterson Road, Suite 140
Linthicum, MD 21090
(301) 684-3400

Lotz, R. James, Jr.
President
International Management
  Advisors, Inc.
767 Third Avenue
New York, NY 10017
(212) 758-7770

Lusk, Theodore E.
Partner
Nadzam, Lusk & Associates, Inc.
3211 Scott Boulevard, Suite 205
Santa Clara, CA 95054
(408) 727-6601

Mangum, William T.
President
Thomas Mangum Company
930 Colorado Boulevard
Los Angeles, CA 90041
(213) 259-0600

Marks, Russell E., Jr.
Vice President
A.T. Kearney, Inc.

875 Third Avenue
New York, NY 10022
(212) 980-5445

Marumoto, William H.
Chairman
The Interface Group, Ltd.
1230 31st Street, N.W.
Washington, DC 20007
(202) 342-7200

Massé, Laurence R.
Partner & Manager
Ward Howell International
1250 Grove Avenue, Suite 201
Barrington, IL 60010
(708) 382-2206

McAulay, Albert L., Jr.
Vice President
Robison & McAulay
1350 First Citizens Plaza
128 South Tryon Street
Charlotte, NC 28202
(704) 376-0059

McCallister, Richard A.
Senior Vice President and
  Managing Director
Boyden International, Inc.
Three Illinois Center
303 East Wacker Drive, Suite 900
Chicago, IL 60601
(312) 565-1300

McCrea, Joan I.
President
Nursing Technomics
814 Sunset Hollow Road
West Chester, PA 19380
(215) 436-4551

Meng, Charles M.
President
Meng, Finseth & Associates, Inc.

4010 Palos Verdes Drive North,
  Suite 204
Rolling Hills, CA 90274
(213) 544-3212

Menzel, Gerald D.
Chairman
Menzel, Robinson, Baldwin, Inc.
550 West Campus Drive
Arlington Heights, IL 60004
(708) 394-4303

Miners, Richard A.
Partner and Chief Operating
  Officer
Goodrich and Sherwood
521 Fifth Avenue
New York, NY 10017
(212) 697-4131

Mingle, Larry D.
Managing Director
Higdon, Joys & Mingle, Inc.
375 Park Avenue, Suite 1601
New York, NY 10152
(212) 752-9780

Mirtz, P. John
President
Martin Mirtz Morice, Inc.
One Dock Street
Stamford, CT 06902
(203) 964-9266

Mitchell, Thomas M.
Managing Partner
Heidrick and Struggles, Inc.
300 South Grand Avenue
Los Angeles, CA 90071
(213) 625-8811

Moody, Norman F.
Chairman
Paul Stafford Associates, Ltd.
261 Madison Avenue

New York, NY 10016
(212) 983-6666

Moore, Thomas R.
Executive Director
Ketchum, Inc.
1030 Fifth Avenue
Pittsburgh, PA 15219
(412) 281-1481

Nitchke, Howard D.
President
Deane, Howard & Simon, Inc.
81 Wethersfield Avenue
Hartford, CT 06114
(203) 727-0721

Ott, George W.
President and Chief Executive
  Officer
Ott & Hansen, Inc.
136 South Oak Knoll, Suite 300
Pasadena, CA 91101
(818) 578-0551

Posner, Gary J.
Vice President
George Kaludis Associates
2505 Hillsboro Road, Suite 302
Nashville, TN 37212
(615) 297-3880

Raben, Steven A.
Partner
Barton Raben, Inc.
Three Riverway, Suite 910
Houston, TX 77056
(713) 961-9111

Rattner, Kenneth L.
Partner
Heidrick and Struggles, Inc.
125 South Wacker Drive, Suite
  2800
Chicago, IL 60606
(312) 372-8811

Raynolds, Eleanor H.
Partner
Ward Howell International, Inc.
99 Park Avenue
New York, NY 10016
(212) 697-3730

Reese, Charles D., Jr.
President
Reese Associates
10475 Perry Highway
Wexford, PA 15090
(412) 935-8644

Reeves, William B.
Managing Vice President and
  Partner
Korn/Ferry International
233 Peachtree, NE, Suite 701
Atlanta, GA 30303
(404) 577-7542

Regehly, Herbert
President
Innkeeper's Management Corp.
14 East 60th Street, Suite 1210
New York, NY 10022
(212) 838-9535

Reynolds, Sydney
President
Sydney Reynolds Associates, Inc.
342 Madison Avenue, Suite 2001
New York, NY 10173
(212) 697-8682

Richard, Albert L., Jr.
President
Human Resources, Inc.
7 James Street
Providence, RI 02903
(401) 861-2550

Richardson, James "Rick" L.
Director
SpencerStuart

695 East Main Street
Stamford, CT 06904
(203) 324-6333

Robertson, Darrell G.
Vice President
Western Reserve Search Associates,
Inc.
843 Ghent Square, Suite 9
Bath, OH 44210
(216) 666-0600

Rollo, Robert S.
Managing Director
Korn/Ferry International
1800 Century Park East
Los Angeles, CA 90067
(213) 879-1834

Rossi, George
Partner
Heidrick and Struggles, Inc.
One Post Office Square
Boston, MA 02109
(617) 423-1140

Ryan, Joseph B.
Vice President
The Cambridge Group Ltd.
830 Post Road East
Westport, CT 06880
(203) 226-4243

Sbarbaro, Richard
President
Lauer, Sbarbaro Associates, Inc.
Three First National Plaza, Suite
650
Chicago, IL 60602
(312) 372-7050

Schmidt, James M.
Vice President
Cejka & Company
222 South Central, Suite 400

St. Louis, MO 63105
(314) 726-1603

Schwartz, Ben
Vice President
Harper Associates
29870 Middlebelt
Farmington Hills, MI 48018
(313) 932-1170

Seiden, Steven A.
President
Seiden Associates, Inc.
375 Park Avenue
New York, NY 10021
(212) 688-8383

Seitchik, Jack
President
Seitchik Corwin and Seitchik
1830 Jackson Street
San Francisco, CA 94109
(415) 928-5717

Silverman, Gary W.
Managing Director
Korn/Ferry International
120 South Riverside Plaza
Chicago, IL 60606
(312) 726-1841

Slowik, Edward C.
Managing Director–U.S. Financial
Services
SpencerStuart
55 East 52nd Street
New York, NY 10055
(212) 407-0221

Splaine, Charles E.
President
Splaine & Associates
15951 Los Gatos Boulevard
Los Gatos, CA 95032
(408) 354-3664

Stanton, John S.
Managing Director
Russell Reynolds Associates, Inc.
200 South Wacker Drive, Suite
    3600
Chicago, IL 60606
(312) 993-9696

Stiles, Linford E.
Partner
Ward Howell International
Four Landmark Square
Stamford, CT 06901
(203) 964-1481

Sur, William K.
President
Stricker, Sur & Associates
717 Fifth Avenue
New York, NY 10022
(212) 308-7272

Sweet, Charles W.
President, Kearney Executive
    Search
A.T. Kearney, Inc.
222 South Riverside Plaza
Chicago, IL 60606
(312) 993-6650

Travis, John A.
President
Travis & Company Inc.
325 Boston Post Road
Sudbury, MA 01770
(508) 443-4000

Tweed, Janet
Principal/Cofounder
Gilbert Tweed Associates
630 Third Avenue
New York, NY 10017
(212) 697-4260

Vernon, Jack H.
Managing Director
Russell Reynolds Associates, Inc.
Old City Hall
45 School Street
Boston, MA 02108
(617) 523-1111

Weiner, Harvey M.
President
Search America
12700 Hillcrest Road, Suite 172
Dallas, TX 75230
(214) 233-3302

Williams, Donald C.
President
Donald Williams Associates, Inc.
303 West Madison Avenue, Suite
    1150
Chicago, IL 60606
(312) 332-6211

Zay, Thomas C.
President
Thomas C. Zay & Company, Inc.
Two Midtown Plaza, Suite 1740
1360 Peachtree Street N.E.
Atlanta, GA 30309
(404) 876-9986

7

Areas of Recruiter Specialization

This chapter categorizes and ranks every recruiter qualifying for this book according to areas of organizational or industry specialization and respective functional competencies. A recruiter's standing in each category is a function of the number of nominating points from both clients and peers, as well as their own individual ranking of organizational and functional skills. Names are listed in order beginning at the top of the left column and continuing down the right. Those individuals whose names appear in boldface type are from the Top 100 group; the others qualify as Top 2 Percenters.

ORGANIZATIONAL OR INDUSTRY SPECIALIZATION
(Sequence of categories)

Categories	
• Aerospace	• Food and kindred products
• Agriculture/Forestry/Fishing	• Government agencies/
• Associations/Societies/Nonprofit organizations	Municipalities
	• Health services/Hospitals
• Banks, savings and loans/Other financial institutions (including investment Banking)	• Holding companies
	• Hotels/Resorts/Clubs
	• Insurance
	• Law/Accounting/Consulting firms
• Chemical and allied products	
• Communications/ Telecommunications	• Lumber and wood products
	• Machinery, except Electrical
• Computer software	• Measuring, analyzing, controlling, and photographic instruments
• Construction	
• Eating and drinking places	
• Electrical and electronic machinery	• Mining
	• Office machinery/Computers
• Energy	• Packaging
• Fabricated metal products	*(continued)*

Categories (*continued*)

- Paper and allied products
- Perfume/Cosmetics/Toilet goods
- Pharmaceutical/Medical products
- Primary metal industries
- Publishing and printing
- Radio and television broadcasting
- Real estate
- Retail
- Rubber and plastic products

- Security and commodity brokers/Dealers and exchanges
- Textiles and apparel
- Tobacco and liquor
- Transportation by air, rail, or water
- Transportation equipment
- Universities/Colleges
- Wholesale trade

AEROSPACE

Frederick W. Wackerle
McFeely Wackerle Jett, Chicago
Otis H. Bowden, II
Bowden & Company, Inc., Cleveland
Paul R. Ray, Sr.
Paul R. Ray & Company, Inc., Fort Worth
Michael S. Dunford
Michael S. Dunford, Inc., Glen Ellyn, IL
Leon A. Farley
Leon A. Farley Associates, San Francisco
Ferdinand Nadherny
Russell Reynolds Associates, Inc., Chicago
Charles P. Beall
Beall & Company, Inc., Roswell, GA
William A. Hertan
Executive Manning Corp., Ft. Lauderdale
Robert Kremple
Kremple & Meade, Malibu, CA
Nelson W. Gibson
N.W. Gibson International, Los Angeles
William C. Houze
William C. Houze & Co., Torrance, CA

E. Pendleton James
Pendleton James & Associates, Inc., New York
Sydney Reynolds
Sydney Reynolds Associates, Inc., New York
Nancy F. Keithley
Ernst & Young, Cleveland
William T. Mangum
Thomas Mangum Company, Los Angeles
George W. Ott
Ott & Hansen, Inc., Pasadena, CA
O.D. "Dan" Cruse
SpencerStuart, Dallas
James M. Montgomery
Houze, Shourds & Montgomery, Inc., Long Beach, CA
Allan D. R. Stern
Haskell & Stern Associates, Inc., New York
J. R. Akin
J. R. Akin & Company, Fairfield, CT
Frederic E. Berman
The Berman Consulting Group, Atlanta
Robert M. Bryza
Robert Lowell International, Inc., Dallas

Richard E. Kinser
  Richard Kinser & Associates, New
  York
David E. Chambers
  David Chambers & Associates, Inc.,
  New York
Theodore E. Lusk
  Nadzam, Lusk & Associates, Inc.,
  Santa Clara, CA
Darrell G. Robertson
  Western Reserve Search Associates,
  Inc., Bath, OH
Richard M. McFarland
  Brissenden, McFarland, Wagoner,
  & Fuccella, Inc., Stamford, CT
Charles M. Meng
  Meng, Finseth & Associates, Inc.,
  Rolling Hills, CA
Lawrence "Larry" W. Hill
  Russell Reynolds Associates, Inc.,
  Houston
Carl W. Menk
  Canny, Bowen Inc., New York
Skott B. Burkland
  Haley BDC, New York
Michael J. Hoevel
  Poirier, Hoevel & Company, Los
  Angeles
Robert G. Cox
  A.T. Kearney, Inc., New York
W. Michael Danforth
  Hyde Danforth & Co., Dallas
Lawrence J. Holmes
  Consulting Associates, Inc.,
  Columbia, MD
John S. Stanton
  Russell Reynolds Associates, Inc.,
  Chicago
Richard C. Slayton
  Slayton International, Inc., Chicago
David H. Charlson
  Chestnut Hill Partners, Deerfield,
  IL
W. Jerry Hyde
  Hyde Danforth & Co., Dallas
William B. Arnold
  William B. Arnold Associates, Inc.,
  Denver

Donald C. Williams
  Donald Williams Associates, Inc.,
  Chicago
P. Anthony Price
  Russell Reynolds Associates Inc.,
  San Francisco
James F. Bishop
  Burke, O'Brien & Bishop
  Associates, Inc., Princeton, NJ
John "Jack" B. Henard, Jr.
  Henard Associates, Dallas
Robert W. Dingman
  Robert W. Dingman Company, Inc.,
  Westlake Village, CA
William H. Marumoto
  The Interface Group, Ltd.,
  Washington, DC
David O. Harbert
  Sweeney Shepherd Bueschel Provus
  Harbert & Mummert, Inc.,
  Chicago
Andrew D. Hart
  Russell Reynolds Associates, Inc.,
  New York
Laurence Massé
  Ward Howell International,
  Barrington, IL
George Rossi
  Heidrick and Struggles, Inc.,
  Boston

AGRICULTURE/FORESTRY/ FISHING

William R. Wilkinson
  Wilkinson & Ives, San Francisco
Dayton Ogden
  SpencerStuart, New York
William B. Arnold
  William B. Arnold Associates, Inc.,
  Denver
Peter D. Crist
  Russell Reynolds Associates, Inc.,
  Chicago

ASSOCIATIONS/SOCIETIES/ NONPROFIT ORGANIZATIONS

Robert W. Dingman
  Robert W. Dingman Company, Inc.,
  Westlake Village, CA

William J. Bowen
Heidrick and Struggles, Inc., Chicago
John S. Lloyd
Witt Associates, Inc., Oak Brook, IL
Michael D. Caver
Heidrick and Struggles, Inc., Chicago
Ira Krinsky
Ira Krinsky Associates, Los Angeles
Janis M. Zivic
The Zivic Group, Inc., San Francisco
Richard M. McFarland
Brissenden, McFarland, Wagoner, & Fuccella, Inc., Stamford, CT
Jacques C. Nordeman
Nordeman Grimm, Inc., New York
Frank A. Garofolo
Garofolo, Curtiss & Company, Ardmore, PA
John H. Callen, Jr.
Ward Howell International, Inc., New York
Stephen A. Garrison
Ward Howell International, Inc., Dallas
Jonathan E. McBride
McBride Associates, Inc., Washington, DC
David R. Peasback
Canny, Bowen Inc., New York
Kenneth L. Rattner
Heidrick and Struggles, Inc., Chicago
Paul R. Ray, Jr.
Paul R. Ray & Company, Inc., Fort Worth
Caroline Ballantine
Heidrick and Struggles, Inc., New York
E. Pendleton James
Pendleton James & Associates, Inc., New York
Judith M. von Seldeneck
Diversified Search, Inc., Philadelphia
William B. Arnold
William B. Arnold Associates, Inc., Denver

Dayton Ogden
SpencerStuart, New York
Thomas R. Moore
Ketchum, Inc., Pittsburgh
Richard Sbarbaro
Lauer, Sbarbaro Associates, Inc., Chicago
Robert M. Flanagan
Paul Stafford Associates, Ltd., New York
Millington F. McCoy
Gould & McCoy, Inc., New York
William H. Willis, Jr.
William H. Willis, Inc., Greenwich, CT
Pierson Keating
Nordeman Grimm, New York
Robert G. Cox
A.T. Kearney, Inc., New York
Eleanor H. Raynolds
Ward Howell International, Inc., New York
William H. Marumoto
The Interface Group, Ltd., Washington, DC
William H. Billington, Jr.
Billington, Fox & Ellis, Inc., Chicago
Russell E. Marks, Jr.
A.T. Kearney, Inc., New York
Jack H. Vernon
Russell Reynolds Associates, Inc., Boston

BANKS/SAVINGS AND LOANS/ OTHER FINANCIAL INSTITUTIONS (*INCLUDING INVESTMENT BANKING*)

Gerard R. Roche
Heidrick and Struggles, Inc., New York
Windle B. Priem
Korn/Ferry International, New York
D. John Ingram
Ingram Inc., New York
Leon A. Farley
Leon A. Farley Associates, San Francisco

George W. Henn, Jr.
G.W. Henn & Company, Columbus, OH

Judith M. von Seldeneck
Diversified Search, Inc., Philadelphia

Jacques C. Nordeman
Nordeman Grimm, Inc., New York

Robert W. Slater
Korn/Ferry International, Dallas

Russell S. Reynolds, Jr.
Russell Reynolds Associates, Inc., New York

Richard Sbarbaro
Lauer, Sbarbaro Associates, Inc., Chicago

Ferdinand Nadherny
Russell Reynolds Associates, Inc., Chicago

Paul R. Ray, Sr.
Paul R. Ray & Company, Inc., Fort Worth

Jacques P. Andre
Paul R. Ray & Company, Inc., New York

David H. Charlson
Chestnut Hill Partners, Deerfield, IL

W. Hoyt Colton
W. Hoyt Colton Associates Inc., New York

H. Leland Getz
Higdon, Joys & Mingle, Inc., New York

Millington F. McCoy
Gould & McCoy, Inc., New York

Robert A. Staub
Staub, Warmbold & Associates, Inc., New York

Robert M. Flanagan
Paul Stafford Associates, Ltd., New York

Richard M. Ferry
Korn/Ferry International, Los Angeles

Caroline Ballantine
Heidrick and Struggles, Inc., New York

Howard Bratches
Thorndike Deland Associates, New York

Michael J. Hoevel
Poirier, Hoevel & Company, Los Angeles

Joseph P. McGinley
SpencerStuart, New York

Lawrence F. Nein
Nordeman Grimm, Inc., Chicago

Thomas H. Ogdon
The Ogdon Partnership, New York

Allan D. R. Stern
Haskell & Stern Associates, Inc., New York

Skott B. Burkland
Haley BDC, New York

Ralph E. Dieckmann
Dieckmann & Associates, Ltd., Chicago

Henry G. Higdon
Higdon, Joys & Mingle, Inc., New York

Roger M. Kenny
Kenny, Kindler, Hunt & Howe, New York

Sydney Reynolds
Sydney Reynolds Associates, Inc., New York

Charles P. Beall
Beall & Company, Inc., Roswell, GA

David E. Chambers
David Chambers & Associates, Inc., New York

William B. Clemens, Jr.
Norman Broadbent International, New York

David H. Hoffmann
DHR International, Inc., Chicago

Durant "Andy" Hunter
Gardiner Stone Hunter International, Boston

Richard E. Kinser
Richard Kinser & Associates, New York

Robert L. Heidrick
The Heidrick Partners, Inc., Chicago

Carl W. Menk
Canny, Bowen Inc., New York
Martin H. Bauman
Martin H. Bauman Associates, Inc.,
New York
Jonathan E. McBride
McBride Associates, Inc.,
Washington, DC
Dayton Ogden
SpencerStuart, New York
W. Michael Danforth
Hyde Danforth & Co., Dallas
Steven M. Darter
People Management Inc., Simsbury,
CT
Jay Gaines
Jay Gaines & Company, Inc., New
York
James E. Hunt
Kenny, Kindler, Hunt & Howe,
New York
Edward R. Howe, Jr.
Diversified Search, Inc.,
Philadelphia
David S. Joys
Higdon, Joys & Mingle, Inc., New
York
Norman F. Moody
Paul Stafford Associates, Ltd., New
York
Albert L. McAulay, Jr.
Robison & McAulay, Charlotte, NC
Frank R. Beaudine
Eastman & Beaudine, Inc., Dallas
Michael S. Dunford
Michael S. Dunford, Inc., Glen
Ellyn, IL
William E. Gould
Gould & McCoy Inc., New York
Mark Lorenzetti
Roberts, Ryan & Bentley,
Linthicum, MD
Howard D. Nitchke
Deane, Howard & Simon, Inc.,
Hartford, CT
James M. Montgomery
Houze, Shourds & Montgomery,
Inc., Long Beach, CA

George W. Ott
Ott & Hansen, Inc., Pasadena, CA
Andrew Sherwood
Goodrich and Sherwood Company,
New York
Charles W. Sweet
A.T. Kearney, Inc., Chicago
William H. Willis, Jr.
William H. Willis, Inc., Greenwich,
CT
J. Alvin Wakefield
Gilbert Tweed Associates, Inc., New
York
James H. Cornehlsen
Heidrick and Struggles, Inc., New
York
W. Jerry Hyde
Hyde Danforth & Co., Dallas
Gary Knisely
Johnson Smith & Knisely Inc., New
York
Thomas C. Zay
Thomas C. Zay & Company, Inc.,
Atlanta
Robert W. Dingman
Robert W. Dingman Company, Inc.,
Westlake Village, CA
Gary R. Barton
Barton Raben, Inc., Houston
Peter D. Crist
Russell Reynolds Associates, Inc.,
Chicago
Jonathan A. Crystal
SpencerStuart, Houston
Robert G. Cox
A.T. Kearney, Inc., New York
Richard A. McCallister
Boyden International, Inc., Chicago
Larry D. Mingle
Higdon, Joys & Mingle, Inc., New
York
Robert S. Rollo
Korn/Ferry International, Los
Angeles
Edward C. Slowik
SpencerStuart, New York
James A. Hayden, Jr.
Hayden Group, Inc., Boston

Gretchen Long
Haskell & Stern Associates, Inc.,
New York
William B. Arnold
William B. Arnold Associates, Inc.,
Denver
William H. Billington, Jr.
Billington, Fox & Ellis, Inc.,
Chicago
Sandford I. Gadient
Huntress Real Estate Executive
Search, Kansas City, MO
Howard D. Nitchke
Deane, Howard & Simon, Inc.,
Hartford, CT
Gardner W. Heidrick
The Heidrick Partners, Inc.,
Chicago
Richard K. Ives
Wilkinson & Ives, San Francisco
Clarence E. McFeely
McFeely Wackerle Jett, Chicago
Mary E. Shourds
Houze, Shourds & Montgomery,
Inc., Long Beach, CA
Douglas H. Gates
Haley BDC, New York
William B. Reeves
Korn/Ferry International, Atlanta
James "Rick" L. Richardson
SpencerStuart, Stamford, CT
Otis H. Bowden, II
Bowden & Company, Inc.,
Cleveland
John R. Ferneborg
Smith, Goerss & Ferneborg, San
Francisco
Nelson W. Gibson
N.W. Gibson International, Los
Angeles
Lawrence J. Holmes
Consulting Associates, Inc.,
Columbia, MD
Darrell G. Robertson
Western Reserve Search Associates,
Inc., Bath, OH
Putney Westerfield
Boyden International Inc., New
York

Pierson Keating
Nordeman Grimm, New York
Joseph E. Griesedieck, Jr.
SpencerStuart, San Francisco
Charles M. Meng
Meng, Finseth & Associates, Inc.,
Rolling Hills, CA
P. Anthony Price
Russell Reynolds Associates Inc.,
San Francisco
John H. Robison
Robison & McAulay, Charlotte, NC
J.R. Akin
J.R. Akin & Company, Fairfield, CT
James R. Clovis, Jr.
Handy Associates, New York
Richard A. Miners
Goodrich and Sherwood, New York
George Rossi
Heidrick and Struggles, Inc.,
Boston
Gary W. Silverman
Korn/Ferry International, Chicago
Janis M. Zivic
The Zivic Group, Inc., San
Francisco
William A. Hertan
Executive Manning Corp., Fort
Lauderdale
John S. Stanton
Russell Reynolds Associates, Inc.,
Chicago
William B. Beeson
Lawrence-Leiter & Company,
Kansas City, MO
Mike Jacobs
Thorne, Brieger Associates Inc.,
New York
Peter G. Grimm
Nordeman Grimm, Inc., New York
Steven A. Seiden
Seiden Associates, Inc., New York
Theodore Jadick
Heidrick and Struggles, Inc., New
York
Andrew D. Hart
Russell Reynolds Associates, Inc.,
New York

Lawrence "Larry" W. Hill
Russell Reynolds Associates, Inc.,
Houston
Steven A. Raben
Barton Raben, Inc., Houston
Brenda L. Ruello
Heidrick and Struggles, Inc., New
York
Janet Tweed
Gilbert Tweed Associates, New
York
Frederick W. Wackerle
McFeely Wackerle Jett, Chicago
E. Pendleton James
Pendleton James & Associates, Inc.,
New York
Eleanor H. Raynolds
Ward Howell International, Inc.,
New York
Thomas M. Mitchell
Heidrick and Struggles, Inc., Los
Angeles
Russell E. Marks, Jr.
A.T. Kearney, Inc., New York
William T. Mangum
Thomas Mangum Company, Los
Angeles
Richard C. Slayton
Slayton International, Inc., Chicago
P. John Mirtz
Martin Mirtz Morice, Inc.,
Stamford, CT
R. James Lotz, Jr.
International Management
Advisors, Inc., New York
Joseph B. Ryan
The Cambridge Group Ltd.,
Westport, CT

CHEMICAL AND ALLIED PRODUCTS

Otis H. Bowden, II
Bowden & Company, Inc.,
Cleveland
Richard M. McFarland
Brissenden, McFarland, Wagoner,
& Fuccella, Inc., Stamford, CT

Nancy F. Keithley
Ernst & Young, Cleveland
Lynn Tendler Bignell
Gilbert Tweed Associates, Inc., New
York
Lawrence F. Nein
Nordeman Grimm, Inc., Chicago
Gerard R. Roche
Heidrick and Struggles, Inc., New
York
William A. Hertan
Executive Manning Corp., Fort
Lauderdale
Gerald D. Menzel
Menzel, Robinson, Baldwin, Inc.,
Arlington Heights, IL
Barbara L. Provus
Sweeney Shepherd Bueschel Provus
Harbert & Mummert, Inc.,
Chicago
Stephen A. Garrison
Ward Howell International, Inc.,
Dallas
Max M. Ulrich
Ward Howell International, Inc.,
New York
William E. Gould
Gould & McCoy Inc., New York
Robert D. Spriggs
Spriggs & Company, Inc., Chicago
R. Paul Kors
Kors Montgomery International,
Houston
David H. Charlson
Chestnut Hill Partners, Deerfield,
IL
Lawrence P. Crowley
Blendow, Crowley & Oliver Inc.,
New York
Martin H. Bauman
Martin H. Bauman Associates, Inc.,
New York
Robert M. Bryza
Robert Lowell International, Inc.,
Dallas
David H. Hoffmann
DHR International, Inc., Chicago
Joseph P. McGinley
SpencerStuart, New York

Andrew D. Hart
Russell Reynolds Associates, Inc., New York
Ferdinand Nadherny
Russell Reynolds Associates, Inc., Chicago
Janet Tweed
Gilbert Tweed Associates, New York
John A. Travis
Travis & Company Inc., Sudbury, MA
William B. Beeson
Lawrence-Leiter & Company, Kansas City, MO
Frederick W. Wackerle
McFeely Wackerle Jett, Chicago
Howard D. Nitchke
Deane, Howard & Simon, Inc., Hartford, CT
David R. Peasback
Canny, Bowen Inc., New York
Paul R. Ray, Sr.
Paul R. Ray & Company, Inc., Fort Worth
Leonard J. Clark, Jr.
Boyden International, New York
David O. Harbert
Sweeney Shepherd Bueschel Provus Harbert & Mummert, Inc., Chicago
Richard J. Cronin
Hodge-Cronin & Associates, Inc., Rosemont, IL
Andrew Sherwood
Goodrich and Sherwood Company, New York
Peter D. Crist
Russell Reynolds Associates, Inc., Chicago
Larry D. Mingle
Higdon, Joys & Mingle, Inc., New York
Michael S. Dunford
Michael S. Dunford, Inc., Glen Ellyn, IL
William K. Sur
Stricker, Sur & Associates, New York

Steven M. Darter
People Management Inc., Simsbury, CT
Douglas H. Gates
Haley BDC, New York
Skott B. Burkland
Haley BDC, New York
Carl W. Menk
Canny, Bowen Inc., New York
Gary R. Barton
Barton Raben, Inc., Houston
Laurence Massé
Ward Howell International, Barrington, IL
Clarence E. McFeely
McFeely Wackerle Jett, Chicago
William H. Willis, Jr.
William H. Willis, Inc., Greenwich, CT
P. John Mirtz
Martin Mirtz Morice, Inc., Stamford, CT
Russell E. Marks, Jr.
A.T. Kearney, Inc., New York
Steven A. Raben
Barton Raben, Inc., Houston
Millington F. McCoy
Gould & McCoy, Inc., New York

COMMUNICATIONS/ TELECOMMUNICATIONS

Gerard R. Roche
Heidrick and Struggles, Inc., New York
Leon A. Farley
Leon A. Farley Associates, San Francisco
Carlton W. "Tony" Thompson
SpencerStuart, New York
Roger M. Kenny
Kenny, Kindler, Hunt & Howe, New York
Gary Knisely
Johnson Smith & Knisely Inc., New York
Charles P. Beall
Beall & Company, Inc., Roswell, GA

Jacques C. Nordeman
  Nordeman Grimm, Inc., New York
James H. Cornehlsen
  Heidrick and Struggles, Inc., New
  York
Gary R. Barton
  Barton Raben, Inc., Houston
Mary E. Shourds
  Houze, Shourds & Montgomery,
  Inc., Long Beach, CA
Robert Kremple
  Kremple & Meade, Malibu, CA
J. R. Akin
  J. R. Akin & Company, Fairfield,
  CT
John R. Ferneborg
  Smith, Goerss & Ferneborg, San
  Francisco
Peter G. Grimm
  Nordeman Grimm, Inc., New York
William A. Hertan
  Executive Manning Corp., Fort
  Lauderdale
Richard Sbarbaro
  Lauer, Sbarbaro Associates, Inc.,
  Chicago
Michael J. Hoevel
  Poirier, Hoevel & Company, Los
  Angeles
Thomas H. Ogdon
  The Ogdon Partnership, New York
William T. Mangum
  Thomas Mangum Company, Los
  Angeles
William K. Sur
  Stricker, Sur & Associates, New
  York
Robert E. Lamalie
  Robert Lamalie Inc., Marco Island,
  FL
Frederic E. Berman
  The Berman Consulting Group,
  Atlanta
John "Jack" B. Henard, Jr.
  Henard Associates, Dallas
Lawrence J. Holmes
  Consulting Associates, Inc.,
  Columbia, MD

William C. Houze
  William C. Houze & Co., Torrance,
  CA
Richard K. Ives
  Wilkinson & Ives, San Francisco
Putney Westerfield
  Boyden International Inc., New
  York
David H. Charlson
  Chestnut Hill Partners, Deerfield,
  IL
Jay Gaines
  Jay Gaines & Company, Inc., New
  York
Nelson W. Gibson
  N.W. Gibson International, Los
  Angeles
Charles E. Splaine
  Splaine & Associates, Los Gatos,
  CA
Clarence E. McFeely
  McFeely Wackerle Jett, Chicago
James M. Montgomery
  Houze, Shourds & Montgomery,
  Inc., Long Beach, CA
Brenda L. Ruello
  Heidrick and Struggles, Inc., New
  York
Allan D. R. Stern
  Haskell & Stern Associates, Inc.,
  New York
George Rossi
  Heidrick and Struggles, Boston
James R. Clovis, Jr.
  Handy Associates, New York
R. G. Finnegan
  Finnegan & Associates, Inc., Palos
  Verdes Estates, CA
David H. Hoffmann
  DHR International, Inc., Chicago
R. James Lotz, Jr.
  International Management
  Advisors, Inc., New York
Robert G. Cox
  A.T. Kearney, Inc., New York
Richard J. Cronin
  Hodge-Cronin & Associates, Inc.,
  Rosemont, IL

Steven A. Raben
   Barton Raben, Inc., Houston
Robert W. Dingman
   Robert W. Dingman Company, Inc.,
      Westlake Village, CA
Richard E. Kinser
   Richard Kinser & Associates, New
      York
Joseph B. Ryan
   The Cambridge Group Ltd.,
      Westport, CT
David F. Smith
   Korn/Ferry International, New
      York
Frank R. Beaudine
   Eastman & Beaudine, Inc., Dallas
Russell E. Marks, Jr.
   A.T. Kearney, Inc., New York
Charles W. Kepler
   Russell Reynolds Associates, Inc.,
      Chicago
Richard C. Slayton
   Slayton International, Inc., Chicago
David E. Chambers
   David Chambers & Associates, Inc.,
      New York
John W. Franklin, Jr.
   Russell Reynolds Associates, Inc.,
      Washington, DC
Leonard J. Clark, Jr.
   Boyden International, New York
David R. Peasback
   Canny, Bowen Inc., New York
Thomas C. Zay
   Thomas C. Zay & Company, Inc.,
      Atlanta
Janet Tweed
   Gilbert Tweed Associates, New
      York
Robert S. Rollo
   Korn/Ferry International, Los
      Angeles
William H. Marumoto
   The Interface Group, Ltd.,
      Washington, DC
Steven A. Seiden
   Seiden Associates, Inc., New York
P. John Mirtz
   Martin Mirtz Morice, Inc.,
      Stamford, CT

Judith M. von Seldeneck
   Diversified Search, Inc.,
      Philadelphia
Robert L. Heidrick
   The Heidrick Partners, Inc.,
      Chicago
E. Pendleton James
   Pendleton James & Associates, Inc.,
      New York
Gardner W. Heidrick
   The Heidrick Partners, Inc.,
      Chicago
Robert M. Bryza
   Robert Lowell International, Inc.,
      Dallas
Donald C. Williams
   Donald Williams Associates, Inc.,
      Chicago
James E. Hunt
   Kenny, Kindler, Hunt & Howe,
      New York
H. Leland Getz
   Higdon, Joys & Mingle, Inc., New
      York

COMPUTER SOFTWARE

Michael S. Dunford
   Michael S. Dunford, Inc., Glen
      Ellyn, IL
J. Gerald Simmons
   Handy Associates, New York
Peter G. Grimm
   Nordeman Grimm, Inc., New York
Theodore E. Lusk
   Nadzam, Lusk & Associates, Inc.,
      Santa Clara, CA
Mary E. Shourds
   Houze, Shourds & Montgomery,
      Inc., Long Beach, CA
James H. Cornehlsen
   Heidrick and Struggles, Inc., New
      York
Pierson Keating
   Nordeman Grimm, New York
Howard D. Nitchke
   Deane, Howard & Simon, Inc.,
      Hartford, CT

Albert L. Richard, Jr.
Human Resources, Inc.,
Providence, RI
David F. Smith
Korn/Ferry International, New
York
Charles E. Splaine
Splaine & Associates, Los Gatos,
CA
R.G. Finnegan
Finnegan & Associates Inc., Palos
Verdes Estates, CA
John R. Ferneborg
Smith, Goerss & Ferneborg, San
Francisco
R. Paul Kors
Kors Montgomery International,
Houston
O.D. "Dan" Cruse
SpencerStuart, Dallas
Robert W. Slater
Korn/Ferry International, Dallas
Gary R. Barton
Barton Raben, Inc., Houston
Jonathan E. McBride
McBride Associates, Inc.,
Washington, DC
James M. Montgomery
Houze, Shourds & Montgomery,
Inc., Long Beach, CA
James E. Hunt
Kenny, Kindler, Hunt & Howe,
New York
Edward A. Raisbeck, Jr.
Thorndike Deland Associates, New
York
Ralph E. Dieckmann
Dieckmann & Associates, Ltd.,
Chicago
Richard K. Ives
Wilkinson & Ives, San Francisco
Robert S. Rollo
Korn/Ferry International, Los
Angeles
William H. Billington, Jr.
Billington, Fox & Ellis, Inc.,
Chicago
George W. Henn, Jr.
G.W. Henn & Company, Columbus,
OH

Michael J. Hoevel
Poirier, Hoevel & Company, Los
Angeles
Robert Kremple
Kremple & Meade, Malibu, CA
W. Michael Danforth
Hyde Danforth & Co., Dallas
Steven A. Raben
Barton Raben, Inc., Houston
George Rossi
Heidrick and Struggles, Inc.,
Boston
W. Jerry Hyde
Hyde Danforth & Co., Dallas
Thomas M. Mitchell
Heidrick and Struggles, Inc., Los
Angeles

CONSTRUCTION

Carl W. Menk
Canny, Bowen Inc., New York
Charles P. Beall
Beall & Company, Inc., Roswell, GA
Richard J. Cronin
Hodge-Cronin & Associates, Inc.,
Rosemont, IL
Richard M. Ferry
Korn/Ferry International, Los
Angeles
Sandford I. Gadient
Huntress Real Estate Executive
Search, Kansas City, MO
Charles M. Meng
Meng, Finseth & Associates, Inc.,
Rolling Hills, CA
Thomas C. Zay
Thomas C. Zay & Company, Inc.,
Atlanta
Jack H. Vernon
Russell Reynolds Associates, Inc.,
Boston
David F. Smith
Korn/Ferry International, New
York
George W. Ott
Ott & Hansen, Inc., Pasadena, CA
Putney Westerfield
Boyden International Inc., New
York

J. Alvin Wakefield
  Gilbert Tweed Associates, Inc., New
    York
Lawrence "Larry" W. Hill
  Russell Reynolds Associates, Inc.,
    Houston
Charles D. Reese, Jr.
  Reese Associates, Wexford, PA
Richard K. Ives
  Wilkinson & Ives, San Francisco
Thomas M. Mitchell
  Heidrick and Struggles, Inc., Los
    Angeles
Otis H. Bowden, II
  Bowden & Company, Inc.,
    Cleveland
Pierson Keating
  Nordeman Grimm, New York
Frank R. Beaudine
  Eastman & Beaudine, Inc., Dallas
Theodore E. Lusk
  Nadzam, Lusk & Associates, Inc.,
    Santa Clara, CA
Richard A. McCallister
  Boyden International, Inc., Chicago

EATING AND DRINKING PLACES

Howard Bratches
  Thorndike Deland Associates, New
    York
Herbert Regehly
  Innkeeper's Management Corp.,
    New York
Ben Schwartz
  Harper Associates, Farmington
    Hills, MI
John "Jack" B. Henard, Jr.
  Henard Associates, Dallas
Robert A. Staub
  Staub, Warmbold & Associates,
    Inc., New York
Putney Westerfield
  Boyden International Inc., New
    York
Harvey M. Weiner
  Search America, Dallas

ELECTRICAL AND ELECTRONIC MACHINERY

Gerard R. Roche
  Heidrick and Struggles, Inc., New
    York
Thomas J. Neff
  SpencerStuart, New York
Donald T. Allerton
  Allerton/Heinze & Associates, Inc.,
    Chicago
John F. Johnson
  Lamalie Associates, Inc., Cleveland
Robert A. Staub
  Staub, Warmbold & Associates,
    Inc., New York
George W. Henn, Jr.
  G.W. Henn & Company, Columbus,
    OH
Frederick W. Wackerle
  McFeely Wackerle Jett, Chicago
Robert L. Heidrick
  The Heidrick Partners, Inc.,
    Chicago
J. Gerald Simmons
  Handy Associates, New York
David O. Harbert
  Sweeney Shepherd Bueschel Provus
    Harbert & Mummert, Inc.,
    Chicago
Michael S. Dunford
  Michael S. Dunford, Inc., Glen
    Ellyn, IL
Leon A. Farley
  Leon A. Farley Associates, San
    Francisco
William E. Gould
  Gould & McCoy Inc., New York
Robert W. Dingman
  Robert W. Dingman Company, Inc.,
    Westlake Village, CA
O.D. "Dan" Cruse
  SpencerStuart, Dallas
Gardner W. Heidrick
  The Heidrick Partners, Inc.,
    Chicago
Richard K. Ives
  Wilkinson & Ives, San Francisco

Theodore E. Lusk
Nadzam, Lusk & Associates, Inc.,
Santa Clara, CA

Clarence E. McFeely
McFeely Wackerle Jett, Chicago

William R. Wilkinson
Wilkinson & Ives, San Francisco

Frederic E. Berman
The Berman Consulting Group,
Atlanta

Otis H. Bowden, II
Bowden & Company, Inc.,
Cleveland

David H. Charlson
Chestnut Hill Partners, Deerfield,
IL

Charles W. Sweet
A.T. Kearney, Inc., Chicago

Skott B. Burkland
Haley BDC, New York

William B. Arnold
William B. Arnold Associates, Inc.,
Denver

Lawrence J. Holmes
Consulting Associates, Inc.,
Columbia, MD

William C. Houze
William C. Houze & Co., Torrance,
CA

Nelson W. Gibson
N.W. Gibson International, Los
Angeles

Darrell G. Robertson
Western Reserve Search Associates,
Inc., Bath, OH

Sydney Reynolds
Sydney Reynolds Associates, Inc.,
New York

Richard Sbarbaro
Lauer, Sbarbaro Associates, Inc.,
Chicago

J.R. Akin
J.R. Akin & Company, Fairfield, CT

Richard J. Cronin
Hodge-Cronin & Associates, Inc.,
Rosemont, IL

R. Paul Kors
Kors Montgomery International,
Houston

William T. Mangum
Thomas Mangum Company, Los
Angeles

Gerald D. Menzel
Menzel, Robinson, Baldwin, Inc.,
Arlington Heights, IL

Mary E. Shourds
Houze, Shourds & Montgomery,
Inc., Long Beach, CA

Charles E. Splaine
Splaine & Associates, Los Gatos,
CA

Richard C. Slayton
Slayton International, Inc., Chicago

John T. Gardner
Lamalie Associates, Inc., Chicago

E. Pendleton James
Pendleton James & Associates, Inc.,
New York

Charles W. Kepler
Russell Reynolds Associates, Inc.,
Chicago

Steven M. Darter
People Management Inc., Simsbury,
CT

R.G. Finnegan
Finnegan & Associates Inc., Palos
Verdes Estates, CA

R. James Lotz, Jr.
International Management
Advisors, Inc., New York

Ralph E. Dieckmann
Dieckmann & Associates, Ltd.,
Chicago

Lynn Tendler Bignell
Gilbert Tweed Associates, Inc., New
York

James H. Cornehlsen
Heidrick and Struggles, Inc., New
York

Robert M. Bryza
Robert Lowell International, Inc.,
Dallas

Mike Jacobs
Thorne, Brieger Associates Inc.,
New York

George W. Ott
Ott & Hansen, Inc., Pasadena, CA

Albert L. Richard, Jr.
Human Resources, Inc.,
Providence, RI
John A. Travis
Travis & Company Inc., Sudbury,
MA
George Rossi
Heidrick and Struggles, Inc.,
Boston
Theodore Jadick
Heidrick and Struggles, Inc., New
York
Richard M. McFarland
Brissenden, McFarland, Wagoner,
& Fuccella, Inc., Stamford, CT
Ferdinand Nadherny
Russell Reynolds Associates, Inc.,
Chicago
William H. Billington, Jr.
Billington, Fox & Ellis, Inc.,
Chicago
Charles D. Reese, Jr.
Reese Associates, Wexford, PA
David E. Chambers
David Chambers & Associates, Inc.,
New York
Leonard J. Clark, Jr.
Boyden International, New York
David S. Joys
Higdon, Joys & Mingle, Inc., New
York
Russell E. Marks, Jr.
A.T. Kearney, Inc., New York
Janet Tweed
Gilbert Tweed Associates, New
York
Linford E. Stiles
Ward Howell International,
Stamford, CT
Ronald Dukes
Heidrick and Struggles, Inc.,
Chicago
James R. Clovis, Jr.
Handy Associates, New York
John "Jack" B. Henard, Jr.
Henard Associates, Dallas
Robert Kremple
Kremple & Meade, Malibu, CA

John Lucht
The John Lucht Consultancy Inc.,
New York
P. Anthony Price
Russell Reynolds Associates Inc.,
San Francisco
Jack H. Vernon
Russell Reynolds Associates, Inc.,
Boston
Richard E. Kinser
Richard Kinser & Associates, New
York

ENERGY

Stephen A. Garrison
Ward Howell International, Inc.,
Dallas
Richard M. McFarland
Brissenden, McFarland, Wagoner,
& Fuccella, Inc., Stamford, CT
Robert W. Slater
Korn/Ferry International, Dallas
Gary R. Barton
Barton Raben, Inc., Houston
Max M. Ulrich
Ward Howell International Inc.,
New York
Steven A. Raben
Barton Raben, Inc., Houston
Robert L. Heidrick
The Heidrick Partners, Inc.,
Chicago
Carl W. Menk
Canny, Bowen Inc., New York
David O. Harbert
Sweeney Shepherd Bueschel Provus
Harbert & Mummert, Inc.,
Chicago
R. Paul Kors
Kors Montgomery International,
Houston
Henry G. Higdon
Higdon, Joys & Mingle, Inc., New
York
Nancy F. Keithley
Ernst & Young, Cleveland
Charles M. Meng
Meng, Finseth & Associates, Inc.,
Rolling Hills, CA

John H. Robison
Robison & McAulay, Charlotte, NC
Gardner W. Heidrick
The Heidrick Partners, Inc.,
Chicago
Richard E. Kinser
Richard Kinser & Associates, New
York
Sydney Reynolds
Sydney Reynolds Associates, Inc.,
New York
Frederic E. Berman
The Berman Consulting Group,
Atlanta
James R. Clovis, Jr.
Handy Associates, New York
Donald C. Williams
Donald Williams Associates, Inc.,
Chicago
Richard M. Ferry
Korn/Ferry International, Los
Angeles
Gretchen Long
Haskell & Stern Associates, Inc.,
New York
Albert L. McAulay, Jr.
Robison & McAulay, Charlotte, NC
Lawrence "Larry" W. Hill
Russell Reynolds Associates, Inc.,
Houston
Paul R. Ray, Jr.
Paul R. Ray & Company, Inc., Fort
Worth
Robert M. Bryza
Robert Lowell International, Inc.,
Dallas
George W. Ott
Ott & Hansen, Inc., Pasadena, CA
Paul R. Ray, Sr.
Paul R. Ray & Company, Inc., Fort
Worth
Jonathan A. Crystal
SpencerStuart, Houston
Richard A. McCallister
Boyden International, Inc., Chicago
Frank R. Beaudine
Eastman & Beaudine, Inc., Dallas
Theodore E. Lusk
Nadzam, Lusk & Associates, Inc.,
Santa Clara, CA

Ferdinand Nadherny
Russell Reynolds Associates, Inc.,
Chicago
H. Leland Getz
Higdon, Joys & Mingle, Inc., New
York
Leon A. Farley
Leon A. Farley Associates, San
Francisco
David E. Chambers
David Chambers & Associates, Inc.,
New York
William H. Willis, Jr.
William H. Willis, Inc., Greenwich,
CT
John "Jack" B. Henard, Jr.
Henard Associates, Dallas
William T. Mangum
Thomas Mangum Company, Los
Angeles
Charles W. Sweet
A.T. Kearney, Inc., Chicago
Russell E. Marks, Jr.
A.T. Kearney, Inc., New York

FABRICATED METAL PRODUCTS

John F. Johnson
Lamalie Associates, Inc., Cleveland
Robert E. Lamalie
Robert Lamalie Inc., Marco Island,
FL
Frederick W. Wackerle
McFeely Wackerle Jett, Chicago
Ferdinand Nadherny
Russell Reynolds Associates, Inc.,
Chicago
Robert D. Spriggs
Spriggs & Company, Inc., Chicago
Richard C. Slayton
Slayton International, Inc., Chicago
Robert L. Heidrick
The Heidrick Partners, Inc.,
Chicago
Nancy F. Keithley
Ernst & Young, Cleveland
Lynn Tendler Bignell
Gilbert Tweed Associates, Inc., New
York

Jack R. Clarey
  Jack Clarey Associates, Inc.,
    Northbrook, IL
William B. Arnold
  William B. Arnold Associates, Inc.,
    Denver
Donald C. Williams
  Donald Williams Associates, Inc.,
    Chicago
Richard J. Cronin
  Hodge-Cronin & Associates, Inc.,
    Rosemont, IL
Gardner W. Heidrick
  The Heidrick Partners, Inc.,
    Chicago
Steven A. Seiden
  Seiden Associates, Inc., New York
William A. Hertan
  Executive Manning Corp., Fort
    Lauderdale
Mike Jacobs
  Thorne, Brieger Associates Inc.,
    New York
Otis H. Bowden, II
  Bowden & Company, Inc.,
    Cleveland
George W. Henn, Jr.
  G. W. Henn & Company,
    Columbus, OH
James F. Bishop
  Burke, O'Brien & Bishop
    Associates, Inc., Princeton, NJ
Lawrence "Larry" W. Hill
  Russell Reynolds Associates, Inc.,
    Houston
Robert M. Bryza
  Robert Lowell International, Inc.,
    Dallas
Herbert T. Mines
  Herbert Mines Associates, Inc.,
    New York
John T. Gardner
  Lamalie Associates, Inc., Chicago
Charles W. Kepler
  Russell Reynolds Associates, Inc.,
    Chicago
Laurence Massé
  Ward Howell International,
    Barrington, IL

Charles D. Reese, Jr.
  Reese Associates, Wexford, PA
William T. Mangum
  Thomas Mangum Company, Los
    Angeles
Andrew Sherwood
  Goodrich and Sherwood Company,
    New York
Martin H. Bauman
  Martin H. Bauman Associates, Inc.,
    New York
William B. Beeson
  Lawrence-Leiter & Company,
    Kansas City, MO
Charles P. Beall
  Beall & Company, Inc., Roswell, GA
Frank R. Beaudine
  Eastman & Beaudine, Inc., Dallas
O.D. "Dan" Cruse
  SpencerStuart, Dallas
Charles W. Kepler
  Russell Reynolds Associates, Inc.,
    Chicago
Robert Kremple
  Kremple & Meade, Malibu, CA
Clarence E. McFeely
  McFeely Wackerle Jett, Chicago
Linford E. Stiles
  Ward Howell International,
    Stamford, CT
Steven M. Darter
  People Management Inc., Simsbury,
    CT
Pierson Keating
  Nordeman Grimm, New York
Charles W. Sweet
  A.T. Kearney, Inc., Chicago
Theodore E. Lusk
  Nadzam, Lusk & Associates, Inc.,
    Santa Clara, CA
Robert W. Dingman
  Robert W. Dingman Company, Inc.,
    Westlake Village, CA
George Rossi
  Heidrick and Struggles, Inc.,
    Boston
Ralph E. Dieckmann
  Dieckmann & Associates, Ltd.,
    Chicago

David S. Joys
    Higdon, Joys & Mingle, Inc., New
    York
Ronald Dukes
    Heidrick and Struggles, Inc.,
    Chicago
Nelson W. Gibson
    N.W. Gibson International, Los
    Angeles
Russell E. Marks, Jr.
    A.T. Kearney, Inc., New York
Jack H. Vernon
    Russell Reynolds Associates, Inc.,
    Boston
William H. Billington, Jr.
    Billington, Fox & Ellis, Inc.,
    Chicago
John W. Franklin, Jr.
    Russell Reynolds Associates, Inc.,
    Washington, DC
Janet Tweed
    Gilbert Tweed Associates, New
    York
Robert G. Cox
    A.T. Kearney, Inc., New York
P. John Mirtz
    Martin Mirtz Morice, Inc.,
    Stamford, CT
J.R. Akin
    J.R. Akin & Company, Fairfield, CT
George W. Ott
    Ott & Hansen, Inc., Pasadena, CA

FOOD AND KINDRED PRODUCTS

Thomas J. Neff
    SpencerStuart, New York
Gerard R. Roche
    Heidrick and Struggles, Inc., New
    York
Robert E. Lamalie
    Robert Lamalie Inc., Marco Island,
    FL
Robert W. Dingman
    Robert W. Dingman Company, Inc.,
    Westlake Village, CA
Paul R. Ray, Sr.
    Paul R. Ray & Company, Inc., Fort
    Worth

Carl W. Menk
    Canny, Bowen Inc., New York
Michael S. Dunford
    Michael S. Dunford, Inc., Glen
    Ellyn, IL
William E. Gould
    Gould & McCoy Inc., New York
Robert D. Spriggs
    Spriggs & Company, Inc., Chicago
Roger M. Kenny
    Kenny, Kindler, Hunt & Howe,
    New York
D. John Ingram
    Ingram Inc., New York
Howard Bratches
    Thorndike Deland Associates, New
    York
Lawrence F. Nein
    Nordeman Grimm, Inc., Chicago
Paul R. Ray, Jr.
    Paul R. Ray & Company, Inc., Fort
    Worth
William R. Wilkinson
    Wilkinson & Ives, San Francisco
William H. Willis, Jr.
    William H. Willis, Inc., Greenwich,
    CT
Andrew D. Hart
    Russell Reynolds Associates, Inc.,
    New York
Millington F. McCoy
    Gould & McCoy, Inc., New York
Frank R. Beaudine
    Eastman & Beaudine, Inc., Dallas
Allan D. R. Stern
    Haskell & Stern Associates, Inc.,
    New York
E. Pendleton James
    Pendleton James & Associates, Inc.,
    New York
Barbara L. Provus
    Sweeney Shepherd Bueschel Provus
    Harbert & Mummert, Inc.,
    Chicago
John F. Johnson
    Lamalie Associates, Inc., Cleveland
William H. Billington, Jr.
    Billington, Fox & Ellis, Inc.,
    Chicago

Jacques P. Andre
Paul R. Ray & Company, Inc., New York

Andrew Sherwood
Goodrich and Sherwood Company, New York

John "Jack" B. Henard, Jr.
Henard Associates, Dallas

Jack R. Clarey
Jack Clarey Associates, Inc., Northbrook, IL

John Lucht
The John Lucht Consultancy Inc., New York

Joseph B. Ryan
The Cambridge Group Ltd., Westport, CT

Charles W. Sweet
A.T. Kearney, Inc., Chicago

Putney Westerfield
Boyden International Inc., New York

Gary R. Barton
Barton Raben, Inc., Houston

Joseph E. Griesedieck, Jr.
SpencerStuart, San Francisco

Theodore Jadick
Heidrick and Struggles, Inc., New York

P. Anthony Price
Russell Reynolds Associates Inc., San Francisco

Michael J. Hoevel
Poirier, Hoevel & Company, Los Angeles

Thomas H. Ogdon
The Ogdon Partnership, New York

David R. Peasback
Canny, Bowen Inc., New York

Edward A. Raisbeck, Jr.
Thorndike Deland Associates, New York

David F. Smith
Korn/Ferry International, New York

William K. Sur
Stricker, Sur & Associates, New York

Donald C. Williams
Donald Williams Associates, Inc., Chicago

Leonard J. Clark, Jr.
Boyden International, New York

William B. Beeson
Lawrence-Leiter & Company, Kansas City, MO

David E. Chambers
David Chambers & Associates, Inc., New York

Richard A. Miners
Goodrich and Sherwood, New York

Gary W. Silverman
Korn/Ferry International, Chicago

O. William Battalia
Battalia & Associates, Inc., New York

Richard E. Kinser
Richard Kinser & Associates, New York

Robert L. Heidrick
The Heidrick Partners, Inc., Chicago

Peter G. Grimm
Nordeman Grimm, Inc., New York

Peter D. Crist
Russell Reynolds Associates, Inc., Chicago

Ralph E. Dieckmann
Dieckmann & Associates, Ltd., Chicago

David S. Joys
Higdon, Joys & Mingle, Inc., New York

David H. Hoffmann
DHR International, Inc., Chicago

Laurence Massé
Ward Howell International, Barrington, IL

Caroline Ballantine
Heidrick and Struggles, Inc., New York

Gardner W. Heidrick
The Heidrick Partners, Inc., Chicago

Gerald D. Menzel
Menzel, Robinson, Baldwin, Inc., Arlington Heights, IL

James F. Bishop
  Burke, O'Brien & Bishop
    Associates, Inc., Princeton, NJ
Douglas H. Gates
  Haley BDC, New York
Gretchen Long
  Haskell & Stern Associates, Inc.,
    New York
Steven A. Raben
  Barton Raben, Inc., Houston
George Rossi
  Heidrick and Struggles, Inc.,
    Boston
Brenda L. Ruello
  Heidrick and Struggles, Inc., New
    York
W. Michael Danforth
  Hyde Danforth & Co., Dallas
W. Jerry Hyde
  Hyde Danforth & Co., Dallas
Dayton Ogden
  SpencerStuart, New York
Judith M. von Seldeneck
  Diversified Search, Inc.,
    Philadelphia
John T. Gardner
  Lamalie Associates, Inc., Chicago
P. John Mirtz
  Martin Mirtz Morice, Inc.,
    Stamford, CT
William H. Marumoto
  The Interface Group, Ltd.,
    Washington, DC
James R. Clovis, Jr.
  Handy Associates, New York
Ronald Dukes
  Heidrick and Struggles, Inc.,
    Chicago
Thomas M. Mitchell
  Heidrick and Struggles, Inc., Los
    Angeles
Janet Tweed
  Gilbert Tweed Associates, New
    York

GOVERNMENT AGENCIES/ MUNICIPALITIES

J. Alvin Wakefield
  Gilbert Tweed Associates, Inc., New
    York

Frederic E. Berman
  The Berman Consulting Group,
    Atlanta
Dayton Ogden
  SpencerStuart, New York
William H. Marumoto
  The Interface Group, Ltd.,
    Washington, DC
Charles M. Meng
  Meng, Finseth & Associates, Inc.,
    Rolling Hills, CA
John H. Robison
  Robison & McAulay, Charlotte, NC

HEALTH SERVICES/ HOSPITALS

Michael C. Kieffer
  Kieffer, Ford & Associates, Inc.,
    Oak Brook, IL
John S. Lloyd
  Witt Associates, Inc., Oak Brook, IL
J. Daniel Ford
  Kieffer, Ford & Associates, Ltd.,
    Oak Brook, IL
Michael D. Caver
  Heidrick and Struggles, Inc.,
    Chicago
William J. Bowen
  Heidrick and Struggles, Inc.,
    Chicago
James N. Heuerman
  Korn/Ferry International, San
    Francisco
Frank A. Garofolo
  Garofolo, Curtiss & Company,
    Ardmore, PA
Judith M. von Seldeneck
  Diversified Search, Inc.,
    Philadelphia
Antoinette "Toni" L. Farley
  Kieffer, Ford & Associates, Ltd.,
    Oak Brook, IL
Robert W. Dingman
  Robert W. Dingman Company, Inc.,
    Westlake Village, CA
Janis M. Zivic
  The Zivic Group, Inc., San
    Francisco

Joan I. McCrea
  Nursing Technomics, West Chester,
  PA
Kenneth L. Rattner
  Heidrick and Struggles, Inc.,
  Chicago
James M. Schmidt
  Cejka & Company, St. Louis
A. Donald Ikle
  Ward Howell International, Inc.,
  New York
Douglas H. Gates
  Haley BDC, New York
Ira Krinsky
  Ira Krinsky Associates, Los Angeles
Richard Sbarbaro
  Lauer, Sbarbaro Associates, Inc.,
  Chicago
Howard Bratches
  Thorndike Deland Associates, New
  York
Robert L. Heidrick
  The Heidrick Partners, Inc.,
  Chicago
Steven M. Darter
  People Management Inc., Simsbury,
  CT
Mark Lorenzetti
  Roberts, Ryan & Bentley,
  Linthicum, MD
Thomas M. Mitchell
  Heidrick and Struggles, Inc., Los
  Angeles
John A. Travis
  Travis & Company, Inc. Sudbury,
  MA
Caroline Ballantine
  Heidrick and Struggles, New York
Thomas R. Moore
  Ketchum, Inc., Pittsburgh
Ben Schwartz
  Harper Associates, Farmington
  Hills, MI
J.R. Akin
  J.R. Akin & Company, Fairfield, CT
Joseph B. Ryan
  The Cambridge Group Ltd.,
  Westport, CT

Gardner W. Heidrick
  The Heidrick Partners, Inc.,
  Chicago
Max M. Ulrich
  Ward Howell International Inc.,
  New York
Stephen A. Garrison
  Ward Howell International, Inc.,
  Dallas
William C. Houze
  William C. Houze & Co., Torrance,
  CA
Jonathan A. Crystal
  SpencerStuart, Houston
Nancy F. Keithley
  Ernst & Young, Cleveland
William T. Mangum
  Thomas Mangum Company, Los
  Angeles
Pierson Keating
  Nordeman Grimm, New York
Robert S. Rollo
  Korn/Ferry International, Los
  Angeles
Jonathan E. McBride
  McBride Associates, Inc.,
  Washington, DC
John R. Ferneborg
  Smith, Goerss & Ferneborg, San
  Francisco
W. Michael Danforth
  Hyde Danforth & Co., Dallas
W. Jerry Hyde
  Hyde Danforth & Co., Dallas
William A. Hertan
  Executive Manning Corp., Fort
  Lauderdale
Richard A. McCallister
  Boyden International, Inc., Chicago
Jack H. Vernon
  Russell Reynolds Associates, Inc.,
  Boston
David H. Hoffmann
  DHR International, Inc., Chicago
P. John Mirtz
  Martin Mirtz Morice, Inc.,
  Stamford, CT

HOLDING COMPANIES

Thomas J. Neff
SpencerStuart, New York

Frederick W. Wackerle
McFeely Wackerle Jett, Chicago

E. Pendleton James
Pendleton James & Associates, Inc.,
New York

Robert L. Heidrick
The Heidrick Partners, Inc.,
Chicago

Paul R. Ray, Sr.
Paul R. Ray & Company, Inc., Fort
Worth

David E. Chambers
David Chambers & Associates, Inc.,
New York

Robert D. Spriggs
Spriggs & Company, Inc., Chicago

Jacques C. Nordeman
Nordeman Grimm, Inc., New York

Jacques P. Andre
Paul R. Ray & Company, Inc., New
York

Gardner W. Heidrick
The Heidrick Partners, Inc.,
Chicago

Clarence E. McFeely
McFeely Wackerle Jett, Chicago

Russell S. Reynolds, Jr.
Russell Reynolds Associates, Inc.,
New York

Richard M. Ferry
Korn/Ferry International, Los
Angeles

Michael J. Hoevel
Poirier, Hoevel & Company, Los
Angeles

David R. Peasback
Canny, Bowen Inc., New York

Millington F. McCoy
Gould & McCoy, Inc., New York

James R. Clovis, Jr.
Handy Associates, New York

Steven A. Seiden
Seiden Associates, Inc., New York

Jack R. Clarey
Jack Clarey Associates, Inc.,
Northbrook, IL

David H. Hoffmann
DHR International, Inc., Chicago

Ralph E. Dieckmann
Dieckmann & Associates, Ltd.,
Chicago

Antoinette "Toni" L. Farley
Kieffer, Ford & Associates, Ltd.,
Oak Brook, IL

Gary R. Barton
Barton Raben, Inc., Houston

Richard A. McCallister
Boyden International, Inc., Chicago

David S. Joys
Higdon, Joys & Mingle, Inc., New
York

William B. Clemens, Jr.
Norman Broadbent International,
New York

Sandford I. Gadient
Huntress Real Estate Executive
Search, Kansas City, MO

Jonathan A. Crystal
SpencerStuart, Houston

James A. Hayden, Jr.
Hayden Group, Inc., Boston

Gretchen Long
Haskell & Stern Associates, Inc.,
New York

Henry G. Higdon
Higdon, Joys & Mingle, Inc., New
York

Nancy F. Keithley
Ernst & Young, Cleveland

Brenda L. Ruello
Heidrick and Struggles, Inc., New
York

H. Leland Getz
Higdon, Joys & Mingle, Inc., New
York

Allan D. R. Stern
Haskell & Stern Associates, Inc.,
New York

Richard Sbarbaro
Lauer, Sbarbaro Associates, Inc.,
Chicago

Nelson W. Gibson
N.W. Gibson International, Los
Angeles

Peter G. Grimm
Nordeman Grimm, Inc., New York
Larry D. Mingle
Higdon, Joys & Mingle, Inc., New York
Steven A. Raben
Barton Raben, Inc., Houston
Robert S. Rollo
Korn/Ferry International, Los Angeles
James E. Hunt
Kenny, Kindler, Hunt & Howe, New York
Charles M. Meng
Meng, Finseth & Associates, Inc., Rolling Hills, CA
William H. Willis, Jr.
William H. Willis, Inc., Greenwich, CT
Barbara L. Provus
Sweeney Shepherd Bueschel Provus Harbert & Mummert, Inc., Chicago
John S. Stanton
Russell Reynolds Associates, Inc., Chicago
Theodore Jadick
Heidrick and Struggles, Inc., New York
Russell E. Marks, Jr.
A.T. Kearney, Inc., New York
P. John Mirtz
Martin Mirtz Morice, Inc., Stamford, CT
Thomas M. Mitchell
Heidrick and Struggles, Inc., Los Angeles
Eleanor H. Raynolds
Ward Howell International, Inc., New York
John W. Franklin, Jr.
Russell Reynolds Associates, Inc., Washington, DC
Richard K. Ives
Wilkinson & Ives, San Francisco
Lawrence "Larry" W. Hill
Russell Reynolds Associates, Inc., Houston

Charles W. Kepler
Russell Reynolds Associates, Inc., Chicago
Robert M. Bryza
Robert Lowell International, Inc., Dallas
David F. Smith
Korn/Ferry International, New York
Joseph E. Griesedieck, Jr.
SpencerStuart, San Francisco
Albert L. McAulay, Jr.
Robison & McAulay, Charlotte, NC
Robert A. Staub
Staub, Warmbold & Associates, Inc., New York
David H. Charlson
Chestnut Hill Partners, Deerfield, IL
Ronald Dukes
Heidrick and Struggles, Inc., Chicago
Caroline Ballantine
Heidrick and Struggles, Inc., New York
Gerald D. Menzel
Menzel, Robinson, Baldwin, Inc., Arlington Heights, IL
William B. Beeson
Lawrence-Leiter & Company, Kansas City, MO

HOTELS/RESORTS/CLUBS

Carol S. Jeffers
John Sibbald Associates, Inc., Chicago
Herbert Regehly
Innkeeper's Management Corp., New York
Robert W. Slater
Korn/Ferry International, Dallas
Harvey M. Weiner
Search America, Dallas
Ben Schwartz
Harper Associates, Farmington Hills, MI
Roger M. Kenny
Kenny, Kindler, Hunt & Howe, New York

Judith M. von Seldeneck
Diversified Search, Inc.,
Philadelphia
W. Michael Danforth
Hyde Danforth & Co., Dallas
Janis M. Zivic
The Zivic Group, Inc., San
Francisco
Michael S. Dunford
Michael S. Dunford, Inc., Glen
Ellyn, IL
Robert W. Dingman
Robert W. Dingman Company, Inc.,
Westlake Village, CA
W. Jerry Hyde
Hyde Danforth & Co., Dallas
Thomas C. Zay
Thomas C. Zay & Company, Inc.,
Atlanta
Gerard R. Roche
Heidrick and Struggles, Inc., New
York
Gary Knisely
Johnson Smith & Knisely Inc., New
York
John R. Ferneborg
Smith, Goerss & Ferneborg, San
Francisco
R. James Lotz, Jr.
International Management
Advisors, Inc., New York
Robert M. Flanagan
Paul Stafford Associates, Ltd., New
York
Howard D. Nitchke
Deane, Howard & Simon, Inc.,
Hartford, CT
Pierson Keating
Nordeman Grimm, New York
Henry G. Higdon
Higdon, Joys & Mingle, Inc., New
York
Robert L. Heidrick
The Heidrick Partners, Inc.,
Chicago
Lawrence J. Holmes
Consulting Associates, Inc.,
Columbia, MD

Charles M. Meng
Meng, Finseth & Associates, Inc.,
Rolling Hills, CA
Frank R. Beaudine
Eastman & Beaudine, Inc., Dallas
Gardner W. Heidrick
The Heidrick Partners, Inc.,
Chicago
Jonathan E. McBride
McBride Associates, Inc.,
Washington, DC
Eleanor H. Raynolds
Ward Howell International, Inc.,
New York
James E. Hunt
Kenny, Kindler, Hunt & Howe,
New York
Lawrence "Larry" W. Hill
Russell Reynolds Associates, Inc.,
Houston
James H. Cornehlsen
Heidrick and Struggles, Inc., New
York

INSURANCE

Thomas J. Neff
SpencerStuart, New York
Windle B. Priem
Korn/Ferry International, New
York
D. John Ingram
Ingram Inc., New York
Lawrence J. Holmes
Consulting Associates, Inc.,
Columbia, MD
Richard Sbarbaro
Lauer, Sbarbaro Associates, Inc.,
Chicago
Ralph E. Dieckmann
Dieckmann & Associates, Ltd.,
Chicago
W. Hoyt Colton
W. Hoyt Colton Associates Inc.,
New York
Joseph B. Ryan
The Cambridge Group Ltd.,
Westport, CT

Edward R. Howe, Jr.
Diversified Search, Inc.,
Philadelphia
Otis H. Bowden, II
Bowden & Company, Inc.,
Cleveland
George W. Henn, Jr.
G.W. Henn & Company, Columbus,
OH
David H. Charlson
Chestnut Hill Partners, Deerfield,
IL
Frank R. Beaudine
Eastman & Beaudine, Inc., Dallas
Andrew D. Hart
Russell Reynolds Associates, Inc.,
New York
Jonathan E. McBride
McBride Associates, Inc.,
Washington, DC
Judith M. von Seldeneck
Diversified Search, Inc.,
Philadelphia
A. Donald Ikle
Ward Howell International, Inc.,
New York
Steven M. Darter
People Management Inc., Simsbury,
CT
J. Gerald Simmons
Handy Associates, New York
Caroline Ballantine
Heidrick and Struggles, Inc., New
York
Albert L. Richard, Jr.
Human Resources, Inc.,
Providence, RI
Sandford I. Gadient
Huntress Real Estate Executive
Search, Kansas City, MO
Richard K. Ives
Wilkinson & Ives, San Francisco
Mark Lorenzetti
Roberts, Ryan & Bentley,
Linthicum, MD
Skott B. Burkland
Haley BDC, New York
Jack R. Clarey
Jack Clarey Associates, Inc.,
Northbrook, IL

Jay Gaines
Jay Gaines & Company, Inc., New
York
Durant "Andy" Hunter
Gardiner Stone Hunter
International, Boston
John Lucht
The John Lucht Consultancy Inc.,
New York
James M. Schmidt
Cejka & Company, St. Louis
Carl W. Menk
Canny, Bowen Inc., New York
William B. Reeves
Korn/Ferry International, Atlanta
Antoinette "Toni" L. Farley
Kieffer, Ford & Associates, Ltd.,
Oak Brook, IL
W. Michael Danforth
Hyde Danforth & Co., Dallas
James E. Hunt
Kenny, Kindler, Hunt & Howe,
New York
Norman F. Moody
Paul Stafford Associates, Ltd., New
York
James A. Hayden, Jr.
Hayden Group, Inc., Boston
Edward C. Slowik
SpencerStuart, New York
Albert L. McAulay, Jr.
Robison & McAulay, Charlotte, NC
Frederic E. Berman
The Berman Consulting Group,
Atlanta
Leon A. Farley
Leon A. Farley Associates, San
Francisco
Joseph E. Griesedieck, Jr.
SpencerStuart, San Francisco
W. Jerry Hyde
Hyde Danforth & Co., Dallas
H. Leland Getz
Higdon, Joys & Mingle, Inc., New
York
Dayton Ogden
SpencerStuart, New York
Robert S. Rollo
Korn/Ferry International, Los
Angeles

322   THE CAREER MAKERS

William H. Willis, Jr.
  William H. Willis, Inc., Greenwich,
  CT
Robert A. Staub
  Staub, Warmbold & Associates,
  Inc., New York
Thomas C. Zay
  Thomas C. Zay & Company, Inc.,
  Atlanta
William B. Clemens, Jr.
  Norman Broadbent International,
  New York
Steven A. Seiden
  Seiden Associates, Inc., New York
E. Pendleton James
  Pendleton James & Associates, Inc.,
  New York
John H. Robison
  Robison & McAulay, Charlotte, NC
David F. Smith
  Korn/Ferry International, New
  York
William B. Beeson
  Lawrence-Leiter & Company,
  Kansas City, MO
Roger M. Kenny
  Kenny, Kindler, Hunt & Howe,
  New York
Peter G. Grimm
  Nordeman Grimm, Inc., New York
Andrew Sherwood
  Goodrich and Sherwood Company,
  New York
Jacques P. Andre
  Paul R. Ray & Company, Inc., New
  York
William A. Hertan
  Executive Manning Corp., Fort
  Lauderdale
Lawrence "Larry" W. Hill
  Russell Reynolds Associates, Inc.,
  Houston
Richard A. McCallister
  Boyden International, Inc., Chicago
Eleanor H. Raynolds
  Ward Howell International, Inc.,
  New York
Douglas H. Gates
  Haley BDC, New York

Gretchen Long
  Haskell & Stern Associates, Inc.,
  New York

LAW/ACCOUNTING/ CONSULTING FIRMS

W. Michael Danforth
  Hyde Danforth & Co., Dallas
William B. Clemens, Jr.
  Norman Broadbent International,
  New York
W. Jerry Hyde
  Hyde Danforth & Co., Dallas
Early, Bert H.
  Bert H. Early Associates, Inc.,
  Chicago
John H. Callen, Jr.
  Ward Howell International, New
  York
Leon A. Farley
  Leon A. Farley Associates, San
  Francisco
William H. Billington, Jr.
  Billington, Fox & Ellis, Inc.,
  Chicago
W. Hoyt Colton
  W. Hoyt Colton Associates Inc.,
  New York
Brenda L. Ruello
  Heidrick and Struggles, Inc., New
  York
Stephen A. Garrison
  Ward Howell International, Inc.,
  Dallas
Ralph E. Dieckmann
  Dieckmann & Associates, Ltd.,
  Chicago
Clarence E. McFeely
  McFeely Wackerle Jett, Chicago
Paul R. Ray, Jr.
  Paul R. Ray & Company, Inc., Fort
  Worth
John "Jack" B. Henard, Jr.
  Henard Associates, Dallas
Charles W. Sweet
  A.T. Kearney, Inc., Chicago
Jacques C. Nordeman
  Nordeman Grimm, Inc., New York

Max M. Ulrich
  Ward Howell International Inc.,
    New York
David O. Harbert
  Sweeney Shepherd Bueschel Provus
    Harbert & Mummert, Inc.,
    Chicago
Jay Gaines
  Jay Gaines & Company, Inc., New
    York
James E. Hunt
  Kenny, Kindler, Hunt & Howe,
    New York
Theodore Jadick
  Heidrick and Struggles, Inc., New
    York
Mark Lorenzetti
  Roberts, Ryan & Bentley,
    Linthicum, MD
Kenneth L. Rattner
  Heidrick and Struggles, Inc.,
    Chicago
Edward R. Howe, Jr.
  Diversified Search, Inc.,
    Philadelphia
Richard A. McCallister
  Boyden International, Inc., Chicago
Larry D. Mingle
  Higdon, Joys & Mingle, Inc., New
    York
John T. Gardner
  Lamalie Associates, Inc., Chicago
William B. Reeves
  Korn/Ferry International, Atlanta
Jonathan E. McBride
  McBride Associates, Inc.,
    Washington, DC
James M. Montgomery
  Houze, Shourds & Montgomery,
    Inc., Long Beach, CA
Gary R. Barton
  Barton Raben, Inc., Houston
H. Leland Getz
  Higdon, Joys & Mingle, Inc., New
    York
Albert L. McAulay, Jr.
  Robison & McAulay, Charlotte, NC
P. Anthony Price
  Russell Reynolds Associates Inc.,
    San Francisco

Richard E. Kinser
  Richard Kinser & Associates, New
    York
R. Paul Kors
  Kors Montgomery International,
    Houston
Edward A. Raisbeck, Jr.
  Thorndike Deland Associates, New
    York
Robert G. Cox
  A.T. Kearney, Inc., New York
Mike Jacobs
  Thorne, Brieger Associates Inc.,
    New York
David S. Joys
  Higdon, Joys & Mingle, Inc., New
    York
John H. Robison
  Robison & McAulay, Charlotte, NC
Henry G. Higdon
  Higdon, Joys & Mingle, Inc., New
    York
Steven A. Raben
  Barton Raben Inc., Houston
George W. Ott
  Ott & Hansen, Inc., Pasadena, CA
Thomas M. Mitchell
  Heidrick and Struggles, Inc., Los
    Angeles
Jacques P. Andre
  Paul R. Ray & Company, Inc., New
    York
Eleanor H. Raynolds
  Ward Howell International, Inc.,
    New York
Richard Sbarbaro
  Lauer, Sbarbaro Associates, Inc.,
    Chicago
P. John Mirtz
  Martin Mirtz Morice, Inc.,
    Stamford, CT

LUMBER AND WOOD PRODUCTS

William R. Wilkinson
  Wilkinson & Ives, San Francisco
Lawrence P. Crowley
  Blendow, Crowley & Oliver Inc.,
    New York

William B. Arnold
William B. Arnold Associates, Inc.,
Denver
Steven A. Seiden
Seiden Associates, Inc., New York
Albert L. McAulay, Jr.
Robison & McAulay, Charlotte, NC
George Rossi
Heidrick and Struggles, Inc.,
Boston
John R. Ferneborg
Smith, Goerss & Ferneborg, San
Francisco
William H. Marumoto
The Interface Group, Ltd.,
Washington, DC

MACHINERY, EXCEPT ELECTRICAL

Frederick W. Wackerle
McFeely Wackerle Jett, Chicago
Robert E. Lamalie
Robert Lamalie Inc., Marco Island,
FL
John F. Johnson
Lamalie Associates, Inc., Cleveland
Barbara L. Provus
Sweeney Shepherd Bueschel Provus
Harbert & Mummert, Inc.,
Chicago
Robert D. Spriggs
Spriggs & Company, Inc., Chicago
Robert M. Flanagan
Paul Stafford Associates, Ltd., New
York
Lynn Tendler Bignell
Gilbert Tweed Associates, Inc., New
York
Richard C. Slayton
Slayton International, Inc., Chicago
Steven A. Seiden
Seiden Associates, Inc., New York
Jack R. Clarey
Jack Clarey Associates, Inc.,
Northbrook, IL
Linford E. Stiles
Ward Howell International,
Stamford, CT

Charles E. Splaine
Splaine & Associates, Los Gatos,
CA
Charles D. Reese, Jr.
Reese Associates, Wexford, PA
Janet Tweed
Gilbert Tweed Associates, New
York
Charles W. Kepler
Russell Reynolds Associates, Inc.,
Chicago
Clarence E. McFeely
McFeely Wackerle Jett, Chicago
Laurence Massé
Ward Howell International,
Barrington, IL
Robert M. Bryza
Robert Lowell International, Inc.,
Dallas
Charles W. Sweet
A.T. Kearney, Inc., Chicago
Gretchen Long
Haskell & Stern Associates, Inc.,
New York
Larry D. Mingle
Higdon, Joys & Mingle, Inc., New
York
Ralph E. Dieckmann
Dieckmann & Associates, Ltd.,
Chicago
Jack H. Vernon
Russell Reynolds Associates, Inc.,
Boston
Ronald Dukes
Heidrick and Struggles, Inc.,
Chicago
George Rossi
Heidrick and Struggles, Inc.,
Boston
Mike Jacobs
Thorne, Brieger Associates Inc.,
New York

MEASURING, ANALYZING, CONTROLLING, AND PHOTOGRAPHIC INSTRUMENTS

George W. Henn, Jr.
G.W. Henn & Company, Columbus,
OH

O.D. "Dan" Cruse
SpencerStuart, Dallas
Lynn Tendler Bignell
Gilbert Tweed Associates, Inc., New
York
William T. Mangum
Thomas Mangum Company, Los
Angeles
Richard C. Slayton
Slayton International, Inc., Chicago
Theodore E. Lusk
Nadzam, Lusk & Associates, Inc.,
Santa Clara, CA
Millington F. McCoy
Gould & McCoy, Inc., New York
Clarence E. McFeely
McFeely Wackerle Jett, Chicago
R. Paul Kors
Kors Montgomery International,
Houston
Jack H. Vernon
Russell Reynolds Associates, Inc.,
Boston
Ronald Dukes
Heidrick and Struggles, Inc.,
Chicago
Laurence Massé
Ward Howell International,
Barrington, IL
William K. Sur
Stricker, Sur & Associates, New
York
Robert Kremple
Kremple & Meade, Malibu, CA

MINING

Stephen A. Garrison
Ward Howell International, Inc.,
Dallas
Lawrence "Larry" W. Hill
Russell Reynolds Associates, Inc.,
Houston
Charles P. Beall
Beall & Company, Inc., Roswell, GA
R. Paul Kors
Kors Montgomery International,
Houston

Robert D. Spriggs
Spriggs & Company, Inc., Chicago
Lynn Tendler Bignell
Gilbert Tweed Associates, Inc., New
York
John F. Johnson
Lamalie Associates, Inc., Cleveland
John T. Gardner
Lamalie Associates, Inc., Chicago
Russell E. Marks, Jr.
A.T. Kearney, Inc., New York
Theodore E. Lusk
Nadzam, Lusk & Associates, Inc.,
Santa Clara, CA
Donald C. Williams
Donald Williams Associates, Inc.,
Chicago

OFFICE MACHINERY/ COMPUTERS

Gerard R. Roche
Heidrick and Struggles, Inc., New
York
J. Gerald Simmons
Handy Associates, New York
O.D. "Dan" Cruse
SpencerStuart, Dallas
Richard K. Ives
Wilkinson & Ives, San Francisco
Theodore E. Lusk
Nadzam, Lusk & Associates, Inc.,
Santa Clara, CA
James M. Montgomery
Houze, Shourds & Montgomery,
Inc., Long Beach, CA
Robert E. Lamalie
Robert Lamalie Inc., Marco Island,
FL
Robert M. Flanagan
Paul Stafford Associates, Ltd., New
York
Leon A. Farley
Leon A. Farley Associates, San
Francisco
Barbara L. Provus
Sweeney Shepherd Bueschel Provus
Harbert & Mummert, Inc.,
Chicago

Donald T. Allerton
Allerton/Heinze & Associates, Inc.,
Chicago
John F. Johnson
Lamalie Associates, Inc., Cleveland
Albert L. Richard, Jr.
Human Resources, Inc.,
Providence, RI
Howard D. Nitchke
Deane, Howard & Simon, Inc.,
Hartford, CT
Mary E. Shourds
Houze, Shourds & Montgomery,
Inc., Long Beach, CA
David F. Smith
Korn/Ferry International, New
York
Charles E. Splaine
Splaine & Associates, Los Gatos,
CA
Richard C. Slayton
Slayton International, Inc., Chicago
James R. Clovis, Jr.
Handy Associates, New York
R.G. Finnegan
Finnegan & Associates Inc., Palos
Verdes Estates, CA
Robert A. Staub
Staub, Warmbold & Associates,
Inc., New York
John R. Ferneborg
Smith, Goerss & Ferneborg, San
Francisco
Nelson W. Gibson
N.W. Gibson International, Los
Angeles
Joseph E. Griesedieck, Jr.
SpencerStuart, San Francisco
Millington F. McCoy
Gould & McCoy, Inc., New York
Charles P. Beall
Beall & Company, Inc., Roswell, GA
George Rossi
Heidrick and Struggles, Inc.,
Boston
Linford E. Stiles
Ward Howell International,
Stamford, CT

J.R. Akin
J.R. Akin & Company, Fairfield, CT
George W. Ott
Ott & Hansen, Inc., Pasadena, CA
Roger M. Kenny
Kenny, Kindler, Hunt & Howe,
New York
Leonard J. Clark, Jr.
Boyden International, New York
Michael S. Dunford
Michael S. Dunford, Inc., Glen
Ellyn, IL
Durant "Andy" Hunter
Gardiner Stone Hunter
International, Boston
P. Anthony Price
Russell Reynolds Associates Inc.,
San Francisco
William A. Hertan
Executive Manning Corp., Fort
Lauderdale
John "Jack" B. Henard, Jr.
Henard Associates, Dallas
R. Paul Kors
Kors Montgomery International,
Houston
William T. Mangum
Thomas Mangum Company, Los
Angeles
Richard A. McCallister
Boyden International, Inc., Chicago
Donald C. Williams
Donald Williams Associates, Inc.,
Chicago
Robert Kremple
Kremple & Meade, Malibu, CA
David R. Peasback
Canny, Bowen Inc., New York
David H. Hoffmann
DHR International, Inc., Chicago
William C. Houze
William C. Houze & Co., Torrance,
CA
John Lucht
The John Lucht Consultancy Inc.,
New York
Gerald D. Menzel
Menzel, Robinson, Baldwin, Inc.,
Arlington Heights, IL

Lawrence J. Holmes
Consulting Associates, Inc.,
Columbia, MD
Richard E. Kinser
Richard Kinser & Associates, New
York
R. James Lotz, Jr.
International Management
Advisors, Inc., New York
James E. Hunt
Kenny, Kindler, Hunt & Howe,
New York
Douglas H. Gates
Haley BDC, New York
Laurence Massé
Ward Howell International,
Barrington, IL
Jack H. Vernon
Russell Reynolds Associates, Inc.,
Boston
Mike Jacobs
Thorne, Brieger Associates Inc.,
New York
Putney Westerfield
Boyden International Inc., New
York

PACKAGING

O. William Battalia
Battalia & Associates, Inc., New
York
Janet Tweed
Gilbert Tweed Associates, New
York
David H. Hoffmann
DHR International, Inc., Chicago
Lawrence P. Crowley
Blendow, Crowley & Oliver Inc.,
New York
Richard J. Cronin
Hodge-Cronin & Associates, Inc.,
Rosemont, IL
Gary W. Silverman
Korn/Ferry International, Chicago
Henry G. Higdon
Higdon, Joys & Mingle, Inc., New
York

Allan D. R. Stern
Haskell & Stern Associates, Inc.,
New York
William T. Mangum
Thomas Mangum Company, Los
Angeles
Steven A. Seiden
Seiden Associates, Inc., New York
Richard A. Miners
Goodrich and Sherwood, New York
Gretchen Long
Haskell & Stern Associates, Inc.,
New York
Andrew Sherwood
Goodrich and Sherwood Company,
New York
William K. Sur
Stricker, Sur & Associates, New
York
Thomas C. Zay
Thomas C. Zay & Company, Inc.,
Atlanta
David F. Smith
Korn/Ferry International, New
York
Eleanor H. Raynolds
Ward Howell International, Inc.,
New York
Ronald Dukes
Heidrick and Struggles, Chicago

PAPER AND ALLIED PRODUCTS

Edward R. Howe, Jr.
Diversified Search, Inc.,
Philadelphia
David R. Peasback
Canny, Bowen Inc., New York
O. William Battalia
Battalia & Associates, Inc., New
York
Darrell G. Robertson
Western Reserve Search Associates,
Inc., Bath, OH
Richard J. Cronin
Hodge-Cronin & Associates, Inc.,
Rosemont, IL

Richard M. McFarland
Brissenden, McFarland, Wagoner, & Fuccella, Inc., Stamford, CT

Robert Kremple
Kremple & Meade, Malibu, CA

John S. Stanton
Russell Reynolds Associates, Inc., Chicago

William A. Hertan
Executive Manning Corp., Fort Lauderdale

Lawrence P. Crowley
Blendow, Crowley & Oliver Inc., New York

Andrew D. Hart
Russell Reynolds Associates, Inc., New York

David E. Chambers
David Chambers & Associates, Inc., New York

Andrew Sherwood
Goodrich and Sherwood Company, New York

George W. Henn, Jr.
G.W. Henn & Company, Columbus, OH

James H. Cornehlsen
Heidrick and Struggles, Inc., New York

James F. Bishop
Burke, O'Brien & Bishop Associates, Inc., Princeton, NJ

Linford E. Stiles
Ward Howell International, Stamford, CT

William K. Sur
Stricker, Sur & Associates, New York

R. James Lotz, Jr.
International Management Advisors, Inc., New York

John F. Johnson
Lamalie Associates, Inc., Cleveland

Thomas C. Zay
Thomas C. Zay & Company, Inc., Atlanta

Gerald D. Menzel
Menzel, Robinson, Baldwin, Inc., Arlington Heights, IL

Peter G. Grimm
Nordeman Grimm, Inc., New York

Richard E. Kinser
Richard Kinser & Associates, New York

Russell E. Marks, Jr.
A.T. Kearney, Inc., New York

William H. Marumoto
The Interface Group, Ltd., Washington, DC

P. John Mirtz
Martin Mirtz Morice, Inc., Stamford, CT

PERFUME/COSMETICS/TOILET GOODS

Robert E. Lamalie
Robert Lamalie Inc., Marco Island, FL

Gerard R. Roche
Heidrick and Struggles, Inc., New York

Robert A. Staub
Staub, Warmbold & Associates, Inc., New York

William E. Gould
Gould & McCoy Inc., New York

Howard Bratches
Thorndike Deland Associates, New York

D. John Ingram
Ingram Inc., New York

J. Alvin Wakefield
Gilbert Tweed Associates, Inc., New York

Paul R. Ray, Jr.
Paul R. Ray & Company, Inc., Fort Worth

John "Jack" B. Henard, Jr.
Henard Associates, Dallas

Jack Seitchik
Seitchik Corwin and Seitchik, San Francisco

Andrew Sherwood
Goodrich and Sherwood Company, New York

John A. Travis
Travis & Company Inc., Sudbury, MA

Harry Bernard
Colton Bernard Inc., San Francisco

Herbert T. Mines
Herbert Mines Associates, Inc.,
New York

James "Rick" L. Richardson
SpencerStuart, Stamford, CT

William K. Sur
Stricker, Sur & Associates, New
York

Martin H. Bauman
Martin H. Bauman Associates, Inc.,
New York

Leonard J. Clark, Jr.
Boyden International, New York

Richard A. Miners
Goodrich and Sherwood, New York

Jacques P. Andre
Paul R. Ray & Company, Inc., New
York

David H. Charlson
Chestnut Hill Partners, Deerfield,
IL

John Lucht
The John Lucht Consultancy Inc.,
New York

Skott B. Burkland
Haley BDC, New York

William B. Reeves
Korn/Ferry International, Atlanta

Putney Westerfield
Boyden International Inc., New
York

R. James Lotz, Jr.
International Management
Advisors, Inc., New York

James F. Bishop
Burke, O'Brien & Bishop
Associates, Inc., Princeton, NJ

Joseph E. Griesedieck, Jr.
SpencerStuart, San Francisco

William H. Marumoto
The Interface Group, Ltd.,
Washington, DC

David R. Peasback
Canny, Bowen Inc., New York

PHARMACEUTICAL/MEDICAL PRODUCTS

William E. Gould
Gould & McCoy Inc., New York

Donald T. Allerton
Allerton/Heinze & Associates, Inc.,
Chicago

Roger M. Kenny
Kenny, Kindler, Hunt & Howe,
New York

Andrew D. Hart
Russell Reynolds Associates, Inc.,
New York

Skott B. Burkland
Haley BDC, New York

Jonathan E. McBride
McBride Associates, Inc.,
Washington, DC

William K. Sur
Stricker, Sur & Associates, New
York

David H. Charlson
Chestnut Hill Partners, Deerfield,
IL

Barbara L. Provus
Sweeney Shepherd Bueschel Provus
Harbert & Mummert, Inc.,
Chicago

William H. Willis, Jr.
William H. Willis, Inc., Greenwich,
CT

R.G. Finnegan
Finnegan & Associates Inc., Palos
Verdes Estates, CA

Judith M. von Seldeneck
Diversified Search, Inc.,
Philadelphia

Carl W. Menk
Canny, Bowen Inc., New York

Michael S. Dunford
Michael S. Dunford, Inc., Glen
Ellyn, IL

Richard M. McFarland
Brissenden, McFarland, Wagoner,
& Fuccella, Inc., Stamford, CT

John A. Travis
Travis & Company Inc., Sudbury,
MA

Frederick W. Wackerle
McFeely Wackerle Jett, Chicago
Lawrence P. Crowley
Blendow, Crowley & Oliver Inc.,
New York
David E. Chambers
David Chambers & Associates, Inc.,
New York
R. James Lotz, Jr.
International Management
Advisors, Inc., New York
Paul R. Ray, Sr.
Paul R. Ray & Company, Inc., Fort
Worth
Robert A. Staub
Staub, Warmbold & Associates,
Inc., New York
John S. Lloyd
Witt Associates, Inc., Oak Brook, IL
Sydney Reynolds
Sydney Reynolds Associates, Inc.,
New York
Clarence E. McFeely
McFeely Wackerle Jett, Chicago
O. William Battalia
Battalia & Associates, Inc., New
York
Millington F. McCoy
Gould & McCoy, Inc., New York
George W. Ott
Ott & Hansen, Inc., Pasadena, CA
Jacques P. Andre
Paul R. Ray & Company, Inc., New
York
Leonard J. Clark, Jr.
Boyden International, New York
E. Pendleton James
Pendleton James & Associates, Inc.,
New York
Lawrence F. Nein
Nordeman Grimm, Inc., Chicago
Peter G. Grimm
Nordeman Grimm, Inc., New York
Robert Kremple
Kremple & Meade, Malibu, CA
Max M. Ulrich
Ward Howell International Inc.,
New York

William R. Wilkinson
Wilkinson & Ives, San Francisco
Mike Jacobs
Thorne, Brieger Associates Inc.,
New York
Theodore Jadick
Heidrick and Struggles, Inc., New
York
Howard Bratches
Thorndike Deland Associates, New
York
Pierson Keating
Nordeman Grimm, New York
Richard Sbarbaro
Lauer, Sbarbaro Associates, Inc.,
Chicago
William B. Clemens, Jr.
Norman Broadbent International,
New York
Putney Westerfield
Boyden International Inc., New
York
Joseph P. McGinley
SpencerStuart, New York
P. Anthony Price
Russell Reynolds Associates Inc.,
San Francisco
J. Alvin Wakefield
Gilbert Tweed Associates, Inc., New
York
James F. Bishop
Burke, O'Brien & Bishop
Associates, Inc., Princeton, NJ
William H. Billington, Jr.
Billington, Fox & Ellis, Inc.,
Chicago
H. Leland Getz
Higdon, Joys & Mingle, Inc., New
York
Richard E. Kinser
Richard Kinser & Associates, New
York
Janet Tweed
Gilbert Tweed Associates, New
York
Donald C. Williams
Donald Williams Associates, Inc.,
Chicago

Jack R. Clarey
  Jack Clarey Associates, Inc.,
    Northbrook, IL
Douglas H. Gates
  Haley BDC, New York
Laurence Massé
  Ward Howell International,
    Barrington, IL
Richard A. Miners
  Goodrich and Sherwood, New York
Janis M. Zivic
  The Zivic Group, Inc., San
    Francisco
Charles E. Splaine
  Splaine & Associates, Los Gatos,
    CA
Robert L. Heidrick
  The Heidrick Partners, Inc.,
    Chicago
John Lucht
  The John Lucht Consultancy Inc.,
    New York
Robert G. Cox
  A.T. Kearney, Inc., New York
Gary Knisely
  Johnson Smith & Knisely Inc., New
    York
James R. Clovis, Jr.
  Handy Associates, New York
Joseph B. Ryan
  The Cambridge Group Ltd.,
    Westport, CT
Andrew Sherwood
  Goodrich and Sherwood Company,
    New York
Gardner W. Heidrick
  The Heidrick Partners, Inc.,
    Chicago
Larry D. Mingle
  Higdon, Joys & Mingle, Inc., New
    York
David O. Harbert
  Sweeney Shepherd Bueschel Provus
    Harbert & Mummert, Inc.,
    Chicago
P. John Mirtz
  Martin Mirtz Morice, Inc.,
    Stamford, CT

J.R. Akin
  J.R. Akin & Company, Fairfield, CT
Lawrence J. Holmes
  Consulting Associates, Inc.,
    Columbia, MD
R. Paul Kors
  Kors Montgomery International,
    Houston
Charles W. Sweet
  A.T. Kearney, Inc., Chicago
Thomas M. Mitchell
  Heidrick and Struggles, Inc., Los
    Angeles
David R. Peasback
  Canny, Bowen Inc., New York
John R. Ferneborg
  Smith, Goerss & Ferneborg, San
    Francisco
William H. Marumoto
  The Interface Group, Ltd.,
    Washington, DC

PRIMARY METAL INDUSTRIES

Edward R. Howe, Jr.
  Diversified Search, Inc.,
    Philadelphia
George W. Henn, Jr.
  G.W. Henn & Company, Columbus,
    OH
David O. Harbert
  Sweeney Shepherd Bueschel Provus
    Harbert & Mummert, Inc.,
    Chicago
Donald C. Williams
  Donald Williams Associates, Inc.,
    Chicago
R. James Lotz, Jr.
  International Management
    Advisors, Inc., New York
Charles D. Reese, Jr.
  Reese Associates, Wexford, PA
Gerald D. Menzel
  Menzel, Robinson, Baldwin, Inc.,
    Arlington Heights, IL
O.D. "Dan" Cruse
  SpencerStuart, Dallas
Jacques P. Andre
  Paul R. Ray & Company, Inc., New
    York

Ronald Dukes
  Heidrick and Struggles, Inc.,
    Chicago
Theodore Jadick
  Heidrick and Struggles, Inc., New
    York
Max M. Ulrich
  Ward Howell International Inc.,
    New York
William H. Billington, Jr.
  Billington, Fox & Ellis, Inc.,
    Chicago
Charles W. Kepler
  Russell Reynolds Associates, Inc.,
    Chicago
Michael S. Dunford
  Michael S. Dunford, Inc., Glen
    Ellyn, IL

PUBLISHING AND PRINTING

James H. Cornehlsen
  Heidrick and Struggles, Inc., New
    York
John Lucht
  The John Lucht Consultancy Inc.,
    New York
Carlton W. "Tony" Thompson
  SpencerStuart, New York
David E. Chambers
  David Chambers & Associates, Inc.,
    New York
J. Gerald Simmons
  Handy Associates, New York
Edward R. Howe, Jr.
  Diversified Search, Inc.,
    Philadelphia
Mark Lorenzetti
  Roberts, Ryan & Bentley,
    Linthicum, MD
Putney Westerfield
  Boyden International Inc., New
    York
John S. Stanton
  Russell Reynolds Associates, Inc.,
    Chicago
R. James Lotz, Jr.
  International Management
    Advisors, Inc., New York

William B. Clemens, Jr.
  Norman Broadbent International,
    New York
James R. Clovis, Jr.
  Handy Associates, New York
Peter G. Grimm
  Nordeman Grimm, Inc., New York
John H. Robison
  Robison & McAulay, Charlotte, NC
Frederick W. Wackerle
  McFeely Wackerle Jett, Chicago
Thomas H. Ogdon
  The Ogdon Partnership, New York
Janis M. Zivic
  The Zivic Group, Inc., San
    Francisco
Sydney Reynolds
  Sydney Reynolds Associates, Inc.,
    New York
Gary Knisely
  Johnson Smith & Knisely Inc., New
    York
Edward A. Raisbeck, Jr.
  Thorndike Deland Associates, New
    York
Robert D. Spriggs
  Spriggs & Company, Inc., Chicago
Allan D. R. Stern
  Haskell & Stern Associates, Inc.,
    New York
Gary W. Silverman
  Korn/Ferry International, Chicago
Linford E. Stiles
  Ward Howell International,
    Stamford, CT
Richard A. Miners
  Goodrich and Sherwood, New York
Richard J. Cronin
  Hodge-Cronin & Associates, Inc.,
    Rosemont, IL
Joseph B. Ryan
  The Cambridge Group Ltd.,
    Westport, CT
Charles W. Sweet
  A.T. Kearney, Inc., Chicago
James F. Bishop
  Burke, O'Brien & Bishop
    Associates, Inc., Princeton, NJ

Douglas H. Gates
  Haley BDC, New York
Richard A. McCallister
  Boyden International, Inc., Chicago
Leonard J. Clark, Jr.
  Boyden International, New York
Joseph E. Griesedieck, Jr.
  SpencerStuart, San Francisco
Andrew D. Hart
  Russell Reynolds Associates, Inc.,
  New York
Millington F. McCoy
  Gould & McCoy, Inc., New York
Ralph E. Dieckmann
  Dieckmann & Associates, Ltd.,
  Chicago

RADIO AND TELEVISION BROADCASTING

Gerard R. Roche
  Heidrick and Struggles, Inc., New
  York
Carlton W. "Tony" Thompson
  SpencerStuart, New York
James H. Cornehlsen
  Heidrick and Struggles, Inc., New
  York
John Lucht
  The John Lucht Consultancy Inc.,
  New York
Gary Knisely
  Johnson Smith & Knisely Inc., New
  York
Carl W. Menk
  Canny, Bowen Inc., New York
Joseph E. Griesedieck, Jr.
  SpencerStuart, San Francisco
Michael J. Hoevel
  Poirier, Hoevel & Company, Los
  Angeles
Clarence E. McFeely
  McFeely Wackerle Jett, Chicago
Peter G. Grimm
  Nordeman Grimm, Inc., New York
William K. Sur
  Stricker, Sur & Associates, New
  York

REAL ESTATE

Dayton Ogden
  SpencerStuart, New York
John R. Ferneborg
  Smith, Goerss & Ferneborg, San
  Francisco
William E. Gould
  Gould & McCoy Inc., New York
Richard M. Ferry
  Korn/Ferry International, Los
  Angeles
Sandford I. Gadient
  Huntress Real Estate Executive
  Search, Kansas City, MO
Thomas H. Ogdon
  The Ogdon Partnership, New York
Windle B. Priem
  Korn/Ferry International, New
  York
W. Hoyt Colton
  W. Hoyt Colton Associates Inc.,
  New York
Lawrence F. Nein
  Nordeman Grimm, Inc., Chicago
Jacques C. Nordeman
  Nordeman Grimm, Inc., New York
Robert M. Flanagan
  Paul Stafford Associates, Ltd., New
  York
Ferdinand Nadherny
  Russell Reynolds Associates, Inc.,
  Chicago
Judith M. von Seldeneck
  Diversified Search, Inc.,
  Philadelphia
Caroline Ballantine
  Heidrick and Struggles, Inc., New
  York
Albert L. McAulay, Jr.
  Robison & McAulay, Charlotte, NC
Paul R. Ray, Sr.
  Paul R. Ray & Company, Inc., Fort
  Worth
Edward R. Howe, Jr.
  Diversified Search, Inc.,
  Philadelphia
Durant "Andy" Hunter
  Gardiner Stone Hunter
  International, Boston

Henry G. Higdon
  Higdon, Joys & Mingle, Inc., New
  York
Frank R. Beaudine
  Eastman & Beaudine, Inc., Dallas
Brenda L. Ruello
  Heidrick and Struggles, Inc., New
  York
William B. Reeves
  Korn/Ferry International, Atlanta
W. Michael Danforth
  Hyde Danforth & Co., Dallas
Jonathan A. Crystal
  SpencerStuart, Houston
W. Jerry Hyde
  Hyde Danforth & Co., Dallas
J. Alvin Wakefield
  Gilbert Tweed Associates, Inc., New
  York
Martin H. Bauman
  Martin H. Bauman Associates, Inc.,
  New York
Otis H. Bowden, II
  Bowden & Company, Inc.,
  Cleveland
Leon A. Farley
  Leon A. Farley Associates, San
  Francisco
David O. Harbert
  Sweeney Shepherd Bueschel Provus
  Harbert & Mummert, Inc.,
  Chicago
H. Leland Getz
  Higdon, Joys & Mingle, Inc., New
  York
Charles M. Meng
  Meng, Finseth & Associates, Inc.,
  Rolling Hills, CA
Norman F. Moody
  Paul Stafford Associates, Ltd., New
  York
Albert L. Richard, Jr.
  Human Resources, Inc.,
  Providence, RI
John H. Robison
  Robison & McAulay, Charlotte, NC
George W. Ott
  Ott & Hansen, Inc., Pasadena, CA

David F. Smith
  Korn/Ferry International, New
  York
William B. Beeson
  Lawrence-Leiter & Company,
  Kansas City, MO
John W. Franklin, Jr.
  Russell Reynolds Associates, Inc.,
  Washington, DC
Robert S. Rollo
  Korn/Ferry International, Los
  Angeles
William H. Willis, Jr.
  William H. Willis, Inc., Greenwich,
  CT
David H. Hoffmann
  DHR International, Inc., Chicago
David S. Joys
  Higdon, Joys & Mingle, Inc., New
  York
Roger M. Kenny
  Kenny, Kindler, Hunt & Howe,
  New York
Gary R. Barton
  Barton Raben, Inc., Houston
Thomas M. Mitchell
  Heidrick and Struggles, Inc., Los
  Angeles
Eleanor H. Raynolds
  Ward Howell International, Inc.,
  New York
Joseph E. Griesedieck, Jr.
  SpencerStuart, San Francisco
Pierson Keating
  Nordeman Grimm, New York
Steven A. Raben
  Barton Raben, Inc., Houston

RETAIL

Herbert T. Mines
  Herbert Mines Associates, Inc.,
  New York
Edward A. Raisbeck, Jr.
  Thorndike Deland Associates, New
  York
Gerald D. Menzel
  Menzel, Robinson, Baldwin, Inc.,
  Arlington Heights, IL

Frank R. Beaudine
   Eastman & Beaudine, Inc., Dallas
Joseph P. McGinley
   SpencerStuart, New York
Andrew D. Hart
   Russell Reynolds Associates, Inc.,
   New York
Paul R. Ray, Sr.
   Paul R. Ray & Company, Inc., Fort
   Worth
Brenda L. Ruello
   Heidrick and Struggles, Inc., New
   York
Joseph B. Ryan
   The Cambridge Group Ltd.,
   Westport, CT
Jack Seitchik
   Seitchik Corwin and Seitchik, San
   Francisco
Joseph E. Griesedieck, Jr.
   SpencerStuart, San Francisco
Skott B. Burkland
   Haley BDC, New York
John Lucht
   The John Lucht Consultancy Inc.,
   New York
Charles M. Meng
   Meng, Finseth & Associates, Inc.,
   Rolling Hills, CA
Gretchen Long
   Haskell & Stern Associates, Inc.,
   New York
Richard M. Ferry
   Korn/Ferry International, Los
   Angeles
Mike Jacobs
   Thorne, Brieger Associates Inc.,
   New York
John T. Gardner
   Lamalie Associates, Inc., Chicago
Barbara L. Provus
   Sweeney Shepherd Bueschel Provus
   Harbert & Mummert, Inc.,
   Chicago
Nelson W. Gibson
   N.W. Gibson International, Los
   Angeles
John "Jack" B. Henard, Jr.
   Henard Associates, Dallas

P. Anthony Price
   Russell Reynolds Associates Inc.,
   San Francisco
David H. Hoffmann
   DHR International, Inc., Chicago
Putney Westerfield
   Boyden International Inc., New
   York
George W. Henn, Jr.
   G.W. Henn & Company, Columbus,
   OH
William B. Beeson
   Lawrence-Leiter & Company,
   Kansas City, MO
James F. Bishop
   Burke, O'Brien & Bishop
   Associates, Inc., Princeton, NJ
H. Leland Getz
   Higdon, Joys & Mingle, Inc., New
   York
David S. Joys
   Higdon, Joys & Mingle, Inc., New
   York
Thomas C. Zay
   Thomas C. Zay & Company, Inc.,
   Atlanta
Thomas M. Mitchell
   Heidrick and Struggles, Inc., Los
   Angeles

RUBBER AND PLASTIC PRODUCTS

John F. Johnson
   Lamalie Associates, Inc., Cleveland
George W. Henn, Jr.
   G.W. Henn & Company, Columbus,
   OH
Richard M. McFarland
   Brissenden, McFarland, Wagoner,
   & Fuccella, Inc., Stamford, CT
Robert M. Flanagan
   Paul Stafford Associates, Ltd., New
   York
Nancy F. Keithley
   Ernst & Young, Cleveland
Robert M. Bryza
   Robert Lowell International, Inc.,
   Dallas

Richard C. Slayton
Slayton International, Inc., Chicago
Otis H. Bowden, II
Bowden & Company, Inc.,
Cleveland
Ferdinand Nadherny
Russell Reynolds Associates, Inc.,
Chicago
Janet Tweed
Gilbert Tweed Associates, New
York
Max M. Ulrich
Ward Howell International Inc.,
New York
Gerald D. Menzel
Menzel, Robinson, Baldwin, Inc.,
Arlington Heights, IL
Barbara L. Provus
Sweeney Shepherd Bueschel Provus
Harbert & Mummert, Inc.,
Chicago
Darrell G. Robertson
Western Reserve Search Associates,
Inc., Bath, OH
Mike Jacobs
Thorne, Brieger Associates Inc.,
New York
Robert Kremple
Kremple & Meade, Malibu, CA
John T. Gardner
Lamalie Associates, Inc., Chicago
Steven M. Darter
People Management Inc., Simsbury,
CT
William B. Beeson
Lawrence-Leiter & Company,
Kansas City, MO
Richard A. McCallister
Boyden International, Inc., Chicago
Laurence Massé
Ward Howell International,
Barrington, IL
O.D. "Dan" Cruse
SpencerStuart, Dallas
Ronald Dukes
Heidrick and Struggles, Inc.,
Chicago
Paul R. Ray, Sr.
Paul R. Ray & Company, Inc., Fort
Worth

SECURITY AND COMMODITY BROKERS/DEALERS AND EXCHANGES

Thomas J. Neff
SpencerStuart, New York
Windle B. Priem
Korn/Ferry International, New
York
Jacques C. Nordeman
Nordeman Grimm, Inc., New York
Jacques P. Andre
Paul R. Ray & Company, Inc., New
York
W. Hoyt Colton
W. Hoyt Colton Associates Inc.,
New York
Russell S. Reynolds, Jr.
Russell Reynolds Associates, Inc.,
New York
Henry G. Higdon
Higdon, Joys & Mingle, Inc., New
York
Jay Gaines
Jay Gaines & Company, Inc., New
York
Dayton Ogden
SpencerStuart, New York
Robert A. Staub
Staub, Warmbold & Associates,
Inc., New York
Stephen A. Garrison
Ward Howell International, Inc.,
Dallas
Ferdinand Nadherny
Russell Reynolds Associates, Inc.,
Chicago
Caroline Ballantine
Heidrick and Struggles, Inc., New
York
Robert M. Flanagan
Paul Stafford Associates, Ltd., New
York
Joseph P. McGinley
SpencerStuart, New York
Durant "Andy" Hunter
Gardiner Stone Hunter
International, Boston

James E. Hunt
  Kenny, Kindler, Hunt & Howe,
    New York
David S. Joys
  Higdon, Joys & Mingle, Inc., New
    York
Norman F. Moody
  Paul Stafford Associates, Ltd., New
    York
Jonathan E. McBride
  McBride Associates, Inc.,
    Washington, DC
Allan D. R. Stern
  Haskell & Stern Associates, Inc.,
    New York
Lawrence J. Holmes
  Consulting Associates, Inc.,
    Columbia, MD
Andrew Sherwood
  Goodrich and Sherwood Company,
    New York
H. Leland Getz
  Higdon, Joys & Mingle, Inc., New
    York
Peter D. Crist
  Russell Reynolds Associates, Inc.,
    Chicago
Larry D. Mingle
  Higdon, Joys & Mingle, Inc., New
    York
Jonathan A. Crystal
  SpencerStuart, Houston
Robert G. Cox
  A.T. Kearney, Inc., New York
Robert S. Rollo
  Korn/Ferry International, Los
    Angeles
William H. Willis, Jr.
  William H. Willis, Inc., Greenwich,
    CT
Steven A. Seiden
  Seiden Associates, Inc., New York
Roger M. Kenny
  Kenny, Kindler, Hunt & Howe,
    New York
Richard A. Miners
  Goodrich and Sherwood, New York
James H. Cornehlsen
  Heidrick and Struggles, Inc., New
    York

David H. Charlson
  Chestnut Hill Partners, Deerfield,
    IL
Joseph B. Ryan
  The Cambridge Group Ltd.,
    Westport, CT

TEXTILES AND APPAREL

John H. Callen, Jr.
  Ward Howell International, New
    York
Jack Seitchik
  Seitchik Corwin and Seitchik, San
    Francisco
Harry Bernard
  Colton Bernard Inc., San Francisco
Herbert T. Mines
  Herbert Mines Associates, Inc.,
    New York
Thomas C. Zay
  Thomas C. Zay & Company, Inc.,
    Atlanta
Gary W. Silverman
  Korn/Ferry International, Chicago
John H. Robison
  Robison & McAulay, Charlotte, NC
Edward A. Raisbeck, Jr.
  Thorndike Deland Associates, New
    York
Robert A. Staub
  Staub, Warmbold & Associates,
    Inc., New York
Andrew D. Hart
  Russell Reynolds Associates, Inc.,
    New York
Albert L. McAulay, Jr.
  Robison & McAulay, Charlotte, NC

TOBACCO AND LIQUOR

Paul R. Ray, Jr.
  Paul R. Ray & Company, Inc., Fort
    Worth
P. Anthony Price
  Russell Reynolds Associates Inc.,
    San Francisco
David F. Smith
  Korn/Ferry International, New
    York

Douglas H. Gates
Haley BDC, New York
Jacques P. Andre
Paul R. Ray & Company, Inc., New
York
William K. Sur
Stricker, Sur & Associates, New
York
James F. Bishop
Burke, O'Brien & Bishop
Associates, Inc., Princeton, NJ
John F. Johnson
Lamalie Associates, Inc., Cleveland
William H. Marumoto
The Interface Group, Ltd.,
Washington, DC
David E. Chambers
David Chambers & Associates, Inc.,
New York
Michael J. Hoevel
Poirier, Hoevel & Company, Los
Angeles
J. R. Akin
J. R. Akin & Company, Fairfield,
CT
Caroline Ballantine
Heidrick and Struggles, Inc., New
York
Carl W. Menk
Canny, Bowen Inc., New York

TRANSPORTATION BY AIR, RAIL, OR WATER

Gerard R. Roche
Heidrick and Struggles, Inc., New
York
Robert W. Slater
Korn/Ferry International, Dallas
D. John Ingram
Ingram Inc., New York
Robert W. Dingman
Robert W. Dingman Company, Inc.,
Westlake Village, CA
E. Pendleton James
Pendleton James & Associates, Inc.,
New York
Martin H. Bauman
Martin H. Bauman Associates, Inc.,
New York

J. Alvin Wakefield
Gilbert Tweed Associates, Inc., New
York
David R. Peasback
Canny, Bowen Inc., New York
Dayton Ogden
SpencerStuart, New York
Henry G. Higdon
Higdon, Joys & Mingle, Inc., New
York
William C. Houze
William C. Houze & Co., Torrance,
CA
Robert D. Spriggs
Spriggs & Company, Inc., Chicago
David O. Harbert
Sweeney Shepherd Bueschel Provus
Harbert & Mummert, Inc.,
Chicago
Gary R. Barton
Barton Raben, Inc., Houston
Leon A. Farley
Leon A. Farley Associates, San
Francisco
Roger M. Kenny
Kenny, Kindler, Hunt & Howe,
New York
William R. Wilkinson
Wilkinson & Ives, San Francisco
John S. Stanton
Russell Reynolds Associates, Inc.,
Chicago
Steven A. Raben
Barton Raben, Inc., Houston
David S. Joys
Higdon, Joys & Mingle, Inc., New
York
John H. Robison
Robison & McAulay, Charlotte, NC
Charles W. Sweet
A.T. Kearney, Inc., Chicago
Richard K. Ives
Wilkinson & Ives, San Francisco
Robert M. Flanagan
Paul Stafford Associates, Ltd., New
York
John R. Ferneborg
Smith, Goerss & Ferneborg, San
Francisco

James E. Hunt
  Kenny, Kindler, Hunt & Howe,
  New York
J. R. Akin
  J. R. Akin & Company, Fairfield,
  CT
William B. Arnold
  William B. Arnold Associates, Inc.,
  Denver
James H. Cornehlsen
  Heidrick and Struggles, Inc., New
  York
Caroline Ballantine
  Heidrick and Struggles, Inc., New
  York
R. Paul Kors
  Kors Montgomery International,
  Houston
Robert G. Cox
  A.T. Kearney, Inc., New York

TRANSPORTATION EQUIPMENT

John F. Johnson
  Lamalie Associates, Inc., Cleveland
Otis H. Bowden, II
  Bowden & Company, Inc.,
  Cleveland
Richard C. Slayton
  Slayton International, Inc., Chicago
William A. Hertan
  Executive Manning Corp., Fort
  Lauderdale
James M. Montgomery
  Houze, Shourds & Montgomery,
  Inc., Long Beach, CA
Laurence Massé
  Ward Howell International,
  Barrington, IL
William H. Billington, Jr.
  Billington, Fox & Ellis, Inc.,
  Chicago
Robert E. Lamalie
  Robert Lamalie Inc., Marco Island,
  FL
Frederick W. Wackerle
  McFeely Wackerle Jett, Chicago

Charles W. Kepler
  Russell Reynolds Associates, Inc.,
  Chicago
Barbara L. Provus
  Sweeney Shepherd Bueschel Provus
  Harbert & Mummert, Inc.,
  Chicago
Gerald D. Menzel
  Menzel, Robinson, Baldwin, Inc.,
  Arlington Heights, IL
Jack R. Clarey
  Jack Clarey Associates, Inc.,
  Northbrook, IL
Ronald Dukes
  Heidrick and Struggles, Inc.,
  Chicago
Donald C. Williams
  Donald Williams Associates, Inc.,
  Chicago
Robert M. Bryza
  Robert Lowell International, Inc.,
  Dallas
Gretchen Long
  Haskell & Stern Associates, Inc.,
  New York
P. Anthony Price
  Russell Reynolds Associates Inc.,
  San Francisco

UNIVERSITIES/COLLEGES

William J. Bowen
  Heidrick and Struggles, Inc.,
  Chicago
Ira Krinsky
  Ira Krinsky Associates, Los Angeles
Gary J. Posner
  George Kaludis Associates,
  Nashville
John S. Lloyd
  Witt Associates, Inc., Oak Brook, IL
Michael D. Caver
  Heidrick and Struggles, Inc.,
  Chicago
Stephen A. Garrison
  Ward Howell International, Inc.,
  Dallas
Frank A. Garofolo
  Garofolo, Curtiss & Company,
  Ardmore, PA

Thomas R. Moore
  Ketchum, Inc., Pittsburgh
Janis M. Zivic
  The Zivic Group, Inc., San
  Francisco
James M. Schmidt
  Cejka & Company, St. Louis
Kenneth L. Rattner
  Heidrick and Struggles, Inc.,
  Chicago
Antoinette "Toni" L. Farley
  Kieffer, Ford & Associates, Ltd.,
  Oak Brook, IL
Judith M. von Seldeneck
  Diversified Search, Inc.,
  Philadelphia
Millington F. McCoy
  Gould & McCoy, Inc., New York
William C. Houze
  William C. Houze & Co., Torrance,
  CA
William E. Gould
  Gould & McCoy Inc., New York
Max M. Ulrich
  Ward Howell International Inc.,
  New York
Frederic E. Berman
  The Berman Consulting Group,
  Atlanta
Robert G. Cox
  A.T. Kearney, Inc., New York
Richard Sbarbaro
  Lauer, Sbarbaro Associates, Inc.,
  Chicago
Pierson Keating
  Nordeman Grimm, New York
Charles M. Meng
  Meng, Finseth & Associates, Inc.,
  Rolling Hills, CA
Dayton Ogden
  SpencerStuart, New York
John Lucht
  The John Lucht Consultancy Inc.,
  New York
John H. Robison
  Robison & McAulay, Charlotte, NC
W. Michael Danforth
  Hyde Danforth & Co., Dallas

W. Jerry Hyde
  Hyde Danforth & Co., Dallas

WHOLESALE TRADE

David O. Harbert
  Sweeney Shepherd Bueschel Provus
  Harbert & Mummert, Inc.,
  Chicago
Martin H. Bauman
  Martin H. Bauman Associates, Inc.,
  New York
Harry Bernard
  Colton Bernard Inc., San Francisco
John H. Callen, Jr.
  Ward Howell International, New
  York
Edward A. Raisbeck, Jr.
  Thorndike Deland Associates, New
  York
Jack Seitchik
  Seitchik Corwin and Seitchik, San
  Francisco
Robert M. Flanagan
  Paul Stafford Associates, Ltd., New
  York
Joseph B. Ryan
  The Cambridge Group Ltd.,
  Westport, CT
Michael J. Hoevel
  Poirier, Hoevel & Company, Los
  Angeles
Thomas C. Zay
  Thomas C. Zay & Company, Inc.,
  Atlanta
Albert L. McAulay, Jr.
  Robison & McAulay, Charlotte, NC
Mike Jacobs
  Thorne, Brieger Associates Inc.,
  New York
William B. Beeson
  Lawrence-Leiter & Company,
  Kansas City, MO
William B. Arnold
  William B. Arnold Associates, Inc.,
  Denver

James R. Clovis, Jr.
  Handy Associates, New York
Steven A. Seiden
  Seiden Associates, Inc., New York

FUNCTIONAL SPECIALIZATION
(Sequence of categories)

Categories

- General management
- Director recruitment
- Administration
- Advertising/Promotion
- Direct Marketing
- Editorial
- Engineering
- Finance and accounting
- Human resources/Personnel
- International
- Legal

- Manufacturing/Production/Operations
- Marketing/Sales–Consumer
- Marketing/Sales–Industrial
- Merchandising
- MIS/Computer operations
- Planning
- Public relations/Government affairs
- Purchasing/Materials
- Research and development

Those recruiters who work essentially only in specific organizational or industry specializations are identified by the following symbols:

(HC)   Health care

(HO)   Hospitality

(LE)   Legal

(ED)   Education and related fields

GENERAL MANAGEMENT

Gerard R. Roche
  Heidrick and Struggles, Inc., New York
Thomas J. Neff
  SpencerStuart, New York
Robert E. Lamalie
  Robert Lamalie Inc., Marco Island, FL

Frederick W. Wackerle
  McFeely Wackerle Jett, Chicago
John F. Johnson
  Lamalie Associates, Inc., Cleveland
Leon A. Farley
  Leon A. Farley Associates, San Francisco
Windle B. Priem
  Korn/Ferry International, New York

Jacques C. Nordeman
   Nordeman Grimm, Inc., New York
Michael C. Kieffer
   Kieffer, Ford & Associates, Inc.,
   Oak Brook, IL (HC)
Donald T. Allerton
   Allerton/Heinze & Associates, Inc.,
   Chicago
John S. Lloyd
   Witt Associates, Inc., Oak Brook, IL
   (HC)
William J. Bowen
   Heidrick and Struggles, Inc.,
   Chicago
D. John Ingram
   Ingram Inc., New York
Otis H. Bowden, II
   Bowden & Company, Inc.,
   Cleveland
Michael D. Caver
   Heidrick and Struggles, Inc.,
   Chicago (HC)
Michael S. Dunford
   Michael S. Dunford, Inc., Glen
   Ellyn, IL
Carol S. Jeffers
   John Sibbald Associates, Inc.,
   Chicago (HO)
William E. Gould
   Gould & McCoy Inc., New York
Robert D. Spriggs
   Spriggs & Company, Inc., Chicago
Robert W. Dingman
   Robert W. Dingman Company, Inc.,
   Westlake Village, CA
George W. Henn, Jr.
   G.W. Henn & Company, Columbus,
   OH
Paul R. Ray, Sr.
   Paul R. Ray & Company, Inc., Fort
   Worth
Robert W. Slater
   Korn/Ferry International, Dallas
Stephen A. Garrison
   Ward Howell International, Inc.,
   Dallas
Roger M. Kenny
   Kenny, Kindler, Hunt & Howe,
   New York

Richard M. McFarland
   Brissenden, McFarland, Wagoner,
   & Fuccella, Inc., Stamford, CT
Harvey M. Weiner
   Search America, Dallas (HO)
Ferdinand Nadherny
   Russell Reynolds Associates, Inc.,
   Chicago
J. Daniel Ford
   Kieffer, Ford & Associates, Ltd.,
   Oak Brook, IL (HC)
Richard M. Ferry
   Korn/Ferry International, Los
   Angeles
Robert A. Staub
   Staub, Warmbold & Associates,
   Inc., New York
Judith M. von Seldeneck
   Diversified Search, Inc.,
   Philadelphia
Carlton "Tony" W. Thompson
   SpencerStuart, New York
Antoinette "Toni" L. Farley
   Kieffer, Ford & Associates, Ltd.,
   Oak Brook, IL (HC)
Robert L. Heidrick
   The Heidrick Partners, Inc.,
   Chicago
Carl W. Menk
   Canny, Bowen Inc., New York
J. Gerald Simmons
   Handy Associates, New York
Richard C. Slayton
   Slayton International, Inc., Chicago
Charles P. Beall
   Beall & Company, Inc., Roswell, GA
Howard Bratches
   Thorndike Deland Associates, New
   York
Gary R. Barton
   Barton Raben, Inc., Houston
David E. Chambers
   David Chambers & Associates, Inc.,
   New York
David H. Charlson
   Chestnut Hill Partners, Deerfield,
   IL
Edward R. Howe, Jr.
   Diversified Search, Inc.,
   Philadelphia

E. Pendleton James
Pendleton James & Associates, Inc.,
New York

Barbara L. Provus
Sweeney Shepherd Bueschel Provus
Harbert & Mummert, Inc.,
Chicago

Lawrence F. Nein
Nordeman Grimm, Inc., Chicago

Russell S. Reynolds, Jr.
Russell Reynolds Associates, Inc.,
New York

Richard Sbarbaro
Lauer, Sbarbaro Associates, Inc.,
Chicago

Lynn Tendler Bignell
Gilbert Tweed Associates, Inc., New
York

James H. Cornehlsen
Heidrick and Struggles, Inc., New
York

Robert M. Flanagan
Paul Stafford Associates, Ltd., New
York

David O. Harbert
Sweeney Shepherd Bueschel Provus
Harbert & Mummert, Inc.,
Chicago

Andrew D. Hart
Russell Reynolds Associates, Inc.,
New York

James N. Heuerman
Korn/Ferry International, San
Francisco (HC)

Millington F. McCoy
Gould & McCoy, Inc., New York

Jacques P. Andre
Paul R. Ray & Company, Inc., New
York

Martin H. Bauman
Martin H. Bauman Associates, Inc.,
New York

Skott B. Burkland
Haley BDC, New York

Nancy F. Keithley
Ernst & Young, Cleveland

Frank R. Beaudine
Eastman & Beaudine, Inc., Dallas

Jack R. Clarey
Jack Clarey Associates, Inc.,
Northbrook, IL

Richard J. Cronin
Hodge-Cronin & Associates, Inc.,
Rosemont, IL

O.D. "Dan" Cruse
SpencerStuart, Dallas

Ralph E. Dieckmann
Dieckmann & Associates, Ltd.,
Chicago

Theodore Jadick
Heidrick and Struggles, Inc., New
York

Durant "Andy" Hunter
Gardiner Stone Hunter
International, Boston

Gardner W. Heidrick
The Heidrick Partners, Inc.,
Chicago

Henry G. Higdon
Higdon, Joys & Mingle, Inc., New
York

Michael J. Hoevel
Poirier, Hoevel & Company, Los
Angeles

Richard K. Ives
Wilkinson & Ives, San Francisco

Robert Kremple
Kremple & Meade, Malibu, CA

John Lucht
The John Lucht Consultancy Inc.,
New York

Theodore E. Lusk
Nadzam, Lusk & Associates, Inc.,
Santa Clara, CA

Jonathan E. McBride
McBride Associates, Inc.,
Washington, DC

Clarence E. McFeely
McFeely Wackerle Jett, Chicago

Joseph P. McGinley
SpencerStuart, New York

James M. Montgomery
Houze, Shourds & Montgomery,
Inc., Long Beach, CA

Dayton Ogden
SpencerStuart, New York

Thomas H. Ogdon
The Ogdon Partnership, New York
David R. Peasback
Canny, Bowen Inc., New York
Paul R. Ray, Jr.
Paul R. Ray & Company, Inc., Fort Worth
H. Leland Getz
Higdon, Joys & Mingle, Inc., New York
Mary E. Shourds
Houze, Shourds & Montgomery, Inc., Long Beach, CA
Allan D. R. Stern
Haskell & Stern Associates, Inc., New York
J. Alvin Wakefield
Gilbert Tweed Associates, Inc., New York
William R. Wilkinson
Wilkinson & Ives, San Francisco
William H. Willis, Jr.
William H. Willis, Inc., Greenwich, CT
Janis M. Zivic
The Zivic Group, Inc., San Francisco
Caroline Ballantine
Heidrick and Struggles, Inc., New York
Max M. Ulrich
Ward Howell International Inc., New York
J.R. Akin
J.R. Akin & Company, Fairfield, CT
William B. Arnold
William B. Arnold Associates, Inc., Denver
O. William Battalia
Battalia & Associates, Inc., New York
Frederic E. Berman
The Berman Consulting Group, Atlanta
Harry Bernard
Colton Bernard Inc., San Francisco
William H. Billington, Jr.
Billington, Fox & Ellis, Inc., Chicago

Robert M. Bryza
Robert Lowell International, Inc., Dallas
John H. Callen, Jr.
Ward Howell International, New York
William B. Clemens, Jr.
Norman Broadbent International, New York
James R. Clovis, Jr.
Handy Associates, New York
Steven M. Darter
People Management Inc., Simsbury, CT
Sandford I. Gadient
Huntress Real Estate Executive Search, Kansas City, MO
Frank A. Garofolo
Garofolo, Curtiss & Company, Ardmore, PA
Nelson W. Gibson
N.W. Gibson International, Los Angeles
Peter G. Grimm
Nordeman Grimm, Inc., New York
John "Jack" B. Henard, Jr.
Henard Associates, Dallas
David H. Hoffmann
DHR International, Inc., Chicago
Lawrence J. Holmes
Consulting Associates, Inc., Columbia, MD
William C. Houze
William C. Houze & Co., Torrance, CA
Richard E. Kinser
Richard Kinser & Associates, New York
R. James Lotz, Jr.
International Management Advisors, Inc., New York
William T. Mangum
Thomas Mangum Company, Los Angeles
Joan I. McCrea
Nursing Technomics, West Chester, PA (HC)
Herbert T. Mines
Herbert Mines Associates, Inc., New York

Howard D. Nitchke
  Deane, Howard & Simon, Inc.,
    Hartford, CT
George W. Ott
  Ott & Hansen, Inc., Pasadena, CA
Edward A. Raisbeck, Jr.
  Thorndike Deland Associates, New
    York
Herbert Regehly
  Innkeeper's Management Corp.,
    New York (HO)
Darrell G. Robertson
  Western Reserve Search Associates,
    Inc., Bath, OH
Steven A. Seiden
  Seiden Associates, Inc., New York
Jack Seitchik
  Seitchik Corwin and Seitchik, San
    Francisco
Andrew Sherwood
  Goodrich and Sherwood Company,
    New York
David F. Smith
  Korn/Ferry International, New
    York
Charles E. Splaine
  Splaine & Associates, Los Gatos,
    CA
William K. Sur
  Stricker, Sur & Associates, New
    York
Charles W. Sweet
  A.T. Kearney, Inc., Chicago
Putney Westerfield
  Boyden International Inc., New
    York
Donald C. Williams
  Donald Williams Associates, Inc.,
    Chicago
P. Anthony Price
  Russell Reynolds Associates Inc.,
    San Francisco
Gerald D. Menzel
  Menzel, Robinson, Baldwin, Inc.,
    Arlington Heights, IL
W. Michael Danforth
  Hyde Danforth & Co., Dallas
R. Paul Kors
  Kors Montgomery International,
    Houston

James M. Schmidt
  Cejka & Company, St. Louis (HC)
Leonard J. Clark, Jr.
  Boyden International, New York
Joseph E. Griesedieck, Jr.
  SpencerStuart, San Francisco
James E. Hunt
  Kenny, Kindler, Hunt & Howe,
    New York
A. Donald Iklé
  Ward Howell International, Inc.,
    New York
Jack H. Vernon
  Russell Reynolds Associates, Inc.,
    Boston
David S. Joys
  Higdon, Joys & Mingle, Inc., New
    York
Gary Knisely
  Johnson Smith & Knisely Inc., New
    York
Charles M. Meng
  Meng, Finseth & Associates, Inc.,
    Rolling Hills, CA
Norman F. Moody
  Paul Stafford Associates, Ltd., New
    York
Sydney Reynolds
  Sydney Reynolds Associates, Inc.,
    New York
Kenneth L. Rattner
  Heidrick and Struggles, Inc.,
    Chicago
John H. Robison
  Robison & McAulay, Charlotte, NC
Brenda L. Ruello
  Heidrick and Struggles, Inc., New
    York
Ben Schwartz
  Harper Associates, Farmington
    Hills, MI (HO)
Janet Tweed
  Gilbert Tweed Associates, New
    York
Thomas C. Zay
  Thomas C. Zay & Company, Inc.,
    Atlanta
Albert L. McAulay, Jr.
  Robison & McAulay, Charlotte, NC

John R. Ferneborg
  Smith, Goerss & Ferneborg, San
  Francisco
Jay Gaines
  Jay Gaines & Company, Inc., New
  York
W. Jerry Hyde
  Hyde Danforth & Co., Dallas
Mike Jacobs
  Thorne, Brieger Associates Inc.,
  New York
William B. Beeson
  Lawrence-Leiter & Company,
  Kansas City, MO
James F. Bishop
  Burke, O'Brien & Bishop
  Associates, Inc., Princeton, NJ
John T. Gardner
  Lamalie Associates, Inc., Chicago
Albert L. Richard, Jr.
  Human Resources, Inc.,
  Providence, RI
James A. Hayden, Jr.
  Hayden Group, Inc., Boston
William A. Hertan
  Executive Manning Corp., Fort
  Lauderdale
Lawrence "Larry" W. Hill
  Russell Reynolds Associates, Inc.,
  Houston
Pierson Keating
  Nordeman Grimm, New York
Charles W. Kepler
  Russell Reynolds Associates, Inc.,
  Chicago
Gretchen Long
  Haskell & Stern Associates, Inc.,
  New York
Laurence Massé
  Ward Howell International,
  Barrington, IL
Richard A. McCallister
  Boyden International, Inc., Chicago
Richard A. Miners
  Goodrich and Sherwood, New York
Larry D. Mingle
  Higdon, Joys & Mingle, Inc., New
  York

Gary J. Posner
  George Kaludis Associates,
  Nashville(ED)
Steven A. Raben
  Barton Raben, Inc., Houston
Charles D. Reese, Jr.
  Reese Associates, Wexford, PA
William B. Reeves
  Korn/Ferry International, Atlanta
James "Rick" L. Richardson
  SpencerStuart, Stamford, CT
George Rossi
  Heidrick and Struggles, Inc.,
  Boston
Gary W. Silverman
  Korn/Ferry International, Chicago
Edward C. Slowik
  SpencerStuart, New York
John S. Stanton
  Russell Reynolds Associates, Inc.,
  Chicago
Linford E. Stiles
  Ward Howell International,
  Stamford, CT
John A. Travis
  Travis & Company Inc., Sudbury,
  MA
Robert G. Cox
  A.T. Kearney, Inc., New York
Peter D. Crist
  Russell Reynolds Associates, Inc.,
  Chicago
Jonathan A. Crystal
  SpencerStuart, Houston
Robert S. Rollo
  Korn/Ferry International, Los
  Angeles
Lawrence P. Crowley
  Blendow, Crowley & Oliver Inc.,
  New York
W. Hoyt Colton
  W. Hoyt Colton Associates Inc.,
  New York
Ronald Dukes
  Heidrick and Struggles, Inc.,
  Chicago
Douglas H. Gates
  Haley BDC, New York

Russell E. Marks, Jr.
   A.T. Kearney, Inc., New York
Thomas R. Moore
   Ketchum, Inc., Pittsburgh
John W. Franklin, Jr.
   Russell Reynolds Associates, Inc.,
   Washington, DC
William H. Marumoto
   The Interface Group, Ltd.,
   Washington, DC
P. John Mirtz
   Martin Mirtz Morice, Inc.,
   Stamford, CT
Thomas M. Mitchell
   Heidrick and Struggles, Inc., Los
   Angeles
Eleanor H. Raynolds
   Ward Howell International, Inc.,
   New York

DIRECTOR RECRUITMENT

Gerard R. Roche
   Heidrick and Struggles, Inc., New
   York
Thomas J. Neff
   SpencerStuart, New York
Ferdinand Nadherny
   Russell Reynolds Associates, Inc.,
   Chicago
Gardner W. Heidrick
   The Heidrick Partners, Inc.,
   Chicago
Richard M. Ferry
   Korn/Ferry International, Los
   Angeles
Russell S. Reynolds, Jr.
   Russell Reynolds Associates, Inc.,
   New York
W. Hoyt Colton
   W. Hoyt Colton Associates, Inc.,
   New York
Max M. Ulrich
   Ward Howell International Inc.,
   New York
Martin H. Bauman
   Martin H. Bauman Associates, Inc.,
   New York

Frederick W. Wackerle
   McFeely Wackerle Jett, Chicago
Robert L. Heidrick
   The Heidrick Partners, Inc.,
   Chicago
John Lucht
   The John Lucht Consultancy Inc.,
   New York
John F. Johnson
   Lamalie Associates, Inc., Cleveland
Andrew Sherwood
   Goodrich and Sherwood Company,
   New York
D. John Ingram
   Ingram Inc., New York
Thomas H. Ogdon
   The Ogdon Partnership, New York
P. Anthony Price
   Russell Reynolds Associates Inc.,
   San Francisco
E. Pendleton James
   Pendleton James & Associates, Inc.,
   New York
Richard E. Kinser
   Richard Kinser & Associates, New
   York
James E. Hunt
   Kenny, Kindler, Hunt & Howe,
   New York
Theodore Jadick
   Heidrick and Struggles, Inc., New
   York
Otis H. Bowden, II
   Bowden & Company, Inc.,
   Cleveland
Robert G. Cox
   A.T. Kearney, Inc., New York
William H. Willis, Jr.
   William H. Willis, Inc., Greenwich,
   CT
Thomas C. Zay
   Thomas C. Zay & Company, Inc.,
   Atlanta
William H. Billington, Jr.
   Billington, Fox & Ellis, Inc.,
   Chicago
Mark Lorenzetti
   Roberts, Ryan & Bentley,
   Linthicum, MD

James A. Hayden, Jr.
Hayden Group, Inc., Boston
Pierson Keating
Nordeman Grimm, New York
George Rossi
Heidrick and Struggles, Inc.,
Boston
Lawrence "Larry" W. Hill
Russell Reynolds Associates, Inc.,
Houston
H. Leland Getz
Higdon, Joys & Mingle, Inc., New
York
Jack H. Vernon
Russell Reynolds Associates, Inc.,
Boston
David R. Peasback
Canny, Bowen Inc., New York
Robert S. Rollo
Korn/Ferry International, Los
Angeles
Thomas M. Mitchell
Heidrick and Struggles, Inc., Los
Angeles
Durant "Andy" Hunter
Gardiner Stone Hunter
International, Boston
Judith M. von Seldeneck
Diversified Search, Inc.,
Philadelphia

ADMINISTRATION

J. Daniel Ford
Kieffer, Ford & Associates, Ltd.,
Oak Brook, IL (HC)
Windle B. Priem
Korn/Ferry International, New
York
Ira Krinsky
Ira Krinsky Associates, Los Angeles
(ED)
Gary J. Posner
George Kaludis Associates,
Nashville (ED)
Kenneth L. Rattner
Heidrick and Struggles, Inc.,
Chicago

Judith M. von Seldeneck
Diversified Search, Inc.,
Philadelphia
Harvey M. Weiner
Search America, Dallas (HO)
Thomas R. Moore
Ketchum, Inc., Pittsburgh
James M. Schmidt
Cejka & Company, St. Louis (HC)
Early, Bert H.
Bert H. Early Associates, Inc.,
Chicago (LE)
Joan I. McCrea
Nursing Technomics, West Chester,
PA (HC)
Herbert Regehly
Innkeeper's Management Corp.,
New York (HO)
W. Hoyt Colton
W. Hoyt Colton Associates Inc.,
New York
William B. Arnold
William B. Arnold Associates, Inc.,
Denver
Caroline Ballantine
Heidrick and Struggles, Inc., New
York
Steven M. Darter
People Management Inc., Simsbury,
CT
Steven A. Seiden
Seiden Associates, Inc., New York
Ben Schwartz
Harper Associates, Farmington
Hills, MI (HO)
Jacques P. Andre
Paul R. Ray & Company, Inc., New
York
David E. Chambers
David Chambers & Associates, Inc.,
New York
Sandford I. Gadient
Huntress Real Estate Executive
Search, Kansas City, MO
A. Donald Iklé
Ward Howell International, Inc.,
New York
Allan D. R. Stern
Haskell & Stern Associates, Inc.,
New York

Janis M. Zivic
  The Zivic Group, Inc., San
    Francisco
William B. Beeson
  Lawrence-Leiter & Company,
    Kansas City, MO
O.D. "Dan" Cruse
  SpencerStuart, Dallas
Michael J. Hoevel
  Poirier, Hoevel & Company, Los
    Angeles
J. Alvin Wakefield
  Gilbert Tweed Associates, Inc., New
    York
O. William Battalia
  Battalia & Associates, Inc., New
    York
William B. Clemens, Jr.
  Norman Broadbent International,
    New York
John R. Ferneborg
  Smith, Goerss & Ferneborg, San
    Francisco
John F. Johnson
  Lamalie Associates, Inc., Cleveland
Mark Lorenzetti
  Roberts, Ryan & Bentley,
    Linthicum, MD
Jack Seitchik
  Seitchik Corwin and Seitchik, San
    Francisco
Edward R. Howe, Jr.
  Diversified Search, Inc.,
    Philadelphia
David O. Harbert
  Sweeney Shepherd Bueschel Provus
    Harbert & Mummert, Inc.,
    Chicago
James N. Heuerman
  Korn/Ferry International, San
    Francisco (HC)
James E. Hunt
  Kenny, Kindler, Hunt & Howe,
    New York
Roger M. Kenny
  Kenny, Kindler, Hunt & Howe,
    New York
Robert M. Bryza
  Robert Lowell International, Inc.,
    Dallas

Jonathan A. Crystal
  SpencerStuart, Houston
David F. Smith
  Korn/Ferry International, New
    York
H. Leland Getz
  Higdon, Joys & Mingle, Inc., New
    York
J.R. Akin
  J.R. Akin & Company, Fairfield, CT
James R. Clovis, Jr.
  Handy Associates, New York
Edward A. Raisbeck, Jr.
  Thorndike Deland Associates, New
    York
Sydney Reynolds
  Sydney Reynolds Associates, Inc.,
    New York
Robert W. Dingman
  Robert W. Dingman Company, Inc.,
    Westlake Village, CA
Paul R. Ray, Sr.
  Paul R. Ray & Company, Inc., Fort
    Worth
Larry D. Mingle
  Higdon, Joys & Mingle, Inc., New
    York
David S. Joys
  Higdon, Joys & Mingle, Inc., New
    York
Jonathan E. McBride
  McBride Associates, Inc.,
    Washington, DC
Charles M. Meng
  Meng, Finseth & Associates, Inc.,
    Rolling Hills, CA
Dayton Ogden
  SpencerStuart, New York
Albert L. McAulay, Jr.
  Robison & McAulay, Charlotte, NC
William H. Billington, Jr.
  Billington, Fox & Ellis, Inc.,
    Chicago
David H. Hoffmann
  DHR International, Inc., Chicago
Charles W. Sweet
  A.T. Kearney, Inc., Chicago
Putney Westerfield
  Boyden International Inc., New
    York

Richard A. McCallister
  Boyden International, Inc., Chicago
Edward C. Slowik
  SpencerStuart, New York
Thomas C. Zay
  Thomas C. Zay & Company, Inc.,
    Atlanta
John W. Franklin, Jr.
  Russell Reynolds Associates, Inc.,
    Washington, DC
Robert Kremple
  Kremple & Meade, Malibu, CA
Leon A. Farley
  Leon A. Farley Associates, San
    Francisco
Richard M. McFarland
  Brissenden, McFarland, Wagoner,
    & Fuccella, Inc., Stamford, CT
Robert A. Staub
  Staub, Warmbold & Associates,
    Inc., New York
Richard Sbarbaro
  Lauer, Sbarbaro Associates, Inc.,
    Chicago
Lynn Tendler Bignell
  Gilbert Tweed Associates, Inc., New
    York
Skott B. Burkland
  Haley BDC, New York
William H. Marumoto
  The Interface Group, Ltd.,
    Washington, DC
Gerald D. Menzel
  Menzel, Robinson, Baldwin, Inc.,
    Arlington Heights, IL
David R. Peasback
  Canny, Bowen Inc., New York
Peter G. Grimm
  Nordeman Grimm, Inc., New York
Lawrence J. Holmes
  Consulting Associates, Inc.,
    Columbia, MD
Russell E. Marks, Jr.
  A.T. Kearney, Inc., New York
Brenda L. Ruello
  Heidrick and Struggles, Inc., New
    York
P. John Mirtz
  Martin Mirtz Morice, Inc.,
    Stamford, CT

ADVERTISING/PROMOTION

D. John Ingram
  Ingram Inc., New York
Richard A. Miners
  Goodrich and Sherwood, New York
James H. Cornehlsen
  Heidrick and Struggles, Inc., New
    York
David E. Chambers
  David Chambers & Associates, Inc.,
    New York
Michael S. Dunford
  Michael S. Dunford, Inc., Glen
    Ellyn, IL
Harry Bernard
  Colton Bernard Inc., San Francisco
Leonard J. Clark, Jr.
  Boyden International, New York
Robert Kremple
  Kremple & Meade, Malibu, CA
Thomas H. Ogdon
  The Ogdon Partnership, New York
Judith M. von Seldeneck
  Diversified Search, Inc.,
    Philadelphia
David F. Smith
  Korn/Ferry International, New
    York
Millington F. McCoy
  Gould & McCoy, Inc., New York
J.R. Akin
  J.R. Akin & Company, Fairfield, CT
W. Michael Danforth
  Hyde Danforth & Co., Dallas
W. Jerry Hyde
  Hyde Danforth & Co., Dallas
Edward C. Slowik
  SpencerStuart, New York
William H. Marumoto
  The Interface Group, Ltd.,
    Washington, DC
Thomas C. Zay
  Thomas C. Zay & Company, Inc.,
    Atlanta
Eleanor H. Raynolds
  Ward Howell International, Inc.,
    New York

DIRECT MARKETING

O.D. "Dan" Cruse
SpencerStuart, Dallas
Howard Bratches
Thorndike Deland Associates, New
York
J. Alvin Wakefield
Gilbert Tweed Associates, Inc., New
York
R.G. Finnegan
Finnegan & Associates, Inc., Palos
Verdes Estates, CA
Charles W. Sweet
A.T. Kearney, Inc., Chicago
Harry Bernard
Colton Bernard Inc., San Francisco
Norman F. Moody
Paul Stafford Associates, Ltd., New
York
Janet Tweed
Gilbert Tweed Associates, New
York
Brenda L. Ruello
Heidrick and Struggles, Inc., New
York
William T. Mangum
Thomas Mangum Company, Los
Angeles
John A. Travis
Travis & Company Inc., Sudbury,
MA
Putney Westerfield
Boyden International Inc., New
York
James "Rick" L. Richardson
SpencerStuart, Stamford, CT
William B. Reeves
Korn/Ferry International, Atlanta
Jack R. Clarey
Jack Clarey Associates, Inc.,
Northbrook, IL
Herbert T. Mines
Herbert Mines Associates, Inc.,
New York
Edward A. Raisbeck, Jr.
Thorndike Deland Associates, New
York

Robert S. Rollo
Korn/Ferry International, Los
Angeles
James E. Hunt
Kenny, Kindler, Hunt & Howe,
New York
Thomas H. Ogdon
The Ogdon Partnership, New York
Edward C. Slowik
SpencerStuart, New York
William K. Sur
Stricker, Sur & Associates, New
York
Roger M. Kenny
Kenny, Kindler, Hunt & Howe,
New York
David F. Smith
Korn/Ferry International, New
York

EDITORIAL

John Lucht
The John Lucht Consultancy Inc.,
New York
Thomas H. Ogdon
The Ogdon Partnership, New York
Richard J. Cronin
Hodge-Cronin & Associates, Inc.,
Rosemont, IL
William A. Hertan
Executive Manning Corp., Fort
Lauderdale
James H. Cornehlsen
Heidrick and Struggles, Inc., New
York
Richard A. McCallister
Boyden International, Inc., Chicago

ENGINEERING

Robert E. Lamalie
Robert Lamalie Inc., Marco Island,
FL
Otis H. Bowden, II
Bowden & Company, Inc.,
Cleveland
George W. Henn, Jr.
G.W. Henn & Company, Columbus,
OH

Carlton W. "Tony" Thompson
SpencerStuart, New York
Lynn Tendler Bignell
Gilbert Tweed Associates, Inc., New York
Robert Kremple
Kremple & Meade, Malibu, CA
Charles P. Beall
Beall & Company, Inc., Roswell, GA
William A. Hertan
Executive Manning Corp., Fort Lauderdale
Richard C. Slayton
Slayton International, Inc., Chicago
Lawrence P. Crowley
Blendow, Crowley & Oliver Inc., New York
Janis M. Zivic
The Zivic Group, Inc., San Francisco
Frederic E. Berman
The Berman Consulting Group, Atlanta
Richard J. Cronin
Hodge-Cronin & Associates, Inc., Rosemont, IL
O.D. "Dan" Cruse
SpencerStuart, Dallas
William T. Mangum
Thomas Mangum Company, Los Angeles
Darrell G. Robertson
Western Reserve Search Associates, Inc., Bath, OH
Max M. Ulrich
Ward Howell International Inc., New York
Robert D. Spriggs
Spriggs & Company, Inc., Chicago
Paul R. Ray, Sr.
Paul R. Ray & Company, Inc., Fort Worth
Nelson W. Gibson
N.W. Gibson International, Los Angeles
R. Paul Kors
Kors Montgomery International, Houston

William C. Houze
William C. Houze & Co., Torrance, CA
Howard D. Nitchke
Deane, Howard & Simon, Inc., Hartford, CT
Richard K. Ives
Wilkinson & Ives, San Francisco
Theodore E. Lusk
Nadzam, Lusk & Associates, Inc., Santa Clara, CA
Steven M. Darter
People Management Inc., Simsbury, CT
Leon A. Farley
Leon A. Farley Associates, San Francisco
R.G. Finnegan
Finnegan & Associates Inc., Palos Verdes Estates, CA
Lawrence J. Holmes
Consulting Associates, Inc., Columbia, MD
Gerald D. Menzel
Menzel, Robinson, Baldwin, Inc., Arlington Heights, IL
Richard M. McFarland
Brissenden, McFarland, Wagoner, & Fuccella, Inc., Stamford, CT
Charles M. Meng
Meng, Finseth & Associates, Inc., Rolling Hills, CA
William B. Arnold
William B. Arnold Associates, Inc., Denver
Charles D. Reese, Jr.
Reese Associates, Wexford, PA
Carl W. Menk
Canny, Bowen Inc., New York
Mike Jacobs
Thorne, Brieger Associates Inc., New York
John H. Robison
Robison & McAulay, Charlotte, NC
Richard Sbarbaro
Lauer, Sbarbaro Associates, Inc., Chicago
Janet Tweed
Gilbert Tweed Associates, New York

R. James Lotz, Jr.
  International Management
    Advisors, Inc., New York
Albert L. McAulay, Jr.
  Robison & McAulay, Charlotte, NC
Charles E. Splaine
  Splaine & Associates, Los Gatos,
    CA
Douglas H. Gates
  Haley BDC, New York
George Rossi
  Heidrick and Struggles, Inc.,
    Boston
Thomas C. Zay
  Thomas C. Zay & Company, Inc.,
    Atlanta
Robert L. Heidrick
  The Heidrick Partners, Inc.,
    Chicago
Robert M. Bryza
  Robert Lowell International, Inc.,
    Dallas
John R. Ferneborg
  Smith, Goerss & Ferneborg, San
    Francisco
Gary R. Barton
  Barton Raben, Inc., Houston
Skott B. Burkland
  Haley BDC, New York
Laurence Massé
  Ward Howell International,
    Barrington, IL
David H. Charlson
  Chestnut Hill Partners, Deerfield,
    IL
Steven A. Raben
  Barton Raben, Inc., Houston
Frank R. Beaudine
  Eastman & Beaudine, Inc., Dallas
William H. Billington, Jr.
  Billington, Fox & Ellis, Inc.,
    Chicago
David H. Hoffmann
  DHR International, Inc., Chicago
P. John Mirtz
  Martin Mirtz Morice, Inc.,
    Stamford, CT
Pierson Keating
  Nordeman Grimm, New York

William H. Marumoto
  The Interface Group, Ltd.,
    Washington, DC
Ronald Dukes
  Heidrick and Struggles, Inc.,
    Chicago
Thomas M. Mitchell
  Heidrick and Struggles, Inc., Los
    Angeles

FINANCE AND ACCOUNTING

Robert E. Lamalie
  Robert Lamalie Inc., Marco Island,
    FL
John F. Johnson
  Lamalie Associates, Inc., Cleveland
Windle B. Priem
  Korn/Ferry International, New
    York
Leon A. Farley
  Leon A. Farley Associates, San
    Francisco
W. Hoyt Colton
  W. Hoyt Colton Associates Inc.,
    New York
Robert W. Dingman
  Robert W. Dingman Company, Inc.,
    Westlake Village, CA
Paul R. Ray, Sr.
  Paul R. Ray & Company, Inc., Fort
    Worth
Robert W. Slater
  Korn/Ferry International, Dallas
Robert A. Staub
  Staub, Warmbold & Associates,
    Inc., New York
Robert D. Spriggs
  Spriggs & Company, Inc., Chicago
Jacques P. Andre
  Paul R. Ray & Company, Inc., New
    York
Judith M. von Seldeneck
  Diversified Search, Inc.,
    Philadelphia
D. John Ingram
  Ingram Inc., New York
Otis H. Bowden, II
  Bowden & Company, Inc.,
    Cleveland

Ferdinand Nadherny
Russell Reynolds Associates, Inc.,
Chicago
Jacques C. Nordeman
Nordeman Grimm, Inc., New York
J. Daniel Ford
Kieffer, Ford & Associates, Ltd.,
Oak Brook, IL ⒣
Russell S. Reynolds, Jr.
Russell Reynolds Associates, Inc.,
New York
David E. Chambers
David Chambers & Associates, Inc.,
New York
Nancy F. Keithley
Ernst & Young, Cleveland
Jay Gaines
Jay Gaines & Company, Inc., New
York
Carl W. Menk
Canny, Bowen Inc., New York
J. Gerald Simmons
Handy Associates, New York
Richard C. Slayton
Slayton International, Inc., Chicago
Carlton W. "Tony" Thompson
SpencerStuart, New York
David O. Harbert
Sweeney Shepherd Bueschel Provus
Harbert & Mummert, Inc.,
Chicago
Andrew D. Hart
Russell Reynolds Associates, Inc.,
New York
James N. Heuerman
Korn/Ferry International, San
Francisco ⒣
Caroline Ballantine
Heidrick and Struggles, Inc., New
York
Max M. Ulrich
Ward Howell International Inc.,
New York
Gary R. Barton
Barton Raben, Inc., Houston
Charles P. Beall
Beall & Company, Inc., Roswell, GA
Howard Bratches
Thorndike Deland Associates, New
York

David H. Charlson
Chestnut Hill Partners, Deerfield,
IL
Ira Krinsky
Ira Krinsky Associates, Los Angeles
ⒺⒹ
Antoinette "Toni" L. Farley
Kieffer, Ford & Associates, Ltd.,
Oak Brook, IL ⒣
Richard Sbarbaro
Lauer, Sbarbaro Associates, Inc.,
Chicago
Martin H. Bauman
Martin H. Bauman Associates, Inc.,
New York
Jack R. Clarey
Jack Clarey Associates, Inc.,
Northbrook, IL
Robert M. Flanagan
Paul Stafford Associates, Ltd., New
York
Henry G. Higdon
Higdon, Joys & Mingle, Inc., New
York
Michael J. Hoevel
Poirier, Hoevel & Company, Los
Angeles
Richard K. Ives
Wilkinson & Ives, San Francisco
Richard M. McFarland
Brissenden, McFarland, Wagoner,
& Fuccella, Inc., Stamford, CT
Joseph P. McGinley
SpencerStuart, New York
Dayton Ogden
SpencerStuart, New York
Thomas H. Ogdon
The Ogdon Partnership, New York
William R. Wilkinson
Wilkinson & Ives, San Francisco
Janis M. Zivic
The Zivic Group, Inc., San
Francisco
Michael S. Dunford
Michael S. Dunford, Inc., Glen
Ellyn, IL
Edward R. Howe, Jr.
Diversified Search, Inc.,
Philadelphia

Lawrence F. Nein
Nordeman Grimm, Inc., Chicago
Robert L. Heidrick
The Heidrick Partners, Inc.,
Chicago
Richard J. Cronin
Hodge-Cronin & Associates, Inc.,
Rosemont, IL
James M. Montgomery
Houze, Shourds & Montgomery,
Inc., Long Beach, CA
David R. Peasback
Canny, Bowen Inc., New York
Gary J. Posner
George Kaludis Associates,
Nashville (ED)
Nelson W. Gibson
N.W. Gibson International, Los
Angeles
Durant "Andy" Hunter
Gardiner Stone Hunter
International, Boston
George W. Ott
Ott & Hansen, Inc., Pasadena, CA
Steven A. Seiden
Seiden Associates, Inc., New York
David F. Smith
Korn/Ferry International, New
York
Donald C. Williams
Donald Williams Associates, Inc.,
Chicago
William A. Hertan
Executive Manning Corp., Fort
Lauderdale
Roger M. Kenny
Kenny, Kindler, Hunt & Howe,
New York
O. William Battalia
Battalia & Associates, Inc., New
York
Frank R. Beaudine
Eastman & Beaudine, Inc., Dallas
Skott B. Burkland
Haley BDC, New York
William B. Clemens, Jr.
Norman Broadbent International,
New York

W. Michael Danforth
Hyde Danforth & Co., Dallas
Ralph E. Dieckmann
Dieckmann & Associates, Ltd.,
Chicago
R.G. Finnegan
Finnegan & Associates Inc., Palos
Verdes Estates, CA
Sandford I. Gadient
Huntress Real Estate Executive
Search, Kansas City, MO
Frank A. Garofolo
Garofolo, Curtiss & Company,
Ardmore, PA
David H. Hoffmann
DHR International, Inc., Chicago
Lawrence J. Holmes
Consulting Associates, Inc.,
Columbia, MD
Richard E. Kinser
Richard Kinser & Associates, New
York
Mark Lorenzetti
Roberts, Ryan & Bentley,
Linthicum, MD
R. James Lotz, Jr.
International Management
Advisors, Inc., New York
Edward A. Raisbeck, Jr.
Thorndike Deland Associates, New
York
Allan D. R. Stern
Haskell & Stern Associates, Inc.,
New York
J. Alvin Wakefield
Gilbert Tweed Associates, Inc., New
York
Theodore Jadick
Heidrick and Struggles, Inc., New
York
Charles M. Meng
Meng, Finseth & Associates, Inc.,
Rolling Hills, CA
Norman F. Moody
Paul Stafford Associates, Ltd., New
York
Albert L. McAulay, Jr.
Robison & McAulay, Charlotte, NC

Howard D. Nitchke
Deane, Howard & Simon, Inc.,
Hartford, CT
Brenda L. Ruello
Heidrick and Struggles, Inc., New
York
Thomas C. Zay
Thomas C. Zay & Company, Inc.,
Atlanta
Peter D. Crist
Russell Reynolds Associates, Inc.,
Chicago
Robert S. Rollo
Korn/Ferry International, Los
Angeles
William B. Arnold
William B. Arnold Associates, Inc.,
Denver
Frederic E. Berman
The Berman Consulting Group,
Atlanta
William H. Billington, Jr.
Billington, Fox & Ellis, Inc.,
Chicago
James R. Clovis, Jr.
Handy Associates, New York
John R. Ferneborg
Smith, Goerss & Ferneborg, San
Francisco
Peter G. Grimm
Nordeman Grimm, Inc., New York
Herbert T. Mines
Herbert Mines Associates, Inc.,
New York
Charles E. Splaine
Splaine & Associates, Los Gatos,
CA
W. Jerry Hyde
Hyde Danforth & Co., Dallas
Jonathan E. McBride
McBride Associates, Inc.,
Washington, DC
Kenneth L. Rattner
Heidrick and Struggles, Inc.,
Chicago
William H. Willis, Jr.
William H. Willis, Inc., Greenwich,
CT

James F. Bishop
Burke, O'Brien & Bishop
Associates, Inc., Princeton, NJ
Douglas H. Gates
Haley BDC, New York
H. Leland Getz
Higdon, Joys & Mingle, Inc., New
York
James A. Hayden, Jr.
Hayden Group, Inc., Boston
Pierson Keating
Nordeman Grimm, New York
Robert Kremple
Kremple & Meade, Malibu, CA
Gretchen Long
Haskell & Stern Associates, Inc.,
New York
Richard A. McCallister
Boyden International, Inc., Chicago
Larry D. Mingle
Higdon, Joys & Mingle, Inc., New
York
William B. Reeves
Korn/Ferry International, Atlanta
Gary W. Silverman
Korn/Ferry International, Chicago
John S. Stanton
Russell Reynolds Associates, Inc.,
Chicago
Robert M. Bryza
Robert Lowell International, Inc.,
Dallas
Joseph E. Griesedieck, Jr.
SpencerStuart, San Francisco
David S. Joys
Higdon, Joys & Mingle, Inc., New
York
Gary Knisely
Johnson Smith & Knisely Inc., New
York
William T. Mangum
Thomas Mangum Company, Los
Angeles
John H. Robison
Robison & McAulay, Charlotte, NC
Andrew Sherwood
Goodrich and Sherwood Company,
New York

John A. Travis
  Travis & Company Inc., Sudbury, MA

Putney Westerfield
  Boyden International Inc., New York

Jonathan A. Crystal
  SpencerStuart, Houston

Lawrence "Larry" W. Hill
  Russell Reynolds Associates, Inc., Houston

John Lucht
  The John Lucht Consultancy Inc., New York

E. Pendleton James
  Pendleton James & Associates, Inc., New York

Steven A. Raben
  Barton Raben, Inc., Houston

Paul R. Ray, Jr.
  Paul R. Ray & Company, Inc., Fort Worth

George W. Henn, Jr.
  G.W. Henn & Company, Columbus, OH

Leonard J. Clark, Jr.
  Boyden International, New York

Mike Jacobs
  Thorne, Brieger Associates Inc., New York

Millington F. McCoy
  Gould & McCoy, Inc., New York

P. Anthony Price
  Russell Reynolds Associates Inc., San Francisco

J. R. Akin
  J. R. Akin & Company, Fairfield, CT

William B. Beeson
  Lawrence-Leiter & Company, Kansas City, MO

John B. Henard, Jr.
  Henard Associates, Dallas

Lawrence P. Crowley
  Blendow, Crowley & Oliver Inc., New York

Charles W. Kepler
  Russell Reynolds Associates, Inc., Chicago

Richard A. Miners
  Goodrich and Sherwood, New York

James "Rick" L. Richardson
  SpencerStuart, Stamford, CT

Edward C. Slowik
  SpencerStuart, New York

Mary E. Shourds
  Houze, Shourds & Montgomery, Inc., Long Beach, CA

Laurence Massé
  Ward Howell International, Barrington, IL

Steven M. Darter
  People Management Inc., Simsbury, CT

William E. Gould
  Gould & McCoy Inc., New York

William K. Sur
  Stricker, Sur & Associates, New York

Lynn Tendler Bignell
  Gilbert Tweed Associates, Inc., New York

James E. Hunt
  Kenny, Kindler, Hunt & Howe, New York

Theodore E. Lusk
  Nadzam, Lusk & Associates, Inc., Santa Clara, CA

Russell E. Marks, Jr.
  A.T. Kearney, Inc., New York

Janet Tweed
  Gilbert Tweed Associates, New York

Harry Bernard
  Colton Bernard Inc., San Francisco

R. Paul Kors
  Kors Montgomery International, Houston

Robert G. Cox
  A.T. Kearney, Inc., New York

John W. Franklin, Jr.
  Russell Reynolds Associates, Inc., Washington, DC

Thomas M. Mitchell
  Heidrick and Struggles, Inc., Los Angeles

Eleanor H. Raynolds
  Ward Howell International, Inc., New York

George Rossi
  Heidrick and Struggles, Inc.,
    Boston
P. John Mirtz
  Martin Mirtz Morice, Inc.,
    Stamford, CT
Charles W. Sweet
  A.T. Kearney, Inc., Chicago
Jack H. Vernon
  Russell Reynolds Associates, Inc.,
    Boston
William H. Marumoto
  The Interface Group, Ltd.,
    Washington, DC
Ronald Dukes
  Heidrick and Struggles, Inc.,
    Chicago

HUMAN RESOURCES/ PERSONNEL

John F. Johnson
  Lamalie Associates, Inc., Cleveland
Donald T. Allerton
  Allerton/Heinze & Associates, Inc.,
    Chicago
Robert E. Lamalie
  Robert Lamalie Inc., Marco Island,
    FL
Michael S. Dunford
  Michael S. Dunford, Inc., Glen
    Ellyn, IL
William E. Gould
  Gould & McCoy Inc., New York
Michael C. Kieffer
  Kieffer, Ford & Associates, Inc.,
    Oak Brook, IL (HC)
Barbara L. Provus
  Sweeney Shepherd Bueschel Provus
    Harbert & Mummert, Inc.,
    Chicago
J. Daniel Ford
  Kieffer, Ford & Associates, Ltd.,
    Oak Brook, IL (HC)
Judith M. von Seldeneck
  Diversified Search, Inc.,
    Philadelphia
Windle B. Priem
  Korn/Ferry International, New
    York

Leon A. Farley
  Leon A. Farley Associates, San
    Francisco
Roger M. Kenny
  Kenny, Kindler, Hunt & Howe,
    New York
Ferdinand Nadherny
  Russell Reynolds Associates, Inc.,
    Chicago
W. Hoyt Colton
  W. Hoyt Colton Associates Inc.,
    New York
Antoinette "Toni" L. Farley
  Kieffer, Ford & Associates, Ltd.,
    Oak Brook, IL (HC)
E. Pendleton James
  Pendleton James & Associates, Inc.,
    New York
Gary J. Posner
  George Kaludis Associates,
    Nashville (ED)
Robert W. Slater
  Korn/Ferry International, Dallas
D. John Ingram
  Ingram Inc., New York
James N. Heuerman
  Korn/Ferry International, San
    Francisco (HC)
Jacques C. Nordeman
  Nordeman Grimm, Inc., New York
David R. Peasback
  Canny, Bowen Inc., New York
Robert W. Dingman
  Robert W. Dingman Company, Inc.,
    Westlake Village, CA
Ralph E. Dieckmann
  Dieckmann & Associates, Ltd.,
    Chicago
Mary E. Shourds
  Houze, Shourds & Montgomery,
    Inc., Long Beach, CA
James R. Clovis, Jr.
  Handy Associates, New York
David O. Harbert
  Sweeney Shepherd Bueschel Provus
    Harbert & Mummert, Inc.,
    Chicago
William C. Houze
  William C. Houze & Co., Torrance,
    CA

R. James Lotz, Jr.
  International Management
    Advisors, Inc., New York
Millington F. McCoy
  Gould & McCoy, Inc., New York
Gary R. Barton
  Barton Raben, Inc., Houston
Jack R. Clarey
  Jack Clarey Associates, Inc.,
    Northbrook, IL
Joseph P. McGinley
  SpencerStuart, New York
James M. Montgomery
  Houze, Shourds & Montgomery,
    Inc., Long Beach, CA
Paul R. Ray, Jr.
  Paul R. Ray & Company, Inc., Fort
    Worth
John "Jack" B. Henard, Jr.
  Henard Associates, Dallas
Janis M. Zivic
  The Zivic Group, Inc., San
    Francisco
Carl W. Menk
  Canny, Bowen Inc., New York
Lynn Tendler Bignell
  Gilbert Tweed Associates, Inc., New
    York
Andrew D. Hart
  Russell Reynolds Associates, Inc.,
    New York
Edward R. Howe, Jr.
  Diversified Search, Inc.,
    Philadelphia
J. R. Akin
  J. R. Akin & Company, Fairfield,
    CT
William B. Clemens, Jr.
  Norman Broadbent International,
    New York
David F. Smith
  Korn/Ferry International, New
    York
Frank R. Beaudine
  Eastman & Beaudine, Inc., Dallas
Gary Knisely
  Johnson Smith & Knisely Inc., New
    York

Robert A. Staub
  Staub, Warmbold & Associates,
    Inc., New York
Thomas C. Zay
  Thomas C. Zay & Company, Inc.,
    Atlanta
Robert M. Flanagan
  Paul Stafford Associates, Ltd., New
    York
Robert L. Heidrick
  The Heidrick Partners, Inc.,
    Chicago
William H. Billington, Jr.
  Billington, Fox & Ellis, Inc.,
    Chicago
Theodore Jadick
  Heidrick and Struggles, Inc., New
    York
Peter G. Grimm
  Nordeman Grimm, Inc., New York
Edward A. Raisbeck, Jr.
  Thorndike Deland Associates, New
    York
Kenneth L. Rattner
  Heidrick and Struggles, Inc.,
    Chicago
Robert D. Spriggs
  Spriggs & Company, Inc., Chicago
Martin H. Bauman
  Martin H. Bauman Associates, Inc.,
    New York
Larry D. Mingle
  Higdon, Joys & Mingle, Inc., New
    York
William B. Reeves
  Korn/Ferry International, Atlanta
Jonathan E. McBride
  McBride Associates, Inc.,
    Washington, DC
Allan D. R. Stern
  Haskell & Stern Associates, Inc.,
    New York
P. John Mirtz
  Martin Mirtz Morice, Inc.,
    Stamford, CT
Joseph E. Griesedieck, Jr.
  SpencerStuart, San Francisco
William R. Wilkinson
  Wilkinson & Ives, San Francisco

Richard Sbarbaro
Lauer, Sbarbaro Associates, Inc.,
Chicago

William A. Hertan
Executive Manning Corp., Fort
Lauderdale

David S. Joys
Higdon, Joys & Mingle, Inc., New
York

John R. Ferneborg
Smith, Goerss & Ferneborg, San
Francisco

Douglas H. Gates
Haley BDC, New York

Lawrence "Larry" W. Hill
Russell Reynolds Associates, Inc.,
Houston

Gretchen Long
Haskell & Stern Associates, Inc.,
New York

Laurence Massé
Ward Howell International,
Barrington, IL

Donald C. Williams
Donald Williams Associates, Inc.,
Chicago

Richard C. Slayton
Slayton International, Inc., Chicago

Skott B. Burkland
Haley BDC, New York

O.D. "Dan" Cruse
SpencerStuart, Dallas

Michael J. Hoevel
Poirier, Hoevel & Company, Los
Angeles

John Lucht
The John Lucht Consultancy Inc.,
New York

Dayton Ogden
SpencerStuart, New York

J. Alvin Wakefield
Gilbert Tweed Associates, Inc., New
York

Theodore E. Lusk
Nadzam, Lusk & Associates, Inc.,
Santa Clara, CA

Gerald D. Menzel
Menzel, Robinson, Baldwin, Inc.,
Arlington Heights, IL

Jacques P. Andre
Paul R. Ray & Company, Inc., New
York

Robert G. Cox
A.T. Kearney, Inc., New York

Richard A. Miners
Goodrich and Sherwood, New York

Edward C. Slowik
SpencerStuart, New York

Steven A. Raben
Barton Raben, Inc., Houston

Nelson W. Gibson
N.W. Gibson International, Los
Angeles

Robert M. Bryza
Robert Lowell International, Inc.,
Dallas

Lawrence J. Holmes
Consulting Associates, Inc.,
Columbia, MD

Richard E. Kinser
Richard Kinser & Associates, New
York

Herbert T. Mines
Herbert Mines Associates, Inc.,
New York

George W. Ott
Ott & Hansen, Inc., Pasadena, CA

Steven A. Seiden
Seiden Associates, Inc., New York

John A. Travis
Travis & Company Inc., Sudbury,
MA

George W. Henn, Jr.
G.W. Henn & Company, Columbus,
OH

William B. Beeson
Lawrence-Leiter & Company,
Kansas City, MO

James F. Bishop
Burke, O'Brien & Bishop
Associates, Inc., Princeton, NJ

Robert S. Rollo
Korn/Ferry International, Los
Angeles

Richard K. Ives
Wilkinson & Ives, San Francisco

Richard M. McFarland
Brissenden, McFarland, Wagoner,
& Fuccella, Inc., Stamford, CT

Max M. Ulrich
Ward Howell International Inc.,
New York
William H. Willis, Jr.
William H. Willis, Inc., Greenwich,
CT
W. Michael Danforth
Hyde Danforth & Co., Dallas
Steven M. Darter
People Management Inc., Simsbury,
CT
Andrew Sherwood
Goodrich and Sherwood Company,
New York
David H. Charlson
Chestnut Hill Partners, Deerfield,
IL
Pierson Keating
Nordeman Grimm, New York
Charles W. Kepler
Russell Reynolds Associates, Inc.,
Chicago
Gary W. Silverman
Korn/Ferry International, Chicago
W. Jerry Hyde
Hyde Danforth & Co., Dallas
Mike Jacobs
Thorne, Brieger Associates Inc.,
New York
P. Anthony Price
Russell Reynolds Associates Inc.,
San Francisco
William H. Marumoto
The Interface Group, Ltd.,
Washington, DC
Thomas M. Mitchell
Heidrick and Struggles, Inc., Los
Angeles
H. Leland Getz
Higdon, Joys & Mingle, Inc., New
York
Richard J. Cronin
Hodge-Cronin & Associates, Inc.,
Rosemont, IL
Richard A. McCallister
Boyden International, Inc., Chicago
James "Rick" L. Richardson
SpencerStuart, Stamford, CT

David H. Hoffmann
DHR International, Inc., Chicago
William B. Arnold
William B. Arnold Associates, Inc.,
Denver
Eleanor H. Raynolds
Ward Howell International, Inc.,
New York
William T. Mangum
Thomas Mangum Company, Los
Angeles
Charles E. Splaine
Splaine & Associates, Los Gatos,
CA
Charles P. Beall
Beall & Company, Inc., Roswell, GA
Jack H. Vernon
Russell Reynolds Associates, Inc.,
Boston
David E. Chambers
David Chambers & Associates, Inc.,
New York
James H. Cornehlsen
Heidrick and Struggles, Inc., New
York
George Rossi
Heidrick and Struggles, Inc.,
Boston

INTERNATIONAL

William E. Gould
Gould & McCoy Inc., New York
William A. Hertan
Executive Manning Corp., Fort
Lauderdale
Durant "Andy" Hunter
Gardiner Stone Hunter
International, Boston
R. Paul Kors
Kors Montgomery International,
Houston
Dayton Ogden
SpencerStuart, New York
H. Leland Getz
Higdon, Joys & Mingle, Inc., New
York
Roger M. Kenny
Kenny, Kindler, Hunt & Howe,
New York

Windle B. Priem
Korn/Ferry International, New
York
Darrell G. Robertson
Western Reserve Search Associates,
Inc., Bath, OH
Ferdinand Nadherny
Russell Reynolds Associates, Inc.,
Chicago
Russell S. Reynolds, Jr.
Russell Reynolds Associates, Inc.,
New York
Ralph E. Dieckmann
Dieckmann & Associates, Ltd.,
Chicago
Robert G. Cox
A.T. Kearney, Inc., New York
O. William Battalia
Battalia & Associates, Inc., New
York
William K. Sur
Stricker, Sur & Associates, New
York
Charles W. Sweet
A.T. Kearney, Inc., Chicago
Putney Westerfield
Boyden International Inc., New
York
David S. Joys
Higdon, Joys & Mingle, Inc., New
York
Andrew D. Hart
Russell Reynolds Associates, Inc.,
New York
Laurence Massé
Ward Howell International,
Barrington, IL
Sandford I. Gadient
Huntress Real Estate Executive
Search, Kansas City, MO
William C. Houze
William C. Houze & Co., Torrance,
CA
Brenda L. Ruello
Heidrick and Struggles, Inc., New
York
Jacques P. Andre
Paul R. Ray & Company, Inc., New
York

Paul R. Ray, Sr.
Paul R. Ray & Company, Inc., Fort
Worth
Albert L. McAulay, Jr.
Robison & McAulay, Charlotte, NC
Thomas H. Ogdon
The Ogdon Partnership, New York
John S. Stanton
Russell Reynolds Associates, Inc.,
Chicago
Max M. Ulrich
Ward Howell International Inc.,
New York
Theodore Jadick
Heidrick and Struggles, Inc., New
York
Albert L. Richard, Jr.
Human Resources, Inc.,
Providence, RI
Gary Knisely
Johnson Smith & Knisely Inc., New
York
John H. Callen, Jr.
Ward Howell International, New
York
David H. Hoffmann
DHR International, Inc., Chicago
Larry D. Mingle
Higdon, Joys & Mingle, Inc., New
York
Jack Seitchik
Seitchik Corwin and Seitchik, San
Francisco
Frank R. Beaudine
Eastman & Beaudine, Inc., Dallas
Allan D. R. Stern
Haskell & Stern Associates, Inc.,
New York
David H. Charlson
Chestnut Hill Partners, Deerfield,
IL
Leon A. Farley
Leon A. Farley Associates, San
Francisco
James H. Cornehlsen
Heidrick and Struggles, Inc., New
York
Robert M. Flanagan
Paul Stafford Associates, Ltd., New
York

Russell E. Marks, Jr.
A.T. Kearney, Inc., New York
Richard A. McCallister
Boyden International, Inc., Chicago
Richard A. Miners
Goodrich and Sherwood, New York
Gary W. Silverman
Korn/Ferry International, Chicago
Edward C. Slowik
SpencerStuart, New York
Richard J. Cronin
Hodge-Cronin & Associates, Inc.,
Rosemont, IL
Joseph E. Griesedieck, Jr.
SpencerStuart, San Francisco
Henry G. Higdon
Higdon, Joys & Mingle, Inc., New
York
John Lucht
The John Lucht Consultancy Inc.,
New York
Robert A. Staub
Staub, Warmbold & Associates,
Inc., New York
John A. Travis
Travis & Company Inc., Sudbury,
MA
Gretchen Long
Haskell & Stern Associates, Inc.,
New York
James "Rick" L. Richardson
SpencerStuart, Stamford, CT
Lynn Tendler Bignell
Gilbert Tweed Associates, Inc., New
York
O.D. "Dan" Cruse
SpencerStuart, Dallas
Richard K. Ives
Wilkinson & Ives, San Francisco
William H. Willis, Jr.
William H. Willis, Inc., Greenwich,
CT
Otis H. Bowden, II
Bowden & Company, Inc.,
Cleveland
Richard E. Kinser
Richard Kinser & Associates, New
York

R. James Lotz, Jr.
International Management
Advisors, Inc., New York
P. Anthony Price
Russell Reynolds Associates Inc.,
San Francisco
Eleanor H. Raynolds
Ward Howell International, Inc.,
New York
Carl W. Menk
Canny, Bowen Inc., New York
Richard C. Slayton
Slayton International, Inc., Chicago
W. Hoyt Colton
W. Hoyt Colton Associates Inc.,
New York
Robert S. Rollo
Korn/Ferry International, Los
Angeles
Harry Bernard
Colton Bernard Inc., San Francisco
John R. Ferneborg
Smith, Goerss & Ferneborg, San
Francisco
William T. Mangum
Thomas Mangum Company, Los
Angeles
John H. Robison
Robison & McAulay, Charlotte, NC

LEGAL

W. Michael Danforth
Hyde Danforth & Co., Dallas
Bert H. Early
Bert H. Early Associates, Inc.,
Chicago(LE)
W. Jerry Hyde
Hyde Danforth & Co., Dallas
E. Pendleton James
Pendleton James & Associates, Inc.,
New York
David R. Peasback
Canny, Bowen Inc., New York
James R. Clovis, Jr.
Handy Associates, New York
Paul R. Ray, Jr.
Paul R. Ray & Company, Inc., Fort
Worth

Otis H. Bowden, II
Bowden & Company, Inc.,
Cleveland
Leon A. Farley
Leon A. Farley Associates, San
Francisco
Barbara L. Provus
Sweeney Shepherd Bueschel Provus
Harbert & Mummert, Inc.,
Chicago
Judith M. von Seldeneck
Diversified Search, Inc.,
Philadelphia
W. Hoyt Colton
W. Hoyt Colton Associates Inc.,
New York
John "Jack" B. Henard, Jr.
Henard Associates, Dallas
Mark Lorenzetti
Roberts, Ryan & Bentley,
Linthicum, MD
Michael J. Hoevel
Poirier, Hoevel & Company, Los
Angeles
Richard C. Slayton
Slayton International, Inc., Chicago
Robert W. Dingman
Robert W. Dingman Company, Inc.,
Westlake Village, CA
Robert A. Staub
Staub, Warmbold & Associates,
Inc., New York
Richard E. Kinser
Richard Kinser & Associates, New
York
Henry G. Higdon
Higdon, Joys & Mingle, Inc., New
York
Richard K. Ives
Wilkinson & Ives, San Francisco
Jonathan E. McBride
McBride Associates, Inc.,
Washington, DC
Max M. Ulrich
Ward Howell International Inc.,
New York
William B. Beeson
Lawrence-Leiter & Company,
Kansas City, MO

William A. Hertan
Executive Manning Corp., Ft.
Lauderdale
James E. Hunt
Kenny, Kindler, Hunt & Howe,
New York
Gretchen Long
Haskell & Stern Associates, Inc.,
New York
Kenneth L. Rattner
Heidrick and Struggles, Inc.,
Chicago
William B. Reeves
Korn/Ferry International, Atlanta
Michael S. Dunford
Michael S. Dunford, Inc., Glen
Ellyn, IL
Millington F. McCoy
Gould & McCoy, Inc., New York
Robert G. Cox
A.T. Kearney, Inc., New York
H. Leland Getz
Higdon, Joys & Mingle, Inc., New
York
Martin H. Bauman
Martin H. Bauman Associates, Inc.,
New York
P. Anthony Price
Russell Reynolds Associates Inc.,
San Francisco
John H. Robison
Robison & McAulay, Charlotte, NC
James F. Bishop
Burke, O'Brien & Bishop
Associates, Inc., Princeton, NJ
George Rossi
Heidrick and Struggles, Inc.,
Boston
Richard Sbarbaro
Lauer, Sbarbaro Associates, Inc.,
Chicago
Andrew D. Hart
Russell Reynolds Associates, Inc.,
New York
Jack R. Clarey
Jack Clarey Associates, Inc.,
Northbrook, IL
Ralph E. Dieckmann
Dieckmann & Associates, Ltd.,
Chicago

Dayton Ogden
SpencerStuart, New York

O. William Battalia
Battalia & Associates, Inc., New York

David S. Joys
Higdon, Joys & Mingle, Inc., New York

Russell E. Marks, Jr.
A.T. Kearney, Inc., New York

Gary R. Barton
Barton Raben, Inc., Houston

John W. Franklin, Jr.
Russell Reynolds Associates, Inc., Washington, DC

Thomas H. Ogdon
The Ogdon Partnership, New York

Donald C. Williams
Donald Williams Associates, Inc., Chicago

Putney Westerfield
Boyden International Inc., New York

Steven A. Raben
Barton Raben, Inc., Houston

Edward C. Slowik
SpencerStuart, New York

William H. Marumoto
The Interface Group, Ltd., Washington, DC

MANUFACTURING/ PRODUCTION/OPERATIONS

Otis H. Bowden, II
Bowden & Company, Inc., Cleveland

Robert E. Lamalie
Robert Lamalie Inc., Marco Island, FL

John F. Johnson
Lamalie Associates, Inc., Cleveland

George W. Henn, Jr.
G.W. Henn & Company, Columbus, OH

Robert W. Dingman
Robert W. Dingman Company, Inc., Westlake Village, CA

Richard C. Slayton
Slayton International, Inc., Chicago

Leon A. Farley
Leon A. Farley Associates, San Francisco

Richard M. McFarland
Brissenden, McFarland, Wagoner, & Fuccella, Inc., Stamford, CT

William A. Hertan
Executive Manning Corp., Fort Lauderdale

Robert D. Spriggs
Spriggs & Company, Inc., Chicago

Lynn Tendler Bignell
Gilbert Tweed Associates, Inc., New York

Robert M. Flanagan
Paul Stafford Associates, Ltd., New York

Carl W. Menk
Canny, Bowen Inc., New York

Richard J. Cronin
Hodge-Cronin & Associates, Inc., Rosemont, IL

James M. Montgomery
Houze, Shourds & Montgomery, Inc., Long Beach, CA

Jacques P. Andre
Paul R. Ray & Company, Inc., New York

Gary R. Barton
Barton Raben, Inc., Houston

David H. Charlson
Chestnut Hill Partners, Deerfield, IL

O.D. "Dan" Cruse
SpencerStuart, Dallas

O. William Battalia
Battalia & Associates, Inc., New York

Robert A. Staub
Staub, Warmbold & Associates, Inc., New York

Nancy F. Keithley
Ernst & Young, Cleveland

Paul R. Ray, Sr.
Paul R. Ray & Company, Inc., Fort Worth

Steven M. Darter
  People Management Inc., Simsbury,
  CT
Frank A. Garofolo
  Garofolo, Curtiss & Company,
  Ardmore, PA
Lawrence J. Holmes
  Consulting Associates, Inc.,
  Columbia, MD
William T. Mangum
  Thomas Mangum Company, Los
  Angeles
Charles P. Beall
  Beall & Company, Inc., Roswell, GA
Howard Bratches
  Thorndike Deland Associates, New
  York
Edward R. Howe, Jr.
  Diversified Search, Inc.,
  Philadelphia
Mike Jacobs
  Thorne, Brieger Associates Inc.,
  New York
Albert L. Richard, Jr.
  Human Resources, Inc.,
  Providence, RI
Harry Bernard
  Colton Bernard Inc., San Francisco
Michael S. Dunford
  Michael S. Dunford, Inc., Glen
  Ellyn, IL
William E. Gould
  Gould & McCoy Inc., New York
Theodore E. Lusk
  Nadzam, Lusk & Associates, Inc.,
  Santa Clara, CA
Gerald D. Menzel
  Menzel, Robinson, Baldwin, Inc.,
  Arlington Heights, IL
George W. Ott
  Ott & Hansen, Inc., Pasadena, CA
Mary E. Shourds
  Houze, Shourds & Montgomery,
  Inc., Long Beach, CA
Charles W. Sweet
  A.T. Kearney, Inc., Chicago
William R. Wilkinson
  Wilkinson & Ives, San Francisco

Robert L. Heidrick
  The Heidrick Partners, Inc.,
  Chicago
Richard Sbarbaro
  Lauer, Sbarbaro Associates, Inc.,
  Chicago
Lawrence P. Crowley
  Blendow, Crowley & Oliver Inc.,
  New York
Robert M. Bryza
  Robert Lowell International, Inc.,
  Dallas
John H. Callen, Jr.
  Ward Howell International, New
  York
David H. Hoffmann
  DHR International, Inc., Chicago
Jack Seitchik
  Seitchik Corwin and Seitchik, San
  Francisco
Martin H. Bauman
  Martin H. Bauman Associates, Inc.,
  New York
Skott B. Burkland
  Haley BDC, New York
Joseph E. Griesedieck, Jr.
  SpencerStuart, San Francisco
Henry G. Higdon
  Higdon, Joys & Mingle, Inc., New
  York
Joseph P. McGinley
  SpencerStuart, New York
Robert Kremple
  Kremple & Meade, Malibu, CA
Jacques C. Nordeman
  Nordeman Grimm, Inc., New York
Paul R. Ray, Jr.
  Paul R. Ray & Company, Inc., Fort
  Worth
Lawrence "Larry" W. Hill
  Russell Reynolds Associates, Inc.,
  Houston
Charles W. Kepler
  Russell Reynolds Associates, Inc.,
  Chicago
Charles D. Reese, Jr.
  Reese Associates, Wexford, PA
J.R. Akin
  J.R. Akin & Company, Fairfield, CT

William B. Arnold
William B. Arnold Associates, Inc.,
Denver

R. Paul Kors
Kors Montgomery International,
Houston

Darrell G. Robertson
Western Reserve Search Associates,
Inc., Bath, OH

Charles E. Splaine
Splaine & Associates, Los Gatos,
CA

Janet Tweed
Gilbert Tweed Associates, New
York

Donald C. Williams
Donald Williams Associates, Inc.,
Chicago

Frank R. Beaudine
Eastman & Beaudine, Inc., Dallas

William B. Beeson
Lawrence-Leiter & Company,
Kansas City, MO

James F. Bishop
Burke, O'Brien & Bishop
Associates, Inc., Princeton, NJ

Jack R. Clarey
Jack Clarey Associates, Inc.,
Northbrook, IL

Richard K. Ives
Wilkinson & Ives, San Francisco

Gretchen Long
Haskell & Stern Associates, Inc.,
New York

Laurence Massé
Ward Howell International,
Barrington, IL

Edward C. Slowik
SpencerStuart, New York

Andrew D. Hart
Russell Reynolds Associates, Inc.,
New York

John H. Robison
Robison & McAulay, Charlotte, NC

William B. Clemens, Jr.
Norman Broadbent International,
New York

W. Michael Danforth
Hyde Danforth & Co., Dallas

John T. Gardner
Lamalie Associates, Inc., Chicago

William C. Houze
William C. Houze & Co., Torrance,
CA

R. James Lotz, Jr.
International Management
Advisors, Inc., New York

Steven A. Raben
Barton Raben, Inc., Houston

George Rossi
Heidrick and Struggles, Inc.,
Boston

Steven A. Seiden
Seiden Associates, Inc., New York

Andrew Sherwood
Goodrich and Sherwood Company,
New York

Linford E. Stiles
Ward Howell International,
Stamford, CT

Janis M. Zivic
The Zivic Group, Inc., San
Francisco

Leonard J. Clark, Jr.
Boyden International, New York

W. Jerry Hyde
Hyde Danforth & Co., Dallas

Richard A. McCallister
Boyden International, Inc., Chicago

Charles M. Meng
Meng, Finseth & Associates, Inc.,
Rolling Hills, CA

Herbert T. Mines
Herbert Mines Associates, Inc.,
New York

P. Anthony Price
Russell Reynolds Associates Inc.,
San Francisco

Durant "Andy" Hunter
Gardiner Stone Hunter
International, Boston

Ronald Dukes
Heidrick and Struggles, Inc.,
Chicago

David O. Harbert
Sweeney Shepherd Bueschel Provus
Harbert & Mummert, Inc.,
Chicago

James "Rick" L. Richardson
SpencerStuart, Stamford, CT
Ralph E. Dieckmann
Dieckmann & Associates, Ltd.,
Chicago
Roger M. Kenny
Kenny, Kindler, Hunt & Howe,
New York
Nelson W. Gibson
N.W. Gibson International, Los
Angeles
John "Jack" B. Henard, Jr.
Henard Associates, Dallas
Richard E. Kinser
Richard Kinser & Associates, New
York
Russell E. Marks, Jr.
A.T. Kearney, Inc., New York
William K. Sur
Stricker, Sur & Associates, New
York
David E. Chambers
David Chambers & Associates, Inc.,
New York
Albert L. McAulay, Jr.
Robison & McAulay, Charlotte, NC
Brenda L. Ruello
Heidrick and Struggles, Inc., New
York
J. Alvin Wakefield
Gilbert Tweed Associates, Inc., New
York
Douglas H. Gates
Haley BDC, New York
William H. Billington, Jr.
Billington, Fox & Ellis, Inc.,
Chicago
John R. Ferneborg
Smith, Goerss & Ferneborg, San
Francisco
John A. Travis
Travis & Company Inc., Sudbury,
MA
Putney Westerfield
Boyden International Inc., New
York
Jack H. Vernon
Russell Reynolds Associates, Inc.,
Boston

Thomas C. Zay
Thomas C. Zay & Company, Inc.,
Atlanta
Robert G. Cox
A.T. Kearney, Inc., New York
Pierson Keating
Nordeman Grimm, New York
P. John Mirtz
Martin Mirtz Morice, Inc.,
Stamford, CT
John Lucht
The John Lucht Consultancy Inc.,
New York
James R. Clovis, Jr.
Handy Associates, New York
Thomas M. Mitchell
Heidrick and Struggles, Los
Angeles

MARKETING/SALES–CONSUMER

Robert E. Lamalie
Robert Lamalie Inc., Inc., Marco
Island, FL
Windle B. Priem
Korn/Ferry International, New
York
D. John Ingram
Ingram Inc., New York
Roger M. Kenny
Kenny, Kindler, Hunt & Howe,
New York
Jacques C. Nordeman
Nordeman Grimm, Inc., New York
Donald T. Allerton
Allerton/Heinze & Associates, Inc.,
Chicago
Michael S. Dunford
Michael S. Dunford, Inc., Glen
Ellyn, IL
Paul R. Ray, Jr.
Paul R. Ray & Company, Inc., Fort
Worth
James H. Cornehlsen
Heidrick and Struggles, Inc., New
York
Edward R. Howe, Jr.
Diversified Search, Inc.,
Philadelphia

Leon A. Farley
Leon A. Farley Associates, San
Francisco
Carl W. Menk
Canny, Bowen Inc., New York
Barbara L. Provus
Sweeney Shepherd Bueschel Provus
Harbert & Mummert, Inc.,
Chicago
Robert D. Spriggs
Spriggs & Company, Inc., Chicago
John F. Johnson
Lamalie Associates, Inc., Cleveland
Carlton "Tony" W. Thompson
SpencerStuart, New York
Robert A. Staub
Staub, Warmbold & Associates,
Inc., New York
Robert W. Dingman
Robert W. Dingman Company, Inc.,
Westlake Village, CA
Jacques P. Andre
Paul R. Ray & Company, Inc., New
York
Howard Bratches
Thorndike Deland Associates, New
York
Robert L. Heidrick
The Heidrick Partners, Inc.,
Chicago
William E. Gould
Gould & McCoy Inc., New York
Millington F. McCoy
Gould & McCoy, Inc., New York
Lawrence F. Nein
Nordeman Grimm, Inc., Chicago
Frank R. Beaudine
Eastman & Beaudine, Inc., Dallas
Andrew D. Hart
Russell Reynolds Associates, Inc.,
New York
Gerald D. Menzel
Menzel, Robinson, Baldwin, Inc.,
Arlington Heights, IL
Paul R. Ray, Sr.
Paul R. Ray & Company, Inc., Fort
Worth
Allan D. R. Stern
Haskell & Stern Associates, Inc.,
New York

Antoinette "Toni" L. Farley
Kieffer, Ford & Associates, Ltd.,
Oak Brook, IL
J. Alvin Wakefield
Gilbert Tweed Associates, Inc., New
York
William H. Willis, Jr.
William H. Willis, Inc., Greenwich,
CT
Judith M. von Seldeneck
Diversified Search, Inc.,
Philadelphia
David E. Chambers
David Chambers & Associates, Inc.,
New York
John R. Ferneborg
Smith, Goerss & Ferneborg, San
Francisco
R.G. Finnegan
Finnegan & Associates, Inc., Palos
Verdes Estates, CA
Mark Lorenzetti
Roberts, Ryan & Bentley,
Linthicum, MD
Caroline Ballantine
Heidrick and Struggles, Inc., New
York
Martin H. Bauman
Martin H. Bauman Associates, Inc.,
New York
Skott B. Burkland
Haley BDC, New York
Henry G. Higdon
Higdon, Joys & Mingle, Inc., New
York
Michael J. Hoevel
Poirier, Hoevel & Company, Los
Angeles
John Lucht
The John Lucht Consultancy Inc.,
New York
Theodore E. Lusk
Nadzam, Lusk & Associates, Inc.,
Santa Clara, CA
Jonathan E. McBride
McBride Associates, Inc.,
Washington, DC
Dayton Ogden
SpencerStuart, New York

Thomas H. Ogdon
The Ogdon Partnership, New York
William R. Wilkinson
Wilkinson & Ives
San Francisco
William H. Billington, Jr.
Billington, Fox & Ellis, Inc.,
Chicago
John H. Callen, Jr.
Ward Howell International, New
York
Peter G. Grimm
Nordeman Grimm, Inc., New York
John "Jack" B. Henard, Jr.
Henard Associates, Dallas
David H. Hoffmann
DHR International, Inc., Chicago
Richard E. Kinser
Richard Kinser & Associates, New
York
Herbert T. Mines
Herbert Mines Associates, Inc.,
New York
Charles E. Splaine
Splaine & Associates, Los Gatos.
CA
William K. Sur
Stricker, Sur & Associates, New
York
Putney Westerfield
Boyden International Inc., New
York
J. R. Akin
J. R. Akin & Company, Fairfield,
CT
Robert M. Bryza
Robert Lowell International, Inc.,
Dallas
Durant "Andy" Hunter
Gardiner Stone Hunter
International, Boston
Robert Kremple
Kremple & Meade, Malibu, CA
Richard Sbarbaro
Lauer, Sbarbaro Associates, Inc.,
Chicago
Andrew Sherwood
Goodrich and Sherwood Company,
New York

John A. Travis
Travis & Company Inc., Sudbury,
MA
Donald C. Williams
Donald Williams Associates, Inc.,
Chicago
Joseph E. Griesedieck, Jr.
SpencerStuart, San Francisco
David F. Smith
Korn/Ferry International, New
York
Leonard J. Clark, Jr.
Boyden International, New York
James N. Heuerman
Korn/Ferry International, San
Francisco (HC)
David S. Joys
Higdon, Joys & Mingle, Inc., New
York
Gary Knisely
Johnson Smith & Knisely Inc., New
York
John H. Robison
Robison & McAulay, Charlotte, NC
George W. Henn, Jr.
G.W. Henn & Company, Columbus,
OH
Charles P. Beall
Beall & Company, Inc., Roswell, GA
Douglas H. Gates
Haley BDC, New York
W. Michael Danforth
Hyde Danforth & Co., Dallas
Frank A. Garofolo
Garofolo, Curtiss & Company,
Ardmore, PA
Edward A. Raisbeck, Jr.
Thorndike Deland Associates, New
York
Mike Jacobs
Thorne, Brieger Associates Inc.,
New York
Charles M. Meng
Meng, Finseth & Associates, Inc.,
Rolling Hills, CA
James M. Montgomery
Houze, Shourds & Montgomery,
Inc., Long Beach, CA

Mary E. Shourds
Houze, Shourds & Montgomery,
Inc., Long Beach, CA

P. Anthony Price
Russell Reynolds Associates Inc.,
San Francisco

Brenda L. Ruello
Heidrick and Struggles, Inc., New
York

Richard A. Miners
Goodrich and Sherwood, New York

James "Rick" L. Richardson
SpencerStuart, Stamford, CT

Edward C. Slowik
SpencerStuart, New York

Nelson W. Gibson
N.W. Gibson International, Los
Angeles

James E. Hunt
Kenny, Kindler, Hunt & Howe,
New York

W. Jerry Hyde
Hyde Danforth & Co., Dallas

R. James Lotz, Jr.
International Management
Advisors, Inc., New York

Steven A. Seiden
Seiden Associates, Inc., New York

Thomas C. Zay
Thomas C. Zay & Company, Inc.,
Atlanta

Gary R. Barton
Barton Raben, Inc., Houston

David H. Charlson
Chestnut Hill Partners, Deerfield,
IL

Ralph E. Dieckmann
Dieckmann & Associates, Ltd.,
Chicago

John T. Gardner
Lamalie Associates, Inc., Chicago

James A. Hayden, Jr.
Hayden Group, Inc., Boston

Richard A. McCallister
Boyden International, Inc., Chicago

David R. Peasback
Canny, Bowen Inc., New York

Robert S. Rollo
Korn/Ferry International, Los
Angeles

George Rossi
Heidrick and Struggles, Inc.,
Boston

Gary W. Silverman
Korn/Ferry International, Chicago

Linford E. Stiles
Ward Howell International,
Stamford, CT

Robert M. Flanagan
Paul Stafford Associates, Ltd., New
York

Ferdinand Nadherny
Russell Reynolds Associates, Inc.,
Chicago

Kenneth L. Rattner
Heidrick and Struggles, Inc.,
Chicago

James F. Bishop
Burke, O'Brien & Bishop
Associates, Inc., Princeton, NJ

Albert L. McAulay, Jr.
Robison & McAulay, Charlotte, NC

Howard D. Nitchke
Deane, Howard & Simon, Inc.,
Hartford, CT

George W. Ott
Ott & Hansen, Inc., Pasadena, CA

William B. Reeves
Korn/Ferry International, Atlanta

Charles W. Sweet
A.T. Kearney, Inc., Chicago

Jack R. Clarey
Jack Clarey Associates, Inc.,
Northbrook, IL

W. Hoyt Colton
W. Hoyt Colton Associates Inc.,
New York

E. Pendleton James
Pendleton James & Associates, Inc.,
New York

William B. Arnold
William B. Arnold Associates, Inc.,
Denver

O. William Battalia
Battalia & Associates, Inc., New
York

Pierson Keating
Nordeman Grimm, New York

Charles W. Kepler
Russell Reynolds Associates, Inc.,
Chicago
Theodore Jadick
Heidrick and Struggles, Inc., New
York
Janis M. Zivic
The Zivic Group, Inc., San
Francisco
James R. Clovis, Jr.
Handy Associates, New York
Ronald Dukes
Heidrick and Struggles, Inc.,
Chicago
Lawrence J. Holmes
Consulting Associates, Inc.,
Columbia, MD
William C. Houze
William C. Houze & Co., Torrance,
CA
Laurence Massé
Ward Howell International,
Barrington, IL
Steven A. Raben
Barton Raben, Inc., Houston
Eleanor H. Raynolds
Ward Howell International, Inc.,
New York
Janet Tweed
Gilbert Tweed Associates, New
York
P. John Mirtz
Martin Mirtz Morice, Inc.,
Stamford, CT
William B. Beeson
Lawrence-Leiter & Company,
Kansas City, MO
Gretchen Long
Haskell & Stern Associates, Inc.,
New York
John W. Franklin, Jr.
Russell Reynolds Associates, Inc.,
Washington, DC
William H. Marumoto
The Interface Group, Ltd.,
Washington, DC
Thomas M. Mitchell
Heidrick and Struggles, Inc., Los
Angeles

MARKETING/SALES–INDUSTRIAL

J. Gerald Simmons
Handy Associates, New York
Robert E. Lamalie
Robert Lamalie Inc., Marco Island,
FL
D. John Ingram
Ingram Inc., New York
Otis H. Bowden, II
Bowden & Company, Inc.,
Cleveland
John F. Johnson
Lamalie Associates, Inc., Cleveland
Skott B. Burkland
Haley BDC, New York
Donald T. Allerton
Allerton/Heinze & Associates, Inc.,
Chicago
Michael S. Dunford
Michael S. Dunford, Inc., Glen
Ellyn, IL
Robert W. Slater
Korn/Ferry International, Dallas
Roger M. Kenny
Kenny, Kindler, Hunt & Howe,
New York
George W. Henn, Jr.
G.W. Henn & Company, Columbus,
OH
Richard M. McFarland
Brissenden, McFarland, Wagoner,
& Fuccella, Inc., Stamford, CT
Charles P. Beall
Beall & Company, Inc., Roswell, GA
Lawrence F. Nein
Nordeman Grimm, Inc., Chicago
Richard Sbarbaro
Lauer, Sbarbaro Associates, Inc.,
Chicago
Paul R. Ray, Sr.
Paul R. Ray & Company, Inc., Fort
Worth
David E. Chambers
David Chambers & Associates, Inc.,
New York
Edward R. Howe, Jr.
Diversified Search, Inc.,
Philadelphia

Gerald D. Menzel
  Menzel, Robinson, Baldwin, Inc.,
    Arlington Heights, IL
Robert D. Spriggs
  Spriggs & Company, Inc., Chicago
Robert W. Dingman
  Robert W. Dingman Company, Inc.,
    Westlake Village, CA
Barbara L. Provus
  Sweeney Shepherd Bueschel Provus
    Harbert & Mummert, Inc.,
    Chicago
Robert L. Heidrick
  The Heidrick Partners, Inc.,
    Chicago
Richard C. Slayton
  Slayton International, Inc., Chicago
James H. Cornehlsen
  Heidrick and Struggles, Inc., New
    York
Theodore E. Lusk
  Nadzam, Lusk & Associates, Inc.,
    Santa Clara, CA
William E. Gould
  Gould & McCoy Inc., New York
Millington F. McCoy
  Gould & McCoy, Inc., New York
John A. Travis
  Travis & Company Inc., Sudbury,
    MA
Robert Kremple
  Kremple & Meade, Malibu, CA
Allan D. R. Stern
  Haskell & Stern Associates, Inc.,
    New York
J. R. Akin
  J. R. Akin & Company, Fairfield,
    CT
Albert L. Richard, Jr.
  Human Resources, Inc.,
    Providence, RI
Jack R. Clarey
  Jack Clarey Associates, Inc.,
    Northbrook, IL
Michael J. Hoevel
  Poirier, Hoevel & Company, Los
    Angeles
Richard K. Ives
  Wilkinson & Ives, San Francisco

William B. Arnold
  William B. Arnold Associates, Inc.,
    Denver
Frederic E. Berman
  The Berman Consulting Group,
    Atlanta
Harry Bernard
  Colton Bernard Inc., San Francisco
Robert M. Bryza
  Robert Lowell International, Inc.,
    Dallas
John R. Ferneborg
  Smith, Goerss & Ferneborg, San
    Francisco
Robert M. Flanagan
  Paul Stafford Associates, Ltd., New
    York
Sandford I. Gadient
  Huntress Real Estate Executive
    Search, Kansas City, MO
Andrew D. Hart
  Russell Reynolds Associates, Inc.,
    New York
Mark Lorenzetti
  Roberts, Ryan & Bentley,
    Linthicum, MD
Sydney Reynolds
  Sydney Reynolds Associates, Inc.,
    New York
Jack Seitchik
  Seitchik Corwin and Seitchik, San
    Francisco
William H. Billington, Jr.
  Billington, Fox & Ellis, Inc.,
    Chicago
John H. Callen, Jr.
  Ward Howell International, New
    York
Martin H. Bauman
  Martin H. Bauman Associates, Inc.,
    New York
Robert A. Staub
  Staub, Warmbold & Associates,
    Inc., New York
Nelson W. Gibson
  N.W. Gibson International, Los
    Angeles
Peter G. Grimm
  Nordeman Grimm, Inc., New York

Henry G. Higdon
Higdon, Joys & Mingle, Inc., New York

R. Paul Kors
Kors Montgomery International, Houston

John Lucht
The John Lucht Consultancy Inc., New York

Lawrence P. Crowley
Blendow, Crowley & Oliver Inc., New York

Jonathan E. McBride
McBride Associates, Inc., Washington, DC

Charles E. Splaine
Splaine & Associates, Los Gatos, CA

William K. Sur
Stricker, Sur & Associates, New York

Putney Westerfield
Boyden International Inc., New York

David O. Harbert
Sweeney Shepherd Bueschel Provus Harbert & Mummert, Inc., Chicago

Janet Tweed
Gilbert Tweed Associates, New York

David H. Charlson
Chestnut Hill Partners, Deerfield, IL

Jonathan A. Crystal
SpencerStuart, Houston

Frank A. Garofolo
Garofolo, Curtiss & Company, Ardmore, PA

Lawrence J. Holmes
Consulting Associates, Inc., Columbia, MD

Durant "Andy" Hunter
Gardiner Stone Hunter International, Boston

Darrell G. Robertson
Western Reserve Search Associates, Inc., Bath, OH

Steven A. Seiden
Seiden Associates, Inc., New York

Andrew Sherwood
Goodrich and Sherwood Company, New York

Donald C. Williams
Donald Williams Associates, Inc., Chicago

Leonard J. Clark, Jr.
Boyden International, New York

O.D. "Dan" Cruse
SpencerStuart, Dallas

Ferdinand Nadherny
Russell Reynolds Associates, Inc., Chicago

John H. Robison
Robison & McAulay, Charlotte, NC

Max M. Ulrich
Ward Howell International Inc., New York

Lynn Tendler Bignell
Gilbert Tweed Associates, Inc., New York

John T. Gardner
Lamalie Associates, Inc., Chicago

George Rossi
Heidrick and Struggles, Inc., Boston

Linford E. Stiles
Ward Howell International, Stamford, CT

W. Michael Danforth
Hyde Danforth & Co., Dallas

Jay Gaines
Jay Gaines & Company, Inc., New York

Mike Jacobs
Thorne, Brieger Associates Inc., New York

Charles M. Meng
Meng, Finseth & Associates, Inc., Rolling Hills, CA

George W. Ott
Ott & Hansen, Inc., Pasadena, CA

P. Anthony Price
Russell Reynolds Associates Inc., San Francisco

Richard J. Cronin
Hodge-Cronin & Associates, Inc., Rosemont, IL

Pierson Keating
Nordeman Grimm, New York
James M. Montgomery
Houze, Shourds & Montgomery,
Inc., Long Beach, CA
Charles D. Reese, Jr.
Reese Associates, Wexford, PA
James "Rick" L. Richardson
SpencerStuart, Stamford, CT
Mary E. Shourds
Houze, Shourds & Montgomery,
Inc., Long Beach, CA
W. Jerry Hyde
Hyde Danforth & Co., Dallas
Steven M. Darter
People Management Inc., Simsbury,
CT
Richard A. McCallister
Boyden International, Inc., Chicago
Ralph E. Dieckmann
Dieckmann & Associates, Ltd.,
Chicago
Paul R. Ray, Jr.
Paul R. Ray & Company, Inc., Fort
Worth
Gary R. Barton
Barton Raben, Inc., Houston
James F. Bishop
Burke, O'Brien & Bishop
Associates, Inc., Princeton, NJ
David S. Joys
Higdon, Joys & Mingle, Inc., New
York
Charles W. Kepler
Russell Reynolds Associates, Inc.,
Chicago
John "Jack" B. Henard, Jr.
Henard Associates, Dallas
David H. Hoffmann
DHR International, Inc., Chicago
William C. Houze
William C. Houze & Co., Torrance,
CA
Howard D. Nitchke
Deane, Howard & Simon, Inc.,
Hartford, CT
Charles W. Sweet
A.T. Kearney, Inc., Chicago

Laurence Massé
Ward Howell International,
Barrington, IL
Frank R. Beaudine
Eastman & Beaudine, Inc., Dallas
Ronald Dukes
Heidrick and Struggles, Inc.,
Chicago
David R. Peasback
Canny, Bowen Inc., New York
William H. Willis, Jr.
William H. Willis, Inc., Greenwich,
CT
O. William Battalia
Battalia & Associates, Inc., New
York
William B. Beeson
Lawrence-Leiter & Company,
Kansas City, MO
W. Hoyt Colton
W. Hoyt Colton Associates Inc.,
New York
E. Pendleton James
Pendleton James & Associates, Inc.,
New York
Larry D. Mingle
Higdon, Joys & Mingle, Inc., New
York
Russell E. Marks, Jr.
A.T. Kearney, Inc., New York
Jack H. Vernon
Russell Reynolds Associates, Inc.,
Boston
Janis M. Zivic
The Zivic Group, Inc., San
Francisco
Steven A. Raben
Barton Raben, Inc., Houston
James R. Clovis, Jr.
Handy Associates, New York
David F. Smith
Korn/Ferry International, New
York
P. John Mirtz
Martin Mirtz Morice, Inc.,
Stamford, CT
Albert L. McAulay, Jr.
Robison & McAulay, Charlotte, NC

William H. Marumoto
  The Interface Group, Ltd.,
    Washington, DC
Richard E. Kinser
  Richard Kinser & Associates, New
    York
James E. Hunt
  Kenny, Kindler, Hunt & Howe,
    New York
Robert G. Cox
  A.T. Kearney, Inc., New York
Douglas H. Gates
  Haley BDC, New York
Robert S. Rollo
  Korn/Ferry International, Los
    Angeles

MERCHANDISING

Edward A. Raisbeck, Jr.
  Thorndike Deland Associates, New
    York
Herbert T. Mines
  Herbert Mines Associates, Inc.,
    New York
Frank R. Beaudine
  Eastman & Beaudine, Inc., Dallas
Jack Seitchik
  Seitchik Corwin and Seitchik, San
    Francisco
Lawrence F. Nein
  Nordeman Grimm, Inc., Chicago
Gerald D. Menzel
  Menzel, Robinson, Baldwin, Inc.,
    Arlington Heights, IL
Harry Bernard
  Colton Bernard Inc., San Francisco
John H. Callen, Jr.
  Ward Howell International, New
    York
Henry G. Higdon
  Higdon, Joys & Mingle, Inc., New
    York
Brenda L. Ruello
  Heidrick and Struggles, Inc., New
    York
Skott B. Burkland
  Haley BDC, New York

Richard A. Miners
  Goodrich and Sherwood Company,
    New York
Peter G. Grimm
  Nordeman Grimm, Inc., New York
William E. Gould
  Gould & McCoy Inc., New York
Mike Jacobs
  Thorne, Brieger Associates Inc.,
    New York
James "Rick" L. Richardson
  SpencerStuart, Stamford, CT
Charles W. Sweet
  A.T. Kearney, Inc., Chicago
H. Leland Getz
  Higdon, Joys & Mingle, Inc., New
    York

MIS/COMPUTER OPERATIONS

Jay Gaines
  Jay Gaines & Company, Inc., New
    York
George W. Henn, Jr.
  G.W. Henn & Company, Columbus,
    OH
Robert W. Slater
  Korn/Ferry International, Dallas
Gary R. Barton
  Barton Raben, Inc., Houston
Jacques C. Nordeman
  Nordeman Grimm, Inc., New York
Mary E. Shourds
  Houze, Shourds & Montgomery,
    Inc., Long Beach, CA
Nancy F. Keithley
  Ernst & Young, Cleveland
J. Daniel Ford
  Kieffer, Ford & Associates, Ltd.,
    Oak Brook, IL (HC)
Joseph B. Ryan
  The Cambridge Group Ltd.,
    Westport, CT
Richard Sbarbaro
  Lauer, Sbarbaro Associates, Inc.,
    Chicago
Joseph P. McGinley
  SpencerStuart, New York

Howard D. Nitchke
Deane, Howard & Simon, Inc.,
Hartford, CT
David H. Charlson
Chestnut Hill Partners, Deerfield,
IL
Gary J. Posner
George Kaludis Associates,
Nashville (ED)
Michael J. Hoevel
Poirier, Hoevel & Company, Los
Angeles
Antoinette "Toni" L. Farley
Kieffer, Ford & Associates, Ltd.,
Oak Brook, IL (HC)
Robert M. Flanagan
Paul Stafford Associates, Ltd., New
York
James E. Hunt
Kenny, Kindler, Hunt & Howe,
New York
A. Donald Iklé
Ward Howell International, Inc.,
New York
Millington F. McCoy
Gould & McCoy, Inc., New York
Robert W. Dingman
Robert W. Dingman Company, Inc.,
Westlake Village, CA
R. James Lotz, Jr.
International Management
Advisors, Inc., New York
George W. Ott
Ott & Hansen, Inc. Pasadena, CA
Albert L. McAulay, Jr.
Robison & McAulay, Charlotte, NC
Jack R. Clarey
Jack Clarey Associates, Inc.,
Northbrook, IL
Roger M. Kenny
Kenny, Kindler, Hunt & Howe,
New York
Judith M. von Seldeneck
Diversified Search, Inc.,
Philadelphia
David O. Harbert
Sweeney Shepherd Bueschel Provus
Harbert & Mummert, Inc.,
Chicago

Steven A. Raben
Barton Raben, Inc., Houston
David H. Hoffmann
DHR International, Inc., Chicago
David F. Smith
Korn/Ferry International, New
York
Douglas H. Gates
Haley BDC, New York
Janis M. Zivic
The Zivic Group, Inc., San
Francisco
James H. Cornehlsen
Heidrick and Struggles, Inc., New
York
James R. Clovis, Jr.
Handy Associates, New York
James A. Hayden, Jr.
Hayden Group, Inc., Boston
Lawrence J. Holmes
Consulting Associates, Inc.,
Columbia, MD
Pierson Keating
Nordeman Grimm, New York
Herbert T. Mines
Herbert Mines Associates, Inc.,
New York
Edward A. Raisbeck, Jr.
Thorndike Deland Associates, New
York
Robert S. Rollo
Korn/Ferry International, Los
Angeles
William K. Sur
Stricker, Sur & Associates, New
York
Joseph E. Griesedieck, Jr.
SpencerStuart, San Francisco
Lawrence "Larry" W. Hill
Russell Reynolds Associates, Inc.,
Houston
Edward R. Howe, Jr.
Diversified Search, Inc.,
Philadelphia
Gary W. Silverman
Korn/Ferry International, Chicago
Thomas C. Zay
Thomas C. Zay & Company, Inc.,
Atlanta

William H. Billington, Jr.
 Billington, Fox & Ellis, Inc.,
  Chicago
W. Michael Danforth
 Hyde Danforth & Co., Dallas
R. G. Finnegan
 Finnegan & Associates Inc., Palos
  Verdes Estates, CA
Peter G. Grimm
 Nordeman Grimm, Inc., New York
R. Paul Kors
 Kors Montgomery International,
  Houston
W. Jerry Hyde
 Hyde Danforth & Co., Dallas
Brenda L. Ruello
 Heidrick and Struggles, Inc., New
  York
Richard C. Slayton
 Slayton International, Inc., Chicago
William B. Arnold
 William B. Arnold Associates, Inc.,
  Denver
Durant "Andy" Hunter
 Gardiner Stone Hunter
  International, Boston
William T. Mangum
 Thomas Mangum Company, Los
  Angeles
Jacques P. Andre
 Paul R. Ray & Company, Inc., New
  York
Charles P. Beall
 Beall & Company, Inc., Roswell, GA
William B. Reeves
 Korn/Ferry International, Atlanta
John Lucht
 The John Lucht Consultancy Inc.,
  New York
Harry Bernard
 Colton Bernard Inc., San Francisco
Robert M. Bryza
 Robert Lowell International, Inc.,
  Dallas
Steven M. Darter
 People Management Inc., Simsbury,
  CT
John "Jack" B. Henard, Jr.
 Henard Associates, Dallas

Robert D. Spriggs
 Spriggs & Company, Inc., Chicago
Donald C. Williams
 Donald Williams Associates, Inc.,
  Chicago
John H. Robison
 Robison & McAulay, Charlotte, NC
Robert L. Heidrick
 The Heidrick Partners, Inc.,
  Chicago
William B. Beeson
 Lawrence-Leiter & Company,
  Kansas City, MO
Eleanor H. Raynolds
 Ward Howell International, Inc.,
  New York
George Rossi
 Heidrick and Struggles, Inc.,
  Boston
Andrew D. Hart
 Russell Reynolds Associates, Inc.,
  New York
Ralph E. Dieckmann
 Dieckmann & Associates, Ltd.,
  Chicago
Robert Kremple
 Kremple & Meade, Malibu, CA
Theodore E. Lusk
 Nadzam, Lusk & Associates, Inc.,
  Santa Clara, CA
Dayton Ogden
 SpencerStuart, New York
J. R. Akin
 J. R. Akin & Company, Fairfield,
  CT
Ronald Dukes
 Heidrick and Struggles, Inc.,
  Chicago
Thomas M. Mitchell
 Heidrick and Struggles, Inc., Los
  Angeles
P. John Mirtz
 Martin Mirtz Morice, Inc.,
  Stamford, CT

PLANNING

J. Daniel Ford
 Kieffer, Ford & Associates, Ltd.,
  Oak Brook, IL (HC)